GW01085571

SQL
Database
Programming
with JAVA

Bill McCarty

CORIOLIS GROUP BOOKS

an International Thomson Publishing company I(T)P®

Albany, NY • Belmont, CA • Bonn • Boston • Cincinnati • Detroit • Johannesburg • London
Madrid • Melbourne • Mexico City • New York • Paris • Singapore • Tokyo • Toronto • Washington

PUBLISHER	KEITH WEISKAMP
PROJECT EDITOR	PAULA KMETZ
PRODUCTION COORDINATOR	KIM EOFF
COVER ARTIST	GARY SMITH
COVER DESIGN	SQUARE ONE DESIGN
INTERIOR DESIGN	NICOLE COLÓN
COMPOSITOR	JIMMIE YOUNG
COPYEDITOR	SUSAN HOLLY
PROOFREADER	BONNIE TRENGA
INDEXER	LUANNE O'LOUGHLIN
CD-ROM DEVELOPMENT	ROBERT CLARFIELD

Visual Developer SQL Database Programming with Java
1-57610-176-2
Copyright © 1998 by The Coriolis Group, Inc.

Limits of Liability and Disclaimer of Warranty

Trademarks

The Coriolis Group, Inc.
An International Thomson Publishing Company
14455 N. Hayden Road, Suite 220
Scottsdale, Arizona 85260

602/483-0192
FAX 602/483-0193
http://www.coriolis.com

Printed in the United States of America
10 9 8 7 6 5 4 3 2 1

CONTENTS

INTRODUCTION

Why I Wrote This Book

I wrote *Visual Developer SQL Database Programming With Java* to help system developers who want to know how to use JDBC (the Java API for accessing relational databases), but aren't familiar with Structured Query Language (SQL). There are many good books on SQL, but almost all focus on interactive SQL, which is not much used outside the training classroom. This book focuses on using SQL with Java and JDBC. So, while you're learning SQL, you'll simultaneously be stretching your Java skills and learning how to apply your newfound SQL knowledge to the world of Java.

I assume you can write, or at least understand, Java programs. I don't assume that you know the ins and outs of JDBC. Along with SQL, this book covers enough JDBC to meet the needs of the typical applications programmer. If you plan to write your own JDBC drivers, you'll need more details than are presented here. But most programmers are quite happy using drivers written by someone else, and prefer to devote their energies to writing better applications. If you're among the many who share this perspective, this book was written for you.

I don't attempt to cover in detail such facilities and protocols as object persistence, Remote Method Invocation (RMI) or Common Object Request Brokering Architecture (CORBA). A solid understanding of SQL is prerequisite to effective use of such technologies; this book aims at helping you satisfy that prerequisite. In any case, these technologies are now in such a rapid state of flux that a book is probably not your best source of information on them.

The source code in the book is based on the 1.1 release of Java, which includes the JDBC API as part of the standard release. Moreover, the example code uses the event-handling mechanisms of Java 1.1 extensively. For these reasons, you would not find it simple to get the example code running under Java 1.0. However, since the example code conforms to the conventions of Java 1.1, it will be more compatible with the coming generation of Java development tools.

If you're still using Java 1.0, you won't find the transition to Java 1.1 especially painful. At the time of writing, both Sun and Microsoft have released free developers' kits for Java; Symantec has just released updated versions of Café, Visual Café, and Visual Café Pro; and Microsoft has provided a plug-in Java Virtual Machine that lets Netscape Navigator run Java 1.1 code. By the time you read these words, tools for Java 1.1 should be widely available at reasonable (or no) cost and fairly stable.

How This Book Is Organized

The book is carefully designed to move gradually from simple material to more complex material. Relational database design theory (often presented in the first or second chapter of books on SQL) is postponed until the middle of the book. The first half of the book addresses the use of existing databases. This material is both more fundamental and of greater relevance to the applications programmer than issues of database design.

The datasheet view and design view facilities of Microsoft Access are presented early, enabling you to perform certain database operations that are cumbersome using SQL but quite simple using Access. Access provides an intuitive visual representation of database structure, simplifying the presentation of fundamental database terms and concepts.

JDBC is presented in abbreviated form, since many of its facilities are not needed by the applications programmer. The presentation of SQL itself follows a fairly typical sequence of development. However, example Java programs and figures are used to avoid the wordy style of the typical SQL book. The text of most chapters is organized around example programs, which introduce concepts within the context of practical examples.

Chapters 1 and 2 present an overview of Internet-based client server systems and show the reader how to use the database maintenance facilities of Microsoft Access. These chapters also introduce basic relational database terminology.

Chapters 3 to 7 show how to use Java's JDBC classes and the JDBC-ODBC bridge to access relational databases and how to use SQL to perform database queries.

Chapters 8 and 9 present the theory behind relational database design and show how to define relational tables using SQL's Data Definition Language statements.

Chapters 10 and 11 present more advanced features and facilities of SQL, including data manipulation and complex queries.

Chapters 12 to 14 cover issues related to real-world use of SQL including views, multiuser considerations, database security, and database integrity.

Three appendixes will help you learn and use SQL. Appendix A gives a convenient alphabetical reference to SQL syntax; Appendix B gives a quick reference to SLQ functions; Appendix C summarizes Microsoft Access data types.

Software And Hardware Requirements

To run the example programs in this book, you'll need an IBM-compatible PC running Microsoft Windows 95 or Windows NT 4.0 or later. Your PC should have at least a 486DX2-66 CPU, or equivalent, and at least 16MB of RAM. Your video card and monitor should support at least 256 colors. Most of the example programs are based on Microsoft Access, version 7.0 or later, and the related ODBC drivers. You'll also need the Java Developer's Kit, version 1.1 or later, which you can download from http://www.javasoft.com.

If you have questions concerning the book or discover any errors, please contact me at bmccarty@crl.com. For help with any technical questions regarding the CD-ROM, send an email to techsupport@coriolis.com.

INTRODUCTION TO DATABASE PROGRAMMING AND CLIENT-SERVER SYSTEMS

1

This chapter presents some background material helpful to understanding how Java, JDBC, SQL, and DBMSs work together to support a typical application. Since you're reading this book, you probably already know something about Java programming, but you may not recall the bigger picture: how Java enables the development of network-based application software. You may or may not be familiar with JDBC, SQL, and DBMSs. If these terms are unfamiliar to you, don't worry. The goal of this chapter is to explain them and show how they fit into network-based application systems.

If these terms *are* familiar to you, I'd suggest you skim this chapter, but don't skip it altogether. You'll probably find useful details that will help you make sense of the following chapters.

This chapter begins with an explanation of how Java is changing the work of client-server application developers, many of whom find that they must now master the special techniques used to create applications that live not only on the corporate intranet, but also on the Internet and the Web. The chapter then turns to the topic of databases and DBMSs, explaining what they are and what they do. Next, I describe SQL, the most popular means of accessing data stored in databases. That is followed by a description of JDBC, a "shim" that allows SQL statements and commands to be issued by a Java program. The chapter concludes with an explanation of several architectures used in building client-server systems.

Java

More and more programmers are learning Java as their first and only programming language. If that's true of you, then mastering this section is especially important. It will help you understand what's special about Java and how it's reshaping the work of client-server application developers.

What Is Java?

Java is a modern, object-oriented language based on C++. For the moment, C++ remains the more popular language, but Java is rapidly gaining ground. Someday soon, you may hear C++ described as the "middle-aged and overweight father" of Java. Already, experienced Java programmers are earning higher wages than experienced C++ programmers (though how a programmer can be "experienced" in using a language that has been publicly available for barely two years is not at all clear).

C++ is undeniably a powerful programming language, but it has proven difficult to learn and less than adequate for creating reliable application software. Simply put, C++ allows the programmer to do dangerous and error-prone things, such as directly manipulating address pointers, that tend to increase the number and severity of program bugs.

The designers of Java sought to create a language that is simpler to learn and use than C++. They wanted a tool better suited than C++ for developing reliable software. To accomplish these goals, they omitted from Java certain C++ capabilities they saw as dangerous and unnecessary. These victims of Occam's razor (William of Occam was a twelfth-century philosopher famous for recommending that "entities should not be multiplied unnecessarily") include operator overloading, pointer manipulation, and multiple inheritance.

Java's designers didn't stop with trimming the waistline of their new language. They added new muscle, including garbage collection, multithreading, and networking. More recently, Javasoft added the JDBC facility, which enables Java programmers to access SQL databases. Together, these well-chosen omissions and additions have produced a language that is easy and fun to learn and use, and well suited for writing reliable applications software. Of course, we will need more substantial experience in developing and using Java applications before we know whether the promises of Java are achievable. Getting there will be more than half the fun.

Why Is Java Important To The Client-Server Developer?

Java's ease of learning and use and its potential for improved software reliability are reasons enough for a high level of interest in the language. But these are secondary issues compared with the central promise of Java: portable software. The Java mantra is "Write once—run anywhere," meaning that a Java program written using (for example) Microsoft Windows NT on an IBM-compatible PC with a Pentium processor is capable of running without modification on a Macintosh, a Sun workstation running Solaris, or many other platforms.

The advent of the Internet and the Web made the once relatively minor issue of portability a central concern. Imagine the chaos that would ensue if Web pages stored on a Sun Solaris server could be viewed only by those using a Sun workstation. Such a balkanization of the Web into distinct realms of Microsoft users, Sun Solaris users, Macintosh users, and so on, would cripple the Web's most useful capability—universality.

Although Web pages have (for the most part) been portable, software programs have not. Converting a program written for one computer system so that it can be run on another has generally been time consuming and costly, often prohibitively so.

Java breaks the portability barrier by relying on an interpreter, which automatically translates Java programs to a form acceptable to a given computer platform. A Java program can be run without modification on any platform for which a Java interpreter has been written. Already, Java interpreters are widely available for most computer platforms.

The significance of Java's portability is that Java programs (more specifically, Java applets) can be included within a Web page and downloaded by a standard Web server to a Web browser, which can execute the Java program (see Figure 1.1). It doesn't matter whether the server and the platform running the browser are the same or even similar; the Java interpreter translates the Java program into a form acceptable for execution on the client platform. If a browser is not a suitable vehicle for hosting a Java program, that program can be written as an application that runs without browser assistance.

Businesses are interested in using Java as a means of protecting themselves against technological change. Writing applications in a portable language reduces dependence on a single computer platform, allowing a business to expand or update its computers by choosing the most cost-effective units available. Writing applications in a nonportable language ties the business to a single platform, which may unexpectedly increase in price or become unavailable through technological obsolescence or business failure of the manufacturer.

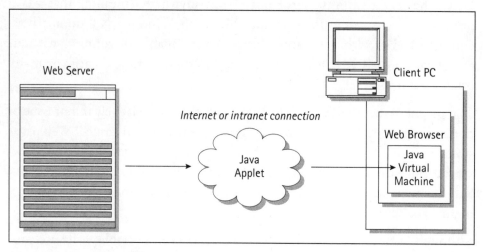

Figure 1.1
Downloading and executing a Java program.

Another attraction of Java for businesses is its ability to build executable content into their Web pages. Many businesses see Web-based sales and customer service as key to building their profitability (latecomers may find that Web technology is key to simply *maintaining* their profitability), so they are scrambling to construct and deploy Web sites intended to entice customers. Java programmers can create interactive, dynamic Web pages that communicate with—and entertain—the customer.

As business interest in the Web increases, the work of software developers is beginning to change. Developers are building more network-based systems, often using the Internet itself, that link dispersed business units. Because of its easy-to-use yet powerful networking API, Java is an ever-more-popular vehicle for writing such systems. Similarly, businesses are increasingly asking developers to construct Web pages and Java programs that are distributed by an intranet or the Internet.

Such Java programs often need to access data held in a database. Data, after all, is the *raison d'être* of most software systems. This is why SQL is an important tool for client-server developers. You probably realize by now that your Java skills are in demand; knowing more about SQL will equip you to construct the application systems of the future and will create even greater demand for your skills and services.

Databases And Database Management Systems

Most modern application software systems store their data in a database, using a database management system to manage the data. To understand the revolution in client-server systems, you need to understand databases. This section describes databases and DBMSs.

What's A Database?

Long ago in a galaxy far, far away, databases did not exist and computer data was stored in files. Actually, it wasn't that long ago—merely a couple of decades—and it happened right here on planet Earth. But we have seen many changes in hardware and software technology in the interim.

Files were important and remain important, because data stored in files is *persistent*. It isn't lost when a program finishes or when you shut down the computer.

Many programming languages (for example, COBOL, FORTRAN, and Basic) provide direct support for reading and writing files; most others (for example, C, C++, and Java) provide libraries that include file input-output routines.

Bitter experience, however, has taught programmers that there are significant drawbacks to storing data in files. Most applications are unable to store all their data in only one file. Files generally contain data on a single type of entity, such as sales or expenses or widget inventories. Since most applications deal with multiple types of entities, they need multiple files to store their data. The problem is that it's altogether too easy for one of these files to get misplaced, confused with an out-of-date version, or corrupted. Such an application system lacks a mechanism for keeping its files in synch.

Most operating systems (for example, MS-DOS and Windows 95) provide no facilities to secure data held in files from unauthorized access or accidental or intentional tampering. No matter how much you want or need to, you simply can't keep every unwanted user out of your files. Worse yet, you can't make your files simultaneously available to multiple authorized users—most operating systems provide no adequate facilities for sharing write access to file data.

Of course, an application programmer can write application code that provides all these necessary facilities, but that significantly increases the cost of developing applications. Moreover, few application programmers have the special expertise needed to implement such facilities efficiently. What's a programmer to do?

Database Management Systems

The solution to the programmers' dilemma is a DBMS that, in effect, extends the operating system to include the facilities needed to manage an application's data. A DBMS stores application information in a database, which is simply a collection of information organized as discrete *tables*. The tables hold the data that would otherwise have been stored in files. These tables may or may not appear as actual files visible to the operating system. A common approach is to store the entire database as a single file, which contains binary data that cannot be (safely) altered using a standard file editor.

The job of the DBMS is to store and protect data, making it available to multiple concurrent users. A typical DBMS provides mechanisms that permit you to use and administer the database. You can:

- retrieve data from tables.

- insert new data into existing tables.

- update data in tables.

- delete data from tables.

A business usually stores all its computerized data in one or only a few data-bases. This makes sharing data among the business's various application systems easier. Rather than having a separate chart-of-accounts file for each application, for example, applications can access the same shared table within the database. This avoids having several distinct and possibly inconsistent versions of the same data, a problem commonly referred to as "the database problem," not because it's *caused* by a database, but because it's *solved* by one.

From time to time, a database must accommodate new information. Similarly, from time to time a database can be purged of information no longer needed. Therefore, a DBMS provides mechanisms that allow you to:

- add new tables.

- change the structure of existing tables.

- remove existing tables.

These operations are normally reserved for a special user, called the *database administrator*, who also defines policies and rules that control access to data and preserve its integrity. For example, the database administrator can specify that employees in the credit or receivables departments can view data on client payment history, but that employees in the human relations department cannot. A DBMS also typically provides a number of utilities that can make backup copies of a database or repair a damaged database.

Other Benefits Of Using A DBMS

Apart from solving problems presented by using ordinary files to store data, use of a DBMS confers a number of further benefits. Among these are:

- Data independence

- Increased efficiency

Data independence is made possible by the DBMS's monopoly hold on data—no application program can obtain data from the database except by the permission and assistance of the DBMS, as shown in Figure 1.2. Because of its strategic position between the data and the program, the DBMS can convert or translate data into a form more convenient to an application program.

Assume, for example, that a table within the database contains a customer address that includes a five-digit postal code and that postal authorities have recently decreed the use of an expanded postal code that adds a four-digit suffix to the original code. Existing programs expect only a five-digit code and may malfunction if the new nine-digit code is presented to them. Nevertheless, the database must store all nine digits.

As shown in Figure 1.3, the DBMS easily resolves this problem by providing the nine-digit code to new programs that need it, but only providing the five-digit code to other programs. Since programs cannot directly access the data in the database, but only via the DBMS, they are unaware of the actual form in which the data is stored. The DBMS can map the stored data into another form more appropriate to the needs of a program.

This decoupling of the form in which data is stored from the form in which it is presented to an application program is a powerful device. It leaves the DBMS

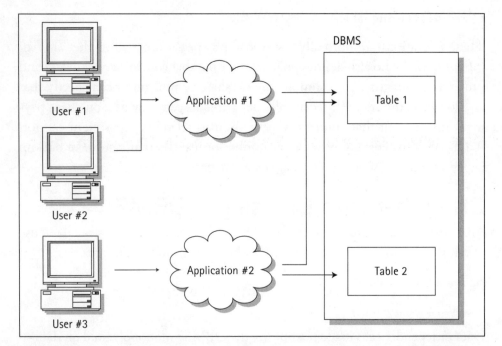

Figure 1.2
A database management system (DBMS).

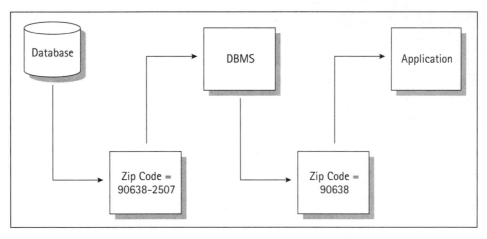

Figure 1.3
Data independence.

free to store data in the most efficient format possible. The DBMS simply reformats data requested by an application program, which remains blissfully unaware of the real form of the data.

Some Real Database Management Systems

Many DBMS vendors and products are available today. Table 1.1 lists some of the more popular ones.

One particularly important DBMS in the world of IBM-compatible PCs is Microsoft Access. It is available at low cost as part of Microsoft Office

TABLE 1.1

SOME POPULAR DBMS VENDORS AND THEIR DBMSS.

Vendor	DBMS
Borland	Interbase
IBM	DB2
Informix	Universal Server, Online Workgroup Server, etc.
Microsoft	Access, SQL Server
Oracle	Oracle Server 7
Sybase	SQL Server

Professional. Although Access has limited capability and performance, it is an excellent tool for learning about databases. Moreover, most software developed to work with Access can be easily modified to work with Microsoft's flagship DBMS, SQL Server. Although the example code in this book is based on Access, the concepts and techniques described apply to a wide range of DBMS products.

Structured Query Language

You might have assumed, based on the previous section, that programmers' problems disappeared with the widespread availability of DBMSs, beginning in the 1970s. Unfortunately, as has so often been the case in the history of software, solving one set of problems merely led to a new, more difficult set of problems.

In the case of database technology, the new problem was difficulty in gaining access to data. As shown in Figure 1.4, databases turned out to resemble medieval castles that securely locked away users' data, protecting it from access and change, whether unwanted or desperately needed. Whenever users had need for data beyond that routinely provided by reports programmed with the application, a new program had to be written. Often, this was expensive. Even more often, by the time the users received their requested data, they could scarcely

Users   Data

Figure 1.4
The data access problem.

recall why they had needed it. In short, the process of accessing the data was too laborious, expensive, and time-consuming.

SQL To The Rescue

In 1974, E. F. Codd of the IBM Research Laboratory, San Jose, proposed a new way of accessing data stored in databases. His innovation was called Structured Query Language, or SQL. Purists correctly insist that the proper pronunciation of SQL is *S-Q-L*, but most programmers today pronounce it as though it were spelled *sequel*.

However one chooses to pronounce it, SQL is a language for accessing databases. Using SQL, a programmer, or even a skilled end user, can retrieve, modify, define, and administer data stored in a database—all without writing a program. At the time of its introduction, SQL was widely seen as the means of breaching the castle walls and achieving quick and easy access to data. Listing 1.1 shows an example SQL query that retrieves data from a relational database table. Notice how much of its meaning is clear, even to those not familiar with SQL.

LISTING 1.1   AN EXAMPLE SQL QUERY.

```
SELECT VendorID, VendorName
    FROM VendorTable
    WHERE DaysSincePurchase <= 90 AND YTDPurchases > 10000
    ORDER BY VendorID;
```

One problem with SQL surfaced early, however: The databases it accesses must be structured according to the so-called *relational model*, which you'll meet in Chapter 2. Unfortunately, at the time SQL was introduced, databases using the relational model were far and away the exception rather than the rule. Worse yet, early relational databases were notorious for poor performance, often requiring significantly longer intervals to access or modify data than required by competing, nonrelational databases.

Happily, neither of these problems is still with us. Increases in computer hardware performance and improved technology for implementing relational databases have combined to leave the relational database the clear winner over alternative models of database organization.

That is not to say that all is now well, however. Many businesses are still saddled with legacy systems implemented prior to the ascendancy of relational technology. Providing flexible and rapid access to data remains a central problem for them and is a major factor driving the move to client-server systems, which we'll discuss later in this chapter.

SQL has other problems as well. For example, the language itself turned out to be less than ideal for use by nonprogrammers. Although SQL avoids the iteration construct (loop) that nonprogrammers often find hard to understand and use, it nevertheless proved difficult even for programmers to use. Effectively using SQL to access data required special training. Of course, that should pose no problem for you, since this book promises to teach you the concepts and skills necessary for using SQL.

Perhaps a more significant problem is that the various vendors who created SQL interpreters for their DBMSs had their own idiosyncratic ideas of the form and meaning of SQL statements. This was partly put to rest by the adoption of an ANSI standard SQL, but dialectical differences remain. For example, vendors create extensions to the SQL standard, necessary to provide access to special facilities peculiar to their DBMSs. A programmer using these extensions may be unaware that they are not part of standard SQL and may be disappointed to find that a SQL command that runs fine on one database won't run at all on another. Other vendors seem bent on "locking in" their customers by adopting dialectical peculiarities that greatly complicate moving an application to another vendor's DBMS.

To minimize such problems in this book, I'll try to avoid (and otherwise point out) any SQL features that are peculiar to Microsoft Access. This will help you get the example code working on the DBMS of your choice. For programmers who are aware of potential differences among dialects, SQL remains a powerful tool for creating portable software.

JDBC And ODBC

SQL was originally designed for interactive use. The idea was that a user would sit at a keyboard and type in statements telling the SQL interpreter what data was required. The interpreter would respond by displaying or printing the requested data. But programmers wanted to use SQL within their programs, not at a keyboard. They wanted a way to simplify the parts of their programs that accessed data stored in databases. SQL as originally conceived did not provide that help.

To address the needs of programmers better, SQL has been extended in various ways. In effect, *embedded SQL* extends a programming language to include new constructs that specify SQL operations, such as retrieving and modifying records. Embedded SQL has long been available for COBOL and has been proposed for Java as well, though no implementation has yet come into widespread use among Java programmers.

A second approach to providing Java with a SQL capability is JDBC, which has been specified by Javasoft and implemented by a number of vendors. JDBC provides a Java-callable application programming interface (API) that programmers can use to access SQL databases. JDBC is based on the 1992 ANSI SQL standard, which helps minimize some of the dialectical differences involved in SQL itself, since vendors have a strong incentive to conform (or at least claim to conform) to the ANSI and JDBC standards. Figure 1.5 shows how a Java program uses JDBC to access a SQL database, and Listing 1.2 shows an excerpt from the JDBC API.

LISTING 1.2   AN EXCERPT FROM THE JDBC API.

```
public interface Connection {
public abstract void clearWarnings( ) throws SQLException;
public abstract void close( ) throws SQLException;
public abstract void commit( ) throws SQLException;
public abstract Statement createStatement( ) throws SQLException;
public abstract boolean getAutoClose( ) throws SQLException;
public abstract boolean getAutoCommit( ) throws SQLException;
public abstract String getCatalog( ) throws SQLException;
// etc.
}
```

Notice in Figure 1.5 the four components of the JDBC system:

- *Data sources*—usually SQL-compliant databases, though drivers have become available for certain other popular data sources as well (for example, Microsoft Excel spreadsheets).

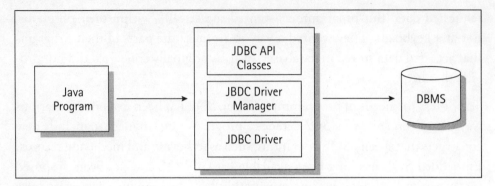

Figure 1.5
Accessing a database via JDBC.

- *Drivers*—provide an interface between a data source and an application program.

- *A driver manager*—selects an appropriate driver to handle each data source.

- *Application programs*—send data to, and receive data from, a data source via a driver.

When using JDBC, an application program requests that the driver manager establish a connection to a specified data source. In response, the driver manager searches its list of registered drivers and selects one appropriate to the type of data source. Once the driver is selected, the application communicates directly with it, sending requests for data and receiving the results.

The design of JDBC is based on that of ODBC, a standard way of accessing SQL-compliant databases that was originally implemented for Microsoft Windows systems. ODBC simply provides a method of connecting an application to a data source. Its significance is that it strives to be open to as many kinds of applications and sources as possible, and does so fairly successfully. Many vendors have adapted their databases for ODBC compliance. Ever since JDK 1.1 included a bridge that allows JDBC access to any ODBC-compliant database, Java programmers have not lacked for data sources. Figure 1.6 shows how a program using JDBC connects to an ODBC-compliant database.

Computing Architectures

Important as they are, such technologies as DBMS, SQL, and JDBC don't in themselves solve information system problems, but the precise way in which

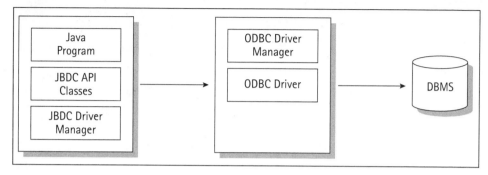

Figure 1.6
Accessing a database via the JDBC/ODBC bridge.

these technologies are used and combined often determines the success or failure of an information system.

The various recurring patterns of use and organization that appear in system after system are referred to as *architectures*. This section describes some common architectures and identifies their strengths and weaknesses. This will help you quickly understand important client-server system design options.

Each architecture includes the same three basic components, but each employs the components in a different configuration. The three components are:

- *The client*—a keyboard and display operated by a user. Typical configurations include multiple clients.

- *The server*—a computer that provides central storage of data. An architecture usually has only a single server, but some employ multiple servers.

- *The network*—a communications link that connects the client and the server. The network may encompass a relatively small geographical area (local area network, or LAN) or a large one (wide area network, or WAN).

Traditional Computing Architecture

Before the advent of the PC, mainframes ruled the earth. It was an era of expensive hardware and, consequently, limited computing functionality. The dominant computing architecture during the mainframe era was known as *traditional computing architecture*, shown in Figure 1.7.

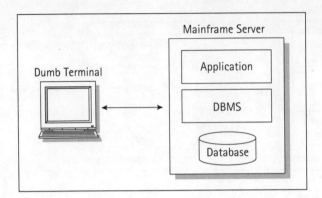

Figure 1.7
Traditional computing architecture.

Clients were typically dumb terminals with monochromatic, text-only displays, because the cost of more sophisticated equipment was prohibitive. The mainframes themselves were used as servers, providing both the data storage and processing capability necessary to obtain input data from clients and transmit appropriate output in response. Networks of both varieties—LAN and WAN—were used to connect multiple clients to (usually) a single server. Traditional computing architecture is sometimes aptly referred to as *dumb-client, smart-server.* Table 1.2 summarizes key advantages and disadvantages of traditional computing architecture.

LAN-Based PC System Architecture

The widespread availability of inexpensive PCs led to *LAN-based PC system architecture,* aimed at overcoming the weaknesses of the traditional architecture. Using PCs as clients provided the users with multicolor, graphical displays. With the advent of Microsoft Windows, the client soon came to support a graphical user interface based on a pointing device, usually a mouse. Compared

TABLE 1.2

ADVANTAGES AND DISADVANTAGES OF TRADITIONAL COMPUTING ARCHITECTURE.

Advantages	Disadvantages
Reliability	High cost of operation
Security	Inflexibility
Ability to handle large transaction volumes well	

with the cumbersome text-only interface provided by clients in the traditional computing architecture, PC clients were a major hit with users, who found them far easier to learn and use.

Figure 1.8 shows a typical LAN-based architecture built around PCs used as clients. PCs were often used both as clients and as the server, but most processing was actually performed by the client. This *smart-client, dumb-server* configuration reversed the client and server roles of traditional computing architecture. Table 1.3 summarizes key advantages and disadvantages of LAN-based PC system architecture.

	TABLE 1.3

ADVANTAGES AND DISADVANTAGES OF THE **LAN**-BASED **PC** SYSTEM ARCHITECTURE.

Advantages	Disadvantages
Low cost	Low reliability
Flexibility	Low security
	Poor scalability
	Inadequate handling of large transaction volumes

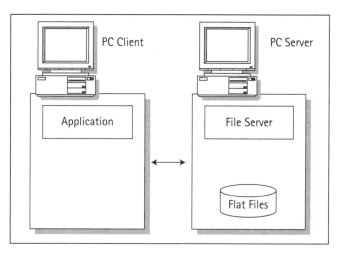

Figure 1.8
LAN-based PC system architecture.

Client-Server Architectures

A more recent set of related architectures, known as *client-server architectures,* attempts to combine the strengths of both the traditional and LAN-based PC architectures. Client-server architectures can be aptly described as *smart-client, smart-server.* They attempt to allocate responsibility between client and server in a less rigid fashion than previous architectures, striving to maintain a balance that optimizes the overall performance and cost effectiveness of the system. Client-server architectures, shown in Figure 1.9, contrast greatly with traditional and LAN-based PC architectures.

The client-server architectures strive to:

- make data more accessible.

- reduce hardware costs.

- support graphical user interfaces.

- build on open, rather than proprietary, technologies.

Client-server architectures have three common forms: the traditional two-tier architecture, the newer three-tier architecture, and the hybrid distributed architecture.

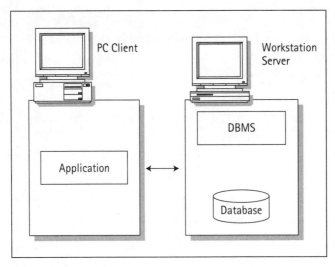

Figure 1.9
A typical client-server architecture.

Two-Tier Architecture

In two-tier client-server architecture (shown in Figure 1.10), a front-end client runs the application software, which obtains its data from a back-end database server. This architecture is superficially similar to LAN-based PC architecture. However, the file server used in the LAN-based system is quite primitive compared with the DBMS in two-tier client-server architecture. The server-based DBMS centralizes control over data and performs much of the data-related processing, leaving the clients mainly responsible for running application code and providing a high-quality user interface.

A common problem with two-tier client-server architecture is that the client must be configured to include a driver for each type of database accessed. This can be costly, since such drivers usually carry a license fee. Moreover, configuration and software maintenance problems often occur with the two-tier architecture. Drivers from various vendors may prove mutually incompatible, and considerable work is involved in keeping clients updated with the latest version of each driver.

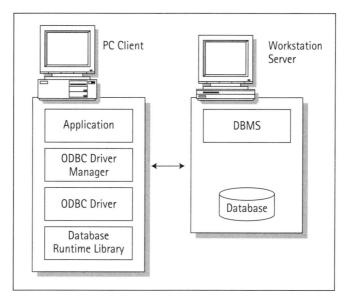

Figure 1.10
Two-tier client-server architecture.

THREE-TIER ARCHITECTURE AND MIDDLEWARE

Three-tier client-server architecture, shown in Figure 1.11, attempts to overcome the shortcomings of two-tier architecture. In three-tier architecture, applications no longer communicate directly with a DBMS. Instead, a *middleware* component is interposed between the application and the database.

Middleware simplifies the configuration of clients, which no longer need a distinct driver for each type of DBMS accessed. Instead, clients need only a single driver that communicates with the middleware server. Some middleware products do not even make this minor demand on their clients, working with any Java-enabled Web browser.

The middleware component also commonly provides a caching facility that speeds access to data and reduces the amount of network traffic flowing to and from clients. Improved network performance is particularly important when

---

TABLE 1.4

KEY ADVANTAGES OF THREE-TIER CLIENT-SERVER ARCHITECTURE.

Simple client management

Scalability

Security

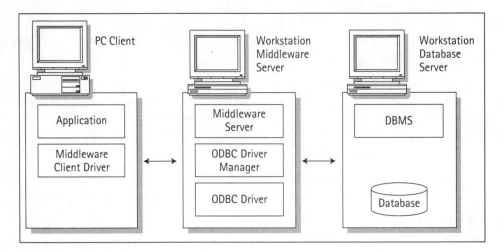

Figure 1.11

Three-tier client-server architecture.

the Internet, rather than a high-speed LAN, is used to connect clients and servers. Table 1.4 summarizes key advantages of three-tier client-server architecture.

DISTRIBUTED SYSTEMS, REMOTE METHOD INVOCATION, AND CORBA

Based on a still more elaborate and sophisticated architecture, distributed systems feature multiple servers. Figure 1.12 shows a typical distributed client-server architecture. Technically, most systems are distributed, since most systems have supplementary servers that perform minor, specialized functions. But the term *distributed system* is more properly applied only when the use of multiple servers is significant.

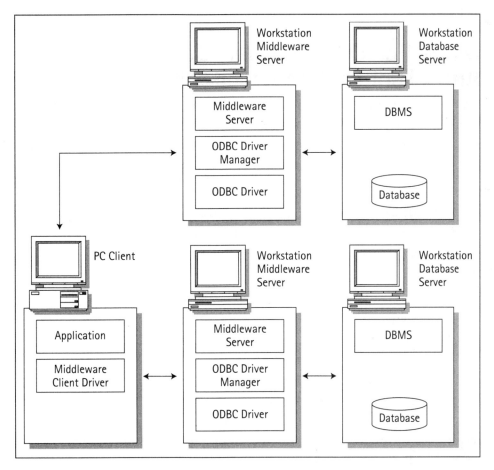

Figure 1.12
Distributed client-server architecture.

Java supports distributed-system architectures by means of its *remote method invocation* (RMI) facility. RMI allows *remote objects,* residing on distinct machines, to invoke methods on one another. Using RMI, remote objects can make method calls that include parameters that may themselves refer to remote objects, allowing sophisticated patterns of data exchange.

Several vendors offer *Common Object Request Broker Architecture (CORBA)* drivers for use with Java. CORBA is a distributed architecture developed by the Object Management Group. Unlike RMI, which can be used only by Java programs, CORBA allows the construction of distributed systems that include multiple platforms and programming languages. CORBA thus provides greater flexibility than RMI, but RMI is simpler to use and a better-performing technology when all parts of a system are implemented in Java.

Made For One Another: Java, JDBC, And Client-Server Architectures

Until the advent of Java, the word *client* in client-server almost always referred to an IBM-compatible PC running Microsoft Windows. Now designers of client-server systems have new options. Java provides a graphical user interface that can be run on almost any computing platform.

One especially interesting platform is the *network computer,* a PC with no disk drive or other local data-storage device. Network computers depend entirely on a central server for all their data-storage needs. Several hardware manufacturers offer Java-based network computers, and others have announced plans to offer them soon.

"But wait!" you protest. "These network computers sound like nothing more than warmed-over dumb terminals. This seems like a disguised return to traditional computing architecture." You're right in all but one important respect. Unlike their dumb-terminal predecessors, network computers sport a very capable, high-speed microprocessor that allows them to run modern, graphical user interfaces. Moreover, their lack of local storage means they are simple to administer; updating a single copy of a driver program or application on the server makes it instantly available to each of the network-computer clients it serves. The future of client-server computing may truly be found in its past.

The combination of Java, JDBC, and RMI is just what the doctor ordered for supporting modern client-server system architectures, including Microsoft Windows clients, network computers, and other client platforms. Java permits the development of reliable and robust software programs that are portable and network-capable. JDBC's support of SQL provides convenient access by Java programs to data stored by most popular DBMSs. RMI provides the ability to build fully distributed Java-based systems configured to balance concerns of performance and reliability. This is truly client-server architecture at its finest.

Summary

Java, a modern, object-oriented language based on C++, offers a rich set of APIs for constructing and deploying portable network-based applications. In particular, Java's JDBC API allows Java programmers to use industry-standard SQL to access database management systems. Using Java, JDBC, and SQL, you can adopt any of several possible client-server architectures, including two-tier and three-tier. The three-tier architecture, which simplifies client configuration and offers potential performance benefits, is becoming more widely used.

RELATIONAL DATA

2

BASICS

Before learning more about SQL, you should understand DBMSs in general and the Microsoft Access DBMS in particular. That's the purpose of this chapter. First, you'll learn important database terms and concepts. Then, you'll learn how to use Microsoft Access to perform useful database tasks. If you're already familiar with relational databases and with Microsoft Access, you can go directly to Chapter 3, which begins the presentation of SQL database programming. Otherwise, you should pay careful attention to the material in this chapter, which forms the foundation on which the remainder of the book is built. Even if you plan on using a DBMS other than Microsoft Access, skim this material to make sure you know how to perform common administrative tasks using your chosen DBMS.

Following widespread custom, the word *database* will refer sometimes to a DBMS and other times to the actual database managed by the DBMS. The difference is seldom crucial to a clear understanding, and context should enable you to determine which meaning is intended in a given reference.

Disassembling A Relational Database

Are you the type of person who disassembles things to learn how they work? If so, you may be familiar with the phenomenon of "extra parts." Often, you may have found that, after reassembling the VCR you disassembled for study, you have parts left over. Here's an interesting question to ponder on such an occasion: How many VCRs would you have to disassemble before you gathered enough leftover parts to build a new VCR?

In this section, I'm going to disassemble a relational database so you can better see how it works. But never fear, one happy advantage of working in the software industry is that there are never any parts left over.

Tables, Rows, And Columns

A relational database consists of a collection of *tables*, also called *files* or *relations*. As shown in Figure 2.1, these tables look a great deal like spreadsheets, consisting of cells organized into rows and columns. Most databases contain several—perhaps many—tables, each holding information about one kind of *object*, such as suppliers, customers, accounts, payments, or invoices. The objects, of course, can be physical or conceptual.

Each *row* within the table describes a single instance of the kind of object represented by the table. For example, each row in the supplier table describes a single supplier; each row in the customer table describes a single customer; and so on. Rows are also called *records* or *tuples*. Truly relational DBMSs detest redundancy and, therefore, do not allow two identical rows in a single table; every row of a table must have a distinct value.

Supplier ID	Supplier Name	Contact	YTD Purchases
1002	Acme Hardware	Fred Smythe	$300.25
1005	Becker Tool & Supply	Bob Becker	$500.55
1006	Carpet King	Mike Morris	$700.24
1007	Davis Furniture	Bill Twomey	$425.31

Figure 2.1
A database table.

Most tables contain multiple *columns*, with each column containing values for some attribute of the object. For example, columns in the supplier table might include a supplier number, the supplier's name, the supplier's address, and the total amount of purchases during the current year. Columns are often called *fields* or *attributes*.

Meta-Data And Schemas

Socrates' advice, "Know thyself," is taken to heart by databases. A database keeps careful track of many important details about itself, such as the names of the tables it contains, and the names of the columns contained in each table. This way, an application program can "ask" the database whether it contains a particular table, and what columns the table contains. Such information, called *meta-data* (data about data), is stored in a part of the database called the *schema*. Very large databases may have multiple schemas, which can be grouped together as a *catalog*.

Domains And Constraints

Data is not useful unless accurate. Fortunately, modern databases have studied their Shakespeare as well as their classical Greek. In "Hamlet," Polonius counsels his son, Laertes, "This above all: To thine own self be true, and it must follow, as the night the day, thou canst not then be false to any man." One way databases heed this advice and keep guard over the accuracy of data they contain is by means of *types*. You're already familiar with types because of the important role they play in Java.

Sometimes, a column of a database holds values of a certain type. For example, a student-information table might include a column for class standing, which could be coded as FRSH, SOPH, JUNR, or SENR. By specifying a *domain*— a set of acceptable values for the column—the DBMS can guard against the possibility of incorrect data entering the database. Domains are used with *constraints*, which are rules restricting the values of data within the database. Constraints, once defined, are enforced by the DBMS, lightening the programmer's workload. For example, you could define a constraint specifying that the value of the class-standing column must be within the domain that consists of FRSH, SOPH, JUNR, or SENR. Once such a constraint has been defined, an attempt to add a student record with the value ELEM for class standing would be rejected by the database, thereby ensuring accuracy of its data.

Indexes And Keys

How would you find the home of a friend whom you had never visited? Would you drive up and down every street until you found the right house? Of course not—you would use an address.

Searching for a row in a large table works the same way. You can find it much more quickly if you have an address. In the world of relational databases, *indexes* perform the function of addresses, helping the DBMS rapidly locate the row you're interested in. Creating an index on a table column allows the DBMS to quickly find all rows in the table that contain a particular value in that column. For example, creating an index on the supplier-number column of the supplier table would hasten the search for a supplier record, as long as you know the supplier's number.

Creating and maintaining an index takes some time, and you must revise it each time a record is added to or deleted from its table. Indexes also take up disk space. Therefore, you should create indexes only where they're needed. The performance difference between a search that has an index to assist it and one that doesn't can be tremendous, however.

Indexes work best when the indexed column has a unique value for every row of the table. In such a case, the index leads directly to the row sought. Most tables are designed to include just such a column, referred to as the *primary key* of the table. For example, the supplier-number column of the supplier table might be its primary key, and the customer-number column of the customer table might be its primary key. No two rows within the supplier table would have the same value of supplier number, and no two rows within the customer table would have the same value of customer number. Note that performance is not guaranteed to improve simply because a column has been designated as the primary key. If you want the improved performance an index provides, you must also create the appropriate index.

Sometimes, no single column within a table has a unique value in each row, ruling out the use of any single column as a primary key. In such a case, you may designate a *composite primary key*, composed of values from multiple columns. In a table containing information on members of neighborhood families, for example, neither LastName nor FirstName is sufficient to uniquely identify an individual. The combination of LastName and FirstName is unique, however, and can be designated as a composite primary key. You can also create indexes on composite primary keys. Figure 2.2 shows a composite primary key.

Often, it's convenient for a table to reference rows of other tables. For example, you may choose to store employee addresses in a special table, and allow the tables containing human-resource data and payroll data to reference employee addresses in the special table. This reduces data-storage requirements, since the addresses are stored only once. This also simplifies the job of keeping addresses up to date, by avoiding the need to revise multiple copies of addresses when they change.

Rows of a table reference rows of other tables using a *foreign key*, which is simply a column that corresponds to, or references, the primary key of another table. Figure 2.3 shows how primary and foreign keys are related. Unlike primary keys, foreign keys do not need unique values. For example, the Skills table may contain entries for computer programming and sky diving, both of which share the foreign key value of 1001, the employee number of Fred Fearless, one of the company's best programmers.

This section has introduced quite a few new terms; Table 2.1 summarizes the most important ones. Check to make sure you understand each of the terms before proceeding to the next section. If a term is unclear, reread its description above. Caution: Do not make the mistake of the programmer found dead in the shower, next to a bottle of shampoo reading, "Lather. Rinse. Repeat." A second reading may clarify the meaning, but if not, push ahead—these new

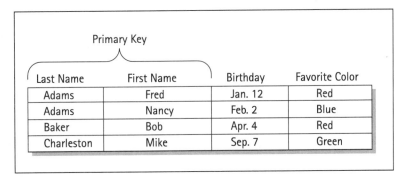

Figure 2.2
A composite primary key.

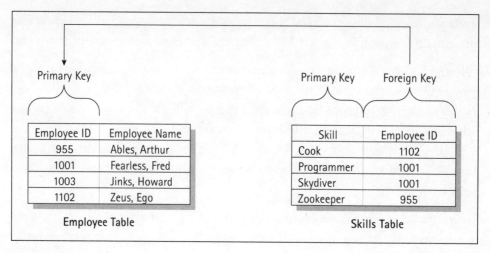

Figure 2.3
Primary and foreign keys.

TABLE 2.1

IMPORTANT RELATIONAL DATABASE TERMS.

Term	Meaning
Table	Describes a single kind of object; consists of rows and columns.
Row	A part of a table that represents some object—physical or conceptual.
Column	A part of a table that holds a single attribute of the table. Attributes describe properties of objects.
Meta-data	Data about data. Allows a database to contain information describing itself.
Schema	Meta-data that describes the contents of a database, including its tables and their structure.
Catalog	A collection of schemas.
Domain	Identifies the acceptable range of values of a column.
Constraint	A rule intended to restrict data values. Enforced by the DBMS.
Index	A table of pointers, used to speed access to rows of a table, given one or more column values.
Primary key	A column (or combination of columns) that yields a value unique to every row within a table.
Foreign key	A column (or combination of columns) that references the primary key of a table.

concepts will probably make more sense when you read the next section, which explains how you can use Microsoft Access to define databases and tables of your own.

Using Microsoft Access

In this section, you'll learn how to use Microsoft Access to create, update, and maintain tables within relational databases. As you'll see in later chapters, you can use SQL to perform most of these tasks, but it's often much more convenient to use Access, which provides an easy-to-use graphical user interface.

If you have an aversion, for whatever reason, to Access, just relax. While you can't actually create an Access database using SQL, you're not forced to use Access itself even for that fundamental purpose. Instead, you can use the Access ODBC driver (available using the ODBC icon in the Control Panel folder) to create your database and then use SQL to set it up just the way you want. You'll learn how to do this in Chapters 9 and 10. However, read on. You'll probably discover that using Access is fun, even for programmers.

Your tour of Access won't be comprehensive, so you may want to consult the Access help files or a reference manual for additional information. This section is intended to jump-start your ability to perform common database tasks with Access. If you're already well versed in Access or prefer to use another database engine, skip ahead to Chapter 3. If you later find you have a question about Access, you can always return to this chapter.

Opening An Existing Database

I'll start the tour by opening an existing Access database. Fire up your computer and perform each step of the tour so your fingers begin to know their way around.

After starting Access using the Windows Start menu, click the radio button marked Open An Existing Database and choose the file that contains the database you want to use, as shown in Figure 2.4. We'll use the Northwind sample database that comes with Access as the setting of our tour. If you didn't install the Northwind database when you installed Access, you can use the Access setup routine now to add it to your system. It requires only a little more than 2MB of disk space. Access databases are stored in files with the .mdb extension.

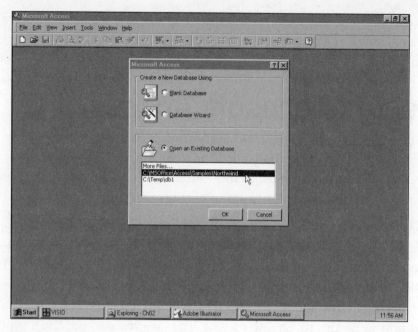

Figure 2.4
Opening an existing database.

If you want to open a database that's not included in the list, select the More Files… option.

Opening A Table And Changing Records

Open the Northwind sample database by selecting its file and clicking the OK button. You should see a Database window like that shown in Figure 2.5. The Tables tab of the Database window lets you see the names of the tables stored in the Northwind database.

You can open one of these tables by selecting its name and clicking open. Select and open the Customers table. You'll see a window with the contents of the table, presented in what's called Datasheet view, as in Figure 2.6. Note how each row describes a customer, identified by a Customer ID in the first column. Datasheet view is both convenient and intuitive, because the form in which the table is displayed exactly matches common relational database terms: *Rows* are actual rows and *columns* are actual columns.

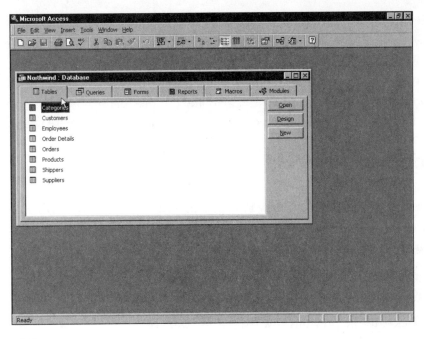

Figure 2.5
The Database window.

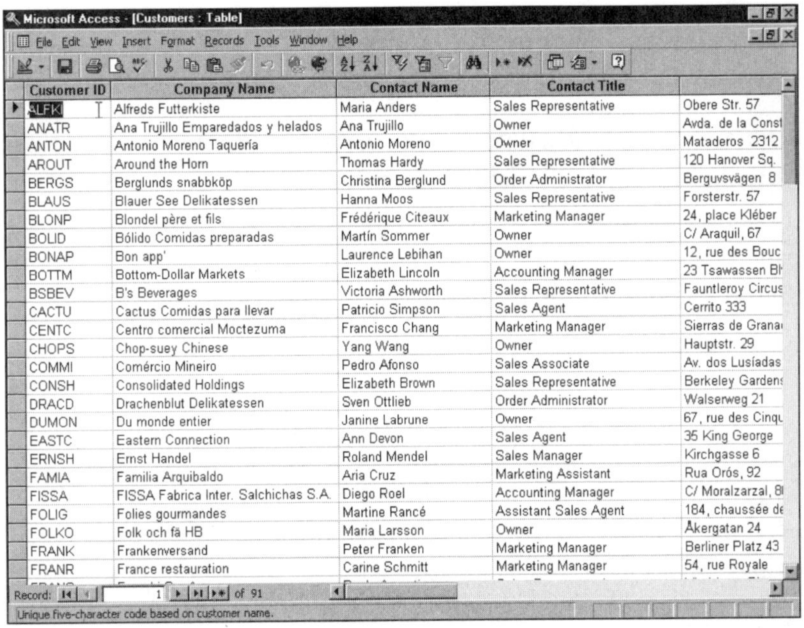

Figure 2.6
Datasheet view of the Customers table.

Using the mouse or the cursor keys, you can scroll down to see additional records (rows) or to the right to see additional fields (columns). Highlight the Contact Name field of the sixth record (for the company Blauer See Delikatessen). Now, revise the Contact Name by typing "Hanna Moose" over the current name, Hanna Moos. Press Enter or scroll off the field and see that the new value replaces the previous one. That's all that's required to change an Access database record.

Adding Table Records

To add a new record, go to the bottom of the table. A quick way to do this is by pressing Ctrl+End, followed by Home, followed by Page Down. Of course, you can use the scroll bar or the Page Down key, but this could grow tiresome if your database is large. An even quicker way is to use the VCR icons at the bottom of the window, shown in Figure 2.7. Here's where they take you:

- **Rewind**—to the first row of the table (the top of the datasheet).

- **Back**—to the previous row (that is, up one row).

- **Forward**—to the next row (that is, down one row).

- **Fast Forward**—to the last row of the table (the bottom of the datasheet).

- **New Record**—to an empty row at the bottom of the datasheet, where you can type in a new record.

To add your record, simply type a value for each field, pressing Enter after each one. Note the Customer ID field includes a constraint that requires your input value to consist of exactly five letters. The fields other than Customer ID and Company Name are optional. When you're done entering the fields you want, you can scroll down to add another record.

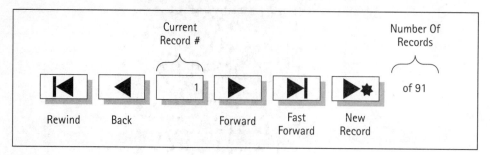

Figure 2.7
The VCR icons.

Deleting Records From A Table

Deleting a record from the table is equally as easy. You can use either Edit|Delete Record or the corresponding tool icon. Notice in Figure 2.8 how Access obligingly asks you to confirm the deletion, since it is irrevocable. Click Yes to delete the record, which is gone forever. Click No to grant the record a reprieve.

Closing The Table And The Database

When you're done adding, changing, and deleting records, you need to close the table and the database. To close the table, click the Close icon in the upper-right corner of the Datasheet window. You should again see the Database window, previously obscured by the Datasheet window.

To close the database, click the Close icon of the Database window. You can now exit Access itself by clicking the Close icon of the Access window. Of course, if you had been in a real hurry to exit, closing the Access window would have automatically closed the Datasheet and Database windows.

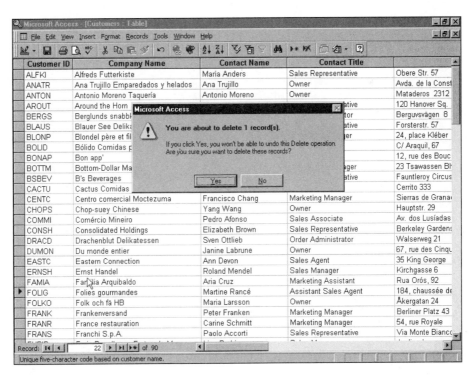

Figure 2.8
Deleting a record.

Creating A Database

You can't create a database using SQL. Fortunately, Access makes this important task very easy. After starting Access, just click the radio button marked Create A New Database Using Blank Database, and then click OK. A dialog prompts you to select a directory and file name for your database, as shown in Figure 2.9. To see how this works, create a database called test and store it in the \Temp directory of your hard drive, giving it the name test.mdb. Note how the Database window shows no tables in your new database. You'll see how to use the New button to create a new table in a moment.

Deleting A Database

When you no longer need a database, you can simply delete the file that contains it, using Windows Explorer or the DOS command line. Of course, you can't do this while Access has the database open (try it if you're unconvinced). So close the Database window or the Access window, and then use Windows Explorer to delete the mdb file containing the database. Delete a database only

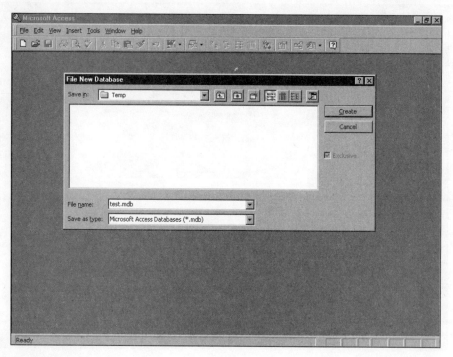

Figure 2.9
Creating a new database.

if you're certain it contains no useful data, and keep a backup or two just in case. Under favorable circumstances, you may be able to recover the file using the Recycle Bin, but don't count on this.

Creating A Table

To learn how to create a table, first use your new Access expertise to create a database called GuestBook and place it in your \Temp directory. Keep this database, since we'll use it in Chapter 3 to build a simple Web guest book that stores its information in the GuestBook database.

When the Database window appears, make sure the Tables tab is active, and then use the New button to tell Access you want to create a new table. Access gives you a choice of several different ways of specifying your new table, including Datasheet View and Design View. Although Datasheet View is the most convenient way of working with an existing table, adding a new table is easiest using Design View. Select the Design View list item and press OK. You'll see the Design window, as shown in Figure 2.10.

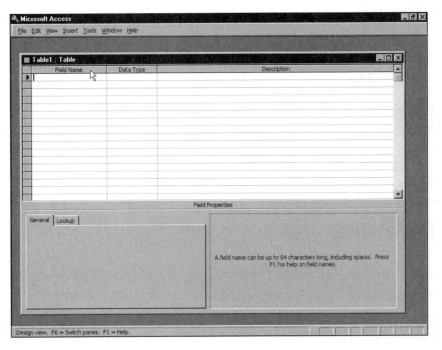

Figure 2.10
The Design window.

Adding Fields To A Table

The Design window lets you specify the fields that will form the columns of your table and the data type of each. As you know from Java, the data type of a field determines the type of contents that the field is allowed. For example, a field with data type Number can contain only digits, not letters.

Create a field called VisitorName by typing the desired field name and pressing Enter. Access automatically creates the field with data type Text, which allows letters, digits, and special characters, with a maximum length of 50 characters. This is an acceptable data type and length for the VisitorName field, so press Enter. You can now enter a descriptive comment for the field, such as: The name of the person who visited the Web page. Press Enter and you're ready to add the next field.

Add another field called VisitorEMail, intended for holding the email address of each visitor. Again use a data type of Text and enter an appropriate description.

Add another field called Comment. A comment may need to be longer than 50 characters, so click on the Field Size text box and change the maximum field size from 50 to 255. Click the mouse button on the Description field of the Design window and enter an appropriate description for the field, which will be used to hold a comment offered by the visitor.

Now add another field, called TimeOfVisit. Make the data type of this field Date/Time by pulling down the list of data types and selecting the corresponding entry. As before, add a description for this field, which will be used to store the date and time at which the Web page was visited. Your Design window should look like that shown in Figure 2.11.

Specifying Keys

As a rule of thumb, every table of a database should have a primary key that contains a unique value for each record. Some tables, such as the Customer table of the sample Northwind database, use an ID field assigned by the user when a new record is created. Other times, the more convenient route is simply to allow Access to assign a sequential number to each record as it's created. This sequence number can be stored in the field designated as the primary key of the table.

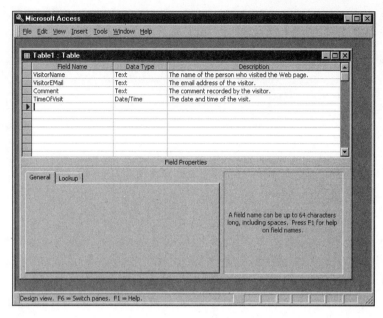

Figure 2.11
Adding a new table and its fields.

To create a sequence-number field for the GuestBook table, tab to the top of the Field Name column and press Insert. Access inserts a new row above the rows for the fields you previously added, as shown in Figure 2.12. Although the primary key does not have to be the first field of a table, this is a common convention, which you should follow when possible.

Simply type SeqNo as the name of the field and press Enter to specify the data type, which should be AutoNumber. Your database design is now complete. Use File|Save to save it. Access prompts you for the name of your new table; call it "Visits" for this sample exercise.

As shown in Figure 2.13, Access immediately responds with a dialog box telling you that the table has no primary key defined. How is this possible, you may ask, since you can see SeqNo, the field you added? This field is indeed contained in the table, but Access was never told that it was to be the primary key. To specify SeqNo as the primary key, simply respond Yes to the question in the dialog box: Do you want to create a primary key now? Access automatically

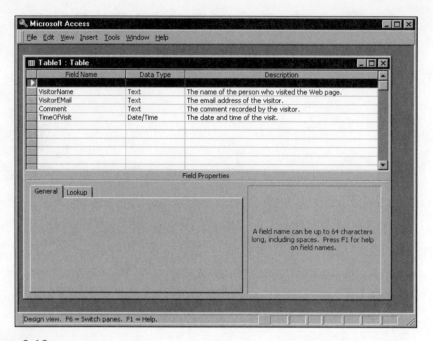

Figure 2.12
Adding a primary key field.

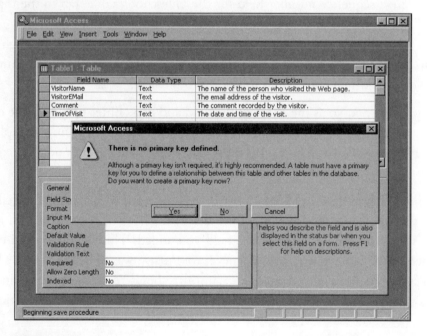

Figure 2.13
Specifying the primary key.

chooses the SeqNo field as the primary key for the table, as shown by the key icon next to the field name, as in Figure 2.14.

Deleting A Field

To see how to delete a field, create a new table using the Design window. Then, create two new fields: GoodField and BadField. To delete the row named BadField, select it by clicking the button at the left end of its row. Now use Edit|Delete Rows to remove the row, as shown in Figure 2.15.

Deleting A Table

Save the table containing GoodField by using File|Save. Give the new table the name Mud, since we don't want it around for long. Note how Access complains about the lack of a primary key. Click Yes, and Access creates a new field called ID—which contains a sequential number—and makes the ID field the primary key of the table. Now, close the table by clicking the Close icon of the Design window. The Database window is now visible again. Select the Mud

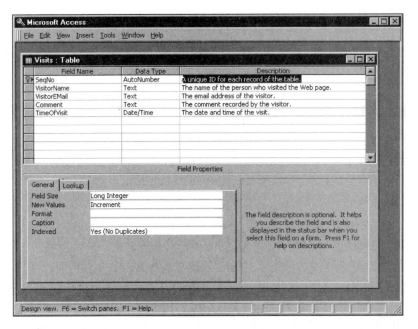

Figure 2.14
Identifying the primary key.

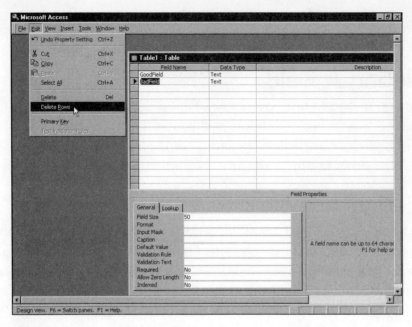

Figure 2.15
Deleting a field.

table and use Edit|Delete to delete it. Access asks you to confirm your action by responding Yes, since deleting the table is an irrevocable action.

Working With Indexes

As explained earlier in this chapter, indexes can improve the performance of table access operations. When you define a primary key for a table, Access automatically creates an index on that field. You can also tell Access to create indexes on other fields. If you wish, you can create an index for each column of a table.

Here's how you create an index. From the Database window, select the Visits table and press the Design button to open the Design window. From the menu, select the View|Indexes menu item. You should see the Indexes window, as shown in Figure 2.16. To create the new index, move the cursor to the second row and enter the name AuxIndex. Now, pull down the Field Name list and select the VisitorEMail field. This designates VisitorEMail as the field indexed by AuxIndex.

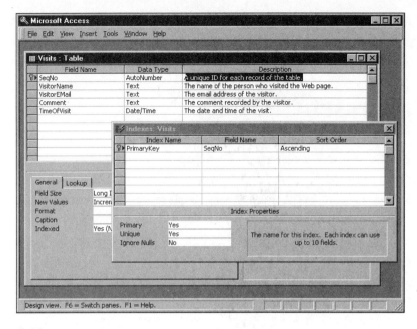

Figure 2.16
The Indexes window.

You can specify additional properties for the new index. The Primary property allows you to make this index the primary key for the table. Do not change this property; leave it set to No.

The Unique property specifies whether multiple table rows can have the same value of the indexed field, VisitorEMail. Leave this property set to No.

If a field is optional, you may want to use the Ignore Nulls property to exclude null values from the index. This makes the index smaller and can improve performance. For the Visits table, leave the property set to No.

Close the Indexes window using its Close icon. Then use the File|Save menu item to save your changes to the GuestBook database.

Deleting An Index

Deleting an index is easy. Open the Indexes window and right-click on the row containing the unwanted index. Select Delete Field from the pop-up menu, and you're done. Go ahead and delete the AuxIndex for practice. Then close the Indexes window and save the revised database.

Your tour of Microsoft Access is complete. You're now well on your way to becoming a database programmer. The next chapter will feature a Java program that uses JDBC to retrieve data from the GuestBook database you just created.

Summary

Relational databases store data in tables, consisting of rows and columns. Each row describes a single object by giving values for properties of the object. The property values are held in the columns of the table. In addition to application data, a database contains a special table, or series of tables, called the schema. The schema describes the database, listing its tables and the names of their columns. Each database table should have a designated primary key, which is a field (or combination of fields) having a unique value for each row of the table. Indexes can be used to rapidly access a particular row of a table by specifying the value of an indexed column. Foreign keys can be used to relate rows of one table to rows of another table.

USING JAVA TO ACCESS DATABASES

3

In this chapter you'll begin your study of SQL database programming. To illustrate the principles of SQL programming, I'll present a Java application that uses an Access database to store data in a guest book of the sort that many people like to provide on their Web home pages. Of course, a real guest book would have to be implemented as an applet, rather than an application, so that it could be automatically downloaded and executed in the user's browser. Building the program as an application rather than an applet avoids some security-related complications, which I'll bring up in Chapter 14.

The emphasis in this chapter is on getting the application up and running and explaining its basic structure. This chapter also explains how the data types provided by SQL correspond to those provided by Access and Java. This information will help you choose the proper Java data types to correctly access values stored in any SQL database. You can then use the example program in this chapter as a pattern for building Java programs that similarly access your own databases.

The following two chapters will address the operation of the application in more detail. Chapter 4 deals with the SQL commands used by the application, and Chapter 5 more fully explains the JDBC API used in accessing the database.

The GuestBook Program

The user interface of the GuestBook application, shown in Figure 3.1, reports entries stored in the GuestBook database designed in Chapter 2. The application displays its output rather primitively; each row of the Visits table is shown as a line within a **TextArea** Abstract Windowing Toolkit (AWT) component. Fields within the row are separated by semicolons. The interface provides no Quit button; the user terminates the program by clicking on the Close icon on the application window's title bar. If this interface isn't exactly what you would enjoy using, never fear. I'll soon show you how to add a more suitable user interface that uses **TextField**s and **Button**s. The application as shown here is indeed clumsy to use, but it's easier to understand than a more attractive one.

Figure 3.2 shows the class hierarchy of the **GuestBook01** class. The application itself is shown beginning in Listing 3.1. It contains a single (public) class named **GuestBook01**, which extends the **Frame** class, as do most other graphical applications. The **GuestBook01** class defines an inner class, called **WindowHandler**, used to process the **windowClosing** message sent when the user wants to close the application window. **WindowHandler** extends the **WindowAdapter** class provided as part of the AWT 1.1 delegation event model. If you're not yet familiar with the delegation event model, you should pay careful attention to the way the application handles events, because the delegation event model is quite different from that used in AWT 1.0.

Just in case your Java is rusty, the explanations in this chapter will be a bit more thorough than those in subsequent chapters. If you find them wordy, just focus on the listings. Listing 3.1 shows the fields defined by the

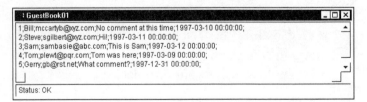

Figure 3.1
Running the GuestBook application.

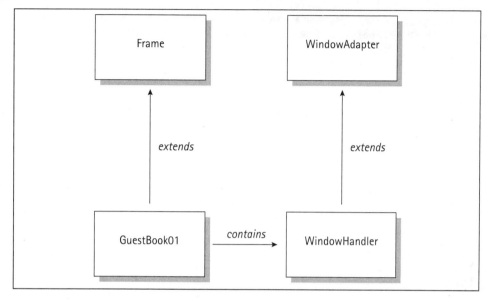

Figure 3.2
Class hierarchy of the **GuestBook01** class.

GuestBook01 class, along with its **main( )** class. The application imports classes from three standard packages:

- **java.awt**—defines the graphical user interface.
- **java.awt.event**—provides support for the AWT 1.1 delegation event model.
- **java.sql**—provides support for JDBC access of SQL databases.

The user interface consists of only two components:

- a **TextArea** named *theVisits*—displays the contents of the database.
- a **TextField** named *theStatus*—displays a message describing any error that occurs.

LISTING 3.1   THE GUESTBOOK APPLICATION.

```
import java.awt.*;
import java.awt.event.*;
import java.sql.*;

class GuestBook01 extends Frame
{
```

```
TextArea   theVisits = new TextArea(6, 80);
TextField  theStatus = new TextField("");

Connection theConnection;
Statement  theStatement;
ResultSet  theResult;
ResultSetMetaData theMetaData;

String theDataSource;
String theUser;
String thePassword;

public static void main(String args[])
{
    new GuestBook01( ).init( );
}
```

The class defines several fields used to support access to the database:

- **theConnection**—a **Connection** object used to represent an open connection to a database.

- **theStatement**—a **Statement** object used to represent a SQL command to be sent to the database for execution.

- **theResult**—a **ResultSet** object used to represent the results returned after execution of a SQL command.

- **theMetaData**—a **ResultSetMetaData** object that contains useful information about results returned after execution of a SQL command, such as the number of records in the result set.

- **theDataSource**—a **String** that contains the name of the database or data source being accessed, in the form of a special type of URL.

- **theUser** and **thePassword**—**Strings** used to gain access to a database that has security restrictions limiting access only to designated users, who must identify themselves and supply a proper password before a connection is established.

The **main( )** method of the class is starkly simple. It creates an anonymous instance of the class and invokes the **init( )** method on it. The arguments passed to **main( )** by the Java interpreter are not used.

Initializing The Application

Listing 3.2 shows the **init( )** method for GuestBook. The default layout manager of the application's frame is **BorderLayout**, so **init( )** places the **TextArea** and **TextField** at the "Center" and "South" positions of the **Frame**, respectively. This way, the **TextArea** will expand to fill any available space, maximizing the room available for displaying database records. Both the **TextArea** and **TextField** are set to be noneditable, since the user doesn't need to type input into either one. An anonymous **WindowHandler** instance is set as a listener for window events, so that it can close the application when the user requests. The **pack( )** and **show( )** methods are invoked on the application frame (the default object) to cause it to resize itself according to the size of its components and display itself on the screen.

The **init( )** method then uses other methods to open a connection to the database, execute a SQL query (the results of which are formatted and displayed in the **TextArea**), and close the database connection. The next section will look at the way window messages are handled, followed by a detailed explanation of the database-related steps.

LISTING 3.2   INITIALIZING THE APPLICATION.

```
public void init( )
{
    setTitle("GuestBook01");
    add("Center", theVisits);
    add("South", theStatus);

    theVisits.setEditable(false);
    theStatus.setEditable(false);
    addWindowListener(new WindowHandler( ));

    pack( );
    show( );

    openConnection( );
    execSQLCommand("Select * from Visits;");
    closeConnection( );
}
```

Handling Window Events

The **init( )** method of the **GuestBook01** class defines an anonymous instance of its **WindowHandler** inner class as a listener for window messages. Details of the inner class are shown in Listing 3.3. Clicking the Close icon of the application window generates a **windowClosing** event. When a **windowClosing** message is received, the **WindowHandler** hides the application frame and terminates the application. Rather than blindly invoking the corresponding methods, it checks to make sure the source of the event is truly a **Frame**, avoiding a possible **ClassCastException** if it turns out the object isn't a **Frame**.

LISTING 3.3   HANDLING WINDOW EVENTS.

```
class WindowHandler extends WindowAdapter
{
    public void windowClosing(WindowEvent event)
    {
        Object source= event.getSource( );
        if (source instanceof Frame)
        {
            ((Frame) source).setVisible(false);
            System.exit(0);
        }
    }
}
```

Opening A Database Connection

Listing 3.4 shows how the program opens its database connection. It first sets values for the fields **theDataSource**, **theUser**, and **thePassword**. The user ID and password should match those associated with the database that is the ODBC data source, as explained in the next section. If the database does not require a user ID or password, each can be specified as an empty string, as done here.

LISTING 3.4   OPENING A DATABASE CONNECTION.

```
public void openConnection( )
{
    theDataSource = "jdbc:odbc:GuestBook";
    theUser = "";
    thePassword = "";

    try
    {
        Class.forName ("sun.jdbc.odbc.JdbcOdbcDriver");
        theConnection =
```

```
            DriverManager.getConnection(theDataSource, theUser,
            thePassword);
        theStatus.setText("Status: OK");
    }
    catch (Exception e)
    {
        handleException(e);
    }
}
```

The string containing the data-source name is formatted as a special URL:

```
jdbc:<subprotocol>:<subname>
```

The protocol name, **jdbc**, is always present. The subprotocol and subname vary depending on the kind of data source used. The JDBC **DriverManager** uses the subprotocol to choose an appropriate driver for the data source. Common values for the subprotocol are "odbc" and "oracle". The subname contains additional information used by the driver. Often, this is a network name, such as that used for other Web services:

```
jdbc:<subprotocol>://<host.domain>:<port>/<databasename>
```

The documentation for your driver should specify the correct form of the subprotocol and subname. With ODBC, the host and port information is unnecessary, since the data source is already configured on the local host. The form used for an ODBC data source is:

```
jdbc:odbc:<data source name>
```

To open the database connection, you must instantiate the proper driver. Again, the documentation for your driver should specify how to do this. If you're using the JDBC-ODBC bridge, you can instantiate the JDBC-ODBC bridge driver by using the **forName( )** method of the class named *Class*:

```
Class.forName ("sun.jdbc.odbc.JdbcOdbcDriver");
```

You can then tell the **DriverManager** to open a connection to your data source by using:

```
theConnection =
    DriverManager.getConnection(theDataSource, theUser, thePassword);
```

The **getConnection( )** method returns a **Connection** object, which you should save, since it becomes your means of accessing the data source. Here, it is saved in the field named *theConnection.*

If an error occurs during the opening of the connection, a **SQLException** is thrown. By enclosing the statements that open the connection within a **try-catch** block, you can handle this contingency gracefully. The GuestBook application simply displays an appropriate message in its **TextField** by means of the **handleException( )** method, shown later.

Closing The Database Connection

When you're done accessing a data source, you should close the database connection, as shown in Listing 3.5, freeing any resources associated with the connection. Any open **ResultSet** or **Statement** objects you've created are closed automatically. Again, a **SQLException** may occur during the closing of a connection, so enclosing the operation in a **try-catch** block is advisable.

LISTING 3.5   CLOSING THE DATABASE CONNECTION.

```
public void closeConnection( )
{
    try
    {
        theConnection.close( );
    }
    catch (Exception e)
    {
        handleException(e);
    }
}
```

Executing A SQL Command

The **execSQLComand( )** method, shown in Listing 3.6, actually issues the SQL command, the most important task of the program. Fortunately, issuing a SQL command is easy with JDBC. In fact, your ability to work with a SQL database has much more to do with the depth of your SQL knowledge than the depth of your JDBC knowledge. JDBC itself is really quite simple to use. That's why this book focuses on SQL, rather than JDBC.

LISTING 3.6   EXECUTING A SQL COMMAND.

```
public void execSQLCommand(String command)
{
    try
    {
        theStatement = theConnection.createStatement();
        theResult = theStatement.executeQuery(command);
        theMetaData = theResult.getMetaData( );
        int columnCount = theMetaData.getColumnCount( );

        theVisits.setText("");

        while (theResult.next( ))
        {
            for (int i = 1; i <= columnCount; i++)
            {
                String colValue = theResult.getString(i);
                if (colValue == null) colValue = "";
                theVisits.append(colValue + ";");
            }
            theVisits.append("\n");
        }
    }
    catch (Exception e)
    {
        handleException(e);
    }
}
```

To perform the command, the program uses the **createStatement( )** method of the **Connection** object to create a **Statement** that can hold the query. Then it invokes the **executeQuery( )** method on the **Statement** object, passing a string containing the SQL query.

Chapter 4 will show how to construct some basic SQL queries. For now, just observe how the **init( )** method passes the query string—"Select * from Visits;"—as an argument. This simple query obtains all the rows of the Visits table and returns a **ResultSet** object. Like most other SQL queries, this one generates a relational table as its result. You can use **ResultSet** to access this result table.

Next the program invokes the **getMetaData( )** method on the **ResultSet** object. This returns a **ResultSetMetaData** value, which the program stores in a variable named *theMetaData*. Much useful data is available using

ResultSetMetaData objects; here, the program uses the **getColumnCount( )** method to obtain the number of columns of the result table.

Finally, the program iterates through the result table, invoking the **next( )** method on **theResult** to obtain each row of the result table. This method eventually returns **false** when it runs out of rows.

Each row is processed using a **for** loop that iterates over the number of columns. The value of each row attribute is obtained using the **getString( )** method, which returns the value of a column as a **String**. As you'll see later in the chapter, there is a whole family of similar methods that return column values as other data types. The **getString( )** method is particularly useful, because almost any SQL value has a **String** representation of some sort. Therefore, the **getString( )** method can be appropriately called on a column of almost any type.

If a database column contains a SQL **null** value, perhaps resulting from an input field omitted by the user, the **getString( )** method returns **null**. The program tests the value returned by **getString( )**, transforming a **null** value to an empty string. Then the value is appended to the contents of the **TextArea**, **theVisits**. The entire operation is enclosed in a **try-catch** block so that a **SQLException** does not unexpectedly terminate the program.

Handling Errors And Exceptions

Listing 3.7 shows the **handleException( )** method, which the program uses to handle errors and exceptions. This method simply sets the status **TextField** to contain the error message related to the exception, which it obtains by using the **getMessage( )** method. It also prints a stack trace on **System.out**.

An interesting property of **SQLException**s is that they can be *chained*—that is, a **SQLException** can be linked to another **SQLException**. The **getNext-Exception( )** method "walks" the exception chain, as shown here. The **handleException( )** method uses this technique to print each chained exception on **System.out**.

LISTING 3.7   HANDLING ERRORS AND EXCEPTIONS.

```
public void handleException(Exception e)
{
    theStatus.setText("Error: " + e.getMessage( ));
```

```
    e.printStackTrace( );
    if (e instanceof SQLException)
    {
        while ((e = ((SQLException) e).getNextException( )) != null)
        {
            System.out.println(e);
        }
    }
}
```

Setting Up The ODBC Data Source

To run the GuestBook application, you must first create an ODBC data source corresponding to the GuestBook Access database. You can use the database you created in Chapter 2 (if you're confident that you created it correctly), or you can copy the database file (GuestBook.mdb) from the CD-ROM directory that contains the source files for this chapter.

To use Access via ODBC, you must install the Access ODBC drivers. If you haven't done so, use the Access setup program to load them onto your system.

To configure the database as an ODBC data source, follow these steps:

1. From the Start menu, select Settings|Control Panel.

2. Click on ODBC-32, the 32-bit ODBC driver. (If this icon is not present, you need to install the Access ODBC drivers.)

3. Click Add and choose Microsoft Access Driver. (If this choice is not present, you need to install the Access ODBC drivers.)

4. Type in a data-source name, such as *Guest Book*, and a suitable description.

5. In the Database frame, click on the Select button.

6. Use the Select Database dialog to select the file that contains your database.

7. If your database is protected with a password, you can click the Advanced button and specify a user name and password.

Your ODBC data source is now configured and ready. This would be a good time for you to execute the GuestBook application and see how it works.

If you later find that you need to change a setting for this data source, follow these steps:

1. From the Start menu, select Settings|Control Panel.

2. Click on ODBC-32, the 32-bit ODBC driver.

3. Select the data source you wish to reconfigure, and click the Setup button.

An Improved GuestBook Program

Upon trying out the GuestBook program, you probably found its output awkward to read. In this section, I'll show how to improve the program's user interface. We'll continue making improvements through the next several chapters until we finally arrive at a program that makes full and effective use of the capabilities of Java and SQL.

Figure 3.3 shows the new version of the program, and Listing 3.8 shows its fields, along with its **main( )** method. The improved version does not make any significant changes to the **main( )** method. The main class is now named **GuestBook02**, to distinguish it from the original version. It implements the **ActionListener** interface, so it can receive and process event messages originating with the two buttons—Next and Quit—added to the user interface.

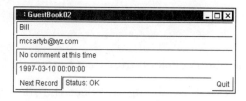

Figure 3.3
The improved GuestBook program.

LISTING 3.8   THE FIELDS AND MAIN( ) METHOD.

```
import java.awt.*;
import java.awt.event.*;
import java.sql.*;

class GuestBook02 extends Frame
implements ActionListener
{

    Panel       theDataPanel = new Panel( );
    TextField   theName      = new TextField("", 32);
    TextField   theEMail     = new TextField("", 32);
    TextField   theComment   = new TextField("", 50);
    TextField   theTime      = new TextField("", 24);

    Panel       theBottomPanel = new Panel( );
    Button      theNextButton  = new Button("Next Record");
    TextField   theStatus      = new TextField("");
    Button      theQuitButton  = new Button("Quit");

    Connection theConnection;
    Statement  theStatement;
    ResultSet  theResult;

    String theDataSource;
    String theUser;
    String thePassword;

    public static void main(String args[])
    {
        new GuestBook02( ).init( );
    }
```

Since the program now displays only a single record at a time, it provides a Next button to allow the user to scroll forward through the database. Note that it has no Previous button; moving backward through the database must await more sophisticated SQL programming techniques, which will be presented in Chapter 4. In addition to the Next button, the program now provides a Quit button, so the novice user can easily figure out how to stop the program.

The init( ) Method

The improved user interface constructed by the **init**( ) method includes two **Panel**s. The center **Panel**, which expands to fill available space, contains

TextFields for the visitor name, email address, comment, and time of visit. These are arranged into four rows—one TextField on each row—using GridLayout.

The bottom Panel is arranged using a BorderLayout. Its center component, the TextField that reports status, expands horizontally to fill available space. The Next and Quit buttons, to the TextField's left and right, respectively, use only enough space to make their labels visible.

Each of the TextFields is set as noneditable, since they're used only for output. Each of the Buttons has the GuestBook02 object set as the listener for any actionPerformed events it generates; the GuestBook02 object is also set as the listener for window events.

The remainder of the init( ) method is little changed. Note, however, that the program no longer invokes the Connection.close( ) method to close the database connection. In the new version of the program, the connection is closed only when the user decides to exit the program.

Listing 3.9 shows the revised init( ) method. The openConnection( ), closeConnection( ), and handleException( ) methods are left exactly as they were in the original version of the program, so they're not shown in the listing.

LISTING 3.9   THE INIT( ) METHOD.

```
public void init( )
{
    setTitle("GuestBook02");
    add("Center", theDataPanel);
    add("South", theBottomPanel);

    theDataPanel.setLayout(new GridLayout(4, 1));
    theDataPanel.add(theName);
    theDataPanel.add(theEMail);
    theDataPanel.add(theComment);
    theDataPanel.add(theTime);

    theBottomPanel.setLayout(new BorderLayout( ));
    theBottomPanel.add("West", theNextButton);
    theBottomPanel.add("Center", theStatus);
    theBottomPanel.add("East", theQuitButton);

    theName.setEditable(false);
    theEMail.setEditable(false);
```

```
    theComment.setEditable(false);
    theTime.setEditable(false);
    theStatus.setEditable(false);

    theNextButton.addActionListener(this);
    theQuitButton.addActionListener(this);
    addWindowListener(new WindowHandler( ));

    pack( );
    show( );

    openConnection( );
    execSQLCommand("Select * from Visits;");
}
```

The execSQLCommand() Method

The **execSQLCommand( )** method, shown in Listing 3.10, appears almost exactly as before. The only change is the addition of a call to a new method, **moveDataToForm( )**, which is invoked if the result set contains at least one row.

LISTING 3.10   THE EXECSQLCOMMAND( ) METHOD.

```
public void execSQLCommand(String command)
{
    try
    {
        theStatement = theConnection.createStatement( );
        theResult = theStatement.executeQuery(command);
        if (theResult.next( )) moveDataToForm( );
    }
    catch (Exception e)
    {
        handleException(e);
    }
}
```

The moveDataToForm( ) Method

The new method, **moveDataToForm( )**, shown in Listing 3.11, is responsible for getting the individual column values from the result set and setting the **TextFields'** contents appropriately. The method uses the **getString( )** method of the **ResultSet** object to obtain a **String** representation of the specified column. A utility method, **noNull( )**, is used to avoid setting a **String** to a **null** value. The

noNull( ) method is shown immediately below the **moveDataToForm( )** method in Listing 3.11.

LISTING 3.11   THE MOVEDATATOFORM( ) AND NONULL( ) METHODS.

```
public void moveDataToForm( )
{
    try
    {
        theName.setText    (noNull(theResult.getString(2)));
        theEMail.setText   (noNull(theResult.getString(3)));
        theComment.setText(noNull(theResult.getString(4)));
        theTime.setText    (noNull(theResult.getString(5)));
    }
    catch (Exception e)
    {
        handleException(e);
    }
}

public String noNull(String s)
{
    return (s != null) ? s : "";
}
```

Note that **moveDataToForm( )** does not include the first column, which contains the primary key of the Visits table. Including the field would have been simple, but the value of the primary key was considered to be of no importance to the user of this program; consequently, the field is not displayed.

The remaining columns are accessed sequentially. Drivers for some ODBC data sources require that columns be accessed only once, and in order. This is a good habit to form at the outset of your JDBC programming career.

The actionPerformed( ) Method

The **actionPerformed( )** method, shown in Listing 3.12, handles events generated when the user clicks either the Next or Quit button. The program establishes the **GuestBook02** object as the listener for all **actionPerformed** events. An alternative would be to create distinct objects to handle the events of each **Button**. This would avoid the need for **if-else** processing and would be quite helpful if the application had many **Buttons**. With only two **Buttons**, however, the simpler course is to handle events from each in a single object and method.

LISTING 3.12   THE actionPerformed( ) METHOD.

```
public void actionPerformed(ActionEvent event)
{
    theStatus.setText("Status: OK");
    Object source = event.getSource( );
    if (source == theNextButton)
    {
        try
        {
            if (theResult.next( )) moveDataToForm( );
            else theStatus.setText("Status: No more records.");
        }
        catch (Exception e)
        {
            theStatus.setText("Error during next: "
              + e.getMessage( ));
        }
    }
    else if (source == theQuitButton)
    {
        destroy( );
    }
}
```

The **getSource( )** method distinguishes which button is the source of the event. If the user clicks the Next button, the routine attempts to obtain and display another row from the result set. A message is displayed if all records have been viewed.

Clicking the Quit button invokes a new method called **destroy( )**, described in the next section. This method has the task of closing down the application.

Notice that the **actionPerformed( )** method sets the status display to Status: OK at the outset of any requested operation. This eliminates "stale" messages caused by transient errors. If the error is "hard," it will recur and the **handleError( )** method will be invoked by the processing method to set the status display appropriately.

The destroy( ) Method

The **destroy( )** method, shown in Listing 3.13, closes down the application. It invokes the **closeConnection( )** method, which frees all JDBC resources and disconnects from the data source. It then hides the application frame and terminates the program.

LISTING 3.13   THE DESTROY( ) METHOD.

```
public void destroy( )
{
    closeConnection( );
    setVisible(false);
    System.exit(0);
}
```

The WindowHandler Inner Class

The **WindowHandler** inner class, shown in Listing 3.14, is little changed from the previous version. Instead of directly invoking the methods to close the data-source connection, it now simply calls the **destroy( )** method. This way, whether the user clicks the Close icon or the Quit button, the result is the same.

LISTING 3.14   THE WINDOWHANDLER.

```
class WindowHandler extends WindowAdapter
{
    public void windowClosing(WindowEvent event)
    {
        Object object = event.getSource( );
        if (object instanceof Frame) destroy( );
    }
}
```

Java And Access Data Types

Now you can use the pattern illustrated by the **GuestBook02** application to create your own SQL database applications, accessing ODBC sources, such as any Access databases you've created. You may want to work with data types other than **String** in your programs. Table 3.1 shows various Access data types, the corresponding Java data types, and the method used to obtain column values of each type. For example,

```
String theString value = getString(1);
```

could obtain the value of result set column 1 as a Java **String**. But

```
int theIntValue = getInt(1);
```

could obtain the value of the same column as an **int**. Chapter 5 will provide a more thorough treatment of Java data types, but Table 3.1 should be enough to get you started writing interesting and useful JDBC programs.

Summary

The most important JDBC data types are **Connection**, which represents connections to data sources; **Statement**, which represents SQL commands; and **ResultSet**, which represents a relational table returned as the result of an executed SQL command. Another important data type is **ResultSetMetaData**, which provides information concerning a **ResultSet**, including the number of columns it contains.

TABLE 3.1

DATA TYPES AND RESULTSET METHODS.

Java Type	Access Type	SQL Type	Method
String	Text	VARCHAR	getString( )
String	Memo	LONGVARCHAR	getASCIIStream( )
java.sql.Numeric	Number	NUMERIC	getNumeric( )
boolean	Yes/No	BIT	getBoolean( )
byte	Byte	TINYINT	getByte( )
short	Integer	SMALLINT	getShort( )
int	Long	INTEGER	getInt( )
long	Long	BIGINT	getLong( )
float	Single	REAL	getFloat( )
double	Double	DOUBLE	getDouble( )
byte[ ]	OLE object	VARBINARY, LONGVARBINARY	getBytes( ), getBinaryStream( )
java.sql.Date	Date/Time	DATE	getDate( )
java.sql.Time	Date/Time	TIME	getTime( )
java.sql.Timestamp	Date/Time	TIMESTAMP	getTimeStamp( )

JDBC data sources are referenced using a special form of URL. The author of the driver used to access the data source specifies the exact syntax.

A SQL command is executed by creating a **Statement** based on an open connection and invoking the **executeQuery( )** method on the **Statement**. The query will generally return a **ResultSet** object, which provides access to the relational table generated by the query. Rows of the table may be accessed sequentially by using the **next( )** method. You can access columns of each row with the **getString( )** method, or a similar method returning a different data type. The columns of each row should be accessed only once and in sequential order. Moving backward through the **ResultSet** requires special techniques.

When a SQL-related error occurs, a **SQLException** is thrown. These exceptions may be caught and handled as other exceptions. **SQLException**s can be chained together; the **getNextException( )** method can be used to walk the chain.

The ODBC driver manager, found in the Control Panel, can configure an ODBC data source. You must install the Access ODBC drivers before JDBC can access data in an Access database.

SQL QUERIES 4

This chapter continues the presentation of SQL, the common language of most modern database systems. The aim of this and the following chapters is to teach you how to access SQL databases from within your Java programs. SQL has quite a few facilities that are needed mainly by interactive users of the SQL interpreter rather than by programmers. Since you are unlikely to need these, I've omitted some of them and covered others only lightly. Many SQL constructs work similarly to familiar Java constructs, so I will point out these similarities to smooth your way. By keeping your focus and building on existing Java knowledge, you'll quickly and easily learn SQL.

In the previous chapter, you learned how to write a Java program that used a simple SQL command to retrieve all the records of a table—more precisely, all the columns of all the records of the table.

Such an approach is acceptable for throw-away programs or for programs that access database tables with few records, but it fails to take full advantage of the power of SQL. If you wrote all your database programs that way, you would soon develop a reputation as a writer of inefficient code. Efficient programs do not send unwanted records from the database, over the network, to an application program. Certainly, an application program is capable of filtering its input data, processing only the records of interest. But sending unwanted data across the network wastes bandwidth and slows response time. This may not have been such a significant problem when networks were high-speed LANs, but Internet and intranet connections often operate at relatively lower speeds. Performance is a greater issue when networks span longer distances.

Fortunately, SQL is a powerful *programming* language, and the SQL programs (called *queries*) you'll soon learn to write are in no way inferior to programs you might write in another language, such as Java. Avoiding inefficiencies, such as sending unwanted records, is little more than child's play.

You'll see that SQL programs are different from those written in more familiar languages. Most programming languages allow programmers to build programs using three basic constructs:

• Sequence

• Selection

• Iteration

In most programming languages, the programmer writes instructions telling the computer *how* to accomplish *what* the programmer wants the program to do. The programmer focuses on the order in which statements should be executed, the conditions under which certain statements should be executed or skipped, and the conditions under which other statements should be executed repeatedly.

SQL programs, in contrast, emphasize the *what*. A SQL programmer writes queries that define *what* is wanted, and the SQL interpreter decides *how* to accomplish the specified results. Once you've gotten used to this idea, you'll probably find it liberating; but to many SQL newcomers the concept seems a little strange at first.

This chapter will focus on overcoming the inefficiencies of the SQL command used in Chapter 3. I will demonstrate how to retrieve from a database only the records an application program actually needs. The technique is simple, but powerful. By the end of this chapter, you'll be writing your own SQL programs for fun and, hopefully, for profit as well.

Query Basics: The Select Verb

Remember the SQL command used in both programs in Chapter 3:

```
Select * from Visits;
```

This is an example of the most basic of SQL commands, the **Select** command. Like Java statements, the **Select** command is terminated by a semicolon. Unlike Java, SQL keywords can be written in either uppercase or lowercase. The following query is considered by the SQL interpreter as equivalent to the first:

```
SELECT * FROM Visits;
```

The table name, *Visits*, on the other hand, should not vary, because it is not a SQL keyword. It should appear in the query the same way it was specified when the table was created, with an uppercase *V* followed by the remaining letters in lowercase. Some DBMSs are more forgiving than others in such matters, but it's best to get in the habit of writing portable queries that will be accepted by a variety of DBMSs.

The **Select** command gives the SQL interpreter three main instructions:

- What table to access

- What columns to retrieve

- What rows to include in the result

You should recall from the previous chapter that the Visits table in this very simple query is part of the GuestBook database, which the program accesses using ODBC. You can't tell anything about the database by inspecting the SQL command, however; the identity of the database is specified in the Java code that establishes the database connection and invokes the SQL command.

One reason this query is so simple is that all rows and columns of the Visits table are included in the result. The next section demonstrates how a somewhat more elaborate **Select** command gives the programmer greater control over the data retrieved.

Choosing Specific Columns: The Column List

Table 4.1 shows an example database table that will be used in this chapter and throughout the rest of the book. The table, part of a human resources database, contains information about the employees of a small software development company.

If you issued a query of this table similar to the query of the Visits table

```
Select * from Employees;
```

you would generate a result set containing all the columns of all the records of the table. The asterisk (*) in such queries means *all columns* to the SQL interpreter. Of course, you may not want to retrieve every column of a table. In place of the asterisk, you can include the name of a table column or a list of column names, separated by commas. For example, the more elaborate query

```
Select EmployeeNo, Name, Address, City, State, Zip, Sex, Salary from
Employees;
```

TABLE **4.1**

THE EMPLOYEES TABLE.

Emp. No	Name	Address	City	State	Zip	Sex	Salary
1	Fred Fearless	711 Danger Way	Tombstone	AZ	71234	M	60000
2	Adam Adams	1 Eden Circle	Paradise	CA	77701	M	120000
3	Eve Adams	1 Eden Circle	Paradise	CA	77701	F	130000
4	Bogus Blitzo	21 High Place	Easy Street	CA	16661	M	150000
5	Jumbo Jones	17 Jungle Way	Redmond	WA	45624	M	65000
6	Sam TheMan	671 Careful Trail	Santa Ona	CA	91732	M	85000
7	Young Tom	5542 Cushy Seat	Overstuff	CA	98235	M	90000
8	Steve Giblet	78 Turkey Plaza	Gravy	CA	93436	M	70000
9	Bill Bonkers	888 Frantic Lane	Anxiety	CA	95632	M	60000
10	Sue Slewfoot	86 Legal Tower	Highrise	CA	97655	F	300000
11	Abigail Honest	111 First Street	Integrity	CA	97633	F	60000
12	Ann Agram	22 Puzzle Box	Intellect	CA	95645	F	75000

produces exactly the same result as the previous simple query. This new syntactic form can be used to exclude unwanted columns from the query result. Suppose you wanted to retrieve only the employees' names and salaries. You would write:

```
Select Name, Salary from Employees;
```

Or perhaps you want salary to be listed in the left-most column in the result set. Simply write:

```
Select Salary, Name from Employees;
```

Explicitly listing the columns to be retrieved can be much more efficient than the all-columns form, especially if the table has many columns that contain long text strings or other large values. But there's a second advantage, often more important than the first: The explicit **Select** is data independent, while the all-columns **Select** is not.

Say you write a query one day, using the all-columns **Select**. Then, the next day you add a new column to the table the query accesses. Now, even though you never changed your query, it behaves differently than before. It retrieves a new field that your Java program may not handle correctly. In the best case, the Java program ignores the new field. In the worst case, the new field causes the Java program to malfunction.

 Although the all-columns **Select** query is convenient to use, you should avoid it in queries that will be executed by programs. It may break the data independence of your program, causing it to fail unexpectedly when the database design is changed.

Figure 4.1 illustrates the all-columns and explicit **Select** queries. The representation used is based on the Microsoft Access Design window, which depicts a table as a vertical list of fields. The name of the table is shown at the top of the list. A key icon identifies key fields. Fields included in the query result are shaded.

Choosing Specific Rows: The Where Clause

The SQL **Select** command is also capable of retrieving only selected rows of a table. This can be an important performance concern, since databases with hundreds of thousands of records, or even millions of records, are not

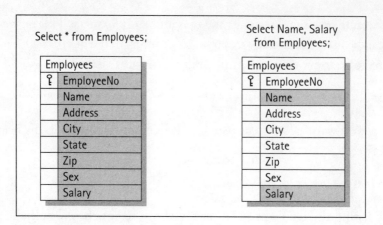

Figure 4.1
Selecting table columns.

uncommon. Sending a million records across the Internet when you need to access only a single record may not be a criminal act, but it won't win you many friends.

To select rows from a table, you simply include a condition in your **Select** statement:

```
Select Name, Salary from Employees Where EmployeeNo = 4;
```

This query returns only those records for which the value of the EmployeeNo field is 4. Executing the query produces a result set containing a single record:

Emp. No	Name	Address	City	State	Zip	Sex	Salary
4	Bogus Blitzo	21 High Place	Easy Street	CA	16661	M	150000

Figure 4.2 illustrates the use of the **Where** clause to select specified table rows. A rectangle containing the comparison value of the EmployeeNo field (4) is connected by a line with the rectangle representing the field, indicating that only selected records are included in the result set.

Of course, you could obtain the same query result in several ways. For example, the following query returns exactly the same result as the first:

```
Select Name, Salary from Employees Where Name = 'Bogus Blitzo';
```

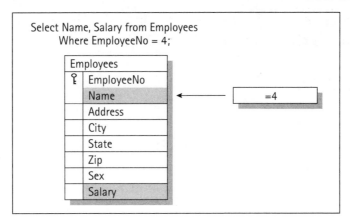

Figure 4.2
Selecting specified table rows.

Although the first query retrieved only those records for which EmployeeNo was 4, this query returns only those records for which Name is 'Bogus Blitzo'. Note how the value of the Name field, which is a text string, is specified using single quotes. Omitting the single quotes, or using double quotes, will cause the query to malfunction.

 In SQL, be sure to enclose text strings using single quotes. Since Java uses double quotes for this purpose, it's easy to write a SQL query that mistakenly uses double quotes.

Each of our last two queries returned only a single record in the result set. Building queries that return multiple records is not any more difficult. The following query would return three records from the table:

```
Select Name, Salary from Employees Where Salary >= 130000;
```

The records returned would be those for Eve Adams, Bogus Blitzo, and Sue Slewfoot. Each has an annual salary of at least $130,000, which is the value specified by the query.

Predicates And Comparisons

The art of writing useful **Where** clauses consists mainly of deciding which records you need and then accurately writing a condition that identifies them. This condition is referred to as a *predicate,* because, for any record, it is either True or False. If the condition tests True for a given record, it will be included; otherwise, it will be excluded. Fortunately, the rules that govern the writing of predicates in SQL are quite similar to those used in writing conditions in Java. Hence, you already know a great deal about writing SQL **Where** clauses.

Comparison Operators

The most common form of SQL predicate is one that compares values. Table 4.2 shows the comparison operators used in writing SQL queries. They are the same as those used in Java, except that nonequality is represented using <> rather than !=.

> Don't use the != operator in a SQL query. The proper SQL operator for testing nonequality is <>.

Most values used in comparisons are either numbers or strings. Both values must have the same type: Numbers should be compared with numbers, and strings with strings. Mixing types leads to errors or wrong results. This mistake is easy for a Java programmer to make, since Java is somewhat friendlier in such matters, allowing such expressions as:

```
String myResult = "The answer is: " + 2;  // Works in Java, but NOT in SQL
```

The Java expression automatically converts the number 2 to a string and appends it to the literal. Don't depend on this behavior in SQL.

	TABLE 4.2

SQL COMPARISON OPERATORS.

Operator	Meaning
=	Equal
<>	Nonequal
<	Less than
>	Greater than
<=	Less than or equal to (i.e., not greater than)
>=	Greater than or equal to (i.e., not less than)

Always compare numbers with numbers, and strings with strings. Don't mix types in a comparison predicate.

String Comparisons

Although writing comparison predicates that use strings is easy, string comparisons involve two subtleties that you need to be aware of: case sensitivity and collating sequences.

CASE SENSITIVITY

In SQL, just as in Java, the string 'ABC' is not the same as the string 'abc'. (Of course, Java strings are written with double quotes, rather than single quotes.) You'll learn in Chapter 6 how you can use SQL functions to perform string comparisons that ignore case.

COLLATING SEQUENCES

Different computers encode character information differently, using *collating sequences*. The collating sequence used by a computer determines which characters are considered greater than others when compared. Everyone expects "B" to be greater than "A", and so every computer collating sequence observes this useful custom. But comparing characters other than letters and digits can lead to unexpected results. Should "%" be considered greater than, or less than, "+"? Even comparing letters and digits is perilous. Some mainframes consider digits as greater than "Z" while most PCs consider digits as less than "A".

Ideally, your SQL queries should not depend upon such considerations, since any query that does so may work on one database host, but fail on another. When your application demands that such comparisons be performed, however, you should consult the documentation for your DBMS or your database administrator to learn how they are handled by your database host.

 Remember that different computer systems sometimes use different collating sequences for comparing characters. Try to write portable queries by avoiding comparisons that depend on the collating sequence used by your database host.

Compound Comparisons

Sometimes, a single predicate is not sufficient to identify the records you're interested in. Suppose you want to retrieve the names of female employees with annual salaries of more than $100,000. Only those records with an "F" in the Sex field and a value greater than 100000 in the Salary field should be included in the query result. SQL provides boolean operators that let you write queries with multiple predicates. SQL's boolean operators work similarly to Java's, though different symbols are used, as shown in Table 4.3.

Using the **And** operator, for example, you could write

```
Select Name From Employees Where Sex = 'F' And Salary > 100000;
```

to generate the needed result. Remember that SQL keywords can be written in uppercase or lowercase, so this same query could be correctly written as:

```
SELECT Name FROM Employees WHERE Sex = 'F' AND Salary > 100000;
```

Use whichever form seems clearest to you. Always use the correct case in writing the names of fields and columns, however.

Figure 4.3 illustrates this query. Figure 4.4 illustrates a different query, using the **Or** operator.

You can use parentheses, as in Java, to control the order in which comparisons are evaluated. This is particularly helpful with the **Not** operator. For example, the query

```
SELECT Name FROM Employees WHERE NOT (Sex = 'M' OR Sex = 'F');
```

would locate employees whose records have an invalid value in the Sex field.

TABLE 4.3

SQL BOOLEAN OPERATORS.

Operator	Result is true if:
AND	Both predicates are true
OR	Either or both predicates are true
NOT	The predicate is false

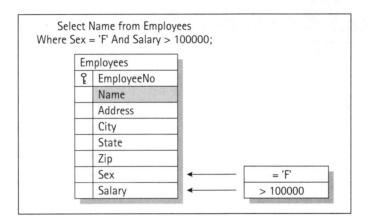

Figure 4.3
A query using **And**.

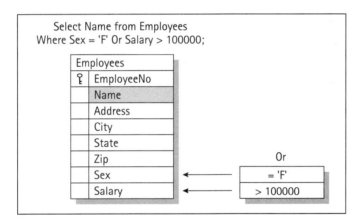

Figure 4.4
A query using **Or**.

Mixing AND And OR

Using both **And** and **Or** in a single compound comparison is possible and often useful. SQL's **And** and **Or** behave similarly to Java's logical operators, && and ||, in such uses. The **And** operator is performed before the **Or** operator, unless parentheses dictate otherwise. For example, the query

```
SELECT Name FROM Employees WHERE Sex = 'F' AND Salary < 70000 OR Salary >
100000;
```

would return records from two groups. The first includes female employees earning less than $70,000 annually. The second includes employees, whether male or female, earning more than $100,000 annually. To find the names of female employees with especially low or especially high salaries, you would write:

```
SELECT Name FROM Employees WHERE Sex = 'F' AND (Salary < 70000 OR Salary >
100000);
```

Figures 4.5 and 4.6, respectively, illustrate these two queries.

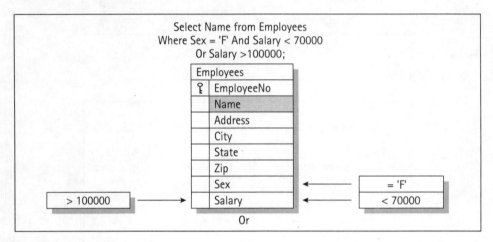

Figure 4.5
Using **And** and **Or** without parentheses.

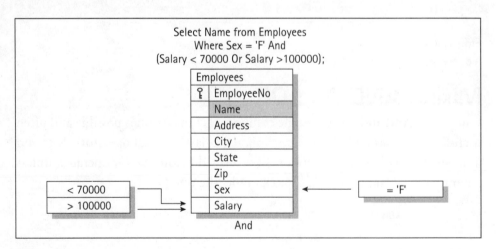

Figure 4.6
Using **And** and **Or** with parentheses.

Be sure to accurately specify compound comparisons including **And** and **Or**, using parentheses when required. You may want to use parentheses all the time, so your intention is clear.

More Predicates

Most SQL implementations include other predicates, which can make it easier to write SQL queries that do just what you want. Table 4.4 summarizes these additional SQL predicates, which are explained in the following sections.

BETWEEN

The **Between** predicate allows you to specify predicates more compactly. Consider the following predicate:

```
Salary >= 100000 AND Salary =< 150000
```

An equivalent predicate can be written in an actual query as:

```
Select Name From Employees Where Salary BETWEEN 100000 AND 150000;
```

A second form of **Between** includes a **Not** that excludes, rather than includes, the specified range. For example, the query

```
Select Name from Employees Where Salary NOT BETWEEN 100000 AND 150000;
```

TABLE 4.4

ADDITIONAL SQL PREDICATES.

Predicate	Meaning
BETWEEN...AND	Include records with field value within specified range.
NOT BETWEEN...AND	Exclude records with field value within specified range.
LIKE	Include records with string field matching pattern.
NOT LIKE	Exclude records with string field matching pattern.
IN	Include records with field value contained in specified list.
NOT IN	Exclude records with field value contained in specified list.
IS NULL	Include records with omitted (null) value for optional field.
IS NOT NULL	Exclude records with omitted (null) value for optional field.

returns exactly those records *not* returned by the earlier query. It's equivalent to the following query:

```
Select Name from Employees Where Salary < 100000 OR Salary > 150000;
```

LIKE

The **Like** predicate allows you to specify wild-card patterns, such as those used for DOS file names. In a pattern, you use an underscore (_) to stand for any single character and a percent sign (%) to stand for any string of characters.

For example, the following query would return all employees named Bob:

```
Select Name From Employees Where Name LIKE 'Bob %';
```

This one would return all employees *not* named Bob:

```
Select Name From Employees Where Name NOT LIKE 'Bob %';
```

IN

The **Or** operator can be used to check whether the value of a column is one of those specified in a list. For example, you could retrieve employees living in Arizona or California by writing:

```
Select Name From Employees Where State = 'AZ' Or State = 'CA';
```

This can grow tedious if the list consists of more than two or three items. The **In** predicate helps out in such situations. You simply write:

```
Select Name From Employees Where State IN ('AZ', 'CA');
```

The **Not In** predicate includes only records with a field value *not* in the specified list.

NULL

When designing a table, you can specify fields to be either required or optional. If a required field is missing from a record sent to the database, the DBMS will not accept the record, generating an error instead. Omitting an optional field causes no error, however. Using the **Is Null** predicate, you can identify stored database records that contain missing optional fields—that is, null fields. Notice that a null field is not the same as a numeric field with zero value or a string field containing an empty string or a blank string. The form of the query is:

```
Select Name From Employees Where Zip IS NULL;
```

This query returns names of employees that have no Zip field in their record. The corresponding **Is Not Null** predicate specifies records that have non-null values in a field. You'll learn more about null values in Chapter 6.

 Remember that the value **Null** is distinct from any other value. Neither a field with the value zero nor a field with a blank string has a **Null** value.

The SQLWindow Application

Now that you've learned some SQL, you need a quick way to try out different SQL commands and view the results. The SQLWindow application is designed to let you do just that. Figure 4.7 shows the SQLWindow application's user interface. The application provides two input **TextField**s, an output **TextArea**, and an output **TextField**. One of the input **TextField**s is used to enter the name of the ODBC data source the application is to access; the other is used to specify a SQL command to be executed. The result set returned by execution of the SQL command is shown in the **TextArea**; each record starts a new line, and

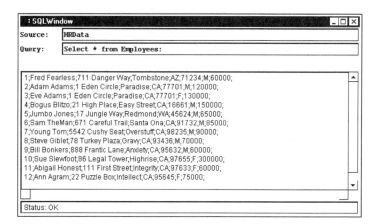

Figure 4.7
The SQLWindow application.

fields are separated by semicolons. The data-source connection is opened and closed for each query, so you can enter a new data-source name at any time. If an error occurs, it is reported using the output **TextField**.

Give the application a try before moving on to study how it was built. Be sure to use the ODBC Control Panel applet to configure your ODBC data source before trying to access it.

To see how the application works, take a look at Listing 4.1, which shows the fields, **main( )** method, and default constructor of the **SQLWindow** class. The user interface is built using five nested panels. The next section, describing the **init( )** method, provides more details. Other than the application-specific user-interface fields, the fields of the **SQLWindow** class are not significantly different from those used in the programs presented in Chapter 3.

LISTING 4.1 THE SQLWINDOW APPLICATION.

```java
import java.awt.*;
import java.awt.event.*;
import java.sql.*;

class SQLWindow extends Frame
implements ActionListener
{
    Panel      topPanel    = new Panel( );
    Panel      mainPanel   = new Panel( );
    Panel      bottomPanel = new Panel( );
    Panel      sourcePanel = new Panel( );
    Panel      queryPanel  = new Panel( );

    Font       topFont = new Font("Courier", Font.BOLD, 12);

    TextArea   theResult = new TextArea(6, 80);
    TextField  theSource = new TextField("");
    TextField  theQuery  = new TextField("");
    TextField  theStatus = new TextField("");

    String theDataSource;
    String theUser;
    String thePassword;

    Connection        theConnection;
    Statement         theStatement = null;
    ResultSet         theResultSet = null;
    ResultSetMetaData theMetaData;
```

```
WindowHandler theWindowHandler = new WindowHandler( );

public static void main(String args[])
{
    SQLWindow theApplication = new SQLWindow( );
    theApplication.init( );
}

public SQLWindow( )
{
    super("SQLWindow");
}
```

The init( ) Method

The **init( )** method, shown in Listing 4.2, builds the user interface using five panels:

- The **topPanel** contains the **sourcePanel** and **queryPanel**.

- The **sourcePanel** holds the **TextField** specifying the data source.

- The **queryPanel** holds the **TextField** specifying the query to be executed.

- The **mainPanel** holds the **TextArea** used to display the query result.

- The **bottomPanel** holds the **TextField** used to display any error messages.

BorderLayout allows the application window to adjust itself to use any extra available space.

LISTING 4.2   THE INIT( ) METHOD.

```
public void init( )
{
    add("North", topPanel);
    add("Center", mainPanel);
    add("South", bottomPanel);

    topPanel.setLayout(new GridLayout(3, 1));
    topPanel.setFont(topFont);
    topPanel.add(sourcePanel);
    topPanel.add(queryPanel);

    sourcePanel.setLayout(new BorderLayout( ));
    sourcePanel.add("West", new Label("Source: "));
    sourcePanel.add("Center", theSource);
```

```
queryPanel.setLayout(new BorderLayout( ));
queryPanel.add("West", new Label("Query:   "));
queryPanel.add("Center", theQuery);

mainPanel.setLayout(new BorderLayout( ));
mainPanel.add("Center", theResult);

bottomPanel.setLayout(new BorderLayout( ));
bottomPanel.add("Center", theStatus);

theResult.setEditable(false);
theStatus.setEditable(false);

addWindowListener(theWindowHandler);
theSource.addActionListener(this);
theQuery.addActionListener(this);

pack( );
show( );
}
```

The openConnection( ) Method

The **openConnection**( ) method, shown in Listing 4.3, is only slightly different
from the form used in Chapter 3. In the SQLWindow application, it takes a
String argument that names the ODBC data source to be opened. The
closeConnection( ) method appears exactly as in Chapter 3 and is not repeated
here. It can be found in the source code on the CD-ROM. The **execSQL-
Command**( ) method, **handleException**( ), and the **WindowHandler** class are
also not shown.

LISTING 4.3   THE OPENCONNECTION( ) METHOD.

```
public void openConnection(String source)
{
    theDataSource = "jdbc:odbc:" + source;
    theUser = "";
    thePassword = "";

    try
    {
        Class.forName ("sun.jdbc.odbc.JdbcOdbcDriver");
        theConnection =
          DriverManager.getConnection(theDataSource, theUser,
          thePassword);
    }
```

```
    catch (Exception e)
    {
        handleException(e);
    }
}
```

The actionPerformed( ) Method

The **actionPerformed**( ) method, shown in Listing 4.4, handles action events generated by either of the two input **TextFields**:

* **theSource**—specifies the ODBC data source name.

* **theQuery**—specifies the SQL query.

A change to the data-source name causes the field containing the query to be blanked. Entry of a new query causes the program to open a database connection, perform the query and display its result, and close the database connection.

LISTING 4.4   THE ACTIONPERFORMED( ) METHOD.

```
public void actionPerformed(ActionEvent e)
{
    Object target = e.getSource( );
    if (target == theSource)
    {
        theQuery.setText("");
    }
    else if (target == theQuery)
    {
        theStatus.setText("Status: OK");
        openConnection(theSource.getText( ));
        execSQLCommand(theQuery.getText( ));
        closeConnection( );
    }
}
```

Another GuestBook Application

The SQLWindow application will help you practice making SQL queries, but you need to write entire programs, not just queries. You can use your new SQL knowledge to extend the capabilities of the GuestBook application from Chapter 3. Recall that the two versions of the GuestBook application you've seen so far have a common fault: Neither is able to move backward through a table to revisit a previously seen record.

JDBC and its underlying ODBC model are at fault here, not SQL. SQL is not bound by the record-at-a-time perspective of application programs. When you tell SQL what result you want, by presenting a legal query, SQL obediently returns the requested result. That's the end of SQL's responsibility in the matter.

Your program inspects the result, a row at a time, using the JDBC API **next( )** method, which it invokes on the object representing the result set. If the JDBC API provided a **previous( )** method, all would be roses. Unfortunately, it doesn't. It's up to you, as the application programmer, to create a mechanism for revisiting the records returned by **next( )**.

The GuestBook03 application neatly solves this problem in its initialization routine, which reads all the records of the Visits table and stores the values of the table's primary key (**SeqNo**) in a **Vector**. Then the application can move forward or backward through the table by simply fetching records in the same order as the **Vector**, based on the stored primary keys. Of course, if other users are accessing the table, adding or deleting records, these updates won't be reflected in the **Vector**. This isn't a problem in many types of applications. If this behavior isn't acceptable to you, don't fret. In Chapter 6 you'll learn a technique that avoids this quirk.

The GuestBook03 Application

Figure 4.8 shows the user interface of the revised GuestBook application, which now sports a team of buttons that lets the user move forward or backward, rewind to the beginning of the table, or fast-forward to the bottom. Take a look at the figure, or better still, try running the application before proceeding.

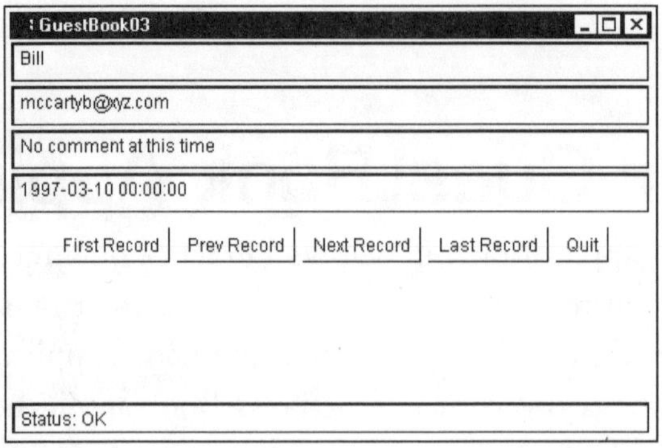

Figure 4.8
The GuestBook03 application.

As you might expect, the new application is quite similar to its ancestral versions of the previous chapter, GuestBook01 and GuestBook02. Listing 4.5 shows the fields of the **GuestBook03** class, along with its **main( )** method and default constructor. As usual, the user interface is built by the **init( )** method, described below. Apart from the new **Button**s allowing the user to navigate the database table, the class also now includes a **Vector**, called *theKeys*, used to hold the primary key values of table records. The class also includes an **int** variable called **theRecNo**, used to hold the index within **theKeys** of the currently displayed record.

LISTING 4.5 THE GUESTBOOK03 APPLICATION.

```
import java.awt.*;
import java.awt.event.*;
import java.sql.*;
import java.util.Vector;

class GuestBook03 extends Frame
implements ActionListener
{

      Panel       theMainPanel = new Panel( );
      Panel       theDataPanel = new Panel( );
      TextField   theName       = new TextField("", 32);
      TextField   theEMail      = new TextField("", 32);
      TextField   theComment    = new TextField("", 50);
      TextField   theTime       = new TextField("", 24);

      Panel       theButtonPanel = new Panel( );
      Button      theFirstButton = new Button("First Record");
      Button      thePrevButton  = new Button("Prev Record");
      Button      theLastButton  = new Button("Last Record");
      Button      theNextButton  = new Button("Next Record");

      Button      theQuitButton  = new Button("Quit");

      Panel       theStatusPanel = new Panel( );
      TextField   theStatus      = new TextField("");

      Connection  theConnection;
      String      theCommand = "";
      Statement   theStatement = null;
      ResultSet   theResult = null;

      int         theRecNo = 0;
```

```
Vector theKeys = new Vector( );

WindowHandler theWindowHandler = new WindowHandler( );

String theDataSource;
String theUser;
String thePassword;

public static void main(String args[])
{
    GuestBook03 theApplication = new GuestBook03( );
    theApplication.init( );
}

public GuestBook03( )
{
    super("GuestBook03");
}
```

The init( ) Method

The **init( )** method of GuestBook04, shown in Listing 4.6, builds the user interface, which includes four nested **Panels**:

- **theMainPanel**—holds **theDataPanel** and **theButtonPanel**.

- **theDataPanel**—holds the **TextFields** that display the current record.

- **theButtonPanel**—holds the **Buttons** that allow the user to navigate the table or quit the program.

- **theStatusPanel**—the only **Panel** not held by **theMainPanel**; it contains the **TextField** used to report status, **theStatus**.

A **try-catch** block encloses the statements that read the records of the Visits table, storing the value of the first column (which contains the primary key, **SeqNo**) in **theKeys**. Note how the **int** returned by **getInt( )** is cast to an **Integer** so it can be stored in the **Vector**. Recall that only objects, not primitive values, can be stored in a **Vector**.

After the key values have been retrieved and stored, the **getFirstRecord( )** method (explained later in this chapter) retrieves and displays the first record of the table. Several methods are not shown, since they are similar to methods shown previously. These include **openConnection( )**, **closeConnection( )**,

execSQLCommand( ), **handleException( )**, and **destroy( )**. The complete source code can be found on the CD-ROM.

LISTING 4.6 THE INIT( ) METHOD.

```
public void init( )
{
    add("Center", theMainPanel);
    add("South", theStatusPanel);

    theMainPanel.setLayout(new GridLayout(2, 1));
    theMainPanel.add(theDataPanel);
    theMainPanel.add(theButtonPanel);

    theDataPanel.setLayout(new GridLayout(4, 1));
    theDataPanel.add(theName);
    theDataPanel.add(theEMail);
    theDataPanel.add(theComment);
    theDataPanel.add(theTime);

    theButtonPanel.setLayout(new FlowLayout( ));
    theButtonPanel.add(theFirstButton);
    theButtonPanel.add(thePrevButton);
    theButtonPanel.add(theNextButton);
    theButtonPanel.add(theLastButton);
    theButtonPanel.add(theQuitButton);

    theStatusPanel.setLayout(new BorderLayout( ));
    theStatusPanel.add("Center", theStatus);

    theName.setEditable(false);
    theEMail.setEditable(false);
    theComment.setEditable(false);
    theTime.setEditable(false);
    theStatus.setEditable(false);

    theFirstButton.addActionListener(this);
    thePrevButton.addActionListener(this);
    theNextButton.addActionListener(this);
    theLastButton.addActionListener(this);
    theQuitButton.addActionListener(this);
    addWindowListener(theWindowHandler);

    pack( );
    show( );
```

```
    try
    {
        theStatus.setText("Status: OK");
        openConnection( );
        execSQLCommand("Select * from Visits;");
        while (theResult.next( ))
        {
        int seqno = theResult.getInt(1);
        theKeys.addElement(new Integer(seqno));
        }
        getFirstRecord( );
    }
    catch (Exception e)
    {
        handleException(e);
    }
}
```

The moveDataToForm( ) Method

The **moveDataToForm**( ) method, shown in Listing 4.7, sets the text of the **TextField**s to reflect the contents of each corresponding database field. Note that the SeqNo field is not shown on the screen. Its function is merely to uniquely identify table records; it has no value or meaning to the user. Of course, displaying it would be simple, if desired.

LISTING 4.7   THE MOVEDATATOFORM( ) METHOD.

```
public void moveDataToForm( )
{
    try
    {
        theName.setText    (theResult.getString(2));
        theEMail.setText   (theResult.getString(3));
        theComment.setText(theResult.getString(4));
        theTime.setText    (theResult.getString(5));
    }
    catch (Exception e)
    {
        handleException(e);
    }
}
```

The actionPerformed( ) Method

The **actionPerformed**( ) method, shown in Listing 4.8, handles events sent by any of the five user-interface **Button**s. Events are handled by invoking an appropriate method to navigate the database or quit the program. The method also resets the displayed error message, so that every requested action has an initial displayed status of "OK". **SQLException**s and other errors are handled by the **handleException**( ) method (not shown), which places a description of any exception or error in the error message **TextField**.

LISTING 4.8   THE ACTIONPERFORMED( ) METHOD.

```
public void actionPerformed(ActionEvent event)
{
    Object target = event.getSource( );
    theStatus.setText("Status: OK");
    if (target == theFirstButton)      getFirstRecord( );
    else if (target == thePrevButton) getPrevRecord( );
    else if (target == theNextButton) getNextRecord( );
    else if (target == theLastButton) getLastRecord( );
    else if (target == theQuitButton) destroy( );
}
```

The getFirstRecord( ) Method

The **getFirstRecord**( ) method, shown in Listing 4.9, is the first of four methods associated with the user-interface **Button**s used to navigate the database table. When the user clicks the First button, this routine is executed under control of the **actionPerformed**( ) method.

Like its siblings—**getNextRecord**( ), **getPrevRecord**( ), and **getLastRecord**( )—**getFirstRecord**( ) depends on the utility method **getRecordByNumber**( ) to do its main work of retrieving the requested record. Here, **getRecordByNumber**( ) is invoked with 0 as its argument. The argument is simply an index into **theKeys** (the **Vector** holding the key values) of the desired record. The argument 0 results in retrieval of the first record.

The **getFirstRecord**( ) method also invokes **moveDataToForm**( ) to display the retrieved record. The **try-catch** block ensures that any exceptions or errors are passed to the **handleException**( ) method, so that an appropriate error message is displayed.

LISTING 4.9   THE GETFIRSTRECORD( ) METHOD.

```
public void getFirstRecord( )
{
    try
    {
        getRecordByNumber(0);
        moveDataToForm( );
    }
    catch (Exception e)
    {
        handleException(e);
    }
}
```

The getNextRecord( ) And getPrevRecord( ) Methods

The **getNextRecord( )** method, shown in Listing 4.10, along with **getPrevRecord( )**, works like the **getFirstRecord( )** method. It uses **getRecordByNumber( )** to retrieve a record specified by its index into **theKeys**. Here, the current record number, contained in **theRecNo**, is incremented to determine the index of the desired record. The "twin" method, **getPrevRecord( )**, decreases the current record number in order to specify backward movement through the database table.

LISTING 4.10   THE GETNEXTRECORD( ) METHOD.

```
public void getNextRecord( )
{
    try
    {
        getRecordByNumber(theRecNo + 1);
        moveDataToForm( );
    }
    catch (Exception e)
    {
        handleException(e);
    }
}

public void getPrevRecord( )
{
    try
    {
```

```
        getRecordByNumber(theRecNo - 1);
        moveDataToForm( );
    }
    catch (Exception e)
    {
        handleException(e);
    }
}
```

The getLastRecord( ) Method

Shown in Listing 4.11, the **getLastRecord**( ) method is the final of the four sibling methods. It uses the **size**( ) method to obtain the current size of the **Vector** containing key values and subtracts one from the result to specify the index of the final record.

LISTING 4.11   THE GETLASTRECORD( ) METHOD.

```
public void getLastRecord( )
{
    try
    {
        getRecordByNumber(theKeys.size( ) - 1);
        moveDataToForm( );
    }
    catch (Exception e)
    {
        handleException(e);
    }
}
```

The getRecordByNumber( ) Method

The **getRecordByNumber**( ) method, shown in Listing 4.12, is the workhorse utility method that does the real work of traversing the database table. It uses a simple **Select** query with a **Where** clause that specifies the **SeqNo** value of the desired record. The query is constructed using a Java **String** expression that concatenates the query text with the **SeqNo** value, obtained by using an index into the **Vector theKeys**. Following a successful query, the current record number, contained in **theRecNo**, is updated to reflect its new value.

Note that the method does not attempt to handle any resulting **SQLException**s. Instead, it passes on a thrown **SQLException** to its caller. Moreover, it generates a **SQLException** in response to any attempt to address a **Vector** element outside the valid range of indexes. This allows the caller to determine how the exception will be handled, making the **getRecordByNumber( )** method better suited to general-purpose use or even reuse.

LISTING 4.12   THE GETRECORDBYNUMBER( ) METHOD.

```
public void getRecordByNumber(int recno)
throws SQLException
{
    try
    {
        execSQLCommand("Select * from Visits WHERE SeqNo = "
          + ((Integer) theKeys.elementAt(recno)).intValue( )
          + ";");
        theResult.next( );
        theRecNo = recno;
    }
    catch (ArrayIndexOutOfBoundsException e)
    {
        throw new SQLException("Record not found");
    }
}
```

 Trying to handle an exception at too low a level can complicate your code and frustrate you. Don't hesitate to use the **Throws** clause to defer handling of exceptions to higher-level methods that are more aware of application-dependent considerations. Your code will often be both clearer and a better candidate for reuse.

Summary

SQL provides the **Select** statement, which specifies the table, columns, and rows a query will return. Columns are specified using a column list or an asterisk (*), which indicates that all columns are to be returned. Rows are selected using the **Where** clause, which introduces a predicate that records must satisfy to be included in the query result set.

You can use comparison predicates based on familiar comparison operators to select records. You can also construct compound predicates that combine several predicates into a more sophisticated predicate expression. SQL also provides several special predicates that allow string pattern matching and testing for null values. Null values result when a database record is stored without any value in an optional field. Null values are distinct from numeric zero and empty text strings.

JDBC API 5

This chapter focuses on the JDBC API, the Java classes that enable your programs to access databases. JDBC provides many features and facilities, most of which are of interest mainly to systems programmers writing new database drivers for use by applications programmers. We'll touch lightly on these aspects of JDBC, since they're occasionally useful to the applications programmer as well.

The primary goal of this chapter, however, is to give you a model that explains how JDBC works and to describe the JDBC features and facilities most used by applications programmers, not to cover JDBC comprehensively. A companion book, *Visual Developer Java Database Programming with JDBC* (Coriolis Group Books), presents the JDBC API in much greater detail. If you're interested in knowing more about the exotica of JDBC, you'll find that book helpful.

Making Your Connection: Accessing A Database

In Chapter 3, you learned how to open a database connection using the JDBC/ODBC driver. The following statements accomplished that purpose:

```
Class.forName ("sun.jdbc.odbc.JdbcOdbcDriver");
theConnection =
    DriverManager.getConnection(theDataSource, theUser,
    thePassword);
```

This section will investigate how these statements work. Figure 5.1 shows the classes involved in opening a database connection. I'll refer to this figure throughout this explanation.

The main players in the task of opening a database connection are database driver classes, the **DriverManager** class, and the client application itself. You need driver classes for each type of database the application accesses. In a three-tier architecture, the client application communicates with a middleware server that mediates access to actual databases. In that configuration, you need only a middleware driver.

The client application opens a database connection by using the static method, **getConnection( )**, of the **DriverManager** class, providing a URL identifying the database, and a user name and password for accessing the database. This is the second of the two Java statements shown previously. I'll get to the first statement in a moment.

In response to invocation of its **getConnection( )** method, the **DriverManager** inspects the URL to discover what sort of database the application wants to ac-

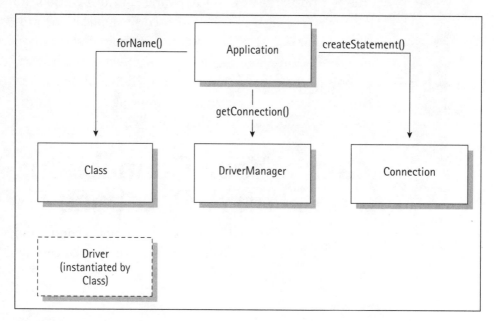

Figure 5.1
Opening a database connection.

cess. The subprotocol field of the URL contains this information. For example, the URL

```
jdbc:odbc:hrdata
```

includes the subprotocol **odbc**, specifying that the JDBC/ODBC bridge driver is to be used. The writer of a database driver decides the subprotocol name used by the drivers. If you're using a driver other than the JDBC/ODBC bridge, you'll need to consult the driver's documentation to learn the proper subprotocol name to use in constructing your URL. Note that the writer of a driver may specify additional attribute values that need to be specified after the host information. Again, the documentation for the driver should tell you what you need to know.

Once the **DriverManager** knows what sort of database the application wants to access, it checks its list of registered drivers for one capable of accessing the database. Suitable drivers are given a chance, one by one, to connect; when a driver succeeds, the **DriverManager** reports success by returning a **Connection** object to the application. If no suitable driver is found, a **SQLException** is thrown.

Loading And Registering A Driver

To open a database connection, an application must load and register a suitable driver with the **DriverManager**. An application can accomplish this task in two ways:

- The simpler and better of the two is simply to create a **Driver** object. Java provides the **forName( )** method of the class named **Class** for such purposes. Calling the method with a **String** containing the name of a class causes Java to instantiate an object of the specified class. The statement

```
Class.forName ("sun.jdbc.odbc.JdbcOdbcDriver");
```

uses the class **sun.jdbc.odbc.JdbcOdbcDriver**, the JDBC/ODBC driver class, to instantiate a driver. The first act of a newborn driver is to register itself with the **DriverManager**; after that, the driver is available for use.

An application program can instantiate multiple drivers by calling the **Class.forName( )** method multiple times. This is necessary if the application needs to access several types of databases, each requiring a distinct driver.

- The other way to load and register a driver is to use the system property **jdbc.drivers**. This property consists of a colon-separated list of driver class names. When **DriverManager** is loaded, it checks the **jdbc.drivers** property and immediately loads and registers any drivers named there. You can set the **jdbc.drivers** system property in the command line that starts your application:

```
java -Djdbc.drivers=sun.jdbc.odbc.JdbcOdbcDriver application class name
```

The advantage of this technique is that you can change the driver used by an application without recompiling the application. On the other hand, it requires access to a preset, persistent environment. If you invoke the application without providing the proper system properties, it will fail.

Several types of JDBC drivers are available:

- *The JDBC/ODBC bridge*—The bridge is convenient to use, since it is provided as part of the JDK and since ODBC drivers exist for many databases. The bridge and the ODBC driver are written in native code, however. That means you must configure client applications to include the necessary driver. Moreover, since native code may open the way to a security breach, Web browsers may not use the ODBC driver and, therefore, cannot host applets that use the JDBC/ODBC bridge.

- *Native-API partly Java driver*—This type of driver translates JDBC calls into native calls for a database using a client API. Like the bridge, this type of driver requires execution of native code.

- *Pure Java driver*—These are becoming widely available. Such drivers do not require execution of native code, simplifying client configuration and allowing the use of general-purpose Web browsers to execute applets that access databases.

DriverManager Methods

The **DriverManager** class and the **Driver** and **Connection** interfaces provide several useful methods for controlling access to a database or reporting status information. The next sections will describe these methods, beginning with those of the **DriverManager** class. Table 5.1 summarizes the key public methods of the **DriverManager** class.

TABLE 5.1

KEY METHODS OF THE DRIVERMANAGER CLASS.

Method	Function
static Connection getConnection (String url, Properties info) throws SQLException	Establishes and returns a Connection to the database specified by the url parameter, using properties specified by the info parameter.
static Connection getConnection(String url, String user, String password) throws SQLException	Establishes and returns a Connection to the database specified by the url parameter, using the specified user name and password.
static Enumeration getDrivers( )	Returns an Enumeration containing a reference to each registered driver.
static int getLoginTimeout( )	Returns the current log-in time-out interval, in seconds.
static PrintStream getLogStream( )	Returns the current log stream or null.
static void println(String message)	Prints a message to the current log stream.
static void setLogStream (PrintStream log)	Sets the value of the current log stream.
static void setLoginTimeout (int seconds)	Sets the log-in time-out interval, in seconds.

You've already seen one form of the **getConnection**( ) method. The new form allows you to pass a **Properties** object that can specify an arbitrary number of properties in addition to the user name and password. For example, you could use the following statements to open a database connection using the more general form of the **getConnection**( ) method:

```
Properties info = new java.util.Properties( );
info.put("user", "Fred");
info.put("password", "sesame");
Connection con = DriverManager.getConnection("jdbc:subname:thebase", info);
```

Here, you access a database known as *thebase*, using a subprotocol known as *subname*. You set only the minimal properties, user and password. You could specify additional properties with additional **put**s. Check your driver's documentation to determine the names and values of properties your driver supports.

Another useful **DriverManager** method is **getDrivers( )**, which returns an **Enumeration** containing a reference to each registered driver. The drivers can then be queried or configured using methods of the **Driver** class, as you'll see shortly.

Establishing a connection to a database, which may be halfway around the world, takes time. A database may even be unavailable because of a hardware failure or another reason. Therefore, an application needs to wait a bit for a connection to be established, but it should not wait indefinitely. The **DriverManager** class supports a time-out value that controls the wait interval. The method **getLoginTimeout( )** can get the current value of the time-out interval, and the **setLoginTimeout( )** method can set the value. The time-out interval is specified in seconds.

JDBC also supports a logging facility that can be useful in troubleshooting database connection and access problems. When active, the facility writes messages to a **PrintStream**, describing every action the JDBC driver takes or attempts, and the responses generated by the database. The log file can become quite large very quickly, so you can turn the log on or off at will. The methods that provide this facility are **getLogStream( )** and **setLogStream( )**. The former returns the **PrintStream**, which is the current log file, or **null** if logging is not enabled. The latter allows you to turn logging on by specifying the **PrintStream** to be used, or to turn it off by specifying **null**.

Driver Methods

Driver is an interface, not a class, implemented by specific database drivers. Table 5.2 shows the key public methods of the **Driver** interface. Using these methods requires a **Driver** reference. One way to obtain such a reference is to save the one returned by the **Class.forName( )** method:

```
Driver theDriver = Class.forName("jdbc.odbc.JDBCOdbcDriver");
```

Another way is to use the **DriverManager** method **getDrivers( )**, which returns an **Enumeration** over all registered drivers. You can then easily access all drivers or select the specific driver you're interested in. An example program later in this chapter will demonstrate this technique.

TABLE 5.2

KEY METHODS OF THE DRIVER INTERFACE.

Method	Function
int getMajorVersion( )	Returns the major version number of the driver.
int getMinorVersion( )	Returns the minor version number of the driver.
DriverPropertyInfo[ ] getPropertyInfo (String url, Properties info) throws SQLException	Returns an array of PropertyInfo objects that may be needed to connect to a database by use of the driver.
boolean jdbcCompliant( )	Returns true if the driver is JDBC compliant, and false otherwise.

Once you have a **Driver** reference, the **getMajorVersion**( ) and **getMinorVersion**( ) methods can determine which version of a driver is loaded, and the **jdbcCompliant**( ) method can verify that the driver is a genuine JDBC COM-PLIANT™ driver. Drivers should report themselves as JDBC compliant only after passing JDBC compliance tests specified by Javasoft.

Application programmers generally don't need the **getPropertyInfo**( ) method, though it may prove useful on occasion. The method is intended to allow a generic tool to discover which properties should be provided when establishing a database connection. It provides the database URL and a **Properties** object that has a proposed list of name/value pairs to be sent using **getConnection**( ). The method returns an array of **DriverProperty** objects that describe possible properties, or an empty array if no additional properties are defined. The **DriverProperty** objects include the public fields described in Table 5.3.

TABLE 5.3

PUBLIC FIELDS OF THE DRIVERPROPERTY CLASS.

Field	Contents Of Field
String name	The name of the property.
String description	A description of the property, possibly null.
boolean required	The value true if the property is required.
String value	The current value of the property.
String [ ] choices	When the value must be selected from a defined set, this array contains the set. Otherwise, it contains null.

Connection Methods

Like **Driver**, **Connection** is an interface implemented by the writer of a database driver. Table 5.4 shows the key public methods of the **Connection** interface.

Some SQL operations result in the throwing of a **SQLException**. When less serious problems occur, a **SQLWarning** is created and posted to the **Connection** or other object responsible for the operation. These **SQLWarning**s accumulate as errors occur and new warnings are posted. The **getWarning( )** method allows a program to determine if warnings have been posted against a **Connection**. The method returns the first posted warning, or **null** if no warnings have been posted. After inspecting the posted warning, a program can clear all posted warnings by calling **clearWarnings( )**.

The **createStatement( )** method is used to obtain a **Statement** object necessary for executing SQL statements. The **Statement** object is described in a later section of this chapter.

You can set a **Connection** to operate in read-only mode, which may improve the performance of some database operations. This is done using the

---

TABLE 5.4

PUBLIC METHODS OF THE CONNECTION INTERFACE.

Method	Function
void clearWarnings( ) throws SQLException	Clears reported warnings for this Connection.
void close( ) throws SQLException	Releases JDBC and database resources held by this Connection.
Statement createStatement( ) throws SQLException	Returns a Statement object used to execute a SQL statement.
DatabaseMetaData getMetaData( ) throws SQLException	Returns information about a database's structure and capabilities.
SQLWarning getWarnings( ) throws SQLException	Returns the first warning reported on this Connection.
boolean isReadOnly( ) throws SQLException	Returns true if the Connection is in read-only mode.
void setReadOnly(boolean readonly) throws SQLException	Sets the read-only mode of the connection to the specified value.

setReadOnly( ) method. A companion method, **getReadOnly**( ), queries whether the **Connection** has been set to read-only mode.

The **getMetaData**( ) method returns a **DatabaseMetaData** object that provides access to a wealth of information about the structure and capabilities of a database. The methods provided by the **DatabaseMetaData** object are described in a later section of this chapter.

The **close**( ) method releases JDBC and database resources held by the **Connection**. When a **Connection** is garbage-collected, its resources are automatically released. Immediately freeing resources that are no longer used may improve program or database performance.

The StudyConnect Program

The StudyConnect program shows how many of the methods provided by **Driver**, **DriverManager**, and **Connection** can be used. Figure 5.2 shows its user interface. When started, the program presents a dialog box that lets the user specify a database URL, user name, and password. It establishes a connection to the database and displays its main window, which provides buttons that allow the user to experiment with the JDBC logging facility, time-out intervals, read-only mode, and SQL warnings. It also allows the user to obtain a list of available JDBC drivers and query their properties.

The StudyConnect program is composed of three classes and one interface:

* *StudyConnect*—the main class, containing the user interface and application processing.

* *WindowHandler*—a subordinate class used to handle window messages, especially the **windowClosing** message.

* *LoginDialog*—a subordinate class that displays the dialog used to obtain log-in properties.

* *Application*—an interface implemented by the main class and used by **WindowHandler**.

I'll explain the subordinate classes and the interface first, followed by the main class.

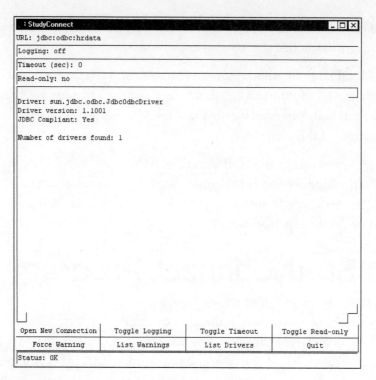

Figure 5.2
The StudyConnect program.

The LoginDialog Class

The **LoginDialog** class, shown in Listing 5.1, displays a dialog that allows the user to enter a database URL, user name, and password. These values are returned by public methods called by the main class: **getURL( )**, **getUser( )**, and **getPassword( )**. The class also provides a **getStatus( )** method that returns **true** if the user clicked the OK button and **false** if the user clicked the Cancel button. **LoginDialog** is used by the StudyConnect application and other example programs.

LISTING 5.1   THE LOGINDIALOG CLASS.

```
import java.awt.*;
import java.awt.event.*;

public class LoginDialog extends Dialog
implements ActionListener
{
    Application theParent;
```

```
Panel[]    thePanel    = new Panel[4];
TextField theSource    = new TextField( );
TextField theUser      = new TextField( );
TextField thePassword  = new TextField( );
Button     btnOK       = new Button("OK");
Button     btnCancel   = new Button("Cancel");
Button     btnQuit     = new Button("Quit");
boolean    statusOK    = false;
String theURL;

public LoginDialog(Application parent, boolean showquit)
{
    super((Frame) parent, "Login", true);
    theParent = parent;

    setFont(new Font("Courier", Font.PLAIN, 12));
    setLayout(new GridLayout(4, 1));
    for (int i = 0; i < 3; i++)
    {
        thePanel[i] = new Panel( );
        thePanel[i].setLayout(new BorderLayout( ));
    }

    thePanel[0].add("West",   new Label("URL:      ", Label.RIGHT));
    thePanel[0].add("Center", theSource);
    add(thePanel[0]);

    thePanel[1].add("West",   new Label("User:     ", Label.RIGHT));
    thePanel[1].add("Center", theUser);
    add(thePanel[1]);

    thePanel[2].add("West",   new Label("Password: ", Label.RIGHT));
    thePanel[2].add("Center", thePassword);
    add(thePanel[2]);

    thePanel[3] = new Panel( );
    thePanel[3].setLayout(new FlowLayout( ));
    thePanel[3].add(btnOK);
    thePanel[3].add(btnCancel);
    if (showquit) thePanel[3].add(btnQuit);
    add(thePanel[3]);

    btnOK.addActionListener(this);
    btnCancel.addActionListener(this);
    btnQuit.addActionListener(this);
    addWindowListener(new WindowHandler(theParent));
```

```
            setSize(400, 150);
    }

    public boolean getStatus( )    { return statusOK; };
    public String  getURL( )       { return theSource.getText( ); }
    public String  getUser( )      { return theUser.getText( ); }
    public String  getPassword( ) { return thePassword.getText( ); }

    public void setVisible(boolean visible)
    {
        if (visible)
        {
            statusOK = false;
            theSource.setText("jdbc:odbc:");
            theUser.setText("");
            thePassword.setText("");
        }
        super.setVisible(visible);
        if (visible) theSource.requestFocus( );
    }

    public void actionPerformed(ActionEvent event)
    {
        Object object = event.getSource( );
        if (object == btnOK) statusOK = true;
        setVisible(false);
        if (object == btnQuit) System.exit(0);
    }
}
```

The class constructor requires two arguments: the **Frame** that hosts the application, and a boolean parameter that specifies whether the dialog should include a Quit button. If the boolean parameter is **true**, the dialog displays a Quit button. The user can click the Quit button to terminate the application.

The dialog is modal, meaning it blocks input to the main application until the user completes the dialog. It is invoked by means of its **setVisible( )** method, passing **true** to show the dialog and **false** to hide it from view. The values of the dialog's input fields are cleared each time it is shown. Although the database URL is initialized using the string "jdbc:odbc:", the dialog can handle non-ODBC data sources without modification.

The WindowHandler Class

The **WindowHandler** class, shown in Listing 5.2, is an adapter class derived from **WindowAdapter**. **WindowHandler** is specialized to handle the **windowClosing** message. In response to a **windowClosing** message, it invokes the **requestClose( )** message on the **Application** object that was provided in the call to its constructor. **Application** can implement any desired behavior in the **requestClose( )** method, but the usual response is to shut down **Application**.

LISTING 5.2   THE WINDOWHANDLER CLASS.

```
import java.awt.*;
import java.awt.event.*;

public class WindowHandler extends WindowAdapter
{
    Application theParent;

    public WindowHandler(Application parent)
    {
        theParent = parent;
    }

    public void windowClosing(WindowEvent event)
    {
        theParent.requestClose( );
    }
}
```

Listing 5.3 shows the **Application** interface used by the **WindowHandler** class. The only method that the interface requires is the **requestClose( )** method, which takes no arguments and returns no value.

LISTING 5.3   THE APPLICATION INTERFACE.

```
public interface Application
{
    public void requestClose( );
}
```

The StudyConnect Class

Listing 5.4 shows the fields and **main( )** method of the **StudyConnect** class, the main class of the **StudyConnect** program. The class uses a default constructor, so no constructor is shown in the listing. The class implements the **Application** interface and, therefore, includes a **requestClose( )** method, described later in this chapter. It also implements the **ActionListener** interface, choosing to handle messages from its **Button**s internally, rather than relying on an adapter class. This simplifies the class, but has the drawback of mingling the user interface and application logic. This drawback, however, is not serious in such a small program. The **main( )** method of the class simply creates an anonymous **StudyConnect** object and invokes its **init( )** method.

Listing 5.4   The StudyConnect class.

```
import java.awt.*;
import java.awt.event.*;
import java.sql.*;
import java.util.*;

class StudyConnect extends Frame
implements Application, ActionListener
{
    Panel           topPanel     = new Panel( );
    Panel           bottomPanel  = new Panel( );
    Panel           buttonPanel  = new Panel( );

    Label           theSource    = new Label("URL: ");
    TextField       theLogger    = new TextField("Logging: ");
    TextField       theTimeout   = new TextField("Timeout: ");
    TextField       theReadOnly  = new TextField("Read-only: ");
    TextArea        theResult    = new TextArea(25, 80);
    TextField       theStatus    = new TextField( );

    Button          btnOpen      = new Button("Open New Connection");
    Button          btnLog       = new Button("Toggle Logging");
    Button          btnTimeout   = new Button("Toggle Timeout");
    Button          btnReadOnly  = new Button("Toggle Read-only");
    Button          btnDoWarn    = new Button("Force Warning");
    Button          btnListWarn  = new Button("List Warnings");
    Button          btnDrivers   = new Button("List Drivers");
    Button          btnQuit      = new Button("Quit");

    Connection      theConnection;
    DatabaseMetaData theDBMetaData;
    Statement       theStatement;
    ResultSet       theResultSet;

    public static void main(String args[])
    {
        new StudyConnect( ).init( );
    }
```

The init( ) Method

The **init( )** method, shown in Listing 5.5, builds the user interface of the application. It also creates an anonymous **WindowHandler** object that handles **windowClosing** messages. After displaying the application window, **init( )** invokes **openConnection( )** to open a database for access. Since an attempt to open a database may fail for a variety of reasons, **init( )** iteratively attempts to open a database until it's successful.

LISTING 5.5   THE INIT( ) METHOD.

```
public void init( )
{
    setTitle("StudyConnect");
    setFont(new Font("Courier", Font.PLAIN, 12));

    add("North", topPanel);
    add("Center", theResult);
    add("South", bottomPanel);

    topPanel.setLayout(new GridLayout(4, 1));
    topPanel.add(theSource);
    topPanel.add(theLogger);
    topPanel.add(theTimeout);
    topPanel.add(theReadOnly);

    bottomPanel.setLayout(new BorderLayout( ));
    bottomPanel.add("Center", buttonPanel);
    bottomPanel.add("South", theStatus);

    buttonPanel.setLayout(new GridLayout(2, 4));
    buttonPanel.add(btnOpen);
    buttonPanel.add(btnLog);
    buttonPanel.add(btnTimeout);
    buttonPanel.add(btnReadOnly);
    buttonPanel.add(btnDoWarn);
    buttonPanel.add(btnListWarn);
    buttonPanel.add(btnDrivers);
    buttonPanel.add(btnQuit);

    theLogger.setEditable(false);
    theTimeout.setEditable(false);
    theReadOnly.setEditable(false);
    theResult.setEditable(false);
    theStatus.setEditable(false);
```

```
    btnOpen.addActionListener(this);
    btnLog.addActionListener(this);
    btnTimeout.addActionListener(this);
    btnReadOnly.addActionListener(this);
    btnDoWarn.addActionListener(this);
    btnListWarn.addActionListener(this);
    btnDrivers.addActionListener(this);
    btnQuit.addActionListener(this);

    addWindowListener(new WindowHandler(this));

    pack( );
    setVisible(true);

    while (!openConnection( )) ; // null statement
}
```

The actionPerformed( ) Method

Listing 5.6 shows the **actionPerformed**( ) method, which handles messages originating with the various **Buttons** displayed by the applications. An appropriate method is invoked to handle each requested action, as distinguished by the **Button** the user clicks. Note that these methods will be executed within the system thread that handles AWT events. Such methods must complete quickly, so that the user interface appears responsive. Instead of doing actual processing, the **actionPerformed**( ) method could control processing performed within another thread. This technique, which yields a more responsive user interface, is demonstrated in Chapter 7.

The actions are wrapped within a **try-catch** block, since the **actionPerformed**() method, which runs in a special AWT thread, should not throw exceptions. Any exceptions that arise are passed to the **handleError**( ) method, which will be shown later in this chapter.

LISTING 5.6   THE ACTIONPERFORMED( ) METHOD.

```
public void actionPerformed(ActionEvent event)
{
    Object source = event.getSource( );
    theStatus.setText("Status: OK");
    try
    {
        if (source == btnOpen)          openConnection ( );
        else if (source == btnLog)      toggleLogging  ( );
```

```
        else if (source == btnTimeout)  toggleTimeout ( );
        else if (source == btnReadOnly) toggleReadOnly ( );
        else if (source == btnDoWarn)   doWarn        ( );
        else if (source == btnListWarn) listWarn      ( );
        else if (source == btnDrivers)  listDrivers   ( );
        else if (source == btnQuit)     requestClose  ( );
    }
    catch (Exception ex)
    {
        handleError(ex);
    }
}
```

The openConnection( ) Method

The task of the **openConnection**( ) method, shown in Listing 5.7, is to deter-mine which database the user wants to access and to open a connection to that database. The **LoginDialog** class obtains the database URL, user name, and password. If the user clicks OK in the dialog, **openConnection**( ) attempts to open the requested database. Otherwise, it simply disposes of the dialog and returns **false**.

The **openConnection**( ) method follows the usual method of opening a data-base connection. **Class.forName**( ) instantiates a driver object, and then the **DriverManager**'s **getConnection**( ) method is invoked. If a **SQLException** is thrown, the **try-catch** block invokes the **handleError**( ) method, displaying an appropriate error message. The **catch** is specified to catch any **Throwable**, especially the **ClassDefNotFound** exception thrown when the specified driver class file cannot be found. This allows **openConnection**( ) to recover from errors of almost any sort, returning **false** to indicate failure. Since **init**( ) loops until **openConnection**( ) returns **true**, the program copes well with most recoverable errors.

When a connection has been established, the current state of the logging facil-ity, the log-in time-out value, and the read-only mode are obtained. The user interface is updated to reflect the obtained values.

LISTING 5.7   THE OPENCONNECTION( ) METHOD.

```
public boolean openConnection( )
{
    LoginDialog theLoginDialog = null;
    try
    {
```

```
theSource.setText("");
theStatus.setText("Status: OK");

theLoginDialog = new LoginDialog(this, true);
theLoginDialog.setVisible(true);
if (theLoginDialog.getStatus( ))
{
    theSource.setText("URL: " + theLoginDialog.getURL( ));
    Class.forName ("sun.jdbc.odbc.JdbcOdbcDriver");
    if (theConnection != null) theConnection.close( );
    theConnection =
      DriverManager.getConnection(theLoginDialog.getURL( ),
        theLoginDialog.getUser( ),
        theLoginDialog.getPassword( ));
    theDBMetaData = theConnection.getMetaData( );

    if (DriverManager.getLogStream( ) != null)
        theLogger.setText("Logging: on");
    else
        theLogger.setText("Logging: off");
    theTimeout.setText("Timeout (sec): "
      + DriverManager.getLoginTimeout( ));
    if (theConnection.isReadOnly( ))
        theReadOnly.setText("Read-only: yes");
    else
        theReadOnly.setText("Read-only: no");
}
theLoginDialog.dispose( );
return true;
}
catch (Throwable t)
{
    handleError(t);
}
if (theLoginDialog != null) theLoginDialog.dispose( );
return false;
}
```

The toggleLogging( ) Method

Listing 5.8 shows the **toggleLogging**( ) method, which the user invokes by clicking the corresponding button. The method toggles the state of connection logging, turning it on if it's currently off, and turning it off if it's currently on. To enable logging, the method specifies **System.out** as the destination **PrintStream** for log messages. Whenever the log status changes, the method uses **DriverManager.println**( ) to log a message that includes the current date and time.

LISTING 5.8   THE TOGGLELOGGING( ) METHOD.

```
public void toggleLogging( )
throws SQLException
{
    if (DriverManager.getLogStream( ) != null)
    {
        DriverManager.println("Logging ended: "
          + new java.util.Date( ));
        DriverManager.setLogStream(null);
    }
    else
    {
        DriverManager.setLogStream(System.out);
        DriverManager.println("Logging started: "
          + new java.util.Date( ));
    }
    if (DriverManager.getLogStream( ) != null)
        theLogger.setText("Logging: on");
    else
        theLogger.setText("Logging: off");
}
```

The toggleTimeout( ) Method

The **toggleTimeout**( ) method, shown in Listing 5.9, switches the log-in time-out interval from 0 to 120 seconds, or back to 0 seconds. Although the convention is not specified in the JDBC specification, many drivers use a log-in time-out interval of 0 seconds to signify that the application is willing to wait indefinitely.

LISTING 5.9   THE TOGGLETIMEOUT( ) METHOD.

```
public void toggleTimeout( )
throws SQLException
{
    if (DriverManager.getLoginTimeout( ) == 0)
    {
        DriverManager.setLoginTimeout(120);
    }
    else
    {
```

```
        DriverManager.setLoginTimeout(0);    }
    theTimeout.setText("Timeout (sec): "
      + DriverManager.getLoginTimeout( ));
}
```

The toggleReadOnly( ) Method

The **toggleReadOnly**( ) method, shown in Listing 5.10, follows the pattern of the two preceding methods. It switches the database connection mode from read-write to read-only, or vice versa.

LISTING 5.10   THE TOGGLEREADONLY( ) METHOD.

```
public void toggleReadOnly( )
{
    try
    {
        if (theConnection.isReadOnly( ))
            theConnection.setReadOnly(false);
        else
            theConnection.setReadOnly(true);
      if (theConnection.isReadOnly( ))
            theReadOnly.setText("Read-only: yes");
        else
            theReadOnly.setText("Read-only: no");
    }
    catch (SQLException sql)
    {
        handleError(sql);
    }
}
```

The doWarn( ) Method

Listing 5.11 shows the **doWarn**( ) method, which generates a **SQLWarning** that the **listWarn**( ) method (shown in the next section) reports. The **doWarn**( ) method uses the **Statement.MaxFieldSize**( ) method to specify that fields returned by a **ResultSet** method should not exceed one character in length. When the data is actually retrieved, it will usually be truncated, resulting in a **SQLWarning**. To choose a suitable table for access, the **doWarn**( ) method uses the **DatabaseMetaData.getTables**( ) method, which returns a result set listing available database tables. This method is further described in a later section of this chapter. Note that the **doWarn**( ) method is not foolproof and may some-times fail to generate the desired warning. Many database drivers, including the

MS Access ODBC driver, do not support the **MaxFieldSize**( ) method. Similarly, a table whose first column contains a one-character field will be correctly handled by the **Select** statement used by **doWarn**( ), so the desired warning will not be posted.

LISTING 5.11   THE doWARN( ) METHOD.

```
public void doWarn( )
{
    try
    {
        ResultSet tables =
          theDBMetaData.getTables(null, null, null, null);
        String table = null;
        String type = null;
        while (tables.next( ))
        {
            table = tables.getString(3);
            type  = tables.getString(4);
            if (type.toUpperCase( ).indexOf("SYSTEM") < 0) break;
        }
        Statement stmt = theConnection.createStatement( );
        stmt.setMaxRows(1);
        stmt.setMaxFieldSize(1);
        ResultSet temp = stmt.executeQuery("Select * from "
          + table + ";");
        temp.next( );
        temp.getString(1);
    }
    catch (SQLException sql)
    {
        handleError(sql);
    }
}
```

The listWarn( ) Method

The **listWarn**( ) method, shown in Listing 5.12, lists warnings posted against the connection. Note that there may be multiple posted warnings. Any warnings issued subsequent to the first warning appear on a chain attached to the first warning returned. The **SQLWarning.getNextWarning**( ) method accesses the elements of the chain; it returns **null** if no chained warnings exist.

LISTING 5.12   THE LISTWARN( ) METHOD.

```
public void listWarn( )
{
    try
    {
        theResult.setText("Connection warnings:\n");
        SQLWarning warn = theConnection.getWarnings( );
        if (warn != null)
        {
            while (warn != null)
            {
                theResult.append("Warning: " + warn.getMessage( ));
                warn = warn.getNextWarning( );
            }
            theConnection.clearWarnings( );
            theResult.append("Warnings now cleared.");
        }
        else theResult.append("(none)");
    }
    catch (SQLException sql)
    {
        handleError(sql);
    }
}
```

The listDrivers( ) Method

The **listDrivers**( ) method, shown in Listing 5.13, uses the **getDrivers**( ) method of the **DriverManager** class to obtain an **Enumeration** over all registered drivers. It then invokes the various information methods of the **Driver** class on each member of the **Enumeration**, displaying the returned results. Note that a given driver may not support the **getPropertyInfo**( ) method. In particular, the MS Access ODBC driver lacks this support. A **try-catch** block deals with the **SQLException** thrown when the method is not supported.

LISTING 5.13   THE LISTDRIVERS( ) METHOD.

```
public void listDrivers( )
throws SQLException
{
    theResult.setText("");
    Enumeration drivers = DriverManager.getDrivers( );
    DriverPropertyInfo[] driver_props;
    Properties proposed_props = new Properties( );
    int i = 0;
```

```
    while (drivers.hasMoreElements( ))
    {
        i++;
        Driver driver = (Driver) drivers.nextElement( );
        theResult.append("\nDriver: "
          + driver.getClass( ).getName( ));
        theResult.append("\nDriver version: "
          + driver.getMajorVersion( )
          + "." + driver.getMinorVersion( ));
        theResult.append("\nJDBC Compliant: "
          + (driver.jdbcCompliant( ) ? "Yes" : "No"));
        theResult.append("\n");

        try
        {
            driver_props = driver.getPropertyInfo(
              theSource.getText( ).substring(5), proposed_props);
            theResult.append("Properties:");
            for (int j=0; j < driver_props.length; j++)
            {
                theResult.append("\n");
                theResult.append("\nName: " + driver_props[j].name);
                theResult.append("\nDescription: "
                  + driver_props[j].description);
                theResult.append("\nValue: "
                  + driver_props[j].value);
                theResult.append("\nRequired: " +
                  ((driver_props[j].required) ? "Yes" : "No"));
                theResult.append("\nChoices: ");
                for (int k=0; k < driver_props[j].choices.length;
                  k++)
                {
                    if (k != 0) theResult.append(", ");
                    theResult.append(driver_props[j].choices[k]);
                }
            }
        }
        catch (SQLException sql) { ; }
    }
    theResult.append("\nNumber of drivers found: " + i);
}
```

The requestClose( ) Method

The **WindowHandler** class invokes the **requestClose( )** method, shown in Listing 5.14, in response to a **windowClosing** message. It simply hides the application

window, closes any open database connection, and terminates the program. Since the **close( )** method may throw a **SQLException**, its invocation is enclosed within a **try-catch** block.

Listing 5.14 The requestClose( ) method.

```
public void requestClose( )
{
    setVisible(false);
    try
    {
        if (theConnection != null) theConnection.close( );
    }
    catch (SQLException sql) { ; }
    System.exit(0);
}
```

The handleError( ) Method

The **handleError( )** method, shown in Listing 5.15, displays an appropriate error message in the application window in response to exceptions or errors detected during program execution. A more elaborate stack trace is also displayed on **System.err** by the **printStackTrace( )** method. This stack trace can investigate the origin of an unexpected exception or error.

Listing 5.15 The handleError( ) method.

```
public void handleError(Throwable t)
{
    theStatus.setText("Error: " + t.getMessage( ));
    t.printStackTrace( );
}
```

Making A Statement: Executing A SQL Statement

The **Statement** object returned by a **Connection** is the JDBC workhorse. It allows you to send SQL queries to a database and receive the results. As you'll see in Chapter 10, you can also use the **Statement** object to change database data, or add or delete rows in a database table. Table 5.5 shows the key methods of the **Statement** interface.

TABLE 5.5

KEY METHODS OF THE STATEMENT INTERFACE.

Method	Function
void cancel( ) throws SQLException	Cancels a SQL query being executed by another thread.
void clearWarnings( ) throws SQLException	Clears reported warnings for this Statement.
void close( ) throws SQLException	Releases JDBC and database resources held by this Statement.
boolean execute (String sql) throws SQLException	Executes an arbitrary SQL command that may return multiple ResultSets and update counts.
ResultSet executeQuery (String sql) throws SQLException	Executes a SQL command that returns a single ResultSet.
int executeUpdate (String sql) throws SQLException	Executes a SQL command that returns a single update count.
int getMaxFieldSize( ) throws SQLException	Returns the maximum number of characters returned for a column value of type BINARY, VARBINARY, LONGVARBINARY, CHAR, VARCHAR, or LONGVARCHAR.
int getMaxRows( ) throws SQLException	Returns the maximum number of rows that a ResultSet can contain.
boolean getMoreResults( ) throws SQLException	Moves to the next ResultSet or update count provided by the execute( ) method, returning true if the next result exists, and false otherwise.
int getQueryTimeout( ) throws SQLException	Returns the number of seconds that the driver will wait for a Statement to execute.
ResultSet getResultSet( ) throws SQLException	Returns the current ResultSet of an execute( ) or executeQuery( ) call.
int getUpdateCount( ) throws SQLException	Returns the current update count of an execute( ) or executeUpdate( ) call. Returns -1 if the result is a ResultSet rather than an update count.
SQLWarning getWarnings( ) throws SQLException	Returns the first warning reported against this Statement, or null if no warnings have been reported.

(continued)

| | TABLE 5.5 |

KEY METHODS OF THE STATEMENT INTERFACE (*CONTINUED*).

Method	Function
void setMaxFieldSize (int max) throws SQLException	Sets the maximum size of data that will be returned for any column value of type BINARY, VARBINARY, LONGVARBINARY, CHAR, VARCHAR, or LONGVARCHAR.
void setMaxRows (int max) throws SQLException	Sets the maximum number of rows that a ResultSet can contain.
void setQueryTimeout (int seconds) throws SQLException	Sets the number of seconds that the driver will wait for a Statement to execute.

The **Statement** interface provides three methods related to the processing of SQL commands:

- **executeQuery( )**

- **executeUpdate( )**

- **execute( )**

The **executeQuery( )** method is the only one of the three you've seen so far. Its job is to execute a SQL command that returns its result as a table, represented as a JDBC **ResultSet** object. SQL queries return tables containing the query result; queries are appropriately executed using **executeQuery( )**. The **ResultSet** generated by **executeQuery( )** is obtained by calling the **getResultSet( )** method.

As you'll see in Chapter 10, JDBC can also write data to databases, adding, deleting, or changing table rows. The result of a write operation is not a table, but simply a count of the number of updated rows. To execute a SQL statement that generates an update count rather than a result set, use the **executeUpdate( )** method.

Occasionally, you may want to write a program that allows a user to enter and execute a SQL statement. Since you might not know ahead of time what sort of statement the user might enter, you wouldn't know whether to use **executeQuery( )** or **executeUpdate( )** to execute the statement. The **execute( )** method resolves this problem. It is capable of generating either a **ResultSet** or an update count, as appropriate to the result of whichever sort of statement is executed. It is even capable of handing SQL statements that access procedures stored in the database, which may return multiple results.

To access the results of the **execute( )** method, you use the **getMoreResults( )** method to move to the **Statement**'s next result, which can be either a **ResultSet** or an update count. By then calling **getUpdateCount( )**, you obtain either the update count, if one exists, or -1, which indicates that a **ResultSet** was generated rather than an update count. You can then access the **ResultSet** in the usual way, by calling **getResultSet( )**.

Several methods provided by **Statement** are similar to those provided by **Connection**. These include **close( )**, **clearWarnings( )**, and **getWarnings( )**. Executing a SQL statement may result in the generation of **SQLWarnings**. You can check for these the same way you check for warnings posted against a **Connection**, by using the **getWarning( )** method and its companion method, **clearWarnings( )**.

The **getQueryTimeout( )** method returns the number of seconds the driver will wait for completion of a query. The related method, **setQueryTimeout( )**, sets the length of the interval. A value of 0 signifies that the application will wait indefinitely.

The maximum number of rows returned as a **ResultSet** is returned by **getMaxRows( )** and can be set by **setMaxRows( )**. The **getMaxFieldSize( )** method returns the maximum number of characters returned as the value of a table column of type BINARY, VARBINARY, LONGVARBINARY, CHAR, VARCHAR, or LONGVARCHAR. This limit can be set to a desired value by using the related method, **setMaxFieldSize( )**.

The **cancel( )** method is useful when a database application has been implemented using Java threads. It allows cancellation of a SQL statement being executed by another thread. Chapter 7 includes an example program demonstrating this capability.

The ResultSet Object

The **ResultSet** object generated by **execute( )** or **executeQuery( )** allows you to access the rows and columns of the table generated by your SQL command. A variety of **ResultSet** methods provides access to the individual fields of the **ResultSet**. These methods map the SQL data types stored by the database to suitable Java data types. Table 5.6 shows the key methods of the **ResultSet** interface.

TABLE 5.6

KEY METHODS OF THE RESULTSET INTERFACE.

Method	Function
void clearWarnings( ) throws SQLException	Clears reported warnings for this ResultSet.
void close( ) throws SQLException	Releases JDBC and database resources held by this ResultSet.
String findColumn(int col) throws SQLException	Returns a column name corresponding to the specified column index.
InputStream getAsciiStream(int col) throws SQLException	Returns a column value as a stream of ASCII characters.
InputStream getAsciiStream(String col) throws SQLException	Returns a column value as a stream of ASCII characters.
BigDecmial getBigDecimal(int col) throws SQLException	Returns a column value as a BigDecimal object.
BigDecmial getBigDecimal(String col) throws SQLException	Returns a column value as a BigDecimal object.
InputStream getBinaryStream(int col) throws SQLException	Returns a column value as a stream of bytes.
InputStream getBinaryStream(String col) throws SQLException	Returns a column value as a stream of bytes.
boolean getBoolean(int col) throws SQLException	Returns a column value as a boolean value.
boolean getBoolean(String col) throws SQLException	Returns a column value as a boolean value.
byte getByte(int col) throws SQLException	Returns a column value as a byte.
byte getByte(String col) throws SQLException	Returns a column value as a byte.
bvte[ ] getBytes(int col) throws SQLException	Returns a column value as a byte array.
byte[ ] getBytes(String col) throws SQLException	Returns a column value as a byte array.
Date getDate(int col) throws SQLException	Returns a column value as a java.sql.Date object.
Date getDate(String col) throws SQLException	Returns a column value as a java.sql.Date object.

(continued)

TABLE 5.6

KEY METHODS OF THE RESULTSET INTERFACE (*CONTINUED*).

Method	Function
double getDouble(int col) throws SQLException	Returns a column value as a double.
double getDouble(String col) throws SQLException	Returns a column value as a double.
float getFloat(int col) throws SQLException	Returns a column value as a float.
float getFloat(String col) throws SQLException	Returns a column value as a float.
int getInt(int col) throws SQLException	Returns a column value as an int.
int getInt(String col) throws SQLException	Returns a column value as an int.
long getLong(int col) throws SQLException	Returns a column value as a long.
long getLong(String col) throws SQLException	Returns a column value as a long.
ResultSetMetaData getMetaData( ) throws SQLException	Returns an object providing access to information about the ResultSet.
Object getObject(int col) throws SQLException	Returns a column value as a Java object.
Object getObject(String col) throws SQLException	Returns a column value as a Java object.
short getShort(int col) throws SQLException	Returns a column value as a short.
short getShort(String col) throws SQLException	Returns a column value as a short.
String getString(int col) throws SQLException	Returns a column value as a String.
String getString(String col) throws SQLException	Returns a column value as a String.
Time getTime(int col) throws SQLException	Returns a column value as a java.sql.Time object.
Time getTime(String col) throws SQLException	Returns a column value as a java.sql.Time object.

(continued)

	TABLE 5.6

KEY METHODS OF THE RESULTSET INTERFACE (CONTINUED).

Method	Function
Timestamp getTimestam(int col) throws SQLException	Returns a column value as a java.sql.Timestamp object.
Timestamp getTimestamp (String col) throws SQLException	Returns a column value as a java.sql.Timestamp object.
InputStream getUnicodeStream(int col) throws SQLException	Returns a column value as a stream of Unicode characters.
InputStream getUnicodeStream (String col) throws SQLException	Returns a column value as a stream of Unicode characters.
SQLWarning getWarnings( ) throws SQLException	Returns the first warning posted against the ResultSet, or null if no warnings are posted.
boolean next( ) throws SQLException	Positions the ResultSet for access to the next row.
boolean wasNull( ) throws SQLException	Returns true if the column last read had the SQL value null.

A prominent **ResultSet** method is **next( )**, which is used to access the rows of a **ResultSet** serially, in much the same way that the members of an **Enumeration** are accessed. It must be called to position the first row as the current row. The second call to **next( )** makes the second row the current row, and so on. The **next( )** method returns **true** if the new current row is valid, and **false** otherwise.

ResultSet supports the now-familiar **close( )**, **clearWarnings( )**, and **get-Warnings( )** methods. A **ResultSet**'s warning chain is automatically cleared when a new row is read.

Most of the other **ResultSet( )** methods are named *getXXXX*, where *XXXX* specifies a Java data type. These methods retrieve a value from the current row of the **ResultSet**. The argument specifies which column to access, and the name of the method matches the data type it returns. The column can be specified using a **String** containing the column name or an **int** with the value of the column index. Column indexes begin with 1, not 0. The form using the **int** argument is the more general, since it can be more confidently used when the **ResultSet** is generated by a SQL **Select** *. A second advantage of the **int** form is that it allows you easily to verify that columns are being retrieved in order from left to right. Many drivers do not support accessing a column out of order or accessing a column more than once, generating a **SQLException** if either is attempted. You can use the **findColumn( )** method to discover the column index corresponding to a specified column name.

Choosing a proper method of matching the SQL data type of a column with the desired Java data type is important. Tables 5.7 and 5.8 show the SQL data types and corresponding Java data types. The class **java.sql.Types** defines a set of public **int** fields whose names correspond to the SQL data types shown in Tables 5.7 and 5.8. The class also defines the field OTHER, used to refer to a database-specific type that can be accessed using the **getObject( )** method. JDBC

TABLE 5.7

SQL DATA TYPES AND THE CORRESPONDING JAVA DATA TYPES.

SQL Type	Java Type
CHAR	String
VARCHAR	String
LONGVARCHAR	String
NUMERIC	java.math.BigDecimal
DECIMAL	java.math.BigDecimal
BIT	boolean
TINYINT	byte
SMALLINT	short
INTEGER	int
BIGINT	long
REAL	float
FLOAT	double
DOUBLE	double
BINARY	byte[ ]
VARBINARY	byte[ ]
LONGVARBINARY	byte[ ]
DATE	java.sql.Date
TIME	java.sql.Time
TIMESTAMP	java.sql.Timestamp

	TABLE 5.8

JAVA DATA TYPES AND THE CORRESPONDING SQL DATA TYPES.

Java Type	SQL Type
String	VARCHAR or LONGVARCHAR
java.math.BigDecimal	NUMERIC
boolean	BIT
byte	TINYINT
short	SMALLINT
int	INTEGER
long	BIGINT
float	REAL
double	DOUBLE
byte[ ]	VARBINARY or LONGVARBINARY
java.sql.Date	DATE
java.sql.Time	TIME
java.sql.Timestamp	TIMESTAMP

methods that return **int** values representing SQL data types can be decoded using the defined field values.

The *getXXXX* methods cannot detect a field that has a SQL null value, meaning the field is optional and has no value in the current row. After accessing the field using an appropriate *getXXXX* method, the programmer should call **wasNull( )**, which returns **true** if the most recently accessed field has a SQL null value.

The **getBinaryStream( )**, **getAsciiStream( )**, and **getUnicodeStream( )** methods can handle fields of arbitrary length. Each can be called using either an **int** argument or a **String** argument to specify the column, resulting in six method signatures. Each of these returns an **InputStream** containing the corresponding type of character values. The stream can be read using the **InputStream** read methods. Conveniently, a call to **next( )** implicitly closes an open stream.

Some Special Types

Several of the types mentioned in Tables 5.7 and 5.8 may be unfamiliar to you. The **BigDecimal** class is part of the **java.math** package and allows you to work with arbitrarily large decimal numbers. The **getBigDecimal( )** methods return a **BigDecimal** value. The **BigDecimal** class includes two constructors: one that creates a **BigDecimal** by the use of a **double** argument, and another that creates a **BigDecimal** by the use of a **String** argument. If the form requiring a **String** is used, the **String** may contain an optional minus sign, followed by 0 or more decimal digits, followed by an optional fractional part, which consists of a decimal point followed by a series of 0 or more decimal digits. A **Number-FormatException** is thrown if the argument is invalid. The scale of a **BigDecimal** is the number of fractional digits it includes. Table 5.9 shows the key methods

TABLE 5.9

KEY METHODS OF THE BIGDECIMAL CLASS.

Method	Function
BigDecimal abs( )	Returns the absolute value of this number.
BigDecimal add(BigDecimal term)	Returns the sum of this number and the specified term.
int compareTo(BigDecimal val)	Returns –1, 0, or 1, indicating that this number is less than, equal to, or greater than val.
BigDecimal divide(BigDecimal val, int scale, int round) throws ArithmeticException, IllegalArgumentException	Returns (this÷val), represented using the specified scale. Rounding is applied as specified.
BigDecimal divide(BigDecimal val, int round) throws ArithmeticException, IllegalArgumentException	Returns (this÷val), applying the specified rounding.
double doubleValue( )	Returns the value of this number converted to a double.
boolean equals(Object x)	Returns true if x is a BigDecimal with the same value as this number.
float floatValue( )	Returns the value of this number converted to a float.
int hashCode( )	Returns a hash code for this object.
int intValue( )	Returns this number converted to an int.

(continued)

TABLE 5.9

KEY METHODS OF THE BIGDECIMAL CLASS (*CONTINUED*).

Method	Function
long longValue( )	Returns this number converted to a long.
BigDecimal max(BigDecimal val)	Returns the larger of this number and the specified number.
BigDecimal min(BigDecimal val)	Returns the smaller of this number and the specified number.
BigDecimal movePointLeft(int *n*)	Returns the value of this number with the decimal point moved the specified number of places to the left.
BigDecimal movePointRight(int *n*)	Returns the value of this number with the decimal point moved the specified number of places to the right.
BigDecimal multiply (BigDecimal val)	Returns the product of this number and val.
BigDecimal negate( )	Returns the arithmetic opposite of this number.
int scale( )	Returns the scale of this number.
BigDecimal setScale(int scale, int round) throws ArithmeticException, IllegalArgumentException	Returns a BigDecimal with the specified scale, the integer value of which is determined by multiplying or dividing this number's integer value by the appropriate power of 10 in order to leave the overall value unchanged.
int signum( )	Returns -1, 0, or 1, as the value of this number is negative, zero, or positive.
BigDecimal subtract (BigDecimal val)	Returns (this - val).
BigInteger toBigInteger( )	Returns this number converted to a BigInteger.
toString( )	Returns a String representation of this number.
BigDecimal valueOf(long val) throws NumberFormatException	Returns a BigDecimal with value equal to val.
BigDecimal valueOf(long val, int scale) throws NumberFormatException	Returns a BigDecimal with value equal to val divided by 10 raised to the scale (val ÷ (10 **scale)).

of the **BigDecimal** class. Several of the methods use special values to specify rounding options applied to calculations, as shown in Table 5.10.

The **Date**, **Time**, and **Timestamp** classes are part of the **java.sql** package. Because they are subclasses of **java.util.Date**, the programmer can use them to convert **Date**, **Time**, and **Timestamp** values to and from **java.util.Date** objects. The constructors and methods of these classes are shown in Tables 5.11, 5.12, and 5.13, respectively. A **Timestamp** object augments a **Date** object with an **int** containing the number of elapsed nanoseconds after the time specified by the **Date**, allowing precise specification of a point in time.

The ResultSetMetaData Method

The **getMetaData( )** method of the **ResultSet** interface returns a **ResultSet-MetaData** object that you can use to discover useful information about a **ResultSet**. Table 5.14 shows key **ResultSetMetaData** methods. Most of the

TABLE 5.10

ROUNDING OPTIONS DEFINED BY THE BIGDECIMAL CLASS.

Option	Meaning
ROUND_CEILING	If the result is positive, behaves as for ROUND_UP; otherwise, behaves as for ROUND_DOWN.
ROUND_DOWN	Truncates a discarded fraction.
ROUND_FLOOR	If the result is positive, behaves as for ROUND_DOWN; otherwise, behaves as for ROUND_UP.
ROUND_HALF_DOWN	Behaves as for ROUND_UP if the discarded fraction is more than 0.5; otherwise, behaves as for ROUND_DOWN.
ROUND_HALF_EVEN	Behaves as for ROUND_HALF_UP if the digit to the left of the discarded fraction is odd; otherwise, behaves as for ROUND_HALF_DOWN.
ROUND_HALF_UP	Behaves as for ROUND_UP if the discarded fraction is greater than or equal to 0.5; otherwise, behaves as for ROUND_DOWN.
ROUND_UNNECESSARY	Performs no rounding.
ROUND_UP	Increments the unit digit any time a nonzero fraction is discarded.

TABLE 5.11

KEY CONSTRUCTORS AND METHODS OF JAVA.SQL.DATE.

Constructor/Method	Function
Date(int yyyy, int mm, int dd)	Creates a Date with the specified value. The month (mm) ranges from 0 to 11, and the day ranges from 1 to 31.
Date(long msec)	Creates a Date with the specified value.
int getHours( )	Returns the hour represented by this Date.
int getMinutes( )	Returns the number of minutes past the hour represented by this Date.
int getSeconds( )	Returns the number of seconds past the minute represented by this Date.
void setHours(int h)	Sets the hour of this date to the specified value.
void setMinutes(int m)	Sets the minutes of this Date to the specified value.
void setSeconds(int s)	Sets the seconds of this Date to the specified value.
void setTime(int msec)	Sets the Date using a millisecond time value.

TABLE 5.12

KEY CONSTRUCTORS AND METHODS OF JAVA.SQL.TIME.

Constructor/Method	Function
Time(int hh, int mm, int ss)	Creates a Time with the specified value.
Time(long msec)	Creates a Time with the specified value.
int getDate( )	Returns the day of month represented by this Time, from 1 to 31.
int getDay( )	Returns the day of week represented by this Time.
int getMonth( )	Returns the month represented by this Time.
int getYear( )	Returns the year represented by this Time, minus 1900.
void setMonth(int mm)	Sets the month of this Time to the specified value. The month ranges from 0 to 11.
void setTime(long msec)	Sets the Time to the specified value.
void setYear(int yyyy)	Sets the year of this Time to the specified value, plus 1900.

TABLE 5.13

KEY CONSTRUCTORS AND METHODS OF JAVA.SQL.TIMESTAMP.

Constructor/Method	Function
Timestamp(int year, int month, int date, int hour, int minute, int second, int nano)	Creates a Timestamp with the specified value.
Timestamp(long msec)	Creates a Timestamp with the specified value.
boolean after(Timestamp t)	Returns true if this Timestamp is later than the argument.
boolean before(Timestamp t)	Returns true if this Timestamp is earlier than the argument.
boolean equals(Timestamp t)	Returns true if this Timestamp is equal to the argument.
int getNanos( )	Returns the Timestamp's nanoseconds value.
void setNanos(int n)	Sets the Timestamp's nanoseconds value.

TABLE 5.14

KEY METHODS OF RESULTSETMETADATA.

Constructor/Method	Function
int getColumnCount( ) throws SQLException	Returns the number of columns in the ResultSet.
int getColumnDisplaySize(int col) throws SQLException	Returns the column's nomal maximum width, in characters.
String getColumnLabel(int col) throws SQLException	Returns the suggested column title.
String getColumnName(int col) throws SQLException	Returns the column's name.
int getColumnType(int col) throws SQLException	Returns the SQL type of the column, using the values defined in java.sql.types.
String getColumnTypeName(int col) throws SQLException	Returns the data-source-specific name using the column's type.
int getPrecisions(int col) throws SQLException	Returns the number of decimal digits defined for column values.
int getScale(int col) throws SQLException	Returns the number of fractional digits defined for column values.
boolean isAutoIncrement(int col) throws SQLException	Returns true if the column is automatically incremented.

(continued)

	TABLE 5.14

KEY METHODS OF RESULTSETMETADATA (*CONTINUED*).

Method	Function
boolean isCaseSensitive(int col) throws SQLException	Returns true if the column is case-sensitive.
boolean isCurrency(int col) throws SQLException	Returns true if the column contains a cash value.
boolean isDefinitelyWritable(int col) throws SQLException	Returns true if the column is definitely writable.
boolean isNullable(int col) throws SQLException	Returns true if SQL null is a legal column value.
boolean isReadOnly(int col) throws SQLException	Returns true if the column is nonwritable.
boolean isSearchable(int col) throws SQLException	Returns true if the column can be used in a SQL WHERE clause.
boolean isSigned(int col) throws SQLException	Returns true if the column is a signed number.
boolean isWritable(int col) throws SQLException	Returns true if the column is possibly writable.

ResultSetMetaData methods use a column index like that used for **ResultSet** methods. The column index starts with 1, not 0. The SQLWindow02 example, presented in the next section, uses several of the methods of the **ResultSet MetaData** interface.

The SQLWindow02 Application

The SQLWindow02 application improves upon the SQLWindow application that was described in Chapter 4. This version uses **ResultSetMetaData** methods to obtain data allowing query results to be displayed in nicely formatted columns, as shown in Figure 5.3. The revised application also uses the **LoginDialog** and **WindowHandler** classes described earlier in this chapter, simplifying the application code. Listing 5.16 shows the fields and the **main( )** method of the **SQLWindow02** class, which follow the pattern of earlier example programs.

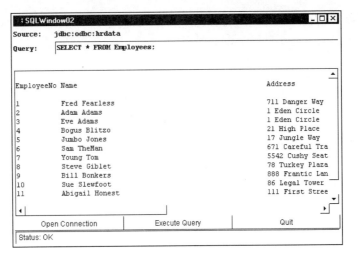

Figure 5.3
The SQLWindow02 application.

When started, the application prompts the user for the database name, log-in user name, and password, using the **LoginDialog**. When a database connection opens, the user can enter a SQL query in the **TextField** and view the results in the **TextArea**. The name of the current data source is displayed in a **Label**, and status information is displayed in a second **TextField**. Execution of the query is initiated by clicking the Execute Query button or by pressing Enter while in the Query **TextField**. The user can open a new database by clicking the Open Connection button or exit the program by clicking the Quit button.

LISTING 5.16   THE SQLWINDOW02 CLASS.

```
import java.awt.*;
import java.awt.event.*;
import java.sql.*;

class SQLWindow02 extends Frame
implements Application, ActionListener
{
    Panel       topPanel    = new Panel( );
    Panel       sourcePanel = new Panel( );
    Panel       queryPanel  = new Panel( );
    Panel       mainPanel   = new Panel( );
    Panel       bottomPanel = new Panel( );
    Panel       buttonPanel = new Panel( );
```

```
Font        topFont    = new Font("Courier", Font.BOLD,  12);
Font        resultFont = new Font("Courier", Font.PLAIN, 12);

Label       theSource  = new Label( );
TextField   theQuery   = new TextField( );
TextArea    theResult  = new TextArea(15, 80);
Button      btnOpen    = new Button("Open Connection");
Button      btnQuery   = new Button("Execute Query");
Button      btnQuit    = new Button("Quit");
TextField   theStatus  = new TextField( );

String theDataSource;
String theUser;
String thePassword;

Connection       theConnection;
Statement        theStatement;
ResultSet        theResultSet;
ResultSetMetaData theMetaData;

public static void main(String args[])
{
    new SQLWindow02( ).init( );
}
```

The init( ) Method

The **init( )** method, shown in Listing 5.17, builds the user interface and opens
the database connection by invoking the **openConnection( )** method. The
method follows the pattern of previous examples.

LISTING 5.17   THE INIT( ) METHOD.

```
public void init( )
{
    setTitle("SQLWindow02");

    topPanel.setFont(topFont);
    theResult.setFont(resultFont);

    add("North", topPanel);
    add("Center", mainPanel);
    add("South", bottomPanel);
```

```
        topPanel.setLayout(new GridLayout(3, 1));
        topPanel.add(sourcePanel);
        topPanel.add(queryPanel);

        sourcePanel.setLayout(new BorderLayout( ));
        sourcePanel.add("West", new Label("Source: "));
        sourcePanel.add("Center", theSource);

        queryPanel.setLayout(new BorderLayout( ));
        queryPanel.add("West", new Label("Query:   "));
        queryPanel.add("Center", theQuery);

        mainPanel.setLayout(new BorderLayout( ));
        mainPanel.add("Center", theResult);

        bottomPanel.setLayout(new BorderLayout( ));
        bottomPanel.add("North", buttonPanel);
        bottomPanel.add("South", theStatus);

        buttonPanel.setLayout(new GridLayout(1, 3));
        buttonPanel.add(btnOpen);
        buttonPanel.add(btnQuery);
        buttonPanel.add(btnQuit);

        theResult.setEditable(false);
        theStatus.setEditable(false);

        addWindowListener(new WindowHandler(this));

        theQuery.addActionListener(this);
        btnOpen .addActionListener(this);
        btnQuery.addActionListener(this);
        btnQuit .addActionListener(this);

        pack( );
        show( );

        while (!openConnection( )) ; // null statement
}
```

The actionPerformed( ) Method

Listing 5.18 shows the **actionPerformed( )** method, which invokes methods in response to user-interface actions. As in the StudyConnect application, a **try-catch** block catches **SQLExceptions** thrown by the invoked methods. Directly invoking the **doQuery( )** method from within the **actionPerformed( )** method causes the former to execute within an AWT thread. While a lengthy query is being processed, the user interface will be unresponsive. Chapter 7 presents an example that shows how to avoid this problem.

LISTING 5.18   THE ACTIONPERFORMED( ) METHOD.

```
public void actionPerformed(ActionEvent event)
{
    try
    {
        theStatus.setText("Status: OK");
        Object source = event.getSource( );
        if (source == btnOpen)          openConnection( );
        else if (source == btnQuery)  doQuery( );
        else if (source == theQuery)  doQuery( );
        else if (source == btnQuit)   requestClose( );
    }
    catch (SQLException sql)
    {
        handleError(sql);
    }
}
```

The openConnection( ) Method

The **openConnection( )** method, shown in Listing 5.19, should seem familiar by now. It directly instantiates an instance of the JDBC/ODBC driver and then establishes a connection to the requested database.

LISTING 5.19   THE OPENCONNECTION( ) METHOD.

```
public boolean openConnection( )
{
    LoginDialog theLoginDialog = null;
    try
    {
        theSource.setText("");
        theResult.setText("");
        theLoginDialog = new LoginDialog(this, true);
```

```
        theLoginDialog.setVisible(true);
        if (theLoginDialog.getStatus( ))
        {
            theSource.setText(theLoginDialog.getURL( ));
            Class.forName ("sun.jdbc.odbc.JdbcOdbcDriver");
            if (theConnection != null) theConnection.close( );
            theConnection =
              DriverManager.getConnection(theLoginDialog.getURL( ),
                theLoginDialog.getUser( ),
                theLoginDialog.getPassword( ));
        }
        theLoginDialog.dispose( );
        return true;
    }
    catch (Throwable t)
    {
        handleError(t);
    }
    if (theLoginDialog != null) theLoginDialog.dispose( );
    return false;
}
```

The doQuery( ) Method

The **doQuery( )** method, shown in Listing 5.20, resembles that used in the original SQLWindow application. Resources associated with the **Statement** and **ResultSet**, which may have been previously used, are immediately released. Garbage collection would force their release, but immediate release can often improve program and database performance. A **DisplayableResultSet** object is constructed using the **ResultSet** obtained from execution of the SQL command. The value returned by the **getString( )** method of the **DisplayableResultSet** is displayed in the **TextArea** known as **theResult**.

Most platforms impose a limit on the amount of text that a **TextArea** can handle. If the query result exceeds this limit, the program will fail. The problem has no simple remedy. One possibility is to limit output to a specified number of rows and provide the user with a pair of buttons that allow forward and backward scrolling among blocks of text, displayed one at a time in the **TextArea**. Another is to create a custom component that presents the same interface as the **TextArea**, but that does not depend upon a native peer component. This, of course, is rather complex. Both remedies are beyond the scope of this book, which focuses on SQL.

LISTING 5.20   THE doQUERY( ) METHOD.

```
public void doQuery( )
throws SQLException
{
    try
    {
        String command = theQuery.getText( );
        theResult.setText("");
        if (theStatement != null) theStatement.close( );
        if (theResultSet != null) theResultSet.close( );
        theStatement = theConnection.createStatement();
        theResultSet = theStatement.executeQuery(command);
        theMetaData = theResultSet.getMetaData( );

        DisplayableResultSet dsr =
          new DisplayableResultSet(theResultSet);
        theResult.setText(dsr.getString( ));
    }
    catch (Exception e)
    {
        handleError(e)
    }
}
```

The requestClose( ) And handleError( ) Methods

The **requestClose**( ) and **handleError**( ) methods, shown together in Listing 5.21, are identical to those used in the **StudyConnect** class.

LISTING 5.2   THE REQUESTCLOSE( ) AND HANDLEERROR( ) METHODS.

```
public void requestClose( )
{
    setVisible(false);
    try
    {
        if (theConnection != null) theConnection.close( );
    }
    catch (SQLException ex)  { ; }
    System.exit(0);
```

```
public void handleError(Throwable t)
{
    theStatus.setText("Error: " + t.getMessage( ));
    t.printStackTrace( );
}
```

The DisplayableResultSet Class

The **DisplayableResultSet** class, shown in Listing 5.22, is the heart of the new capabilities of the SQLWindow02 application. Fortunately, the new capabilities are simple to achieve with the help of **ResultSetMetaData** methods. The constructor for the class simply saves a reference to the provided **ResultSet** in a field for subsequent access by the **getString( )** method. The **getString( )** method obtains a **ResultSetMetaData** object from the **ResultSet** and uses it to obtain the following information on the columns of the **ResultSet**:

- Display column size
- Column label
- Column type
- Column type name
- Precision
- Scale

These values are stored in a set of parallel arrays, each having one cell for each column of the **ResultSet**. The program actually uses only the column name and column size. The remaining values are retrieved simply to demonstrate how to obtain them.

The column size determines the width of each display column. Column labels are concatenated onto the result string to serve as report headings, and then the actual data values are appended. Column labels and data values are truncated or right-padded with spaces to fill the width of each column exactly as specified by **ResultSetMetaData**. Truncated data values are transformed to asterisks to call attention to any formatting problems. This also avoids the possible right truncation of a numeric value, which might result in it being misread. Note that text and numeric values are treated identically. The availability of type, precision, and scale information, however, allows you to extend this method fairly easily so it can handle numeric data values more appropriately.

The **TextArea** used for output in the **SQLWindow02** class is configured to use the monospaced Courier font, which displays each character at the same size. For example, the lowercase *i* and the uppercase *W* occupy the same screen width. The result is that the **String** returned by **getString** displays the **ResultSet** output in neatly arranged columns.

LISTING 5.22   THE DISPLAYABLERESULTSET CLASS.

```java
import java.sql.*;

class DisplayableResultSet extends Object
{   ResultSet theResultSet;
    String    theResult;

    public DisplayableResultSet(ResultSet result)
    {
        theResultSet = result;
    }

    public String getString( )
    throws SQLException
    {
        theResult = "";

        ResultSetMetaData metaData = theResultSet.getMetaData( );
        int colCount = metaData.getColumnCount( );

        int    colSize  [ ]  = new int    [colCount];
        String colLabel [ ]  = new String [colCount];
        int    colType  [ ]  = new int    [colCount];
        String colTName [ ]  = new String [colCount];
        int    colPrec  [ ]  = new int    [colCount];
        int    colScale [ ]  = new int    [colCount];

        theResult += "\n";
        for (int i = 1; i <= colCount; i++)
        {
            colSize [i - 1] = metaData.getColumnDisplaySize(i);
            colLabel[i - 1] = metaData.getColumnLabel        (i);
            colType [i - 1] = metaData.getColumnType         (i);
            colTName[i - 1] = metaData.getColumnTypeName     (i);
            colPrec [i - 1] = metaData.getPrecision          (i);
            colScale[i - 1] = metaData.getScale              (i);

            if (colSize[i - 1] < 1 + colLabel[i - 1].length( ))
                colSize[i - 1] = 1 + colLabel[i - 1].length( );
```

```
            theResult += rightPad(colLabel[i - 1], colSize[i - 1]);

        }
        theResult += "\n\n";

        while (theResultSet.next( ))
        {
            for (int i = 1; i <= colCount; i++)
            {
                String colvalue = theResultSet.getString(i);
                if (colvalue == null) colvalue = "";
                theResult += rightPad(colvalue, colSize[i - 1]);
            }
            theResult += "\n";
        }
        return theResult;
    }

    public String rightPad(String s, int len)
    {
        int curlen = s.length( );
        if (curlen > len) return repString("*", len);
        return s + repString(" ", (len - curlen));
    }

    public String repString(String s, int times)
    {
        String result = "";
        for (int i = 0; i < times; i++)
        {
            result += s;
        }
        return result;
    }
}
```

The SQLException And SQLWarning Classes

You're familiar by now with both **SQLException** and **SQLWarning**, but the former has a few tricks not yet mentioned. Table 5.15 shows the key methods of the **SQLException** class, and Table 5.16 shows the key method of the **SQLWarning** class.

	TABLE 5.15

KEY METHODS OF THE SQLEXCEPTION CLASS.

Method	Function
int getErrorCode( )	Returns the database-vendor-specific error code.
SQLException getNextException( )	Returns the next SQLException chained to this one, or null if no further SQLExceptions are on the chain.
String getSQLState( )	Returns the SQLState, as described in the XOPEN SQLState conventions.

	TABLE 5.16

KEY METHOD OF THE SQLWARNING CLASS.

Method	Function
SQLException (getNextWarning)	Returns the next SQLWarning chained to this one, or null if no further SQLWarnings are on the chain.

The DatabaseMetaData Object

The **Connection getMetaData( )** method returns a **DatabaseMetaData** object that provides access to many methods that return information on database structure and capability. This information is potentially useful in coping with differences between SQL dialects. Although the "main and plain" SQL syntax is standard across many databases, a number of vendors have yet to bring the advanced features of their databases into conformance with the SQL standard. By using the methods of **DatabaseMetaData**, you can explore the features supported by a given database. A related JDBC facility, escape syntax (discussed in Chapter 6), will help you form SQL statements that can be portably executed across many databases.

Of course, an easier way to discover the peculiarities of a given database is by referring to its documentation. The SQL-related methods of **DatabaseMetaData** are primarily of value to systems programmers creating tools that must work across a variety of databases, which cannot always be identified at the time the tool is written. Consequently—and because the focus of this book is SQL, not JDBC—I don't present these methods here. A program included on the CD-ROM, DBAnalyzer, demonstrates how to use these methods. Figure 5.4 shows

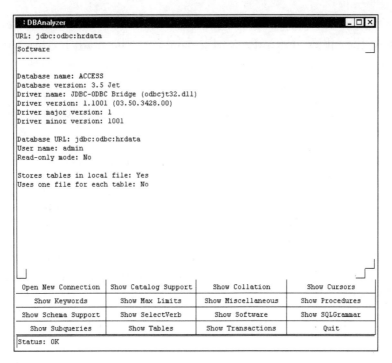

Figure 5.4
A DBAnalyzer run.

an example DBAnalyzer screen. DBAnalyzer has buttons that let the user select from among different categories of information. The program uses the **DatabaseMetaData** object to extract the selected category of information and display it in the application window.

You can use DBAnalyzer in two ways:

- Run it on your databases to learn more about their capabilities.

- Study its source code to see how to call **DatabaseMetaData** methods in your programs, if you need the capabilities they offer.

The **DatabaseMetaData** object also provides access to information on database structure. In particular, it allows you to programmatically determine the tables and indexes included within a database and useful information about their contents.

Listing 5.23 shows the DBExplorer application, which uses **DatabaseMetaData** to explore the tables and indexes of a database. The main methods used by DBExplorer to accomplish its purpose are:

- **getTables( )**, which obtains a **ResultSet** describing the database tables. The table names are loaded into a **Choice** that allows the user to select a database table for exploration.

- **getColumns( )**, which obtains a **ResultSet** describing the columns of a database table.

- **getIndexInfo( )**, which obtains a **ResultSet** describing the indexes related to a database table.

By following the example of DBExplorer, you should be able to understand the JDBC documentation well enough to work with these facilities in your programs when needed.

LISTING 5.23   THE DBEXPLORER APPLICATION.

```
import java.awt.*;
import java.awt.event.*;
import java.sql.*;
import java.util.*;

class DBExplorer extends Frame
implements Application, ActionListener
{
    Panel     topPanel    = new Panel( );
    Panel     sourcePanel = new Panel( );
    Panel     tablePanel  = new Panel( );
    Panel     buttonPanel = new Panel( );
    Panel     bottomPanel = new Panel( );

    Label     theSource   = new Label( );
    Choice    theTables    = new Choice( );
    TextArea  theResult   = new TextArea( );
    Button    btnOpen      = new Button("Open New Connection");
    Button    btnShowCol   = new Button("Show Columns");
    Button    btnShowIndex = new Button("Show Indexes");
    Button    btnQuit      = new Button("Quit");
    TextField theStatus    = new TextField( );

    Connection        theConnection;
    DatabaseMetaData  theDBMetaData;
```

```
public static void main(String args[])
throws SQLException, ClassNotFoundException
{
    new DBExplorer( ).init( );
}

public void init( )
{
    setTitle("DBExplorer");
    setFont(new Font("Courier", Font.PLAIN, 12));
    add("North",  topPanel);
    add("Center", theResult);
    add("South",  bottomPanel);

    topPanel.setLayout(new GridLayout(2, 1));
    topPanel.add(sourcePanel);
    topPanel.add(tablePanel);

    sourcePanel.setLayout(new BorderLayout( ));
    sourcePanel.add("West", new Label("URL:    "));
    sourcePanel.add("Center", theSource);

    tablePanel.setLayout(new BorderLayout( ));
    tablePanel.add("West", new Label("Table: "));
    tablePanel.add("Center",  theTables);

    bottomPanel.setLayout(new GridLayout(2, 1));
    bottomPanel.add(buttonPanel);
    bottomPanel.add(theStatus);

    buttonPanel.setLayout(new FlowLayout( ));
    buttonPanel.add(btnOpen);
    buttonPanel.add(btnShowCol);
    buttonPanel.add(btnShowIndex);
    buttonPanel.add(btnQuit);

    theResult.setEditable(false);
    theStatus.setEditable(false);

    btnOpen.addActionListener(this);
    btnShowCol.addActionListener(this);
    btnShowIndex.addActionListener(this);
    btnQuit.addActionListener(this);

    addWindowListener(new WindowHandler(this));
```

```
        pack( );
        setVisible(true);

        while (!openConnection( )) ; // null statement
    }

    public void actionPerformed(ActionEvent event)
    {
        theStatus.setText("Status: OK.");
        Object source = event.getSource( );
        try
        {
            if (source == btnOpen)              openConnection( );
            else if (source == btnShowIndex) showIndexes   ( );
            else if (source == btnShowCol)   showColumns   ( );
            else if (source == btnQuit)      requestClose  ( );
        }
        catch (Exception ex)
        {
            handleError(ex);
        }
    }

    public boolean openConnection( )
    {
        LoginDialog theLoginDialog = null;
        try
        {
            theSource.setText("");
            theTables.removeAll( );
            theResult.setText("");
            theStatus.setText("Status: OK.");
            theLoginDialog = new LoginDialog(this, true);
            theLoginDialog.setVisible(true);
            if (theLoginDialog.getStatus( ))
            {
                theSource.setText("URL: " + theLoginDialog.getURL( ));
                Class.forName ("sun.jdbc.odbc.JdbcOdbcDriver");
                if (theConnection != null) theConnection.close( );
                theConnection =
                  DriverManager.getConnection(theLoginDialog.getURL( ),
                    theLoginDialog.getUser( ),
                    theLoginDialog.getPassword( ));
                theDBMetaData = theConnection.getMetaData( );

                ResultSet result = theDBMetaData.getTables(
                  null, null, null, null);
                ResultSetMetaData rsmeta = result.getMetaData( );
```

```
        while (result.next( ))
        {
            String catalog
              = result.getString(1);
            String schema
              = result.getString(2);
            String table
              = result.getString(3);
            String type
              = (result.getString(4)).toUpperCase( );
            String remarks
              = result.getString(5);

            if (type.indexOf("SYSTEM") < 0) theTables.add(
              table + ((remarks != null) ? ": "
                  + remarks : ""));
        }
    }
    theLoginDialog.dispose( );
    return true;
}
catch (Exception ex)
{
    handleError(ex);
}
if (theLoginDialog != null) theLoginDialog.dispose( );
return false;
}

public void showIndexes( )
throws SQLException
{
    if (theConnection == null) return;
    String table = theTables.getSelectedItem( );
    ResultSet result = theDBMetaData.getIndexInfo(
      null, null, table, false, true);
    theResult.setText("Indexes for table: " + table + "\n\n");
    while (result.next( ))
    {
        String   catalog_name = result.getString(1);
        String   schema_name  = result.getString(2);
        String   table_name   = result.getString(3);
        boolean non_unique    = result.getBoolean(4);
        String   index_qual   = result.getString(5);
        String   index_name   = result.getString(6);
        short    index_type   = result.getShort(7);
        short    index_pos    = result.getShort(8);
```

```
            String  col_name      = result.getString(9);
            String  asc_or_desc   = result.getString(10);
            String  cardinality   = result.getString(11);
            String  pages_used    = result.getString(12);
            String  filter_cond   = result.getString(13);

            if (index_type != DatabaseMetaData.tableIndexStatistic)
            {
                theResult.append(index_name);
                theResult.append(" Component=" + index_pos);
                theResult.append(" Col=" + col_name);
                theResult.append(" Seq=" + asc_or_desc);
                theResult.append(" Unique="
                   + (non_unique ? "no" : "yes"));
                theResult.append("\n");
            }
        }
    }
}

public void showColumns( )
throws SQLException
{
    if (theConnection == null) return;
    String table
      = theTables.getSelectedItem( );
    ResultSet result
      = theDBMetaData.getColumns(null, null, table, null);
    theResult.setText("Columns for table: " + table + "\n\n");

    while (result.next( ))
    {
        String  catalog_name = result.getString(1);
        String  schema_name  = result.getString(2);
        String  table_name   = result.getString(3);
        String  col_name     = result.getString(4);
        String  data_type    = result.getString(6);
        int     col_size     = result.getInt(7);
        int     dec_digits   = result.getInt(9);
        int     radix        = result.getInt(10);
        int     nullable     = result.getInt(11);
        String  remarks      = result.getString(12);
        int     table_pos    = result.getInt(13);

        theResult.append("" + table_pos + ": ");
        theResult.append(col_name);
        theResult.append(" Type=" + data_type);
```

```
                theResult.append(" Size=" + col_size + "." + dec_digits);
                theResult.append(" Radix=" + radix);
                theResult.append(" Nullable=" + nullable);
                theResult.append(" Remarks=" + remarks);
                theResult.append("\n");
            }
        }

        public void displayResultSet(ResultSet result)
        throws SQLException
        {
            ResultSetMetaData metaData = result.getMetaData( );
            int columnCount = metaData.getColumnCount( );

            theResult.setText("");
            while (result.next( ))
            {
                for (int i = 1; i <= columnCount; i++)
                {
                    theResult.append(result.getString(i) + ";");
                }
                theResult.append("\n");
            }
        }

        public void requestClose( )
        {
            setVisible(false);
            try
            {
                if (theConnection != null) theConnection.close( );
            }
            catch (SQLException ex)
            {
                // null statement
            }
            System.exit(0);
        }

        public void handleError(Throwable t)
        {
            theStatus.setText("Error: " + t.getMessage( ));
            t.printStackTrace( );
        }
    }
```

Summary

A JDBC program accesses a database through a **Driver** managed by the **DriverManager** class. In response to a request to access a database, the **DriverManager** selects an appropriate **Driver** that opens access to the database and returns a **Connection** object. The **Connection** object creates a **Statement** object that handles execution of SQL statements using its execute methods.

The **executeQuery( )** method returns a **ResultSet** object that provides access to the table generated by a SQL query. A variety of methods is available to access the data types that may be found in a **ResultSet** column. The **ResultSet** is accessed column by column with each row; new rows are obtained using the **next( )** method.

You can obtain useful information about the database from a **DatabaseMetaData** object returned by the **getMetaData( )** method of the **Connection** interface. You can obtain useful information about a **ResultSet** from a **ResultSetMetaData** object returned by the **getResultSetMetaData( )** method of the **ResultSet** interface.

Special types provided by Java for handling SQL data types include **BigDecimal**, **Date**, **Time**, and **Timestamp**. Errors and warnings may result in the throwing of **SQLException**s or the posting of **SQLWarning**s against a responsible object.

SORTING AND GROUPING 6

Now that you know a bit more about the JDBC API, it's time to return to this book's primary focus—SQL. In this chapter you'll learn how to write queries that cause the DBMS to return your results in a form closer to what your application needs. For example, you'll learn how to use **Order By** to obtain a sorted **ResultSet** and how to use **Group By** to generate a summary table. You'll also learn how to form expressions that manipulate the raw values contained in database tables, returning computed results ready for use.

Of course, you can perform these operations yourself in your Java program. But these SQL facilities are easy to use and often lead to improved system performance, since you may not need to send as much data across the network that links your clients with their servers.

Some of these facilities are not yet standard and must be accessed differently for different databases. Fortunately, JDBC includes an escape facility that allows you to write more portable queries.

You'll also learn more about SQL nulls. Understanding nulls is important in writing queries that count table records. You also need to know how nulls behave when used in expressions.

The chapter's example programs include further improvements to the GuestBook and SQLWindow programs. Let's get started!

Putting Things In Order: The Order By Clause

So far, the **ResultSets** returned in response to your SQL queries have had no particular order. Often, however, you may want to display or report data in some predetermined sequence—for example, a list of employees in ascending or descending order by employee number, or alphabetical by name. This is simple to achieve using the SQL **Order By** clause of the **Select** statement.

This chapter will use the Employees table introduced in Chapter 4. For convenience, the contents of the table are shown again in Table 6.1.

TABLE 6.1

THE EMPLOYEES TABLE.

Emp. No	Name	Address	City	State	Zip	Sex	Salary
1	Fred Fearless	711 Danger Way	Tombstone	AZ	71234	M	60000
2	Adam Adams	1 Eden Circle	Paradise	CA	77701	M	120000
3	Eve Adams	1 Eden Circle	Paradise	CA	77701	F	130000
4	Bogus Blitzo	21 High Place	Easy Street	CA	16661	M	150000
5	Jumbo Jones	17 Jungle Way	Redmond	WA	45624	M	65000
6	Sam TheMan	671 Careful Trail	Santa Ona	CA	91732	M	85000
7	Young Tom	5542 Cushy Seat	Overstuff	CA	98235	M	90000
8	Steve Giblet	78 Turkey Plaza	Gravy	CA	93436	M	70000
9	Bill Bonkers	888 Frantic Lane	Anxiety	CA	95632	M	60000
10	Sue Slewfoot	86 Legal Tower	Highrise	CA	97655	F	300000
11	Abigail Honest	111 First Street	Integrity	CA	97633	F	60000
12	Ann Agram	22 Puzzle Box	Intellect	CA	95645	F	75000

Suppose you want to retrieve the name and salary of each employee, but you want the **ResultSet** to be ordered by employee name. The following query would do just that, as shown by the output following the query:

```
Select Name, Salary From Employees Order By Name;
```

Results:

```
Name              Salary

Abigail Honest    60000
Adam Adams        120000
Ann Agram         75000
Bill Bonkers      60000
Bogus Blitzo      150000
Eve Adams         130000
Fred Fearless     60000
Jumbo Jones       65000
Sam TheMan        85000
Steve Giblet      70000
Sue Slewfoot      300000
Young Tom         90000
```

The query and results are shown as the SQLWindow program would display them, with the query at the top and the results below. Of course, in your program the query is returned as a **ResultSet**, which you use to obtain the values shown.

In the output, note that (perhaps to your surprise and dismay) the employees are sorted by *first* name rather than last name. SQL sorts by examining the characters of a field one by one, from left to right. It has no way of knowing that each field value includes the first name, followed by a space, followed by the last name.

You can cope with this problem in several ways. The simplest is to enter the employee names with the last name first, followed by a comma, and then the first name. A better solution is to redesign the database to include separate fields for first and last names. You can also use a SQL expression to "crack" the employee name into a first and last name. You'll see how to do that in a later section of this chapter.

Sorting on more than one field is easy. Suppose you want a list of employees by state and that you want the employees within each state to be ordered by name. The following query does the job:

```
Select Name, State From Employees
Order By State, Name;
```

Results:

```
Name            State

Fred Fearless   AZ
Abigail Honest  CA
Adam Adams      CA
Ann Agram       CA
Bill Bonkers    CA
Bogus Blitzo    CA
Eve Adams       CA
Sam TheMan      CA
Steve Giblet    CA
Sue Slewfoot    CA
Young Tom       CA
Jumbo Jones     WA
```

The query has been written across two lines for ease of reading. Do not, however, embed a newline character in the query executed by a **Statement** object in your program, because that will cause a syntax error.

Of course, if you wanted the state to appear in the left column and the name to appear in the right column, you could write:

```
Select State, Name From Employees Order By State, Name;
```

A sorted column normally appears in ascending sequence, with the lowest values at the top of the column and the highest values at the bottom. A descending order is also possible:

```
Select Name From Employees
Order By Name Desc;
```

Results:

```
Name
```

```
Young Tom
Sue Slewfoot
Steve Giblet
Sam TheMan
Jumbo Jones
Fred Fearless
Eve Adams
Bogus Blitzo
Bill Bonkers
Ann Agram
Adam Adams
Abigail Honest
```

You can use the **Order By** clause and the **Where** clause together to produce a sorted result that includes only selected records. For example, to obtain a result sorted by name that includes only the California employees, you could write:

```
Select Name From Employees
Where State = 'CA'
Order By Name;
```

Results:

```
Name

Abigail Honest
Adam Adams
Ann Agram
Bill Bonkers
Bogus Blitzo
Eve Adams
Sam TheMan
Steve Giblet
Sue Slewfoot
Young Tom
```

Remember, unlike Java, SQL requires that string literals be enclosed in single quotes. If you use double quotes, your query will be rejected because of incorrect syntax.

One place where using double quotes is appropriate is in the **As** clause. What if you want to use *select* as the heading for a column, as in the following query:

```
Select Name As select From Employees;
```

This query will fail due to a syntax error, because *select* is a SQL keyword. To outsmart the SQL interpreter, you can use:

```
Select Name As "select" From Employees;
```

By surrounding the column name with double quotes, you prevent the SQL interpreter from peeking inside and realizing that the contents resemble a keyword. You *could* use single quotes for the same purpose

```
Select Name As 'select' From Employees;
```

but single quotes used this way actually appear in the column name—probably not what you want in most cases.

Getting It Together: Aggregates

Suppose you want to discover the highest salary paid to any employee. One way to do this would be to generate an employee list sorted by salary and inspect the last entry. This method, however, would send each employee record across the network—a wasteful exercise when all you want is the highest salary. SQL solves your problem:

```
Select Max(Salary) From Employees;
```

Results:

```
Expr1000
```

```
300000
```

One problem with the output is that the SQL interpreter has assigned a name to the result of the **Max** function, *Expr1000*. If you're dissatisfied with this nondescript name, you can modify the query slightly:

```
Select Max(Salary) As BigBucks From Employees;
```

Results:

```
BigBucks

300000
```

The original name may not pose a real problem, since your program receives a **ResultSet**, not a printed display. If you want a more descriptive column name to be available in the **ResultSetMetaData**, however, the **As** clause is exactly your ticket.

Of course, what you probably want to know is not only the largest salary amount, but which employee earns that amount. I'll get to that in the next section of this chapter, but first I want to explore some further aspects of SQL's *aggregate functions*, which combine and summarize data from table rows. Table 6.2 describes these aggregate functions.

Here's a query that returns the average salary of California employees, who appear as a group to be quite well paid:

```
Select Avg(Salary) As Average From Employees
Where State = 'CA';
```

Results:

```
Average

114000.0
```

	TABLE 6.2

SQL's AGGREGATE FUNCTIONS.

Name	Function
Avg	Computes the average (mean) of a column.
Count	Counts the number of non-null entries in a column.
Max	Finds the maximum value in a column.
Min	Finds the minimum value in a column.
Sum	Computes the sum of a column.

Of course, that isn't to say that every California employee is getting rapidly wealthy. The following query shows that some employees are paid only a little more than half the average:

```
Select Min(Salary) As Poverty From Employees
Where State = 'CA';
```

Results:

```
Poverty

60000
```

You can find the total annual salary for employees outside the state of California using this query:

```
Select Sum(Salary) As Budget From Employees
Where State <> 'CA';
```

Results:

```
Budget

125000.0
```

The **Count** function is one of the most versatile SQL functions. It counts the number of non-null values in a column. The following query finds the number of California employees:

```
Select Count(EmployeeNo) As Staff From Employees
Where State = 'CA';
```

Results:

```
Staff

10
```

By choosing **EmployeeNo** as the column, you make sure that all employees are counted. Because **EmployeeNo** is the primary key of the Employees table, it can never be null, and so the count will be correct. If you had used the query

```
Select Count(Address) As Staff From Employees
Where State = 'CA';
```

then the count would not have included any employee with a missing address. A special form of the **Count** function eliminates this problem. The query

```
Select Count(*) As Staff From Employees
Where State = 'CA';
```

will include all rows in the count.

When you use an aggregate function in the column list of the **Select** statement, all other columns selected must also be aggregates. For example, you can't write

```
Select EmployeeNo, Sum(HoursPerWeek) From Assignments;
```

because **Sum(HoursPerWeek)** is an aggregate, and **EmployeeNo** is not. Also, aggregates cannot be included in a **Where** clause, so you can't write:

```
Select State From Employees Where Sum(Salary) > 60000;
```

Don't fret. You'll soon learn the correct way to accomplish such queries.

Microsoft Access SQL Extensions: Distinct, Top, And Top *n* Percent

What if you want to know the number of states in which the company has employees? The obvious query

```
Select Count(State) As States From Employees;
```

won't deliver the correct result. Though it may seem right at first, it actually counts the number of non-null values of the state column. A second, special form of the **Count** function solves this problem:

```
Select Count(Distinct State) From Employees;
```

One unfortunate shortcoming of the Microsoft Jet database engine used by Microsoft Access is that it does not support **Count(Distinct)**, even though this form is part of ANSI-standard SQL. (Microsoft SQL Server's Transact-SQL also lacks support for **Count(Distinct)**.) Access does support a non-ANSI

Select Distinct, which includes in the result only those rows that have a unique combination of values for the specified field(s). For example, the query

```
Select Distinct State From Employees;
```

obtains the result

```
State

AZ
CA
WA
```

which includes only one row for each state. This doesn't provide the count of states originally sought, but it gets you most of the way there. A few lines of Java, or some more sophisticated SQL that you'll learn about in Chapter 11, can do the rest.

Access supports two other handy, though nonstandard, forms of the **Select** statement. The first lets you select a specified number of records from among those returned by the query. For example, the query

```
Select Top 5 Name, Salary From Employees
Where State = 'CA'
Order By Salary Desc;
```

obtains the result

```
Name            Salary

Sue Slewfoot    300000
Bogus Blitzo    150000
Eve Adams       130000
Adam Adams      120000
Young Tom       90000
```

which returns only the first five records satisfying the **Where** clause. This way, you can easily see who's making the big bucks.

A related form returns a specified percentage of the records that would otherwise have appeared in the result:

```
Select Top 25 Percent Name, Salary From Employees
Where State = 'CA'
Order By Salary Desc;
```

Results:

```
Name            Salary

Sue Slewfoot    300000
Bogus Blitzo    150000
Eve Adams       130000
```

Remember that **Select Distinct**, **Select Top** *n*, and **Select Top** *n* **Percent** are nonstandard Microsoft Access forms that most SQL interpreters do not handle. You can use the **Count(Distinct)** aggregate function with most ANSI-compliant SQL interpreters. Duplicating the function of Access's **Select Top** *n* and **Select Top** *n* **Percent** forms is also possible using standard SQL forms, as you'll see in Chapter 11.

Subtotals, Group By Group

The Assignments table (Table 6.3) shows how employees have been assigned to departments. For example, employee 10 (Sue Slewfoot, per Table 6.1) is assigned to department 1 for 40 hours per week. Employee 6 (Sam TheMan) is assigned to department 2, and so on.

TABLE **6.3**

THE ASSIGNMENTS TABLE.

EmployeeNo	DeptNo	HoursPerWeek
10	1	40
6	2	40
9	3	20
7	1	40
1	2	40
5	2	40
9	2	40
3	3	40
9	1	20
2	3	40
12	3	40

Determining the total number of assigned hours for all employees is easy, using the query:

```
Select Sum(HoursPerWeek) From Assignments;
```

But what if you want to know the number of assigned hours for each department, rather than for the whole company? The **Group By** clause fills this need:

```
Select Sum(HoursPerWeek) From Assignments Group By Deptno;
```

Results:

```
DeptNo      TotalHours

1           100.0
2           160.0
3           140.0
```

The **Group By** clause controls the level at which aggregate functions are computed. In the previous example, they are computed separately for each department. Use of **Group By** places some restrictions on the columns that can appear in the column list of the **Select** statement. Only aggregates and columns specified in **Group By** can be selected for retrieval. For example, the query

```
Select DeptNo, EmployeeNo, Sum(HoursPerWeek) From Assignments
Group By DeptNo
```

is invalid, because the column Employeeno is neither an aggregate nor included in **Group By**.

Here's a query that reports total staff and assigned hours by department:

```
Select DeptNo,
  Count(*) As Staff,
  Sum(HoursPerWeek) As Hours
From Assignments
Group By DeptNo;
```

Results:

```
DeptNo      Staff      Hours

1           3          100.0
```

```
2          4          160.0
3          4          140.0
```

Of course, you can include multiple columns within a **Group By** clause when you want groups within groups. For example, you can write:

```
Select DeptNo,
  EmployeeNo,
  Sum(HoursPerWeek) As Hours
From Assignments
Group By DeptNo, EmployeeNo;
```

Results:

```
DeptNo     EmployeeNo  Hours

1          7           40.0
1          9           20.0
1          10          40.0
2          1           40.0
2          5           40.0
2          6           40.0
2          9           40.0
3          2           40.0
3          3           40.0
3          9           20.0
3          12          40.0
```

This way, if an employee has more than one assignment within a department, the employee's assignments will all be combined into a single subtotal of hours, displayed by employee number within a department.

Having It Your Way: Selecting Groups

Earlier in the chapter, you saw that you cannot use an aggregate function in a **Where** clause. How, then, do you write a query that lists the states where employees have total salaries of more than $60,000? The **Having** clause can be used with the **Group By** clause to write such a query.

```
Select State From Employees
Group By State
Having Sum(Salary) > 60000;
```

Results:

```
State

CA
WA
```

The **Having** clause works with **Group By** in much the same way as the **Where** clause works with the **Select** statement. **Where** determines which table rows are included in the result. **Having** determines which *groups* of table rows are included in the result. Here, only groups (by state) having total salaries greater than $60,000 are included.

How about a query that returns departments with more than two employees? This can be written as follows:

```
Select DeptNo, Count(*) As Staff From Assignments
Group By DeptNo
Having Count(*)>2;
```

Results:

```
DeptNo    Staff

1         3
2         4
3         4
```

Expressing Yourself With Expressions

Now that you're a pro at selecting data using SQL queries, you may yearn to express yourself more flexibly. Good news awaits: Your **Select** statements can select from more than table columns. You can include literals, expressions, and functions in your **Select**s. For example, to provide the boss with a script for greeting the employees each morning, you can write:

```
select 'Hi, ' As "Greet", Name, '. How are you?' As "Question" From
Employees;
```

Results:

```
Greet    Name               Question

Hi,      Fred Fearless      . How are you?
Hi,      Adam Adams         . How are you?
Hi,      Eve Adams          . How are you?
Hi,      Bogus Blitzo       . How are you?
Hi,      Jumbo Jones        . How are you?
Hi,      Sam TheMan         . How are you?
Hi,      Young Tom          . How are you?
Hi,      Steve Giblet       . How are you?
Hi,      Bill Bonkers       . How are you?
Hi,      Sue Slewfoot       . How are you?
Hi,      Abigail Honest     . How are you?
Hi,      Ann Agram          . How are you?
```

As another example, suppose you wanted to give every employee a 10 percent raise. You could use this query to report the old and new salary amounts:

```
Select Name, Salary As OldSalary, Salary * 1.1 As NewSalary From Employees;
```

Results:

```
Name             OldSalary   NewSalary

Fred Fearless    60000       66000.0
Adam Adams       120000      132000.0
Eve Adams        130000      143000.0
Bogus Blitzo     150000      165000.0
Jumbo Jones      65000       71500.0
Sam TheMan       85000       93500.0
Young Tom        90000       99000.0
Steve Giblet     70000       77000.0
Bill Bonkers     60000       66000.0
Sue Slewfoot     300000      330000.0
Abigail Honest   60000       66000.0
Ann Agram        75000       82500.0
```

The ordinary arithmetic operations of addition (+), subtraction (-), multiplication (*), and division (/) are available in SQL. You can also use parentheses to group the operations where necessary. For example, to give everyone a $500 salary increase and then increase their salary by 10 percent, you could write:

```
Select Name, Salary As OldSalary, 1.1 * (Salary + 500) As NewSalary From
Employees;
```

Results:

```
Name            OldSalary  NewSalary

Fred Fearless   60000      66550.0
Adam Adams      120000     132550.0
Eve Adams       130000     143550.0
Bogus Blitzo    150000     165550.0
Jumbo Jones     65000      72050.0
Sam TheMan      85000      94050.0
Young Tom       90000      99550.0
Steve Giblet    70000      77550.0
Bill Bonkers    60000      66550.0
Sue Slewfoot    300000     330550.0
Abigail Honest  60000      66550.0
Ann Agram       75000      83050.0
```

This result is different from that obtained by use of

```
Select Name, Salary As OldSalary, 1.1 * Salary + 500 As NewSalary From
Employees;
```

which would give everyone a 10 percent raise and then an additional $500. The parentheses are important: This query gives everyone a $50 smaller raise than the former one.

Fun With Functions

Most SQL interpreters include a variety of useful functions you can use to form new values from the values in table columns. Unfortunately, the names and arguments of these functions are largely nonstandardized. Even those functions specified by the ANSI standard continue to be supported only in nonstandard ways by many popular databases. Table 6.4 shows the functions provided by Microsoft Access. Consult the documentation for your database to determine which functions are available and how they are used.

TABLE 6.4

Microsoft Access SQL functions.

Name	Meaning
Abs(x)	Returns the absolute value of the number x.
Ascii(x)	Returns the numeric value of the ASCII character x.
AtanN(x)	Returns the angle (in radians) whose tangent is the number x.
Ceiling(x)	Returns the smallest integer not less than the number x.
Char(x)	Returns the character whose ASCII code is given by the number x.
Concat(x, y)	Returns the result of concatenating string y onto the end of string x.
Cos(x)	Returns the cosine of the angle given by x (in radians).
Curdate(x)	Returns the current date.
Curtime(x)	Returns the current time.
Dayofmonth(x)	Returns the day of month (1–31) specified by the date x.
Dayofweek(x)	Returns the number that represents the day of week (Sunday = 1) specified by the date x.
Dayofyear(x)	Returns the day of year (1–366) specified by the date x.
Exp(x)	Returns the base of natural logarithms (e) raised to the power x.
Floor(x)	Returns the largest integer not greater than the number x.
Hour(x)	Returns the hour specified by the time x.
Lcase(x)	Returns the result of converting string x to lowercase.
Left(x, y)	Returns the leftmost y characters of string x.
Length(x)	Returns the length of string x.
Locate(x, y)	Returns the index of string y in string x, or 0 if y is not found in x.
Log(x)	Returns the natural logarithm of x.
Ltrim(x)	Returns the string x with any leading (left) spaces removed.
Minute(x)	Returns the minute specified by the time x.
Mod(x, y)	Returns the remainder of the division of x by y.
Month(x)	Returns the month (1–12) specified by the date x.
Now(x)	Returns a timestamp containing the current date and time.

(continued)

	TABLE 6.4

MICROSOFT ACCESS SQL FUNCTIONS (*CONTINUED*).

Name	Meaning
Power*(x, y)*	Returns the number *x* raised to the power *y*.
Rand( )	Returns a random number from 0.0 (inclusive) to 1.0 (exclusive).
Right*(x, y)*	Returns the rightmost *y* characters of string *x*.
Rtrim*(x)*	Returns the string *x* with any trailing (right) spaces removed.
Second*(x)*	Returns the number of seconds specified by the time *x*.
Sign*(x)*	Returns -1, 0, or 1 according to the sign of *x*.
Sin*(x)*	Returns the sine of the angle given by *x* (in radians).
Space*(x)*	Returns a string containing the number of spaces specified by *x*.
Sqrt*(x)*	Returns the square root of the number *x*.
Substring*(x, y, z)*	Returns the substring of string *x*, beginning at position *y* and having length *z*.
Tan*(x)*	Returns the tangent of the angle given by *x* (in radians).
Ucase*(x)*	Returns the result of converting string *x* to uppercase.
Week*(x)*	Returns the week of year (1-53) specified by the date *x*.
Year*(x)*	Returns the year specified by the date *x*.

JDBC does provide some help, by defining a special escape syntax for calling functions. The escape syntax specifies function calls in a standard way and lets the driver for a particular database map function calls—expressed using the escape syntax—into the proper form for the database it supports. This helps make SQL queries that include function calls more portable.

The JDBC escape syntax for functions is

```
{ fn name (arglist) }
```

where *name* stands for the name of the function and *arglist* stands for its argument list. For example, to give every employee a new salary equal to the natural logarithm of his or her current salary, you could write:

```
Select Name,
   Salary As OldSalary,
   {fn Log(Salary)} As NewSalary
From Employees;
```

Results:

Name	OldSalary	NewSalary
Fred Fearless	60000	11.0020998412042
Adam Adams	120000	11.6952470217642
Eve Adams	130000	11.7752897294377
Bogus Blitzo	150000	11.9183905730784
Jumbo Jones	65000	11.0821425488778
Sam TheMan	85000	11.3504065354725
Young Tom	90000	11.4075649493124
Steve Giblet	70000	11.1562505210315
Bill Bonkers	60000	11.0020998412042
Sue Slewfoot	300000	12.6115377536383
Abigail Honest	60000	11.0020998412042
Ann Agram	75000	11.2252433925184

To separate an employee's first and last names, you could use this query:

```
Select {fn Length(name)} As Len,
       {fn Locate(' ', Name)} As Break,
       {fn Left(Name, Break)} As First,
       {fn Right(Name, Len - Break)} As Last
From Employees ;
```

Results:

Len	Break	First	Last
13	5	Fred	Fearless
10	5	Adam	Adams
9	4	Eve	Adams
12	6	Bogus	Blitzo
11	6	Jumbo	Jones
10	4	Sam	TheMan
9	6	Young	Tom
12	6	Steve	Giblet
12	5	Bill	Bonkers
12	4	Sue	Slewfoot
14	8	Abigail	Honest
9	4	Ann	Agram

Unfortunately, if you try to use **Order By Last** to sort the results of the previous query, you'll be disappointed. Named expressions cannot be used in the **Order By** clause. You can still accomplish your purpose, however, by using column numbers, rather than column names, in the **Order By** clause:

```
Select {fn Length(Name)} as Len,
       {fn Locate(' ', Name)} As Break,
       {fn Left(Name, Break)} As First,
       {fn Right(Name, Len - Break)} As Last
From Employees
Order By 4, 3;
```

Results:

Len	Break	First	Last
10	5	Adam	Adams
9	4	Eve	Adams
9	4	Ann	Agram
12	6	Bogus	Blitzo
12	5	Bill	Bonkers
13	5	Fred	Fearless
12	6	Steve	Giblet
14	8	Abigail	Honest
11	6	Jumbo	Jones
12	4	Sue	Slewfoot
10	4	Sam	TheMan
9	6	Young	Tom

Escaping Your Dates

The syntax used to express dates and times is another area, like function syntax, that tends to differ from database to database. JDBC helps out with an escape syntax for specifying date and time literals, as shown in Table 6.5.

For example, to retrieve from the Visits table of the GuestBook database only those rows describing visits after December 31, 1997, you could write:

```
Select VisitorName From visits Where TimeOfVisit >= {d '1997-12-31'};
```

Two methods of the **java.sql.Date** class are helpful in working with JDBC-escaped dates. The **toString( )** method formats the **Date** as a JDBC-escaped **String**. The **valueOf( )** static method returns a **Date** value when passed a **String** containing a JDBC-escaped date.

	TABLE 6.5

JDBC ESCAPE SYNTAX FOR DATE AND TIME LITERALS.

Literal Type	Escape Syntax
Date	{d 'yyyy-mm-dd'}, where yyyy gives the year, mm gives the month, and dd gives the day.
Time	{t 'hh:mm:ss'}, where hh gives the hour, mm gives the minute, and ss gives the second.
Timestamp	{ts 'yyyy-mm-dd hh:mm:ss[.fff ...]'}, where yyyy gives the year, mm gives the month, dd gives the day, hh gives the hour, mm gives the minute, ss gives the second, and fff ... gives the fractional seconds.

For example, to convert a **Date** to a **String** containing a JDBC-escaped date, you can use:

```
java.sql.Date theDate = // some value
String escapedDate = theDate.toString( );
```

To convert a **String** containing a JDBC-escaped date to a **Date**, you can use:

```
String escapedDate = // some value
java.sql.Date theDate = java.sql.Date.valueOf(escapedDate);
```

Nulls

We've briefly mentioned SQL nulls on several previous occasions. Recall that SQL nulls are placeholder values that indicate the absence of a valid column value. They often result from the user's decision to omit an optional field during data input. In Chapter 5, you learned that you can test for a null column in a **ResultSet** by calling **wasNull( )** after fetching the data using one of the **ResultSet.getXXXX( )** methods.

Now that you know how to form expressions using column values, you need to know a bit more about SQL nulls. Unfortunately, various databases treat nulls quite differently. For example, if you use an **Order By** clause to sort a query result by a particular column that contains null values, some databases will place the rows containing the null at the top of the result, and some will put them at the bottom.

Computations involving numeric columns including null values also cause problems. Many databases report the result of any computation on a null column as null, but this is not guaranteed to be true for every database.

The bottom line with nulls is that you must get acquainted with the database system you're using. Study its documentation to learn the rules it follows when working with null values. This can save you a great deal of late-night head scratching down the road.

The GuestBook04 Application

The time has come to revisit the database browsing problem. Chapter 4 presented the GuestBook03 application, which allowed the user to browse forward and backward through a database table. However, the technique used in GuestBook03—storing primary keys in a **Vector** object—had a significant drawback in a multiuser environment. The records visible to GuestBook03 are "frozen" when the program is started and key values are loaded into the **Vector**. Any records added to the database by other users after GuestBook03 is started are "invisible" to it. Similarly, the program continues to "see" records that were deleted after it began.

One remedy would be to provide a Refresh button that allows the user to reload the **Vector** so that it's up to date. But this is not a very satisfactory solution, because the user doesn't know *when* a refresh is needed. Even worse, the refresh forces the user to restart browsing from the first table record.

The new and improved version of the application, named GuestBook04, uses the SQL **Order By** clause to remedy this situation. It moves forward in the table by retrieving records having primary key values greater than the current value, or backward by retrieving records having primary key values less than the current value. This causes considerably more activity on the database server and network than did the technique used by GuestBook03, but if the user's view of the data must be as up to date as possible, the price can be worthwhile.

Listing 6.1 shows the fields of the GuestBook04 application and its **main( )** method. Several things are new. Three **static final int** fields define values used to set an **int** named **browseStatus**, which indicates whether the user is currently browsing forward or backward through the table. Along with the values denoting forward and backward movement, a third value indicates that the last attempt to fetch a record was unsuccessful.

GuestBook04 also has a new **int** (**theSeqNo**) and four new **String** fields (**theName**, **theEMail**, **theComment**, and **theTime**) that act as a buffer, holding data obtained from the **ResultSet**, but not yet displayed on the screen. The four **TextField**s have been renamed to avoid conflicts with the names of the buffer fields.

LISTING 6.1   THE GUESTBOOK04 APPLICATION.

```java
import java.awt.*;
import java.awt.event.*;
import java.sql.*;

class GuestBook04 extends Frame
implements ActionListener
{
    static final int BROWSING_FORWARD  = +1;
    static final int BROWSING_BACKWARD = -1;
    static final int BROWSING_INVALID  =  0;

    Panel       theMainPanel = new Panel( );
    Panel       theDataPanel = new Panel( );

    TextField   txtName      = new TextField("", 32);
    TextField   txtEMail     = new TextField("", 32);
    TextField   txtComment   = new TextField("", 50);
    TextField   txtTime      = new TextField("", 24);

    String      theName;
    String      theEMail;
    String      theComment;
    String      theTime;

    Panel       theButtonPanel = new Panel( );
    Button      theFirstButton = new Button("First Record");
    Button      thePrevButton  = new Button("Prev Record");
    Button      theLastButton  = new Button("Last Record");
    Button      theNextButton  = new Button("Next Record");

    Button      theQuitButton  = new Button("Quit");

    Panel       theStatusPanel = new Panel( );
    TextField   theStatus      = new TextField("");
```

```
Connection theConnection;
Statement  theStatement;
ResultSet  theResult;

int        theSeqNo = 0;
int        browseStatus;

String theDataSource;
String theUser;
String thePassword;

public static void main(String args[])
{
    new GuestBook04( ).init( );
}
```

The init( ) Method

The **init**( ) method is shown in Listing 6.2. If you look back at GuestBook03 in Chapter 4, you'll find that little has changed.

LISTING 6.2   THE INIT( ) METHOD.

```
public void init( )
{
    setTitle("GuestBook04");
    add("Center", theMainPanel);
    add("South",  theStatusPanel);

    theMainPanel.setLayout(new GridLayout(2, 1));
    theMainPanel.add(theDataPanel);
    theMainPanel.add(theButtonPanel);

    theDataPanel.setLayout(new GridLayout(4, 1));
    theDataPanel.add(txtName);
    theDataPanel.add(txtEMail);
    theDataPanel.add(txtComment);
    theDataPanel.add(txtTime);

    theButtonPanel.setLayout(new FlowLayout( ));
    theButtonPanel.add(theFirstButton);
    theButtonPanel.add(thePrevButton);
    theButtonPanel.add(theNextButton);
    theButtonPanel.add(theLastButton);
    theButtonPanel.add(theQuitButton);
```

```
theStatusPanel.setLayout(new BorderLayout( ));
theStatusPanel.add("Center", theStatus);

txtName    .setEditable(false);
txtEMail   .setEditable(false);
txtComment.setEditable(false);
txtTime    .setEditable(false);
theStatus .setEditable(false);

theFirstButton.addActionListener(this);
thePrevButton .addActionListener(this);
theNextButton .addActionListener(this);
theLastButton .addActionListener(this);
theQuitButton .addActionListener(this);

addWindowListener(new WindowHandler( ));

pack( );
show( );

try
{
    openConnection( );
    getFirstRecord( );
    moveDataToForm( );
}
catch (Exception e)
{
    handleException(e);
}
}
```

The actionPerformed ( ) Method

Listing 6.3 shows the **actionPerformed**( ) method. This now separately invokes the method to fetch a new table row and the method to display the result of a fetch.

LISTING 6.3   THE ACTIONPERFORMED( ) METHOD.

```
public void actionPerformed(ActionEvent event)
{
    statusOK( );

    Object source = event.getSource( );
    if (source == theFirstButton)
    {
```

```
        getFirstRecord( );
        moveDataToForm( );
    }
    else if (source == thePrevButton)
    {
        getPrevRecord( );
        moveDataToForm( );
    }
    else if (source == theNextButton)
    {
        getNextRecord( );
        moveDataToForm( );
    }
    else if (source == theLastButton)
    {
        getLastRecord( );
        moveDataToForm( );
    }
    else if (source == theQuitButton) destroy( );
}
```

The getColumns( ) Method And Related Methods

The **getColumns( )** method is shown in Listing 6.4, along with the related methods, **noNull( )** and **moveDataToForm( )**. The **getColumns( )** method retrieves column values from the **ResultSet**, storing them in the fields designated for that purpose. It uses the **noNull( )** method to ensure that each **String** reference is non-null. The **moveDataToForm( )** method simply uses the buffer fields to set the value of the related **TextField**s.

LISTING 6.4   THE GETCOLUMNS( ) METHOD AND RELATED METHODS.

```
public boolean getColumns( )
{
    try
    {
        if (!theResult.next( )) return false;

        theSeqNo = theResult.getInt(1);

        theName   = noNull(theResult.getString(2));
        theEMail  = noNull(theResult.getString(3));
```

```
        theComment = noNull(theResult.getString(4));
        theTime    = noNull(theResult.getString(5));
    }
    catch (Exception e)
    {
        handleException(e);
    }
    return true;
}

public String noNull(String s)
{
    return (s != null) ? s : "";
}

public void moveDataToForm( )
{
    txtName    .setText(theName);
    txtEMail   .setText(theEMail);
    txtComment.setText(theComment);
    txtTime    .setText(theTime);
}
```

The openConnection( ) Method And The closeConnection( ) Method

Listing 6.5 shows the methods used to open and close the database connection. Since the **Statement** object can be reused, the **openConnection**( ) method creates it and saves its reference in a field. The **closeConnection**( ) method is, as usual, quite simple.

LISTING 6.5   THE OPENCONNECTION( ) METHOD AND THE CLOSECONNECTION( ) METHOD.

```
public void openConnection( )
throws SQLException, ClassNotFoundException
{
    statusOK( );

    theDataSource = "jdbc:odbc:GuestBook";
    theUser = "";
    thePassword = "";

    Class.forName ("sun.jdbc.odbc.JdbcOdbcDriver");
    theConnection =
```

```
    DriverManager.getConnection(theDataSource, theUser,
        thePassword);
    theStatement = theConnection.createStatement();
}

public void closeConnection( )
throws SQLException
{
    theConnection.close( );
}
```

The execSQLCommand( ) Method

Listing 6.6 shows the **execSQLCommand**( ) method, which is simpler here than in some programs you've seen so far. It depends on **openConnection**( ) having stored a reference to a **Statement** in the field named **theStatement**. It explicitly closes any open **ResultSet**, immediately freeing database and JDBC resources, to improve program performance.

LISTING 6.6   THE EXECSQLCOMMAND( ) METHOD.

```
public void execSQLCommand(String command)
throws SQLException
{
    if (theResult != null)    theResult.close();
    theResult = theStatement.executeQuery(command);
}
```

The getFirstRecord( ) Method

The first of the four database navigation methods, **getFirstRecord**( ), is shown in Listing 6.7. It simply uses an all-column **Select** query to generate a result table containing all records from the Visits table. It sets **browseStatus** to indicate that forward browsing is in progress. The value of **browseStatus** is tested in each of the remaining three database navigation methods.

LISTING 6.7   THE GETFIRSTRECORD( ) METHOD.

```
public void getFirstRecord( )
{
    browseStatus = BROWSING_FORWARD;
    try
    {
        execSQLCommand("SELECT * FROM Visits ORDER BY SeqNo;");
        if (!getColumns( )) noRecordFound( );
    }
```

```
catch (Exception e)
{
    handleException(e);
}
}
```

The getNextRecord( ) Method

The **getNextRecord**( ) method, shown in Listing 6.8, first checks to see if forward browsing is in progress. If not, a SQL query is used to establish a **ResultSet** for forward browsing, the first record of which is the next record in primary key sequence. The query uses a **Where** clause and an **Order By** clause to accomplish this result.

Once forward browsing is ensured, **getNext Record**( ) uses the **getColumns**( ) method to load the next record into the buffer fields. If no such record exists, **getColumns**( ) returns **false**. In this event, **getNextRecord**( ) uses the **noRecordFound**( ) method to display an appropriate error message.

LISTING 6.8   THE GETNEXTRECORD( ) METHOD.

```
public void getNextRecord( )
{
    try
    {
        if (browseStatus != BROWSING_FORWARD)
        {
            execSQLCommand("SELECT * FROM Visits WHERE SeqNo > "
            + theSeqNo + " ORDER BY SeqNO;");
            browseStatus = BROWSING_FORWARD;
        }
        if (!getColumns( )) noRecordFound( );
    }
    catch (Exception e)
    {
        handleException(e);
    }
}
```

The getPrevRecord( ) Method

Listing 6.9 shows the **getPrevRecord**( ) method, which functions similarly to **getNextRecord**( ). The difference is that **getPrevRecord**( ) browses backward and therefore uses a SQL query that includes the **Desc** modifier in its **Order By** clause.

LISTING 6.9   THE GETPREVRECORD( ) METHOD.

```
public void getPrevRecord( )
{
    try
    {
        if (browseStatus != BROWSING_BACKWARD)
        {
            execSQLCommand("SELECT * FROM Visits WHERE SeqNo < "
            + theSeqNo + " ORDER BY SeqNO DESC;");
            browseStatus = BROWSING_BACKWARD;
        }
        if (!getColumns( )) noRecordFound( );
    }
    catch (Exception e)
    {
        handleException(e);
    }
}
```

The getLastRecord( ) Method

The **getLastRecord**( ) method, shown in Listing 6.10, is the most complex of
the four database navigation routines. It is patterned after **getNextRecord**( ),
but uses a loop to iteratively move forward a row at a time, until there are no
more rows. It saves the relevant values from each row retrieved, restoring these
after it reaches the end of the table. In effect, it travels one row too far, and then
backs up.

LISTING 6.10   THE GETLASTRECORD( ) METHOD.

```
public void getLastRecord( )
{
    try
    {
        if (browseStatus != BROWSING_FORWARD)
        {
            execSQLCommand("SELECT * FROM Visits WHERE SeqNo >= "
            + theSeqNo + " ORDER BY SeqNO;");
            browseStatus = BROWSING_FORWARD;
        }
        if (getColumns( ))
        {
            int seqno;
            String name;
            String email;
```

```
            String comment;
            String time;
            do
            {
                seqno    = theSeqNo;
                name     = theName;
                email    = theEMail;
                comment = theComment;
                time     = theTime;
            }
            while (getColumns( ));

            theSeqNo    = seqno;
            theName     = name;
            theEMail    = email;
            theComment = comment;
            theTime     = time;
        }
        else noRecordFound( );
    }
    catch (Exception e)
    {
        handleException(e);
    }
}
```

The Remaining Methods

The remaining methods of GuestBook04, shown in Listing 6.11, include **statusOK( )** and **noRecordFound( )**, for displaying status messages; **destroy( )**, for terminating the application; and **handleException( )**, for reporting **SQLException**s. The latter two methods are identical to forms previously shown, as is the **WindowHandler** class (Listing 6.12).

Taking into account other methods similar to those in previous versions of the program, little of GuestBook04 is completely new. This is true of many Java and SQL client-server applications. Often, only a few changes can create significant new functionality.

LISTING 6.11   REMAINING METHODS OF GUESTBOOK04.

```
public void statusOK( )
{
    theStatus.setText("Status: OK.");
}
```

```
public void noRecordFound( )
{
    theStatus.setText("Status: No record found.");
    browseStatus = BROWSING_INVALID;
}

public void destroy( )
{
    try
    {
        closeConnection( );
        setVisible(false);
        System.exit(0);
    }
    catch (Exception e)
    {
        handleException(e);
    }
}

public void handleException(Exception e)
{
    theStatus.setText("Error: " + e.getMessage( ));
    e.printStackTrace( );
    if (e instanceof SQLException)
    {
        while ((e = ((SQLException) e).getNextException( )) != null)
        {
            System.out.println(e);
        }
    }
}
```

LISTING 6.12   THE WINDOWHANDLER CLASS.

```
class WindowHandler extends WindowAdapter
{
    public void windowClosing(WindowEvent event)
    {
        Object object = event.getSource( );
        if (object instanceof Frame) destroy( );
    }
}
```

Summary

This chapter has introduced clauses that let you write sophisticated **Select** queries that return only the data you need, thereby speeding processing and reducing network bandwidth requirements. The **Order By** clause lets you specify an order for retrieval of records via the result set. The aggregate functions (**Average**, **Count**, **Max**, **Min**, and **Sum**) can be used with the **Group By** clause to retrieve summary data, rather than large result sets requiring programmatic summarization. The **Having** clause allows you to select groups in much the same way that the **Where** clause allows you to select records. Expressions and functions let you manipulate stored data before it ever reaches your program. JDBC escapes let you write more portable queries; this is especially helpful in writing queries that include date and time literals. SQL nulls can have interesting consequences, since they are handled differently by many popular database systems.

JOINS AND UNIONS 7

As you'll learn in Chapter 8, relational databases are carefully designed so that each table contains data on only a single type of entity. So far, all the SQL queries you've written have retrieved rows from only a single table. That means they're capable of retrieving data on only a single type of entity: You can write queries that access supplier data, or queries that access order data, but you cannot yet write queries that access supplier *and* order data.

Of course, you frequently need to retrieve data that relates entities of one type to entities of another type. This chapter shows you how to do so, using *joins*. A join is simply a query that accesses data in multiple tables. The good news is that joining tables does not require you to use any unfamiliar SQL verbs. Your friend, the **Select** statement, is more powerful than you may have imagined, as you'll soon see.

Because a clear understanding of the **Select** statement is so important, this chapter begins with a review of the clauses that can be used inside **Select**. This is followed by an explanation of how to write a SQL query that joins two tables. You'll then learn how to refer more conveniently to tables and columns used in a query, by means of aliases and qualified names. We then move on to more advanced forms of the join, including the three-way join, self-joins, and outer joins. We'll also cover the **Union**, a SQL technique that lets you combine the results of two or more queries.

Finally, we present the example program for the chapter, an improved version of the SQLWindow application. This version uses Java threads to enable you to interrupt queries in process. It also uses a new class that enables you to send query results to a printer. You'll be able to make good use of the improved SQLWindow application by trying out sophisticated queries based on the techniques given in this chapter.

A Select Summary

The clauses that can be attached to a **Select** verb make the **Select** statement a powerful and flexible SQL form. Because this book has introduced these clauses one at a time, you may find it helpful to see the complete pattern. Here's **Select**, as you've learned it so far, in its full glory:

```
SELECT [DISTINCT] select_list
FROM table
WHERE where_condition
GROUP BY group_list
HAVING having_condition
ORDER BY order_list
```

Table 7.1 summarizes the purpose of each clause appearing in **Select**. Recall that most of the clauses are optional. Only *select_list* and *table* are required.

TABLE 7.1

CLAUSES OF THE SELECT STATEMENT.

Clause	Form And Purpose
Distinct	Specifies that only distinct rows are to be returned as part of the query result. Any duplicate rows will be suppressed.
select_list	A comma-separated list of columns (and expressions) that specifies the columns included in the query result. The special value * is used to indicate that all columns of the table are included in the query result.
table	The name of the table accessed by the query. As shown in this chapter, this can take the form of a comma-separated list of table names.
where_condition	A true-false condition that determines which rows of the table are included in the query result.
group_list	A comma-separated list of columns that specifies that groups of rows, rather than individual rows, are to be returned in the query result.

(continued)

TABLE 7.1

CLAUSES OF THE SELECT STATEMENT (*CONTINUED*).

Clause	Form And Purpose
having_condition	A true-false condition that specifies which groups of rows are to be returned. Used only with Group By.
order_list	A comma-separated list of columns that specifies the order in which query result rows are sorted. An entry can be followed by Desc, indicating that it is sorted in descending order—that is, with higher values near the beginning (top) of the table.

The power of the **Select** statement comes from the various clauses and the various types of lists and expressions the clauses contain. Note that the clauses must appear in fixed order. You cannot write a query that puts the **Where** clause after the **Order By** clause. To avoid this mistake, you may want to memorize a nonsense sentence containing the first letter of the name of each clause. This will help you remember the proper order of the clauses. Such mnemonic devices usually work best if you make them up yourself, but if nothing else occurs to you, try this: "Short Firemen Were Gobbling Huge Oysters." Admittedly, it's no literary pearl, but it may serve its purpose. Picture the scene to lock it in your mind, and we'll move on.

Joins

Say you are assigned the task of writing a SQL query to produce a list of employees by department. You fire up your SQL-writing skills and produce this piece of code:

```
Select * From Assignments Order By DeptNo, EmployeeNo;
```

Results:

```
EmployeeNo   DeptNo    HoursPerWeek

7            1         40
9            1         20
10           1         40
1            2         40
5            2         40
```

6	2	40
9	2	40
2	3	40
3	3	40
9	3	20
12	3	40
8	4	40
11	4	40

Unfortunately, your boss is not impressed. She wants the *names* of the employees in each department, not their numbers—and she wants them *now*. Undaunted, you return to your PC and issue the following query:

```
Select EmployeeNo, Name From Employees Order By EmployeeNo;
```

Results:

```
EmployeeNo Name

1          Fred Fearless
2          Adam Adams
3          Eve Adams
4          Bogus Blitzo
5          Jumbo Jones
6          Sam TheMan
7          Young Tom
8          Steve Giblet
9          Bill Bonkers
10         Sue Slewfoot
11         Abigail Honest
12         Ann Agram
```

Stapling the printout of the results of the new query to those of the previous one, you rush back into the boss's office. Later, over a hot-dog lunch in the park, you scan the classified ads looking for openings for SQL programmers. "How was I supposed to know," you ask yourself, "that she wanted *both* queries in a single report?"

Users want data that is timely, accurate, and convenient. Asking a user, particularly your boss, to thumb through several reports and mentally associate related records, is risky business—assuming you value your job.

The SQL join is the solution to this problem. A join, as mentioned, is simply a **Select** statement that retrieves data from multiple tables. In this case, you needed data from the Assignments table and data from the Employees table. The Assignments table tells you which employees are assigned to a department by storing their employee numbers. The Employees table tells you an employee's name given the employee's number. Put these two tables together and you have everything you need.

Here's a query that does the job:

```
Select DeptNo, Assignments.EmployeeNo, Name
From Assignments, Employees
Where Assignments.EmployeeNo = Employees.EmployeeNo
Order By DeptNo, Assignments.EmployeeNo;
```

Results:

DeptNo	EmployeeNo	Name
1	7	Young Tom
1	9	Bill Bonkers
1	10	Sue Slewfoot
2	1	Fred Fearless
2	5	Jumbo Jones
2	6	Sam TheMan
2	9	Bill Bonkers
3	2	Adam Adams
3	3	Eve Adams
3	9	Bill Bonkers
3	12	Ann Agram
4	8	Steve Giblet
4	11	Abigail Honest

Notice that the results are ordered by department number and the employees within each department are ordered by employee number. If the employee number were not needed in the result, you could have written

```
Select DeptNo, Name
From Assignments, Employees
Where Assignments.EmployeeNo = Employees.EmployeeNo
Order By DeptNo, Assignments.EmployeeNo;
```

which would have worked just as you desired.

Compare the results of this query with those of the two previous queries, which show the contents of the Assignments table and the Employees table, respectively.

Take a closer look at the join, as such a multitable query is called. Notice the **From** clause, which lists two tables. Data for this query is taken from both the Assignments table and the Employees table. That proves this is, in fact, a join.

Now, take a look at the **Where** clause:

```
Where Assignments.EmployeeNo = Employees.EmployeeNo
```

You've not previously seen such forms as **Assignments.EmployeeNo** or **Employees.EmployeeNo**, which are called *qualified references*. Since the column **EmployeeNo** appears in both the Assignments table and the Employees table, SQL can't tell which is meant if you just write **EmployeeNo**. Instead, you prefix the column name with the name of the containing table and a period (.), much the same way you form qualified names in Java.

If you forget to qualify an ambiguous name, SQL will generate an exception. For example, if you'd written:

```
Select DeptNo, EmployeeNo, Name From Assignments, Employees Order By
DeptNo, EmployeeNo;
```

SQL might have responded with this message:

```
The specified field 'EmployeeNo' could refer to more than one table
listed in the FROM clause of your SQL statement.
```

How Joins Work

Now that you know how to specify a join, this section will focus on how the join does its work. The join example used in the previous section had two interesting parts that work together to accomplish the join: a **From** clause that specified two tables, and a **Where** condition that rejected rows where the employee number from the Assignments table was different in value from the employee number from the Employees table. You can imagine a join as concatenating table rows much the same way that SQL and Java concatenate strings. Figure 7.1 shows how this concatenation works for our example query.

To gain a better understanding of joins, let's experiment with the example query. First, omit the **Where** clause and see what happens:

```
Select DeptNo, Assignments.EmployeeNo, Name
From Assignments, Employees
Order By DeptNo, Assignments.EmployeeNo;
```

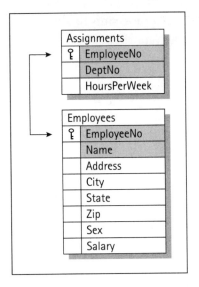

Figure 7.1
A join concatenates table rows.

Results:

```
DeptNo      EmployeeNo   Name

1           7            Fred Fearless
1           7            Ann Agram
1           7            Adam Adams
1           7            Eve Adams
1           7            Bogus Blitzo
1           7            Jumbo Jones
1           7            Young Tom
1           7            Steve Giblet
1           7            Bill Bonkers
1           7            Sue Slewfoot
1           7            Abigail Honest
1           7            Sam TheMan
1           9            Abigail Honest
[and so on]
```

Instead of the original output, this query produces an avalanche of data. The query result table has 156 rows. (If you're skeptical, you don't have to count them; the improved SQLWindow application presented later in the chapter will do this for you.)

Why so many rows? What's going on? To find out, consider a similar query executed using two small, hypothetical tables. Assume the first table looks like this:

```
Select * From TableA
```

Results:

```
Column1

1
2
```

Assume the second table looks like this:

```
Select * From TableB
```

Results:

```
Column1

3
4
5
```

Now, run the following join on the two tables:

```
Select * From TableA, TableB
```

Results:

```
Column1    Column1

1          3
2          3
1          4
2          4
1          5
2          5
```

Notice how the query result pairs every record of the first table with every record of the second table. Each possible combination appears in the query result. So, if the first table has *m* records and the second table has *n* records, the result will be $n * m$ records. That's why the previous experiment produced so many output records. The Assignments table has 13 rows, and the Employees table has 12. Joining the two tables produces a result set with 12 * 13 = 156 rows.

Imagine what would occur if the company had 300 employees and about one-third of them had multiple assignments. The result table would contain about 300 * 300 * (1.3) = 117,000 rows. Retrieving this result could put a considerable, unnecessary strain on the database server and the network.

The role of the **Where** clause, as usual, is to pare down the result table so it includes only rows of interest, and thereby to improve system performance. Here, you want only *corresponding* rows from the Assignments table and Employees table, specifically those rows that share a common employee number. The technique is to use the employee number in the Assignments table to obtain the employee name from the corresponding row in the Employees table. This is the most usual type of join, sometimes called an *equi-join* because it is expressed using an equality condition, such as the one used here:

```
Assignments.EmployeeNo = Employees.EmployeeNo
```

Figure 7.2 illustrates how an equi-join connects two tables.

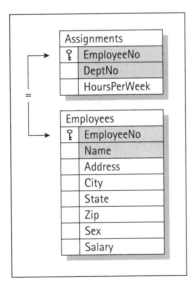

Figure 7.2
A SQL equi-join.

To Join Or Not To Join

Joins are used to relate relational tables. You may recall from Chapter 2 that foreign keys serve the same purpose. This might lead you to suspect a relationship exists between joins and foreign keys. If so, pack your violin—you're ready for residence at 221B Baker Street, along with Sherlock Holmes and Dr. Watson.

As you may have guessed, joins usually relate a foreign key in one table to a primary key in another. In the example query, **employeeno** was a foreign key of the Assignments table and a primary key of the Employees table.

Joined columns do not have to be foreign or primary keys. Joined fields do not need to have similar names, though they often do. You can join tables using any columns you like. However, the fact that the database designer went to the trouble of identifying a column as a foreign key suggests that a relationship exists between the table that contains it and the table that contains the corresponding primary key. So, it naturally works out that most joins involve primary keys and foreign keys, and these usually have similar names.

Strictly speaking, all that's necessary in a join is that the joined columns have compatible types. Compatibility in SQL basically means that you should join numeric columns only with other numeric columns, and text columns only with other text columns. You don't have to be concerned about whether a numeric column is represented as a small precision integer or as a large precision floating-point value. SQL will perform the necessary conversions, joining the columns wherever possible.

You can also join fields using a comparison operator other than the equality operator. Such a join is sometimes called a *non-equijoin*. You'll see an example of this later in the chapter, in the section on self-joins.

Compound Join Conditions

The **Where** condition used to establish a join can include additional terms beyond that used to join the tables. For example, take a look at the following query:

```
Select DeptNo, Assignments.EmployeeNo, Name
From Employees, Assignments
Where
```

```
   State In ('AZ', 'CA')
    And Employees.EmployeeNo = Assignments.EmployeeNo
Order By DeptNo, Employees.EmployeeNo;
```

Results:

DeptNo	EmployeeNo	Name
1	7	Young Tom
1	9	Bill Bonkers
1	10	Sue Slewfoot
2	1	Fred Fearless
2	6	Sam TheMan
2	9	Bill Bonkers
3	2	Adam Adams
3	3	Eve Adams
3	9	Bill Bonkers
3	12	Ann Agram
4	8	Steve Giblet
4	11	Abigail Honest

Here the condition limits the query result to only those rows that represent employees living in the states of Arizona or California. The result is an employee list, by department, of only those employees living in either of those states. Figure 7.3 illustrates this join, which uses a compound condition.

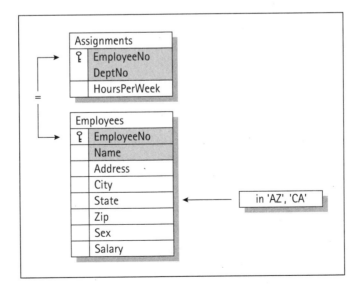

Figure 7.3
A SQL join with a compound condition.

Aliases

The qualified names that must be used in joins to avoid ambiguous column references can be cumbersome, particularly if you're an inaccurate typist. SQL provides a special syntax that lets you create an alias, or second identity, for a table. Here's an example:

```
Select DeptNo, A.EmployeeNo, Name
From Assignments As A, Employees As E
Where A.EmployeeNo = E.EmployeeNo
Order By DeptNo, A.EmployeeNo;
```

Results:

DeptNo	EmployeeNo	Name
1	7	Young Tom
1	9	Bill Bonkers
1	10	Sue Slewfoot
2	1	Fred Fearless
2	5	Jumbo Jones
2	6	Sam TheMan
2	9	Bill Bonkers
3	2	Adam Adams
3	3	Eve Adams
3	9	Bill Bonkers
3	12	Ann Agram
4	8	Steve Giblet
4	11	Abigail Honest

Notice that the query result is unchanged, even though the form of the query has changed. The query uses the **As** clause to establish new names for the tables. An **As** clause establishes **A** as an alternate name for the Assignments table and **E** as an alternate name for the Employees table. Having assigned these aliases, they can be used in more compact qualified references. **A.EmployeeNo** now refers to the employee number column of the Assignments table and **E.EmployeeNo** to the employee number column of the Employees table.

The aliases don't need to be single letters. However, since the main purpose of using an alias is to permit a more compact statement of the query, single-letter aliases are common.

Three-Way Joins

"If a little bit is good, a lot is better," insist some hot-pepper aficionados. Others, not enamored of the potent habanero, insist to the contrary that moderation is the ticket. In the case of SQL joins, you can have it as you like it. You can stick to "mild" joins that combine two tables (*two-way joins*), or you can go wild with *three-way joins*.

What might tempt you to sample the three-way join? Say you wanted to produce a departmental staffing report, like that produced by the queries we've been studying, only you want the result to show a department name, rather than number.

Assume your database contains a Departments table, like the following:

```
Select DeptNo, DeptName From Departments;
```

Results:

```
DeptNo      DeptName

1           Business Analysis
2           Development
3           Testing
4           Quality Assurance
```

All you need to do is grab rows from the Assignments table, relating each row's employee number to the Employees table to access the employee name, and each row's department number to the Departments table to access the department name. Such a query is called a three-way join, simply because it joins three tables—in this case, Assignments, Employees, and Departments.

Here's how you could write the necessary query:

```
Select DeptName, Name
From Employees E, Assignments A, Departments D
Where E.EmployeeNo = A.EmployeeNo And A.DeptNo = D.DeptNo
Order By DeptName, E.EmployeeNo;
```

Results:

```
DeptName            Name

Business Analysis   Young Tom
Business Analysis   Bill Bonkers
```

```
Business Analysis      Sue Slewfoot
Development            Fred Fearless
Development            Jumbo Jones
Development            Sam TheMan
Development            Bill Bonkers
Quality Assurance      Steve Giblet
Quality Assurance      Abigail Honest
Testing                Adam Adams
Testing                Eve Adams
Testing                Bill Bonkers
Testing                Ann Agram
```

The three-way join is really not that complex, as shown in Figure 7.4. The **Where** clause simply specifies the desired relationships between the columns of the Assignments table and those of the other tables.

Here's another example of a useful three-way join. The Departments table contains a column named **ManagerID**, which contains the employee number of the department manager. You can use this column to obtain a report showing who manages whom, by department. You can accomplish this with employee numbers or employee names. Because the simpler method is with employee numbers, I'll show that first:

```
Select A.DeptNo, D.Managerid, A.EmployeeNo
From Assignments A, Departments D, Employees E
Where A.DeptNo = D.DeptNo And D.ManagerID = E.EmployeeNo;
```

Results:

DeptNo	ManagerID	EmployeeNo
1	10	10
2	6	6
3	9	9
4	8	8
2	6	1
2	6	5
2	6	9
3	9	3
1	10	9
4	8	11
3	9	12

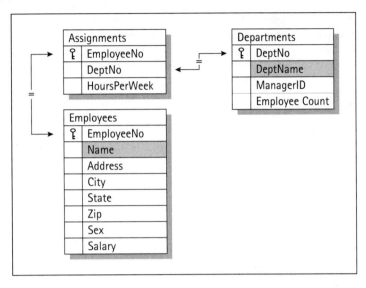

Figure 7.4
A three-way join.

Here's the revised version that puts names in the result set:

```
Select Deptname As "Department",
  Mgr.Name as "Manager",
  Sub.Name as "Subordinate"
From Assignments A,
  Departments D,
  Employees Mgr,
  Employees Sub
Where
  A.Deptno = D.DeptNo
  And D.ManagerID = Mgr.EmployeeNo
  And A.EmployeeNo = Sub.EmployeeNo
Order By DeptName, Sub.Name;
```

Results:

```
Department          Manager          Subordinate

Business Analysis   Sue Slewfoot     Bill Bonkers
Business Analysis   Sue Slewfoot     Sue Slewfoot
Business Analysis   Sue Slewfoot     Young Tom
Development         Sam TheMan       Bill Bonkers
Development         Sam TheMan       Fred Fearless
Development         Sam TheMan       Jumbo Jones
```

```
Development          Sam TheMan      Sam TheMan
Quality Assurance    Steve Giblet    Abigail Honest
Quality Assurance    Steve Giblet    Steve Giblet
Testing              Bill Bonkers    Adam Adams
Testing              Bill Bonkers    Ann Agram
Testing              Bill Bonkers    Bill Bonkers
Testing              Bill Bonkers    Eve Adams
```

The report could be made more compact by eliminating the lines with the same name under "Manager" and "Subordinate." You could do this by adding a term to the **Where** condition:

```
And Mgr.Employee <> Sub.EmployeeNo
```

Another example of a sophisticated join is a query that reports for each department the number of staff and their assigned weekly hours. Here's the query:

```
Select
  A.DeptNo,
  D.ManagerID,
  Count(A.EmployeeNo) As Staff,
  Sum(A.HoursPerWeek) As Hours
From Assignments A, Departments D, Employees E
Where
  A.DeptNo = D.DeptNo
  And D.ManagerID = E.EmployeeNo
Group By A.DeptNo, D.ManagerID;
```

Results:

```
DeptNo    ManagerID  Staff    Hours

1         10         3        100.0
2         6          4        160.0
3         9          4        140.0
4         8          2        80.0
```

Outer Joins

The join queries you've built so far function fine for some purposes, but fall short for others. For example, what if an employee has not yet been assigned to a department? The queries we've built entirely ignore such individuals, which is sometimes, but not always, what's wanted. Similarly, departments without employees fall through these same cracks.

SQL provides a special form of query, called an *outer join*, that joins two tables, but includes in the result set any rows that lack a matching row in the paired table. By contrast, the queries we've seen so far are known as *inner joins*, because they include rows only when a match exists.

Outer joins come in two flavors:

- *Left join*—includes rows from the first table that lack a matching row in the second table

- *Right join*—includes rows from the second table that lack a matching row in the first table

Unfortunately, not every database supports outer joins. Worse, the syntax used by many databases to specify outer joins does not conform to the ANSI 92 standard. JDBC rescues you, however, by providing a special escape syntax for specifying outer joins:

```
{OJ table Left Outer Join table On condition }
```

For example, you can write a left outer join of the Employees table on the Assignments table with a query like this:

```
Select E.EmployeeNo, A.DeptNo
From
{
  OJ Employees As E Left Outer Join Assignments As A
  On E.EmployeeNo = A.EmployeeNo
}
Order By E.EmployeeNo;
```

Results:

```
EmployeeNo DeptNo

1          2
2          3
3          3
4
5          2
6          2
7          1
8          4
9          1
```

```
9        2
9        3
10       1
11       4
12       3
```

Even an employee with no assignments will be included in the result set, as shown by employee number 4. Figure 7.5 illustrates the left outer join.

A right outer join can be written similarly. The following right outer join includes rows from the Assignments table even if no matching row appears in the Employees table:

```
Select A.DeptNo, E.EmployeeNo
From
{
  OJ Employees As E Right Outer Join Assignments As A
  On E.EmployeeNo = A.EmployeeNo
}
Order By A.DeptNo;
```

Results:

```
DeptNo      EmployeeNo

1           7
1           9
1           10
2           9
2           5
2           1
2           6
3           2
3           12
3           3
3           9
4           11
4           8
```

Figure 7.6 depicts the right outer join.

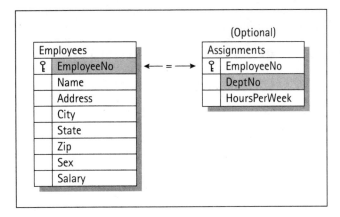

Figure 7.5
A left outer join.

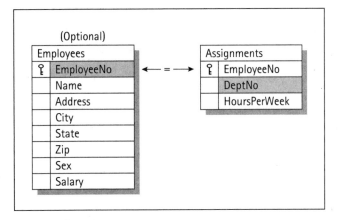

Figure 7.6
A right outer join.

Self-Joins

It's possible, sometimes even useful, to join a table with itself. Suppose you wanted to create a report that showed, for each employee, the names of all employees who earn more. Here's a query that does exactly that:

```
Select E1.Name, E1.Salary, E2.Name, E2.Salary
From Employees E1, Employees E2
Where E1.Salary < E2.Salary
Order By 1;
```

Results:

Name	Salary	Name	Salary
Abigail Honest	60000	Sam TheMan	85000
Abigail Honest	60000	Eve Adams	130000
Abigail Honest	60000	Steve Giblet	70000
Abigail Honest	60000	Adam Adams	120000
Abigail Honest	60000	Young Tom	90000
Abigail Honest	60000	Sue Slewfoot	300000
Abigail Honest	60000	Ann Agram	75000
Abigail Honest	60000	Jumbo Jones	65000
Abigail Honest	60000	Bogus Blitzo	150000
Adam Adams	120000	Eve Adams	130000
Adam Adams	120000	Bogus Blitzo	150000
Adam Adams	120000	Sue Slewfoot	300000

[and so on]

Name	Salary	Name	Salary
Steve Giblet	70000	Ann Agram	75000
Steve Giblet	70000	Adam Adams	120000
Steve Giblet	70000	Sue Slewfoot	300000
Steve Giblet	70000	Sam TheMan	85000
Steve Giblet	70000	Bogus Blitzo	150000
Steve Giblet	70000	Eve Adams	130000
Steve Giblet	70000	Young Tom	90000
Young Tom	90000	Bogus Blitzo	150000
Young Tom	90000	Eve Adams	130000
Young Tom	90000	Adam Adams	120000
Young Tom	90000	Sue Slewfoot	300000

Figure 7.7 depicts the self-join. Notice that two aliases are established for the table, so that unambiguous reference can be made to the employee number column in each. There's really nothing new here, beyond the bold idea of naming the same table twice in the **From** clause.

In addition to demonstrating a self-join, this example demonstrates a non-equijoin, since it uses the greater than operator (>) to form the join condition, rather than the equality operator (=). You can use any of the other comparison operators (<, <=, >=, or <>) to form similar non-equijoins.

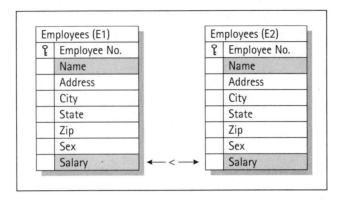

Figure 7.7
A self-join.

Unions

Unions, like joins, combine things. But, where joins combine database tables, unions combine query results. Remembering that query results are themselves a table, you can see that both joins and unions combine tables. Joins combine database tables, while unions combine query result tables.

Another difference exists between unions and joins: While a join adds the joined table as new *columns* of the original table, a union adds the unioned table as new *rows* of the original table. Figure 7.8 illustrates this difference between unions and joins; Figure 7.9 shows the details of a union operation.

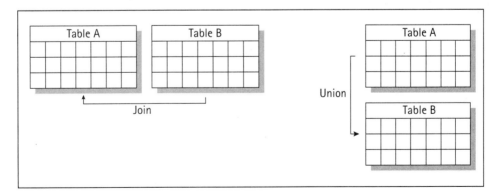

Figure 7.8
Unions and joins contrasted.

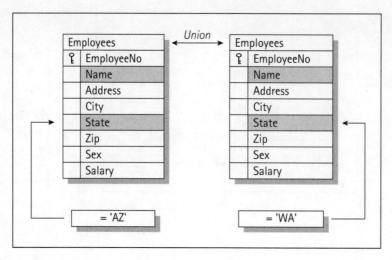

Figure 7.9
A union.

To create a union, just place the SQL keyword **Union** between two **Select** statements:

```
Select EmployeeNo, State
From Employees
Where State = 'AZ'

Union

Select EmployeeNo, State
From Employees
Where State = 'WA';
```

Results:

```
EmployeeNo State

1          AZ
5          WA
```

The query result includes any row returned by either of the component queries. Duplicate rows are omitted. If you want duplicate rows to appear in the result, you can write **Union All** in place of **Union**.

A union can simplify queries that might otherwise be complex or cumbersome. For example, assume you wanted to give a 5 percent raise to California employees, a 10 percent raise to Arizona employees, and a 15 percent raise to Washington employees. The following query would show the new salaries:

```
Select State, Name, Salary, Salary * 1.05 As "New Salary"
From Employees
Where State = 'CA'

Union

Select State, Name, Salary, Salary * 1.10 as "New Salary"
From Employees
Where State = 'AZ'

Union

Select State, Name, Salary, Salary * 1.15 As "New Salary"
From Employees
Where State = 'WA'
```

Results:

State	Name	Salary	New Salary
AZ	Fred Fearless	60000	66000.0
CA	Abigail Honest	60000	63000.0
CA	Adam Adams	120000	126000.0
CA	Ann Agram	75000	78750.0
CA	Bill Bonkers	60000	63000.0
CA	Bogus Blitzo	150000	157500.0
CA	Eve Adams	130000	136500.0
CA	Sam TheMan	85000	89250.0
CA	Steve Giblet	70000	73500.0
CA	Sue Slewfoot	300000	315000.0
CA	Young Tom	90000	94500.0
WA	Jumbo Jones	65000	74750.0

The SQLWindow03 Application

Now that you have an improved repertoire of queries, you deserve an improved tool with which to practice them. The SQLWindow03 application fits that bill. Its user interface, shown in Figure 7.10, provides two **TextField**s for entering queries. You can use copy, cut, and paste operations to alternate between the two **TextField**s, refining queries until they're right. You can also use the Print

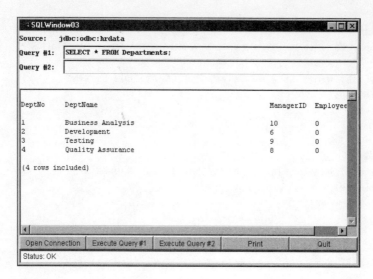

Figure 7.10
The SQLWindow03 user interface.

button to send your query results to a printer. What's more, the application is implemented using Java's thread facilities, so issuing a new query while another is running automatically cancels the running query. If you change your mind about a query, you don't have to wait for it to complete before issuing a new one.

Listing 7.1 shows the fields of the new SQLWindow03 application, along with its **main( )** method. The application has several new features, in addition to the new **TextField**s and **Button**s:

- First, note that the class now implements **Runnable**, promising that it includes a **run( )** method that allows it to be used as a **Thread**.

- Second, it includes a **FocusHandler** object. I'll provide its class definition in a moment. Its purpose is to remove highlighting from a **TextField** when the user tabs to another component. Otherwise, several **TextField**s may be simultaneously highlighted, which is distracting to the user (though it causes no other problem).

- Finally, it has a field named **theThread**, intended for holding a reference to an executing **Thread**.

LISTING 7.1   THE SQLWINDOW03 APPLICATION.

```java
import java.awt.*;
import java.awt.event.*;
import java.sql.*;

class SQLWindow03 extends Frame
implements Application, ActionListener, Runnable
{
    Panel       topPanel    = new Panel( );
    Panel       sourcePanel = new Panel( );
    Panel       query1Panel = new Panel( );
    Panel       query2Panel = new Panel( );
    Panel       mainPanel   = new Panel( );
    Panel       bottomPanel = new Panel( );
    Panel       buttonPanel = new Panel( );

    Font        topFont     = new Font("Courier", Font.BOLD, 12);
    Font        resultFont  = new Font("Courier", Font.PLAIN, 12);
    Font        printFont   = new Font("Courier", Font.PLAIN, 12);

    Label       theSource   = new Label( );
    TextField   theQuery1   = new TextField( );
    TextField   theQuery2   = new TextField( );
    TextArea    theResult   = new TextArea(15, 80);
    Button      btnOpen     = new Button("Open Connection");
    Button      btnQuery1   = new Button("Execute Query #1");
    Button      btnQuery2   = new Button("Execute Query #2");
    Button      btnPrint    = new Button("Print");
    Button      btnQuit     = new Button("Quit");
    TextField   theStatus   = new TextField( );

    FocusHandler theFocusHandler = new FocusHandler( );

    String theDataSource;
    String theUser;
    String thePassword;
    String theQuery;

    Connection        theConnection;
    Statement         theStatement;
    ResultSet         theResultSet;
    ResultSetMetaData theMetaData;

    Thread theThread = null;
```

```
public static void main(String args[])
{
    new SQLWindow03( ).init( );
}
```

The init( ) Method

The **init**( ) method, shown in Listing 7.2, does its usual job of creating the user interface. It has a bit more to do than usual, owing to the additional components. Otherwise, all that's new is setting up the **FocusListener** queues for the **TextField**s, which is done using the **addFocusListener**( ) method.

LISTING 7.2   THE INIT( ) METHOD.

```
public void init( )
{
    setTitle("SQLWindow03");

    topPanel.setFont(topFont);
    theResult.setFont(resultFont);

    add("North",  topPanel);
    add("Center", mainPanel);
    add("South",  bottomPanel);

    topPanel.setLayout(new GridLayout(4, 1));
    topPanel.add(sourcePanel);
    topPanel.add(query1Panel);
    topPanel.add(query2Panel);

    sourcePanel.setLayout(new BorderLayout( ));
    sourcePanel.add("West", new Label("Source: "));
    sourcePanel.add("Center", theSource);

    query1Panel.setLayout(new BorderLayout( ));
    query1Panel.add("West", new Label("Query #1:"));
    query1Panel.add("Center", theQuery1);

    query2Panel.setLayout(new BorderLayout( ));
    query2Panel.add("West", new Label("Query #2:"));
    query2Panel.add("Center", theQuery2);

    mainPanel.setLayout(new BorderLayout( ));
    mainPanel.add("Center", theResult);
```

```
    bottomPanel.setLayout(new BorderLayout( ));
    bottomPanel.add("North", buttonPanel);
    bottomPanel.add("South", theStatus);

    buttonPanel.setLayout(new GridLayout(1, 5));
    buttonPanel.add(btnOpen);
    buttonPanel.add(btnQuery1);
    buttonPanel.add(btnQuery2);
    buttonPanel.add(btnPrint);
    buttonPanel.add(btnQuit);

    theResult.setEditable(false);
    theStatus.setEditable(false);

    addWindowListener(new WindowHandler(this));

    theQuery1.addActionListener(this);
    theQuery2.addActionListener(this);
    btnOpen  .addActionListener(this);
    btnQuery1.addActionListener(this);
    btnQuery2.addActionListener(this);
    btnPrint .addActionListener(this);
    btnQuit  .addActionListener(this);

    theQuery1.addFocusListener(theFocusHandler);
    theQuery2.addFocusListener(theFocusHandler);
    theResult.addFocusListener(theFocusHandler);

    while (!openConnection( )) ; // null statement

    pack( );
    show( );
}
```

The actionPerformed( ) Method

Listing 7.3 shows the **actionPerformed**( ) method, which handles the **ActionEvents** resulting from button clicks or pressing Enter within a **TextField**. It uses the **startQuery**( ) method to initiate a query; otherwise, it calls **openConnection**( ), **printResult**( ), or **closeConnection**( ) as appropriate.

LISTING 7.3   THE ACTIONPERFORMED( ) METHOD.

```
public void actionPerformed(ActionEvent event)
{
    theStatus.setText("Status: OK");
    Object source = event.getSource( );
```

```
      if (source == btnOpen)        openConnection( );
      else if (source == btnQuery1)  startQuery(theQuery1.getText( ));
      else if (source == btnQuery2)  startQuery(theQuery2.getText( ));
      else if (source == theQuery1)  startQuery(theQuery1.getText( ));
      else if (source == theQuery2)  startQuery(theQuery2.getText( ));
      else if (source == btnPrint)   printResult( );
      else if (source == btnQuit)    requestClose( );
}
```

The startQuery( ) Method

The **startQuery( )** method, shown in Listing 7.4, stops any existing query by means of the **killThread( )** method. It then creates and starts a new **Thread** for the query specified in the **String** parameter provided by **actionPerformed( )**. The method is synchronized to prevent conflicts between multiple **Threads**.

LISTING 7.4   THE STARTQUERY( ) METHOD.

```
synchronized public void startQuery(String query)
{
    killThread( );
    theThread = new Thread(this);
    theQuery = query;
    theThread.start( );
}
```

The run( ) Method

Listing 7.5 shows the **run( )** method, which processes a query in a private **Thread**. The method of doing so is no different than shown in previous programs, even though it now operates asynchronously.

LISTING 7.5   THE RUN( ) METHOD.

```
public void run( )
{
    try
    {
        String command = theQuery;
        theResult.setText("");
        if (theStatement != null) theStatement.close( );
        if (theResultSet != null) theResultSet.close( );

        theStatement = theConnection.createStatement();
        theResultSet = theStatement.executeQuery(command);
```

```
        DisplayableResultSet dsr =
          new DisplayableResultSet(theResultSet);
        theResult.setText(dsr.getString( ));
    }
    catch (SQLException e)
    {
        handleError(e);
    }
    catch (NoClassDefFoundError err) { ; }
}
```

The killThread( ) Method

The **killThread( )** method, shown in Listing 7.6, is responsible for stopping a running query so that a new one can be started. It checks whether a live **Thread** exists. If so, it uses the **cancel( )** method to interrupt the query and then stops the **Thread**.

LISTING 7.6   THE KILLTHREAD( ) METHOD.

```
public void killThread( )
{
    if (theThread != null && theThread.isAlive( ))
    {
        if (theStatement != null)
        {
            try
            {
                theStatement.cancel( );
            }
            catch (SQLException sql) { ; }
        }
        theThread.stop( );
        theThread = null;
    }
}
```

The openConnection( ) Method

The **openConnection( )** method, shown in Listing 7.7, is similar to versions used in previous applications. It uses a new version of the login dialog, christened **LoginDialog02**, which allows specification of a default data source. The user can type over the default, or click OK to accept it. The source code for **LoginDialog02** appears later in the chapter.

LISTING 7.7   THE openConnection( ) METHOD.

```
public boolean openConnection( )
{
    killThread( );
    LoginDialog02 theLoginDialog02 = null;
    try
    {
        theSource.setText("");
        theResult.setText("");
        theLoginDialog02
          = new LoginDialog02("SQLWindow03: "
            + "Please select the data source:",
            "jdbc:odbc:Northwind", this, true);
        theLoginDialog02.setVisible(true);
        if (theLoginDialog02.getStatus( ))
        {
            theSource.setText(theLoginDialog02.getURL( ));
            Class.forName ("sun.jdbc.odbc.JdbcOdbcDriver");
            if (theConnection != null) theConnection.close( );
            theConnection =
              DriverManager.getConnection(theLoginDialog02.getURL( ),
                theLoginDialog02.getUser( ),
                theLoginDialog02.getPassword( ));
        }
        theLoginDialog02.dispose( );
        return true;
    }
    catch (Throwable t)
    {
        handleError(t);
    }
    if (theLoginDialog02 != null) theLoginDialog02.dispose( );
    return false;
}
```

The printResult( ) Method

Listing 7.8 shows the **printResult**( ) method, invoked by **actionPerformed**( ) in response to the user's click of the Print button. The **printResult**( ) method uses a new class, **PrintReport**, to send the contents of the **TextArea** to the printer. The source code for **PrintReport** is shown later in the chapter. Its **print**( ) method requires the **String** to be printed, the font to be used, and the vertical and horizontal page margins to be used. The margins are specified in pixels.

LISTING 7.8   THE PRINTRESULT( ) METHOD.

```
public void printResult( )
{
    new PrintReport( ).print(theResult.getText( ), printFont, 30, 20);
}
```

The requestClose( ) Method

The **requestClose**( ) method, shown in Listing 7.9, performs its usual function of shutting down the application. It is invoked by the **WindowHandler** object in response to the user clicking the application window's close icon.

LISTING 7.9   THE REQUESTCLOSE( ) METHOD.

```
public void requestClose( )
{
    setVisible(false);
    try
    {
        if (theConnection != null) theConnection.close( );
    }
    catch (SQLException ex)  { ; }
    System.exit(0);
}
```

The handleError( ) Method

The familiar **handleError**( ) method is shown in Listing 7.10. As usual, it simply displays an error message and prints a stack trace.

LISTING 7.10   THE HANDLEERROR( ) METHOD.

```
public void handleError(Throwable t)
{
    theStatus.setText("Error: " + t.getMessage( ));
    t.printStackTrace( );
}
```

The FocusHandler Class

The **FocusHandler** class, shown in Listing 7.11, handles messages sent when a component gains or loses keyboard focus. In response to loss of keyboard focus by a **TextComponent** (that is, a **TextField** or **TextArea**), the **focusLost**( ) method unselects the text of the **TextComponent**. This makes the screen less confusing to the user.

LISTING 7.11   THE FOCUSHANDLER CLASS.

```java
import java.awt.*;
import java.awt.event.*;

public class FocusHandler extends FocusAdapter
{
    public void focusLost(FocusEvent event)
    {
        Object source = event.getSource( );
        if (source instanceof TextComponent)
        {
            TextComponent text = (TextComponent) source;
            int caret = text.getCaretPosition( );
            text.setSelectionStart(caret);
            text.setSelectionEnd  (caret);
        }
    }
}
```

The LoginDialog02 Class

The revised login dialog, **LoginDialog02**, is shown beginning in Listing 7.12, which presents its fields and constructor. The constructor requires four arguments: a **String** holding a title for the dialog, a **String** holding a default data source name, a reference to the parent **Application** object, and a **boolean**, which indicates whether a Quit button should be shown. Note that this version of the login dialog uses a **WindowHandler** to handle its window messages.

LISTING 7.12   THE LOGINDIALOG02 CLASS.

```java
import java.awt.*;
import java.awt.event.*;

public class LoginDialog02 extends Dialog
implements ActionListener, Application
{
    String       theDefaultSource;
    Application  theParent;

    Panel[]    thePanel      = new Panel[4];
    TextField  theSource     = new TextField(35);
    TextField  theUser       = new TextField( );
    TextField  thePassword   = new TextField( );
    Button     btnOK         = new Button("OK");
    Button     btnCancel     = new Button("Cancel");
```

```
Button    btnQuit    = new Button("Quit");
boolean   statusOK   = false;
String theURL;

public LoginDialog02(String title, String source,
  Application parent, boolean showquit)
{
    super((Frame) parent, title, true);
    theDefaultSource = source;
    theParent = parent;

    setFont(new Font("Courier", Font.PLAIN, 12));
    setLayout(new GridLayout(4, 1));
    for (int i = 0; i < 3; i++)
    {
        thePanel[i] = new Panel( );
        thePanel[i].setLayout(new BorderLayout( ));
    }

    thePanel[0].add("West",   new Label("URL:      ", Label.RIGHT));
    thePanel[0].add("Center", theSource);
    add(thePanel[0]);

    thePanel[1].add("West",   new Label("User:     ", Label.RIGHT));
    thePanel[1].add("Center", theUser);
    add(thePanel[1]);

    thePanel[2].add("West",   new Label("Password: ", Label.RIGHT));
    thePanel[2].add("Center", thePassword);
    add(thePanel[2]);

    thePanel[3] = new Panel( );
    thePanel[3].setLayout(new FlowLayout( ));
    thePanel[3].add(btnOK);
    thePanel[3].add(btnCancel);
    if (showquit) thePanel[3].add(btnQuit);
    add(thePanel[3]);

    btnOK.addActionListener(this);
    btnCancel.addActionListener(this);
    btnQuit.addActionListener(this);
    addWindowListener(new WindowHandler(this));

    pack( );
}
```

The Accessor Methods

The accessor methods of the **LoginDialog02** class are shown in Listing 7.13. The application uses these methods to obtain the results of the dialog.

LISTING 7.13 THE ACCESSOR METHODS.

```
public boolean getStatus( )    { return statusOK; };
public String  getURL( )       { return theSource.getText( ); }
public String  getUser( )      { return theUser.getText( ); }
public String  getPassword( ) { return thePassword.getText( ); }
```

The setVisible( ) Method

The **setVisible( )** method, as seen in Listing 7.14, is used to show or hide the dialog. It includes new lines that center the dialog in a pleasing position on the screen.

LISTING 7.14 THE SETVISIBLE( ) METHOD.

```
public void setVisible(boolean visible)
{
    if (visible)
    {
        statusOK = false;
        theSource.setText(theDefaultSource);
        theUser.setText("");
        thePassword.setText("");

        Dimension screenSize
          = Toolkit.getDefaultToolkit().getScreenSize();
        int x = (screenSize.width/2) -(getSize( ).width/2);
        int y = (screenSize.height/3)-(getSize( ).height/2);

        setBounds(x,y,getSize( ).width, getSize( ).height);
    }
    super.setVisible(visible);
    if (visible)
    {
        theSource.requestFocus( );
    }
}
```

The actionPerformed( ) Method And requestClose( ) Method

Listing 7.15 shows the **actionPerformed( )** and **requestClose( )** methods of **LoginDialog02**. The **requestClose( )** method does nothing, which prevents the user from using the dialog's close icon to close the dialog. The user must click the OK button or the Cancel button to close the dialog.

LISTING 7.15   THE ACTIONPERFORMED( ) METHOD AND REQUESTCLOSE( ) METHOD.

```
public void actionPerformed(ActionEvent event)
{
    Object object = event.getSource( );
    if (object == btnOK) statusOK = true;
    setVisible(false);
    if (object == btnQuit) System.exit(0);
}


public void requestClose( )  { ; }
```

The DisplayableResultSet02 Class

The revised **DisplayableResultSet02** class is shown in Listing 7.16. The new version of the class includes in its formatted output a count of the number of **ResultSet** records.

LISTING 7.16   THE DISPLAYABLERESULTSET02 CLASS.

```
import java.sql.*;

class DisplayableResultSet02 extends Object
{
    ResultSet theResultSet;
    String    theResult;

    public DisplayableResultSet02(ResultSet result)
    {
        theResultSet = result;
    }

    public String getString( )
    throws SQLException, NoClassDefFoundError
    {
        theResult = "";
```

```
ResultSetMetaData metaData = theResultSet.getMetaData( );
int colCount = metaData.getColumnCount( );

int    colSize  [ ]  = new int    [colCount];
String colLabel [ ]  = new String [colCount];
int    colType  [ ]  = new int    [colCount];
String colTName [ ]  = new String [colCount];
int    colPrec  [ ]  = new int    [colCount];
int    colScale [ ]  = new int    [colCount];

theResult += "\n";
for (int i = 1; i <= colCount; i++)
{
    colSize [i - 1] = metaData.getColumnDisplaySize(i);
    colLabel[i - 1] = metaData.getColumnLabel       (i);
    colType [i - 1] = metaData.getColumnType        (i);
    colTName[i - 1] = metaData.getColumnTypeName     (i);
    colPrec [i - 1] = metaData.getPrecision         (i);
    colScale[i - 1] = metaData.getScale             (i);

    if (colSize[i - 1] < 1 + colLabel[i - 1].length( ))
        colSize[i - 1] = 1 + colLabel[i - 1].length( );

    theResult += rightPad(colLabel[i - 1], colSize[i - 1]);

}
theResult += "\n\n";

int rows = 0;

while (theResultSet.next( ))
{
    rows++;
    for (int i = 1; i <= colCount; i++)
    {
        String colvalue = theResultSet.getString(i);
        if (colvalue == null) colvalue = "";
        theResult += rightPad(colvalue, colSize[i - 1]);
    }
    theResult += "\n";
}

theResult += "\n(" + rows + " rows included)\n";
return theResult;
}
```

```
    public String rightPad(String s, int len)
    {
        int curlen = s.length( );
        if (curlen > len) return repString("*", len);
        return s + repString(" ", (len - curlen));
    }

    public String repString(String s, int times)
    {
        String result = "";
        for (int i = 0; i < times; i++)
        {
            result += s;
        }
        return result;
    }
}
```

The PrintReport Class

The **PrintReport** class, shown in Listing 7.17, provides a **print( )** method that prints a **String** passed as a parameter. The **String** is printed using a **Font** that is also specified as a parameter. The **print( )** method keeps track of the height of each printed line and skips to a new page when necessary. It does not, however, wrap lines longer than the output page width. Lines that do not fit are truncated without warning.

LISTING 7.17 THE PRINTREPORT CLASS.

```
import java.awt.*;
import java.awt.event.*;
import java.util.*;

public class PrintReport extends Frame
{
    public void print(String text, Font font, int vmargin, int hmargin)
    {
        Properties props = null;
        PrintJob   pjob =
          getToolkit( ).getPrintJob( this, "Java Report", props);
        int pageNo = 1;

        do
        {
            System.out.println("Printing page #" + pageNo++ + ".");
            Graphics pg = pjob.getGraphics();
```

```
            pg.setFont(font);
            pg.setColor(Color.black);

            int pixPerInch      = pjob.getPageResolution( );
            Dimension pageSize  = pjob.getPageDimension( );
            int width           = pageSize.width - pixPerInch;
            int height          = pageSize.height - pixPerInch;
            FontMetrics metrics = pg.getFontMetrics( );
            int lineHeight      = metrics.getHeight( )
              + metrics.getLeading( );
            int linePos         = vmargin;

            if (text.charAt(text.length( ) - 1) != '\n') text += '\n';

            int lineEnd;
            while ((lineEnd = text.indexOf('\n')) >= 0)
            {
                String line = text.substring(0, lineEnd);
                if (linePos + lineHeight > height) break;
                pg.drawString(line, hmargin, linePos);
                linePos += lineHeight;
                if (lineEnd >= text.length( ) - 1)
                    text = "";
                else
                    text = text.substring(lineEnd + 1);
            }
            pg.dispose( );

        }
        while (text.length( ) > 0);
        System.out.println("Printing complete.");

        pjob.end();
    }
}
```

SQLWindow03 uses the **WindowHandler** class, but without change from previous uses. Therefore, its source code is not shown here. The source code does appear in the CD-ROM directory that corresponds to this chapter.

Summary

SQL queries can retrieve data from multiple tables by specifying the table names in the **From** clause of the **Select** statement. The **Where** clause specifies a correspondence between table rows that eliminates unwanted records. Foreign keys and primary keys are often used in forming the **Where** condition of a join. Table names can be aliased using **As**, and column names can be qualified using table names or aliases. Joins are usually performed on two tables, but can be performed on a single table (a self-join) or multiple tables. Special forms of the join, called left outer joins and right outer joins, allow join query results to include rows that would otherwise be omitted owing to the absence of a corresponding record in the joining or joined table. Unions allow queries to be built in steps, the results of which are combined as a single query result.

8
DESIGNING DATABASES

U p to this point, you've been using databases designed by others. Your database world has included only those columns, tables, and relationships the designer of the database provided on your behalf. Somewhat akin to running only programs written by others, this is no life for a programmer. The time has come to break free and express yourself. This chapter and the next will equip you to design and create your own databases. You'll soon be able to have it your way, creating columns, tables, and relationships that do your bidding.

This chapter explains the technique of database design. The next chapter will show you how to implement your design by means of SQL's Data Definition Language, which lets you create columns, tables, and relationships.

After an introduction to database design, this chapter teaches you the technique of Entity-Relationship diagramming. E-R diagramming, as it's often called, lets you conveniently represent the structure of a database on paper. Then, with the aid of E-R diagrams, the chapter examines in detail the concept of relationships. As you'll see, the greater part of the power of a relational database system is rooted in its ability to define various types of relationships between the tables it contains. Next,

223

the chapter turns to the topic of database normalization, teaching you how to improve your database designs, making your databases more usable and reliable. Finally, this chapter deals with the important topic of referential integrity, showing you how to specify constraints that protect your database against changes that could break important relationships.

Database Stew

By now, you're accustomed to working with relational databases. You understand what tables, columns, and relationships are all about. In designing your own databases, you'll draw on your familiarity with these "ingredients" that make up the "database stew." Cooking, however, is somewhat different from tasting, as many a beginning chef can attest. One key element of success is a keen knowledge of ingredients. You can't make a world-class ratatouille without using first-rate, fresh eggplant. To obtain the best eggplant, you must know how eggplant looks, how eggplant smells, and how eggplant responds to a probing touch, both when fresh and when stale.

The same is true of your "database stew." The quality of your database design crucially depends on your knowledge of the design ingredients: tables, columns, and relationships. This section reviews these important concepts before moving on to the topic of E-R diagramming.

Tables

A relational database table contains information about one type of entity. These entities may be real, such as physical objects, or conceptual, such as events. SQL tables resemble Java classes. Classes are used to build Java programs, and tables are used to build relational databases. If you know something about object-oriented programming and design, you already know something about database design. The two are quite similar. In your Java program, you might have a class corresponding to suppliers; in your relational database, you might have a suppliers table. Both the class and the table correspond to a type of real-world entity—namely, suppliers.

Just as classes have instances, tables have rows. Your supplier class can be used to instantiate supplier objects, and your supplier table can contain rows, each describing a distinct supplier. An object corresponds to an individual entity, as does a row. Every object belongs to some class; similarly, every row belongs to some table. Classes can have no associated objects, one associated object, or many associated objects. Tables can have no rows, one row, or many rows. Objects come and go, as they are created and destroyed during program execution. Rows, too, come and go, as they are added to and deleted from tables over time.

The basic property shared by objects and rows is identity. Each represents a distinct individual. A useful adjunct to identity is a name. Within a Java program, each object is known by a unique reference. Within a relational database table, each row is known by a unique value of its primary key.

In writing a Java program, you decide which classes to create by asking yourself which objects in the real world need to be represented in your program. In designing a relational database, you ask yourself the same question: "Which entities in the real world need to be represented in my database?" Then, you include in your design exactly those tables that represent the relevant entities.

Columns

Neither classes nor tables are atomic; each has components. A class identifies fields and methods, which describe the state and behavior of class instances. A table identifies columns, which describe characteristics of the type of entity stored in the table.

Just as Java fields have data types, table columns have domains. Data types and domains limit the range of values stored in a field or a table column.

In designing a Java class, you include a field for each relevant item of information about objects of the class. In designing a relational table, you include a column for each relevant item of information about individual rows. Columns define the characteristics shared by all individuals belonging to a given entity type. For example, your suppliers table might include columns for a supplier ID number, name, and address. You might also include some historical information on the supplier, such as the amount of total purchases from the supplier during the current year.

You choose data types for Java fields based on the sort of information the field must hold. Numeric information is stored in numeric fields, and text information is stored in String fields. You choose a type large enough to accommodate the values you anticipate, but not so large that program performance suffers. Similarly, in designing a relational database, you choose the domain of a column based on the sort of information the column must store, taking care not to wastefully overallocate. You would define a Char column to hold the supplier's name, but you would probably limit the size of the column to 50 characters or so. Defining a 512-character supplier name would be unnecessary and inefficient.

Relationships

You can do only so much with a single class or a single table. Without relationships, even multiple classes or tables provide little capability. Just as teamwork makes a sports team more than a mere collection of individuals, relationships make object-oriented programs and relational databases powerful and flexible.

Relational databases are called relational because they handle relationships in a distinctive way. Flat-file systems, on the other hand, deal with relationships the way insects deal with their skeletons. The design of a flat-file system determines the relationships it supports, much the same way the exoskeleton of an insect determines its form. The price in each case is rigidity. A flat-file system can no more accommodate a new relationship than an insect can swivel its hips. Both are limited by an excess of structure.

Well-designed relational databases have just the right amount of relational structure—not so much that they become rigid like the insect, but not so little that they're weak and formless like the jellyfish. Knowing how to balance these contrasting concerns is an important aspect of the art of relational database design.

Relationships within a relational database are defined by pairs of primary and foreign keys. These pairs make joining a pair of distinct tables and exploring the resulting relationship easy and efficient. However, you can also join tables that are not related by a primary-foreign key pair. Thus, it's possible to explore relationships that the database designer did not provide for, or even anticipate. This gives relational databases unequaled power for coping with ad hoc queries, those unplanned and unanticipated forays into the data jungle. Flat-file systems, in contrast, deal well only with queries that are carefully planned and programmed in advance.

Logical Vs. Physical Design

Remember that database management systems conceal the physical structure of data, allowing the designer and programmer to deal with convenient abstractions.

The relational database designer need not be concerned with the sizes of disk pages and file clusters. These details are handled by the database management system, though many systems give the database administrator some degree of control over such matters.

During database design, you're concerned with a logical view of the data—how the data appears from the standpoint of a SQL query, not how the operating system perceives it. In fact, as you'll learn in Chapter 12, many relational databases support multiple views of their data, allowing different users to see the same data differently. In designing a database, the designer can compose the database to suit general needs. Later, the designer can define views that map the database in ways that are more appropriate to specific needs. This makes the task of the designer considerably easier.

Design Goals And Design Quality

In designing a relational database, the programmer seeks to identify a database structure that:

- Ensures data integrity

- Controls data redundancy

- Accommodates ad hoc queries

- Permits modification of the database to support changing requirements

Ensuring data integrity is a vital database design consideration. If the design permits inaccurate data to enter the database or data on the database to become inaccurate, inconsistent, or corrupt, the database fails in its central purpose.

Controlling data redundancy is an important design task. If a given piece of information appears in several database rows or tables, each of these locations must be updated when the information changes. If unchecked, this leads to complicated programs and poor system performance. In the worst case, it can lead to a lack of data integrity—for example, when one location is updated but others are not.

Accommodating ad hoc queries is necessary since no one can predict tomorrow's information needs. A database design that does not allow for data to be accessed in new ways may be an investment in the present, but not in the future. Good database designs stock the data warehouse in such a way that the system can satisfy unanticipated demands for information.

A database that cannot be easily modified is one that is—or soon will be—out of date. The real world that the database models is in continuous flux. Previously irrelevant entity types become matters of concern. Previously ignored characteristics of entities become mission-critical items that must be tracked, recorded, and reported if the business entity is to survive and prosper. A good database design is one that allows new entities and new characteristics to be added without upsetting the structural "apple cart."

E-R Diagrams

The basic activity of any relational database design is choosing components—and relationships between components—that balance a set of concerns. In database design, you choose columns, tables, and relationships. You also strive to strike a balance between low redundancy (which improves data integrity, accommodates ad hoc queries, improves update performance, and facilitates modification of the database) and high redundancy (which can improve query performance).

One of the best tools for database design is E-R modeling, which lets you sketch the tables and relationships that make up your data. You can modify a pencil-and-paper sketch more easily than a real database. Of course, if you can afford one, several good software packages let you create E-R diagrams using your computer. These make your diagrams look more professional, and some can even automatically generate the SQL statements needed to create your database.

E-R diagrams allow you to use the visually oriented parts of your mind that have a special knack for understanding relationships. Explaining a database design to someone is easier if you show an E-R diagram rather than the SQL statements used to create the database. The mind perceives graphical information holistically and textual information serially. Simply put, the E-R diagram lets you see more things at once than is possible with textual information. When you have a satisfactory E-R diagram—whether developed with pencil and paper or a fancy software tool—creating a SQL script to build the database is easy. The next chapter will show you how.

I have described E-R diagrams as showing tables and relationships. You may have noticed something missing: columns. E-R diagrams don't normally show the columns of each database table. Omitting details is one important technique in coping with complexity. By focusing on just tables and relationships, the database design problem becomes simpler. After you have decided on the tables and relationships, you can add the columns. Sometimes, this step points out a need to change the tables or relationships. That's normal. Design is an iterative process that may need to cycle again and again before a satisfactory result is achieved. That's why a visual technique such as E-R diagramming is helpful.

Understanding E-R Diagrams

Figure 8.1 shows an E-R diagram that depicts the Employees table , the Departments table, and relationships between them. The rectangles represent tables, and the diamonds represent relationships between tables. Lines connect diamonds to rectangles, showing the tables that participate in each relationship.

Each rectangle is labeled with the name of the corresponding table. Each diamond is labeled with two phrases that describe the corresponding relationship. Two phrases are needed, since you can view each relationship two ways. For example, the relationship that joins the Employees table with the Departments

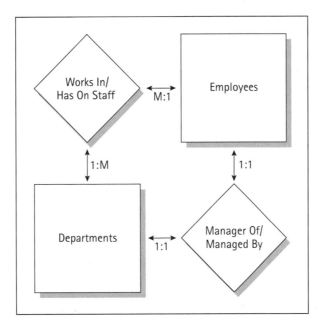

Figure 8.1
An E-R diagram.

table can be seen as meaning that a given employee works in a given Department, or that a given Department has a given employee on its staff. You could describe this relationship in either of the following two ways:

- *Works-in relationship*—if it's viewed from the standpoint of the employee

- *Has-on-staff relationship*—if it's viewed from the standpoint of the department

Therefore, each diamond is labeled with a pair of phrases so the reader can sort out the relationship, no matter which side of the relationship is read first.

The diagram also includes decorations that indicate each relationship's *cardinality*—the number of records from each table that participate in the relationship. For example, an employee can be assigned to multiple departments; hence, each record of the Employees table can be related to multiple records of the Departments table. Such a relationship is called a 1:M relationship, since one employee record is related to an indefinite number (M) of department records. Another way of saying this is a *one-to-many* relationship. Of course, viewed from the perspective of the Departments table, this is an M:1, or *many-to-one*, relationship. To show the cardinality of the Works-in/Has-on-staff relationship, the decorations 1 and M appear near the lines that join the tables to it.

A 1:1 *(one-to-one)* relationship is also possible. Each department has exactly one manager, and each Departments table record contains a ManagerID field with the employee number of the department's manager. The lines that depict the Manager-of/Managed-by relationship are decorated with 1s, showing that it is a 1:1 relationship.

You may be curious about the possibility of *many-to-many*, or M:N, relationships. Any M:N relationships that turn up during the design process are removed and replaced by a pair of 1:M relationships. When a design is finished, you'll not see any M:N relationships, only 1:1 and 1:M relationships. This is described in more detail later in this chapter.

Drawing E-R Diagrams

If you're drawing an E-R diagram that represents an existing database, you know what the tables are. In such a case, starting with the tables is the easiest course. When you're designing a database, however, you don't know what the tables are. You first need to know what characteristics the database must contain. Only then can you identify the tables and begin to draw the E-R diagram.

To learn what characteristics the database must contain, you need help. Unless you thoroughly and accurately understand the data, you're not qualified to decide how the database should be organized—you need the assistance of a user. Fortunately, because an E-R diagram is simple to understand, it's a great tool for working with users.

A useful approach is to gather a couple of programmers and a couple of users in a private conference room equipped with a whiteboard. Designate one of the programmers as the moderator, who will draw large E-R diagrams on the whiteboard. This way, everyone can see the design and contribute corrections and additions. With the whiteboard, you can easily accommodate these changes, since a swish of the eraser makes errors vanish forever.

Whether you identify the database columns first or the tables and relationships first really doesn't matter. Good design is "round trip;" that is, it continues cycling until you achieve the desired quality. You may identify the tables and relationships, identify the columns, add and change a few tables and relationships, and then add and change a few columns. Or, you may identify the columns, identify the tables and relationships, add and change a few columns, and then add and change a few tables and relationships. You may cycle only twice, or you may cycle three times, four times, or a dozen times. Although starting with the tables and relationships may be easier because they're less numerous, remember that design is a contingent process, meaning it's best done any way that actually works.

Identifying Columns

Assume that you've decided to tackle the columns first. Divide the whiteboard into two sections—one for tables and one for columns. Brainstorm as a group, listing possible columns until you're unable to come up with any new ones. Then, go through the list and eliminate any duplicates—that is, different names that refer to the same piece of data. This can be a little tricky. Your list of possible columns may include employee name, manager name, customer name, and so on. For now, even though they may be distinct, put a single "name" item on the list and remove any variant forms.

Next, assign names more appropriate for use in SQL commands and Java programs. The names should be short, but descriptive, and should follow any established programming standards or other local conventions that govern capitalization and so on. While you're at it, purge the list of any names that do not refer to characteristics. For example, the name of a possible table may have gotten mixed with the column names. Remove it from the column list, adding it to the opposite side of the whiteboard, which will contain the E-R diagram.

Once you're done with the list of columns, begin grouping them under implied subjects. These subjects will shortly become tables in your E-R diagram. For example, you might group name, address, and salary under the subject Employee, which will later become the Employees table. Feel free to include a single column name under multiple subjects. For example, Name can be included under the subject Employee, as well as Customer. As you did with the columns, assign short, descriptive names to the subjects you find. Then, go back and "customize" any column names that were used multiple times, so that they include their subject as part of the name. You should end up with such columns as EmployeeName and CustomerName where before you had only Name.

Finally, transfer the names of the subjects to the side of the whiteboard reserved for drawing the E-R diagram. Put a rectangle around each name and move on to establish the database relationships.

Now, consider each pair of tables in turn. Ask yourself what important relationships, if any, hold between the members of the pair. For each such relationship, add a diamond to the E-R diagram. Label the diamond with both names of the relationship, one from the standpoint of each participant, and draw lines connecting the participating tables (rectangles) with the relationship (diamond).

For the moment, don't worry about the cardinality of the relationships. Just focus on identifying the tables and relationships. You'll refine the relationships and specify their cardinalities soon.

You may run into some difficulties in identifying the tables and relationships. For example, an object may have several subtypes. In your real-estate database you may have single-family homes, townhouses, and apartments. Initially, you should create one table, perhaps called Residences, intended to hold information on all these subtypes. When you later elaborate your design to include the columns, you can include a column named ResidenceType that distinguishes a single-family home from a townhouse or apartment. To remind yourself to do so, jot yourself a note right on the E-R diagram.

As you move from identifying tables to identifying their relationships, you may find that the relationships pertaining to a single-family home are different from those pertaining to a townhouse. When you discover this, it's your clue to break the single table into separate tables—one for single-family homes and one for townhouses. As long as relationships apply equally to all the subtypes stored in the table, however, the best course is usually to keep them together.

Assigning Primary Keys

Now that you've identified the tables of your database, make sure each one has a primary key. Write the name of a table's primary key on the E-R diagram, beside the rectangle representing the table.

Three types of primary keys are possible:

- *An existing column that uniquely identifies each row.* For example, you might use Social Security Number as the primary key of a table that describes employees.

- *A combination of existing columns that uniquely identifies each row.* For example, you might use the combination of first and last names.

- *An artificial key (sometimes called a surrogate key), which is a new column you add expressly to serve as a primary key.* For example, you might define an employee number field.

The third of these options is usually the best. By assigning your own identifiers, you can ensure that each table row has a unique primary key. Better still, most databases have a facility, such as Access's AUTONUMBER data type, that can automatically assign unique identifiers to rows as they're added to the table. By all means, use that facility when it's available.

Although the first option sounds good, supposedly unique identifiers often turn out to be anything but unique. For example, because of data-entry errors, more than one person could end up with the same driver's license number or Social Security Number, or have automobiles with the same vehicle license number. Although a good database design should allow the user to detect such anomalies, it generally shouldn't force the user to resolve them before adding records to the database. Often, resolving such anomalies is beyond the power of the user. Prohibiting the entry of information until errors are fixed delays updating of the database, which is not always desirable.

The second option presents similar perils. Combinations that seem unique may not be in every instance. First and last names serve to uniquely identify employees only until a second John Smith is hired. By then, changing the database structure is difficult. You should avoid this possibility entirely.

Managing Relationships

Some relationships are easy to spot, because they're natural relationships between the tables you've identified. You've probably already identified these among those you've written on the whiteboard. Other relationships are less natural than designer-made. These you must work to find.

Suppose you've identified a Managers table, a Departments table, and an Employees table. Since managers manage departments, a natural relationship exists between the Managers table and the Departments table. Call this the Manages/Managed-by relationship. Similarly, since managers are employees, a natural relationship exists between the Managers table and the Employees table. Call this relationship Is-also-employee/Is-also-manager. Since employees are assigned to departments, there's a third natural relationship—between the Employees table and the Departments table. Call this final relationship Assigned-to/Has-on-staff. Figure 8.2 shows the related E-R diagram.

ONE-TO-ONE RELATIONSHIPS

The Manages/Managed-by relationship between Managers and Departments is a one-to-one relationship, assuming that each manager manages a single department, and each department has a single manager. Is-also-employee/Is-also-manager is another one-to-one relationship. For a manager, the Managers table and the Employees table record different information about the same individual.

However, these two one-to-one relationships are different from each other. Manages/Managed-by is a *required* relationship that holds for every row of the Departments table and the Managers table. Every department has a corresponding manager, and every manager has a corresponding department. The Is-also-employee/Is-also manager relationship, in contrast, holds for only selected employees. Only those employees who are also managers have rows in the Managers table, and most employees are not managers. This is an *optional* relationship—one that holds sometimes, but not always.

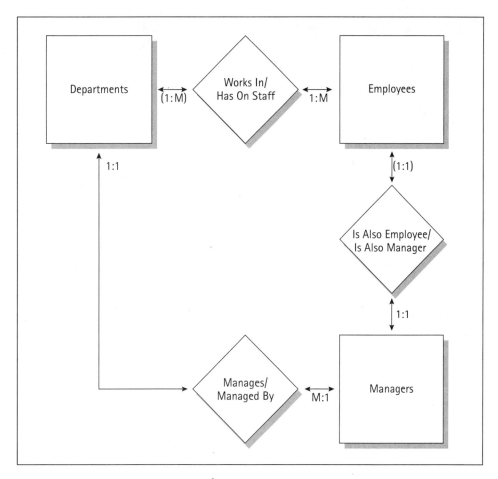

Figure 8.2
The E-R diagram for the Managers, Departments, and Employees database.

A good way to indicate an optional relationship on an E-R diagram is to put its cardinality in parentheses.

Some programmers would refer to this optional relationship as a zero-to-one relationship between the Employees table and the Managers table. This can become confusing, however, if you turn the relationship around and consider what might be meant by a one-to-zero relationship between the Managers table and the Employees table. In fact, an entry in the Managers table *must* have a corresponding entry in the Employees table. The better approach, therefore, is to think of the relationship as a one-to-one relationship that may or may not hold—that is, an optional relationship.

A one-to-one relationship can be an early sign of a database design problem. Often, one side of the relationship should simply be a characteristic of the other, rather than a table. In the case of the Manages/Managed-by relationship, you should consider whether the manager of a department is better seen as a characteristic of the department, or whether the department managed by an employee is better seen as a characteristic of the employee.

Since every department has a manager, but only a few employees manage departments, you should view the manager of a department as a characteristic of the department. Therefore, dispense with the Managers table and simply add ManagersName as a new column of the Departments table. Figure 8.3 shows the result.

Now, consider the manager once named Jeff Tode, who married Ima Gladd. They jointly decided that the custom of the wife taking the husband's family name would not be in her interest, since she would then be named Ima Tode. Instead, Jeff Tode became Jeff Gladd. The payroll clerk changed Jeff's name in the Employees table, but no one changed his name in the Managers table. Jeff continues to appear on company reports as Tode, when everyone now knows him as Gladd.

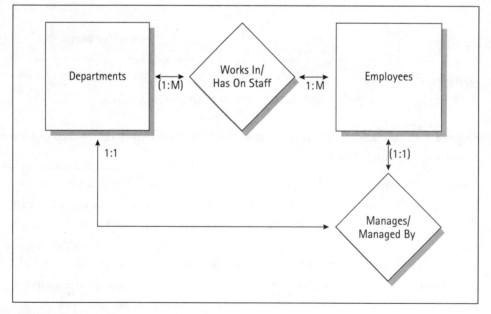

Figure 8.3
The Departments and Employees database.

This problem occurred as a result of redundant data—the same piece of data appearing in two locations. In this case, Jeff's name appeared in both the Managers table and the Employees table. Invariably, some such instances will acquire inconsistent data. At best, the work of maintaining the database is increased, since changes must be made in several locations, rather than one.

The solution is to store a foreign key in place of the redundant data. Rather than putting the manager's name in the Departments table, put the manager's employee number in the Departments table. Then, the manager's name appears only once in the database, in the Employees table. The name cannot become inconsistent because it's stored only once. Changing the Employees table is all that's necessary to update the company's records. It's often handy to annotate the E-R diagram with the name of the foreign key used by a relationship. Figure 8.4 shows the result.

One-to-one relationships do not represent the only situation in which foreign keys are needed. Every relationship in your database will be associated with a primary-foreign key pair. The next section explains how this plays out with many-to-many relationships.

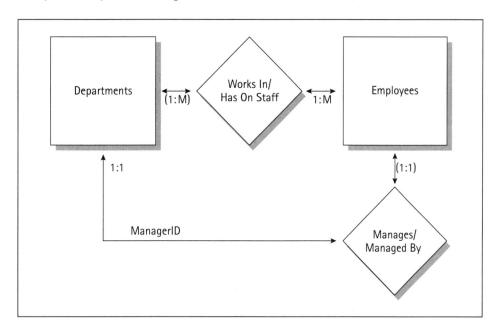

Figure 8.4
The Departments and Employees database with a foreign key.

MANY-TO-MANY RELATIONSHIPS

Many-to-many relationships are commonly found during database design, but must be removed to complete the design. Wherever you find a many-to-many relationship in your design, create a new table—often called a *connecting table*— and give it a name appropriate to the many-to-many relationship. For example, the Departments table and the Employees table are related by a many-to-many relationship called Works-in/Has-on-staff. The connecting table created to deal with this many-to-many relationship might be called Assignments.

Separately connect the new table to each of the tables in the many-to-many relationship using two new one-to-many relationships. For example, you might connect the Employees table and the Assignments table using a Has-assignment/ Assignment-of relationship, and you might connect the Departments table and the Assignments table using an Assignment-of/Has-assignment relationship. Figure 8.5 shows the result.

Now, you need to determine the columns that belong in the connecting table. These will usually be foreign keys that point to the related tables. For example, the Assignments table might include an employee-number foreign key pointing to the Employees table, and a department-number key pointing to the Departments table.

The primary key of a connecting table is usually the combination of its foreign keys. For example, the Assignments table might use the combination of employee number and department number as its primary key. If the combination of foreign keys is not unique, this is a clue to rethink your design. Usually, you'll find that something is amiss.

Once you've identified the key fields of the connecting table, consider whether it will need any previously unknown columns. For example, you might decide that it's useful to store the date on which an employee was assigned to a department or the number of hours per week the employee works in the department. The proper place to store this information is in the connecting table, Assignments.

ONE-TO-MANY RELATIONSHIPS

One-to-many relationships are the bread and butter of relational database design; most database relationships are one-to-many (or many-to-one, if viewed

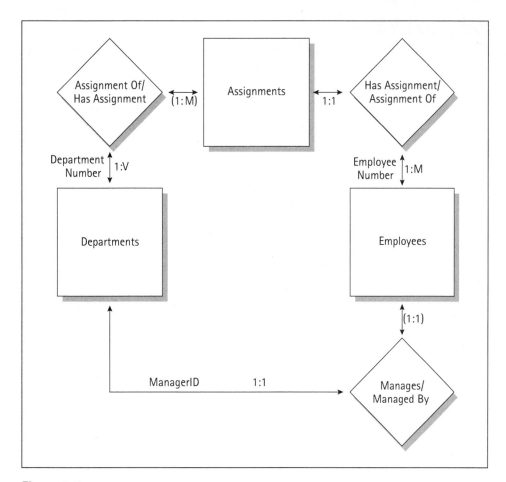

Figure 8.5
Replacing a many-to-many relationship.

from the opposite perspective). These relationships require no special handling. Each such relationship should be associated with a paired primary-foreign key combination. If you find a relationship that lacks the necessary keys, add them to the E-R diagram, restructuring tables if necessary. Indicate optional one-to-many relationships on the E-R diagram by placing the cardinality in parentheses.

The one-to-many relationship anticipates the use of a SQL join that uses the primary-foreign key to combine information from the related tables. Optional one-to-many relationships correspond to situations where outer joins may be used to retrieve rows that lack a matching row in the related table.

SELF-RELATIONSHIPS

The correspondence between relationships and joins applies to more than one-to-many joins. Just as self-joins are possible (as explained in Chapter 7), self-relationships are possible. For example, in a company in which every employee has one immediate superior, it might be handy to store the superior's employee number in each table row representing a subordinate. This can be shown in an E-R diagram, as seen in Figure 8.6.

Self-relationships can be one-to-one, one-to-many, and either required or optional. A self-relationship that is many-to-many should be factored using a connecting table, the same as for any other type of relationship.

Programmers often find self-relationships confusing. Don't hesitate to represent a self-relationship using an auxiliary table, if you find that's clearer. To store the employee numbers of superiors and subordinates, for example, you might define a table, named SupervisedBy, that has one entry for each employee. The table would contain the employee number of the subordinate, used as the primary key of the table, and the employee number of the superior. Of course, you would have to give each column a distinct name, such as SubEmployeeNo and

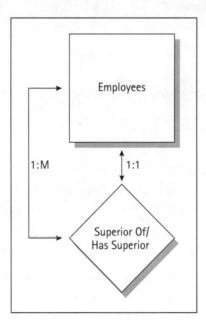

Figure 8.6
A self-relationship.

SupEmployeeNo. Each of these columns would be a foreign key related to the employee-number primary key of the Employees table.

Reiterate

Now that you're done identifying the tables, columns, and relationships, go back to the beginning and reconsider each step. You'll probably find items you've missed and better ways of doing things. Keep cycling until you're confident that no further "trips" through the process are likely to improve the result. Then, move on to database normalization.

Database Normalization

Database normalization is a process that helps further refine your design. The immediate effect of normalization will be to cause you to break some of your tables into smaller tables. The ultimate effect will be that your database will be more flexible and robust.

What's Wrong With Being Abnormal?

A non-normalized database is prey to a host of problems, called *anomalies*. To understand the risks to your data of using a non-normalized database, consider the hypothetical table shown in Table 8.1.

TABLE 8.1

A NON-NORMALIZED TABLE.

Customer #	City	Part#	Quantity
101	New York	1	100
101	New York	2	200
102	Boston	1	100
103	Los Angeles	2	200
103	Los Angeles	3	100
103	Los Angeles	4	500
104	Chicago	3	100
104	Chicago	4	100

Since no single column of the table is obviously unique, assume that the primary key is the combination of all four columns.

The three types of anomalies that plague such a table are:

- *The insert anomaly*—Assume you want to record that a new customer, #105, is based in Detroit. You can't do so until the customer places an order, because until then, you have no values for part number and quantity. (The components of a primary key must never be null.)

- *The delete anomaly*—If the shipment for customer #102 was really intended for customer #103, you can't delete the erroneous shipment. Doing so would also delete the record that customer #102 is based in Boston.

- *The update anomaly*—If customer #103 moves from Los Angeles to Dallas, you have to search through the entire database and change every record pertaining to that customer, or live with the fact that the customer's city may be reported incorrectly from time to time.

The problem in each case is that the table contains too many columns. To avoid anomalies, it needs to be split into separate tables. For example, assume the same data is organized as shown in Tables 8.2 and 8.3.

Now the three anomalies no longer exist:

- To record that customer #105 is based in Detroit, simply add an appropriate record to the Customers table. You don't need to wait until the first shipment is made.

TABLE 8.2

THE NORMALIZED CUSTOMERS TABLE.

Customer #	City
101	New York
102	Boston
103	Los Angeles
104	Chicago

	TABLE 8.3

THE NORMALIZED SHIPMENTS TABLE.

Customer #	Part #	Quantity
101	1	100
101	2	200
102	1	100
103	2	200
103	3	100
103	4	500
104	3	100
104	4	100

- You can safely delete the erroneous shipment to customer #102, without losing your record that the customer is based in Boston, since the city is now in the Customers table.

- To update customer #103 to reflect the move from Los Angeles to Dallas, all you have to do is change a single record in the Customers table. You don't have to search the entire database, and data is never reported incorrectly or inconsistently.

The normalization process helps you discover tables that need to be split, so you can be spared the heartbreak of insert, delete, and update anomalies. As a bonus, normalized databases are often easier to understand and explain, easier to query, and easier to modify.

About the only drawback of normalization is that it results in more, smaller tables. This may increase database response time for some queries. The wrong response to this bit of knowledge, however, is to skip database normalization. The correct response is to normalize, then selectively denormalize the database to improve response to critical queries. That way, the greater part of the database remains normalized.

The Normal Forms

Normalization involves checking your database design against a set of rules. The three rules explained in this chapter are called:

- 1st normal form
- 2nd normal form
- 3rd normal form

Each rule fixes the form of each database table. It does this by ruling out certain inappropriate forms that lead to anomalies. The rules build on one another. For a database table to be in 2nd normal form, it must also be in 1st normal form. Similarly, for a database table to be in 3rd normal form, it must also be in 1st and 2nd normal forms.

Additional rules have been proposed in the database literature. In practice, however, most programmers work with only these three rules. Most table designs that are in 3rd normal form are entirely satisfactory. Moreover, some of the more advanced normal forms exact significant performance penalties. Consequently, this book will not present these advanced forms.

1st Normal Form: No Multiple Values

A database table in 1st normal form must contain no repeating groups. In Java, a repeating group would be referred to as an array, so 1st normal form says that a table should not contain a column that holds an array of values.

This might occur, for example, if you decided to store the departments to which an employee is assigned in the Employees table. Since, as you'll learn in the next chapter, you cannot actually define an array in SQL, you might compose an artificial array by defining several numeric columns named Dept01, Dept02, Dept03, Dept04, and Dept05. Then, you could put the department numbers of an employee's assignments in these columns.

Not only does this break the rule for 1st normal form, it also unnecessarily imposes a limit on the number of departments to which an employee can be assigned. If anyone works in more than five departments, your database design won't allow this to be recorded. The assignment information really belongs in a separate table, perhaps called Assignments, where it won't be subject to this arbitrary limit. By relating this new table to the original Employees table, you establish a master-detail relationship between the master table (Employees) and the detail table (Assignments).

A database in 1st normal form cannot contain any columns that have compound values. Remember the problems with the Name column of the Employees table in Chapter 6? It contained a compound value consisting of a first name and a last name. Although the SQL Substring function helped us cope, it was inconvenient. Worse yet, it's a violation of 1st normal form. A table that contains a compound column, such as the Name column of the Employees table, is not in 1st normal form. You should break such a column into distinct columns. Then, your database table will be in 1st normal form, and you can move on to assess whether it also meets the test for 2nd normal form.

2nd Normal Form: Depend On The Primary Key

The 2nd normal form places restrictions on the structure of tables that have composite primary keys. If the primary key of your table is not a composite key, your table is automatically in 2nd normal form (so long as it is also in 1st normal form).

To determine whether a table with a composite primary key is in 2nd normal form, make sure that every nonkey column depends on the entire primary key. If only a portion of the primary key would be enough to uniquely identify the value of a nonkey column, your table is not in 2nd normal form.

For example, assume that the composite primary key of the Assignments table includes the employee number and the department number. Assume that the Assignments table contains one additional column, employee date of birth. Intuitively, you know that the date of birth belongs in the Employees table, not the Assignments table. That's exactly what 2nd normal form asserts. The date of birth relates to employee number, a portion of the composite primary key. You don't really need to know the department number to which an employee is assigned in order to know the employee's date of birth.

When you find a column that violates the 2nd normal form, move it to a more appropriate table that has a noncomposite primary key or that has a composite primary key on which the column fully depends. If necessary, create a new table to hold the recalcitrant column. When you've done this, your table is in 2nd normal form. You should now proceed to check whether it's in 3rd normal form.

3rd Normal Form: Don't Depend On Nonkey Columns

The 3rd normal form applies the principle behind the 2nd normal form to all tables, not merely those that have composite primary keys. To be in 3rd normal form, a table must have no nonkey columns that depend on anything other than the primary key. Each nonkey column must be a characteristic that tells something about the primary key column.

For example, assume that in a given company, employees are assigned to only a single department. In the Employees table, the columns include employee number, department number, and department name. The primary key is employee number. Intuitively, you know that it's not necessary to store both the department number and the department name in the Employees table. That's what 3rd normal form says. The department name depends on the department number (or vice versa, if you want to look at it the other way), not on the primary key. The department name is redundant and should be moved to a Departments table.

Normal Forms Summed Up

William Kent, a prominent writer and thinker on database issues, wrote that the essence of normalization is simply this: "Every nonkey column provides a fact about the key, the whole key, and nothing but the key." It's altogether too easy to get caught up in the technique of normalization, forgetting that simple common sense is behind each of the normal forms. Avoid mechanical application of the rules of database normalization. The rules cannot be used to prove that your database actually is in 3rd normal form, only that there are no known exceptions. You must understand your data to massage it into normal form. Also use common sense in dealing with violations of normal form. Normalization is a tool, not a goal.

As an example, consider a database that records the parts used in constructing a two-story building. Assume that the room number is the primary key and the part number is the only data column. Now consider the parts used in constructing room 105, a first-floor restroom. One of these parts is a valve of a sort used only on the first floor; a special type of valve is needed above the first floor. Note that the room number is actually a compound column, consisting of the number of the floor and the number of the room within the floor. This means that the part number for the valve depends on only part of the room number, the number of the room within the floor. This is true because the valve cannot be used except on the first floor, so the number of the floor where the valve is used must always be 1.

Such a database, while not fully normalized, is probably quite satisfactory for actual use. Putting first-floor parts in a separate table would be a cure worse than the disease.

Choosing Data Types

The next step in designing your database is choosing an appropriate data type for each column. For some data types, you'll also need to decide length, precision, or scale. *Length* refers to the number of characters or digits the column can hold. *Precision* refers to the number of digits allowed, and *scale* refers to the number of fractional digits. Think carefully before assigning a data type to a column, because databases often provide no way to change the data type of a column. SQL supports five main categories of data types:

- Character

- Whole number

- Decimal

- Date and time

- Binary

The following sections describe each main category, identifying the specific data types it includes, providing hints concerning when each is useful, and identifying the options that must be specified along with the data type. The names of data types sometimes vary from database to database; those shown here are used by Microsoft Access. Consult your database documentation to verify the specific names used by your database. Table 8.4 summarizes the SQL data types.

TABLE 8.4

THE SQL DATA TYPES.

Data Type	Description
BIT(n)	A bit string of the specified fixed length.
BIT	A single-bit value.
BIT VARYING(n)	A bit string of the specified maximum length.
CHAR(n)	A character string of specified length, right-padded with spaces.
DATE	A date, including year, month, and day.
DECIMAL(p,s)	A decimal number of specified precision and scale. Maximum precision and scale depend on the implementation. The system may substitute a greater precision.
DECIMAL(p)	A decimal number of specified precision and default scale. Maximum precision and default scale depend on the implementation. The system may substitute a greater precision.
DECIMAL	A decimal number of default precision and scale. Default precision and scale depend on the implementation. The system may substitute a greater precision.
DOUBLE	A double-precision floating-point number. The precision depends on the implementation.
FLOAT(p)	A floating-point number with either single- or double-precision.
INTEGER	A whole number. The precision depends on the implementation.
NUMERIC(p,s)	A decimal number of specified precision and scale. Maximum precision and scale depend on the implementation.
NUMERIC(p)	A decimal number of specified precision and default scale. Maximum precision and default scale depend on the implementation.
NUMERIC	A decimal number of default precision and scale. Default precision and scale depend on the implementation.
REAL	A single-precision floating-point number. The precision depends on the implementation.
SMALLINT	A whole number. The precision depends on the implementation, but is never greater than that of the INTEGER data type.

(continued)

TABLE 8.4

THE SQL DATA TYPES (*CONTINUED*).

Data Type	Description
TIME(p)	A time, including hour, minutes, seconds, and a number of fractional seconds with the specified number of digits.
TIME	A time, including hour, minutes, and seconds.
TIMESTAMP(p)	A date and time, with fractional seconds having the specified number of digits.
TIMESTAMP	A date and time, with six fractional second digits.
VARCHAR(n)	A character string of specified maximum length.

Character Data Types

SQL supports two main character data types, CHAR and VARCHAR. Like Java's **String** type, each can hold letters, digits, and special characters. CHAR specifies a fixed-length character string that is automatically right-padded with spaces to fill the specified length. VARCHAR specifies a variable-length character string that is not automatically padded. Each is specified along with the desired length of the string.

The character data types are often useful for storing data that at first seems to be numeric—for example, phone numbers—but that contains hyphens or parentheses in addition to digits.

Whole-Number Data Types

Most SQL implementations provide at least two whole-number data types: INTEGER and SMALLINT. Many provide additional data types, such as BYTE and TINYINT. The precision of whole-number data types is determined by the implementation. However, the SMALLINT data type never has greater precision than the INTEGER data type.

Decimal Data Types

Decimal data types, unlike whole-number data types, include fractional digits. They come in two categories:

- *Exact decimal data types*—These include NUMERIC and DECIMAL. They allow you to express the value of a decimal number exactly.

- *Approximate decimal data types*—These include REAL, DOUBLE, and FLOAT. They allow you to express the value of a decimal number only approximately, but can readily handle very large or very small numbers by use of exponents. The FLOAT data type is especially useful if your database may someday be moved to a different platform, since it allows you some control over the precision of the stored values.

Date And Time Data Types

Date and time data types include DATE, TIME, and TIMESTAMP. Both TIME and TIMESTAMP can optionally include fractional seconds, allowing considerable precision in specifying time values.

Binary Data Types

The binary data types are BIT, a fixed-length string of bits; and BIT VARYING, a variable-length string of bits.

Create A Prototype Of The Database, And Experiment

Although the previous steps—using E-R diagrams, normalizing your database, and choosing data types—help ensure that your database will provide every needed function, the performance of your database is still at issue. So, you should create a prototype of your database, as you'll learn how to do in Chapter 9. Then, you should experiment with the database and assess its performance. If time-critical operations cannot be completed as quickly as needed, you can attempt to revise the database structure to improve performance. Describing the specific measures you should use is beyond the scope of this book, in part because they depend to a considerable degree on implementation details of your database system. But, generally, you must add indexes and/or selectively denormalize strategically chosen tables. At its best, the process is largely trial and error, so don't hesitate to play a hunch. The reward may be a handsome one.

Database Design Case Study

The best way, perhaps the only way, to learn database design is by doing it. This section presents a case study in database design, showing you step by step what's involved. You should read through the case study, referring back to the earlier parts of the chapter to clarify the details of each step.

Assemble Your Team

Pretend you've settled into a comfortable swivel chair in the conference room, along with another programmer and a couple of users from the order department. It's 10:00 a.m. and a full pot of freshly brewed coffee sits on the table next to you. You pour yourself a cup of French Extra Roast and grab one of the nearby doughnuts. Taking a generous bite, you discover it's filled with vanilla cream. As the others help themselves to the refreshments, your eyes gaze through the large, tinted windows of the conference room to the panorama of nearby mountains, wrapped in fluffy clouds. Isn't database design wonderful!

Identify The Columns

Your fellow programmer, already acquainted with the two users, introduces you and hands the meeting over to you. Taking the last bite of your doughnut, you rise and stride to the whiteboard, moving your coffee mug to your left hand to make room for a blue erasable marker, which you use to divide the board into two areas. At the top of the left side you write in large block letters "Characteristics" and at the top of the right side you write "E-R diagram."

As the sugar high from your doughnut builds to full pitch, one of the users, a middle-aged and balding fellow with a grim expression, asks what an E-R diagram is. You respond with a joke about an emergency room doctor and patient, which, oddly, no one finds very funny. Users never seem to have a sense of humor, you remind yourself.

Buckling down to the task at hand, you solicit everyone's ideas on data needed in the database. As they begin to quickly call out a mixture of characteristics and subjects, you just as quickly scribble their ideas verbatim on the board. After a time, the flow dwindles. Your colleague asks a couple of questions, causing the flow to resume, but only briefly. Soon, even this second flow has subsided.

Reaching to refill your empty mug, you view the left half of the board from a distance of several feet, seeing it as the others have seen it all along. Table 8.5 shows the list of characteristics contributed by the group.

Identify The Tables

Grabbing another doughnut, this one a cake doughnut with little sprinkles, you tentatively group the characteristics under their implied subjects, thereby designating the tables. You tweak the names of several of the columns and add a few you believe the group has missed.

You ask for the group's approval, getting a noncommittal grunt from your colleague, but the users are silent. Studying their faces, you note that their eyes are glazed over. Passing the remaining doughnuts in their direction, you explain what you've done and why. This time they readily assent to your call for approval. You hope the change was as much due to your explanation as the additional round of doughnuts. Table 8.6 shows the results of your efforts.

TABLE 8.5

THE LIST OF CHARACTERISTICS FOR THE CASE STUDY.

Order

Customer

Stock #

Date

Quantity

Amount

Name

Shipping Address

Billing Address

Purchase Order #

Sales Order #

Description

YTD Purchases

TABLE 8.6

THE LIST OF TABLES FOR THE CASE STUDY.

Table	Characteristic
Customers	Customer #
	Customer name
	Billing address
	Billing city
	Billing state
	Billing zip
	YTD purchases
Orders	Sales order #
	Customer #
	PO #
	Shipping address
	Shipping city
	Shipping state
	Shipping zip
	Order date
Order Details	Sales order #
	Stock #
	Description
	Unit price
	Quantity ordered
	Quantity shipped
	Date shipped

Assign Primary Keys

Assigning primary keys to the Customers table and the Orders table is easy; the customer number and sales-order number are perfectly suited. You circle each and step back to ponder what to use as a key for the Order Details table.

Ultimately, you decide on a composite key consisting of the sales-order number and stock number. You place a large circle around both column names, disappointed that no one applauds.

Identify Relationships

Scanning for relationships, you begin sketching an E-R diagram on the right half of the whiteboard. You find a one-to-many relationship between Customers and Orders, and another between Orders and Order Details. Pondering momentarily, you decide that the former is an optional relationship and the latter is required. You name the relationship between Customers and Orders the Ordered/Ordered-by relationship. You name the other relationship Has-Detail/Detail-of, adding labeled diamonds to your E-R diagram. You note the cardinalities of the relationships on the E-R diagram, which resembles Figure 8.7.

It's now 11:20 a.m. and one of the two users begs off, citing an important meeting. You're not overly concerned, because you seem now to have an adequate understanding of what's needed. You press on, hoping to finish in time for lunch.

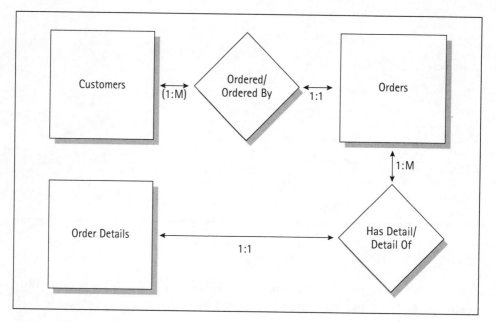

Figure 8.7
The E-R diagram for the case study.

Define Foreign Keys

You now designate the customer number column of the Orders table as a foreign key that references the customer number primary key of the Customers table. You also designate the sales-order number column of the Order Details table as a foreign key that references the sales-order number primary key of the Orders table. You annotate the E-R diagram with these tidbits and pick up the pace, concerned that time is slipping away.

Review One-To-One Relationships

You're relieved to note that no one-to-one relationships appeared in the design. You know they often spell trouble, and it would have taken time to determine whether they were appropriate and to revise the design if they weren't.

Replace Many-To-Many Relationships

You're also relieved to see that no many-to-many relationships are involved. These are not as troublesome as one-to-one relationships, but they must be replaced by a pair of one-to-many relationships, and that takes time. You relinquish your almost empty coffee cup to permit an even faster pace of work.

Normalize The Database

As the remaining user departs for a restroom break, you note that the time is 11:35 a.m. Not bothering to wonder if she will return, you set about normalizing the database, knowing that time is short, yet hoping to finish before lunch.

The Customers table and the Orders table look fine, but the Order Details table has a problem. The description depends only on the stock number, not on the composite key consisting of the sales-order number and the stock number. The table is not in 2nd normal form. You quickly define a new Items table and move the description column into the new table. You establish the stock number as the primary key of the new table and make the stock number column within the Order Details table a foreign key that references it.

You ponder whether you should also move the unit price into the Items table. Eventually, you decide to retain it as a column in the Order Details table, but also include it as a column within the Items table. That way, when the unit price is changed, the Order Details table will still reflect the price prevailing at the time of shipment. You reconsider the decision to place the description column in the Items table, ultimately deciding to leave it. When a description is changed, it is best to change every occurrence.

When you're done, the list of database tables looks like Table 8.7, and the revised E-R diagram looks like that shown in Figure 8.8.

TABLE 8.7

THE REVISED LIST OF TABLES FOR THE CASE STUDY.

Table	Characteristic
Customers	Customer #
	Customer name
	Billing address
	Billing city
	Billing state
	Billing zip
	YTD purchases
Orders	Sales order #
	Customer #
	PO #
	Shipping address
	Shipping city
	Shipping state
	Shipping zip
	Order date
Items	Stock #
	Description
	Unit price
Order Details	Sales order #
	Stock #

(continued)

TABLE 8.7

THE REVISED LIST OF TABLES FOR THE CASE STUDY (*CONTINUED*).

Table	Characteristic
Order Details *(continued)*	Unit price
	Quantity ordered
	Quantity shipped
	Date shipped

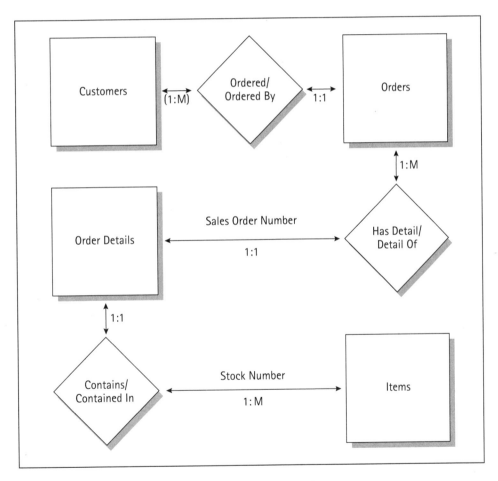

Figure 8.8
The revised E-R diagram for the case study.

Assign Data Types

Noting the time as 11:50 a.m., you decide the second user won't be back. Putting on a final burst of speed, you decorate the tables list with appropriate data types for each column. The result is shown in Table 8.8.

TABLE 8.8

THE REVISED LIST OF TABLES FOR THE CASE STUDY.

Table	Characteristic	Data Type
Customers	Customer#	INTEGER
	Customer name	VARCHAR(35)
	Billing address	VARCHAR(35)
	Billing city	VARCHAR(15)
	Billing state	CHAR(2)
	Billing zip	CHAR(5)
	YTD purchases	DECIMAL(8,2)
Orders	Sales order #	INTEGER
	Customer #	INTEGER
	PO #	VARCHAR(35)
	Shipping address	VARCHAR(35)
	Shipping city	VARCHAR(15)
	Shipping state	CHAR(2)
	Shipping zip	CHAR(5)
	Order date	DATE
Items	Stock #	INTEGER
	Description	VARCHAR(20)
	Unit price	DECIMAL(6,2)
Order Details	Sales order #	INTEGER
	Stock #	INTEGER
	Unit price	DECIMAL(6,2)
	Quantity ordered	DECIMAL(3,0)
	Quantity shipped	DECIMAL(3,0)
	Date shipped	DATE

Experiment With A Prototype

A glance at your wristwatch reveals the time is now 12:05 p.m. You discover that your fellow programmer has left the room without a goodbye, taking apparent advantage of your deep concentration to achieve a place ahead of you in the cafeteria lunch line. Just as well, you think, since meatloaf is on the menu today. All morning you've had your appetite set on a healthy, steaming tofu burger of the sort only available at JJ's down the street.

To ensure your work isn't in vain, you write "Do not erase" several places on the whiteboard. Then you take your digital camera from your shirt pocket and snap a couple of photos just to be sure. Promising yourself that you'll have only a single strawberry smoothie so you can be back in time to do some prototyping before the weekly staff meeting, you exit the room with a feeling of accomplishment and professional pride. As they say, another day, another database; a million days, a million databases.

Summary

The journey has been a long one and you may be forgiven if some of the twists and turns are less than clearly remembered. To help you find your way back through the thickets, here's a review of the steps of the database design process:

1. Assemble a team that includes programmers and users, and retire as a group to a private location equipped with a whiteboard.

2. Identify the columns and place them on a list.

3. Allocate the columns into tables, and place the tables on the E-R diagram.

4. Make sure each table has a suitable primary key.

5. Add relationships to the E-R diagram.

6. Locate one-to-many relationships between tables and define an appropriate foreign key on the "many" side of the relationship.

7. Locate one-to-one relationships and consider whether they should be removed.

8. Locate many-to-many relationships and replace each with a pair of one-to-many relationships with a new connecting table. Add any necessary foreign keys.

9. Normalize the database design.

10. Assign a suitable data type to each column.

11. Prototype and experiment. Denormalize to improve performance, as needed.

This chapter has taught you how to design a database. The next chapter introduces SQL Data Definition Language (DDL), the SQL statements you use to actually create a database from your design.

SQL DATA DEFINITION LANGUAGE

9

Now that you know how to design a relational database, you're ready to learn how to implement your design. Of course, you can use Microsoft Access to create your database, by following the instructions given in Chapter 2. But using the SQL commands is a better way, because they work for many databases, not just Access.

This chapter presents SQL's Data Definition Language (DDL), which is used to define the structure of a relational database. Chapter 10 presents Data Manipulation Language (DML), which is used to add, change, and delete table rows.

You'll first learn how to use the DBMaker application, a Java program that makes it a little easier to issue the SQL commands used to build a database. DBMaker lets you display the structure of the database you're working on, so you know that your commands have had the desired effects. It also provides menus and dialogs that simplify common operations.

After touring DBMaker, you'll learn how to create, delete, and alter database tables, using SQL commands. You'll then learn how to create and delete indexes, and how to create and delete constraints that enforce rules protecting your data. Finally, you'll get a look at the source code for DBMaker, which shows how to issue SQL DDL commands from within your Java programs.

Up to this point, I've presented no programs or SQL commands that alter the structure or contents of a database. DBMaker and the SQL DDL commands *do* make such changes. A program bug or a mistyped DDL command can wipe out important data. Before trying the examples in this chapter, be sure your important data is securely backed up. Creating a special database just for working with DDL is a good idea. You can simply copy an Access MDB file and use the ODBC Administration Applet in the Control Panel to configure the copied file as a new ODBC data source. By taking these extra steps, you're less likely to accidentally delete your income tax records or other important data.

The DBMaker Application

Figure 9.1 shows the user interface of the DBMaker application, which will execute the SQL commands described in this chapter. The application is easy to use because it's menu-driven. Clicking a menu brings up a series of menu items. When you select an item, a dialog box appears, prompting you for the information needed to complete the operation you chose. Table 9.1 describes the available menu items.

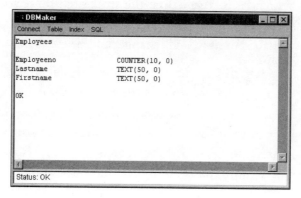

Figure 9.1
The DBMaker user interface.

TABLE 9.1

SUMMARY OF DBMAKER MENU ITEMS.

Menu Item	Function
Connection|Open Connection	Opens a connection to a database.
Connection|Close Connection	Closes an open database connection.
Connection|Exit	Exits the application.
Table|Show Table	Displays the columns of a table, and their parameters.
Table|Create Table	Creates a new table.
Table|Add Column	Adds a new column to a table.
Table|Drop Column	Drops a column from a table.
Table|Drop Table	Drops a table.
Index|Show Indexes	Displays information about the defined indexes.
Index|Create Index	Creates a new index.
Index|Drop Index	Drops an index.
SQL|Execute Query	Executes a SQL statement and displays the **ResultSet** or update count, as appropriate to the statement type.

The menu items used in executing the examples include: Show Table, which displays the structure of a selected database table; Show Indexes, which displays the structure of all indexes defined in the database; and Execute Query, which lets you type and execute a SQL command.

You can't use SQLWindow (or any of the other applications presented so far) to execute SQL DDL commands, because they don't return a **ResultSet**. Instead, they return an update count and must be executed using **Statement.execute( )** or **Statement.executeUpdate( )**, rather than **Statement.executeQuery( )**. The difference is small, but significant, as you'll see when I explain the source code for DBMaker.

The remaining menu items appear in DBMaker for two reasons. First, you may tire of typing DDL commands once you've mastered them; instead, you may prefer to use the dialogs provided by DBMaker. Second, the common DDL operations illustrated by DBMaker enable you to study its source code and learn how to include these operations in programs you write.

Defining Tables

Before you can define database tables, you must have a database. You can copy an MDB file or use the ODBC Data Source Administrator to create a new database. If you copy an MDB file, your new database won't start out empty; it will contain the same tables as the original database. In a moment, you'll learn how to delete these unwanted tables, so don't be concerned about them. Be sure the ODBC data source you're using points to an MDB file that contains no important data. Damaging a database is altogether too easy when using DDL. Unlike Access, which regularly prompts, "Are you sure?", DDL simply does what you've asked. If you told the SQL interpreter to delete a table, it's gone forever, unless you have a backup.

Creating A Table

Once you have a database to work with, the next step is to create its tables. Start DBMaker and open a connection to your working database. Use the Execute SQL menu item to enter and execute the following SQL command:

```
Create Table Employees(EmployeeNo Int) ;
```

This command creates a new table named Employees, which contains a single column named EmployeeNo. The data type of the column is INT, which is short for integer. As you recall from the last chapter, the INT data type stores whole numbers in an implementation-defined precision.

Unless you've made a syntax error, the command produces no output. How are you to know whether it succeeded or not? Simple. Use the Show Table menu item, which displays a dialog that includes a **List** that shows every table in the database. You should see the Employees table listed; select it and click OK. DBMaker displays a short report that shows the structure of the Employees table:

```
Employees

EmployeeNo          LONG(10, 0)

OK
```

From the report, you can see that the table does contain a single field, named Employeeno. The data type is shown as LONG, which is a "flavor" of INT that has about 10 decimal digits of precision. DBMaker does not report the SQL-92 data type names; it reports those used by the local database. Table 9.2 shows data type names reported by Access and how they correspond to standard SQL data type names. When issuing DDL commands to Access, you can use names from either column of Table 9.2. When issuing DDL commands to a database other than Access, you should use the SQL data type names shown in the second column.

Dropping A Table

Now that you know how to create a simple table, you need to know how to delete a table so that, when you make a mistake or change your mind, you can put things back as they were. To delete the Employees table, use the Execute SQL menu item of DBMaker to type and execute the following DDL command:

```
Drop Table Employees ;
```

TABLE 9.2

ACCESS AND SQL DATA TYPE NAMES.

Access Type	SQL Type
BINARY	BIT, BIT VARYING
BIT	N/A
BYTE	N/A
COUNTER	N/A
DATETIME	DATE, TIME, TIMESTAMP
SINGLE	REAL
DOUBLE	FLOAT, DOUBLE PRECISION
SHORT	SMALLINT
LONG	INTEGER
LONGBINARY	N/A
LONGTEXT	N/A
TEXT	CHARACTER, CHARACTER VARYING
VALUE	N/A

That's all there is to it. If the table had contained rows, they would now be gone. Be certain you want to drop a table before issuing this command, and double-check what you've typed before allowing the command to execute.

Use the Show Table menu item to prove that the table is gone. When the table selection list appears, the Employees table should not be listed. Just click Cancel to dispose of the dialog.

Creating More Elaborate Tables

Single-field tables are simple and, therefore, well suited as an introductory example. But you need to be able to create industrial-strength, nuclear-grade, super tables. This section moves on to some more interesting examples.

Try the following DDL command to create an improved Employees table, with two columns of different data types:

```
Create Table Employees(EmployeeNo Int, EmployeeName Char(50)) ;
```

As before, use Show Table to check your results. You should see this:

```
Employees

EmployeeNo            LONG(10, 0)
EmployeeName          CHAR(50, 0)

OK
```

The database you created in Chapter 2 featured a column, **SeqNo**, that contained an automatically updated serial number that uniquely identified each row of the Visits table. Can you use DDL to create an Employees table with such a column? Absolutely. The trick is to use COUNTER as the data type. Be sure to drop the Employees table before trying to create this version:

```
Create Table Employees(EmployeeNo Counter, EmployeeName Char(50)) ;
```

Here's what Show Table should report:

```
Employees

EmployeeNo            COUNTER(10, 0)
```

```
EmployeeName              CHAR(50, 0)
```

OK

Altering A Table

Dropping a table every time you want to change it is a nuisance. It's an even greater nuisance if the table is populated with rows, which you must somehow read from the table and save, so you can put them back after you re-create the table.

As you might hope, there's a better way. Assume you had created the Employees table, but forgotten to include the EmployeeName field:

```
Create Table Employees (EmployeeNo Counter) ;

Employees

EmployeeNo                COUNTER(10, 0)
```

OK

You can use the **Alter Table** DDL command to add the EmployeeName column after the table has been created:

```
Alter Table Employees Add Column EmployeeName Char(50) ;

Employees

EmployeeNo                COUNTER(10, 0)
EmployeeName              CHAR(50, 0)
```

OK

You can use **Alter Table** to drop columns, much the same as you use it to add them:

```
Alter Table Employees Drop Column EmployeeName;

Employees

EmployeeNo                COUNTER(10, 0)
```

OK

As you can see, SQL DDL is really quite simple.

Defining Indexes

Most database tables hold data, but you probably recall from Chapter 2 that databases also include special tables, called indexes, that improve data-retrieval performance. You can use SQL DDL to create and delete indexes.

Dropping an unneeded index may improve database update performance, so balancing retrieval performance against update performance is one of the challenges of database design. Without a detailed knowledge of your database system, the only effective way to tune the performance of a database is by experimentation. (That's one good reason to learn more about how your database system organizes its data internally.) Adding and dropping indexes is central to such experimentation. Fortunately, using SQL DDL to add and drop indexes is simple.

Creating An Index

Delete the Employees table from your working database and create a table that matches this one:

```
Employees

EmployeeNo              COUNTER(10, 0)
Lastname                CHAR(50, 0)
Firstname               CHAR(50, 0)

OK
```

Now, create an index on the EmployeeNo column of the Employees table:

```
Create Index EmployeeIndex On Employees (EmployeeNo) ;
```

To use the DDL command to create an index, you must provide the name your new index is to have (EmployeeIndex), the table you wish it to index (Employees), and the field you wish to be indexed (EmployeeNo). When you've issued the command, you can use DBMaker's Show Indexes menu item to report the result:

```
Indexes

Table          Index               Column          Flags
employees      EmployeeIndex(1)    EmployeeNo      A

OK
```

As you can see, you successfully created the index. The (1) after the name of the index indicates that EmployeeNo is the first column of the index. Since you indexed only one column, it is also the only column. The column number is valuable when creating multicolumn indexes, as I'll show you in a moment.

The A in the Flags column indicates that the index is in ascending order. DBMaker uses a D to indicate an index in descending order.

Dropping An Index

Before going on to create more sophisticated indexes, I'll show you how to delete an index, so that you can eliminate any mistakes. To drop the EmployeeIndex that was just created, execute the following DDL command:

```
Drop Index EmployeeIndex On Employees ;
```

By using Show Indexes, you can see that the index has indeed been dropped:

```
Indexes

(no indexes listed)

OK
```

Creating More Elaborate Indexes

Now you can create some more interesting and elaborate indexes for the Employees table. Here's how to create a multicolumn index on Lastname and Firstname:

```
Create Index Nameindex On Employees (Lastname, Firstname) ;
```

The Show Indexes output numbers each component of the index, so you can tell the order of its columns:

```
Indexes

Table          Index            Column          Flags
Employees      Nameindex(1)     Lastname        A
Employees      Nameindex(2)     Firstname       A

OK
```

As mentioned, it's simple to create an index that sorts in descending order, rather than ascending. Delete the Nameindex and re-create it as an index that sorts on Lastname ascending and Firstname descending:

```
Create Index Nameindex On Employees (Lastname Asc, Firstname Desc) ;
```

Here's the report showing the results:

```
Indexes

Table          Index            Column           Flags
Employees      Nameindex(1)     Lastname         A
Employees      Nameindex(2)     Firstname        D

OK
```

The indexes created so far allow multiple records to share the same indexed value. You can use an index to ensure that each row has a unique indexed value by simply specifying that the index is **Unique**. Once this has been done, the database will reject any attempt to add a table row that duplicates an existing value in the index. Here's the DDL form:

```
Create Unique Index Employeeindex On Employees (EmployeeNo) ;

Indexes
```

Note that the Show Indexes report includes **Unique** under the Flags column. Now, no two rows in the Employees table may have the same value of EmployeeNo.

```
Table          Index              Column           Flags
Employees      EmployeeIndex(1)   EmployeeNo       A Unique

OK
```

You can use a unique index to define a primary key for a table. Since a primary key must always be unique, the **Unique** keyword is not used; the **Primary** keyword implies that the index is unique. Here's how to create the index (be sure to drop the existing EmployeeIndex before trying this):

```
Create Index EmployeeIndex On Employees (EmployeeNo) With Primary ;
```

Here's the Show Indexes report:

```
Indexes

Table          Index              Column          Flags
Employees      EmployeeIndex(1)   EmployeeNo      A Unique

OK
```

You're probably surprised and annoyed to find that the report is no different than before. The Access ODBC driver does not support certain Level 2 ODBC API calls necessary to report the result accurately. So, even though JDBC has a **DatabaseMetaData.getExportedKeys( )** method, Access will not respond. Instead, it throws a **SQLException** that explains the driver is not capable of executing the requested function.

How can you verify that the DDL command did its job? One way is to use Access. By opening the database and using View|Indexes, you can verify that the primary key was established. As you can see in Figure 9.2, a key icon appears at the left of the EmployeeNo row. This proves the DDL command did its job.

You can use either of two other options in creating indexes. Each specifies a different way of dealing with SQL null values in the indexed column. Since a primary key column can never be null, neither of these options is needed, or can be used, with the **Primary** option.

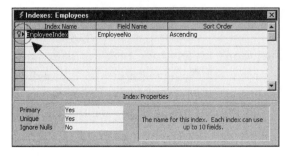

Figure 9.2
Verifying the creation of the primary index.

- The first option specifies that SQL nulls are not allowed in the indexed column. Any attempt to add a table row with a null value in the indexed column will be rejected by the database. Here's how it's done:

```
Create Index EmployeeIndex On Employees (EmployeeNo) With Disallow Null ;
```

- The second option specifies that SQL nulls are allowed, but shouldn't appear in the index. This makes the index more compact. The drawback is that the index cannot be used to speed retrieval of the rows having the null value. Here's the DDL command:

```
Create Index EmployeeIndex On Employees (EmployeeNo) With Ignore Null ;
```

The Show Indexes report is not capable of reporting the use of **Disallow Null** or **Ignore Null**. If you're concerned that your command may not have worked, you'll have to use Access to verify that the index was properly built.

Defining Constraints

In addition to letting you define tables and indexes, SQL DDL lets you specify *constraints*—rules that table rows must follow. If you try to add a table row that violates a constraint, the row is rejected. Similarly, any changes or deletions of table rows are first checked against any applicable constraints. The change or deletion will be allowed only if no constraints are violated.

Why Be Constrained?

Constraints keep watch over the database, helping ensure the data is accurate and consistent. They don't do anything magical; you can write application code that does the same work that constraints do. If you did so, however, you would be forced to include the related checks in *every* program that changes the database. This would be difficult if you were working with several programmers; the checks would have to be included in their code as well as your own. Even if they agreed to include the checks in their programs, they might forget or might misuse them. Either way, database accuracy and consistency could be compromised.

By creating centralized constraints, you can be certain that no change to the database violates the constraints you've defined. Moreover, constraints are applied comprehensively. If you write checks into your Java application, anyone with the ability to change the database by means of SQL commands could circumvent them. When you define database constraints, *everyone* is ruled by them.

Variations In Constraint Syntax

Unfortunately, most databases have yet to bring their syntax for defining database constraints into conformance with SQL-92. This means you have to write somewhat different DDL commands for each database system. This book follows the syntax used by Microsoft Access; the syntax used by Microsoft SQL Server is similar. If you're using some other database, you'll need to consult your reference manual or online help file to learn the proper syntax.

Access supports two kinds of constraints: The first applies to a single field, and the second applies to multiple fields, such as the components of a composite key. Each uses a similar syntax.

Defining Field Constraints

When you create a table, you can specify a field constraint for any columns you desire. You can also specify a field constraint when you add a column to an existing table. There are four possible kinds of constraints:

- *Primary Key*—Identifies the related column as the primary key of the table. Since a table can have only one primary key, this constraint can be applied to only a single column. If you want to identify a composite key as the primary key, you must use a multifield constraint. These are described in the next section.

- *Unique*—Prohibits two rows within the table from having the same value in the related column.

- *Not Null*—Prohibits the column from containing a SQL null value.

- *References*—Identifies the related column as a foreign key and specifies the table and primary key referenced by the foreign key.

The following example shows how to define constraints. Assume that, in addition to the Employees table, you have an Assignments table, created like this:

```
Create Table Assignments (EmployeeNo Int, DeptNo Int, HoursPerWeek Int) ;
```

Here's the table structure report for the Assignments table, as provided by DBMaker:

```
Assignments

EmployeeNo              LONG(10, 0)
DeptNo                  LONG(10, 0)
HoursPerWeek            LONG(10, 0)

OK
```

Now, define a Departments table and include a constraint that identifies the department number as its primary key:

```
Create Table Departments (
  DeptNo Counter Constraint Itsthekey Primary Key,
  DeptName Char(50) Not Null
) ;
```

Here's the indexes report, showing that the constraint caused the automatic creation of the index used by the primary key:

```
Indexes

Table           Index           Column          Flags
Departments     Itsthekey(1)    DeptNo          A Unique

OK
```

The constraints provided by Access are like "smart indexes." They establish relationships between tables and build indexes that make it easier to access data using the relationships. Note that the constraint was given a name, Itsthekey. You can use this name to drop the constraint:

```
Alter Table Departments Drop Constraint Itsthekey ;
```

The **Unique** or **Not Null** constraint could be used in place of the **Primary Key** constraint. However, only one constraint can be specified for each field.

Now, turn your attention to the **References** constraint. First, you need to define a primary key for the Employees table. To do so, drop the Employees table and then re-create it as follows:

```
Drop Table Employees;
Create Table Employees
  (EmployeeNo Counter Constraint Pk Primary Key,
   EmployeeName char(50)
) ;
```

Now, drop and re-create the Assignments table:

```
Drop Table Assignments;
Create Table Assignments (
  EmployeeNo Int Constraint Fk1 References Employees(EmployeeNo),
  DeptNo Int Constraint Fk2 References Departments(DeptNo),
  HoursPerWeek Int
) ;
```

This DDL command defines two field constraints: one for the Employeeno column and one for the Deptno column. Each is a **References** constraint that identifies its related column as a foreign key, and gives the table and column of the corresponding primary key. Here's the indexes report from DBMaker, showing what happened:

```
Indexes

Table            Index           Column          Flags
Assignments      Fk1(1)          EmployeeNo      A
Assignments      Fk2(1)          DeptNo          A
Departments      Itsthekey(1)    DeptNo          A Unique
Employees        Pk(1)           EmployeeNo      A Unique

OK
```

You can also specify a **References** constraint for a field that references a composite primary key. Just include a comma-separated list of fields inside the parentheses of the **References** clause:

```
… Constraint constraintname References tablename (key1, key2, key3) ;
```

Defining Table Constraints

You can also define constraints that apply to the entire table, rather than to a single field. The syntax is similar to the single-field form. Re-create the Assignments table, this time identifying its primary key by using a table constraint:

```
Drop Table Assignments;
Create Table Assignments (
    EmployeeNo Int Constraint Fk1 References Employees(EmployeeNo),
    DeptNo Int Constraint Fk2 References Departments(DeptNo),
    HoursPerWeek Int,
    Constraint Pk Primary Key (EmployeeNo, DeptNo)
) ;
```

Here's the report from DBMaker, showing what actually happened:

```
Indexes

Table            Index            Column           Flags
Assignments      Pk(1)            EmployeeNo       A Unique
Assignments      Pk(2)            DeptNo           A Unique
Assignments      Fk1(1)           EmployeeNo       A
Assignments      Fk2(1)           DeptNo           A
Departments      Itsthekey(1)     DeptNo           A Unique
Employees        Pk(1)            EmployeeNo       A Unique

OK
```

You can specify each of the field constraints (**Primary Key, Unique, Not Null,** and **References**) as a table constraint. For **Primary Key, Unique,** and **Not Null,** the constraint type name is immediately followed by parentheses that enclose a comma-separated list of fields to which the constraint applies. For the **References** constraint, a slightly more complex form is used

```
Foreign Key (field1, field2, …) References foreigntable (key1, key2, …)
```

where *field1, field2,* … refer to columns in the current table, and *key1, key2,* … refer to columns in the table referenced by fields of the current table.

DDL Summary

Table 9.3 summarizes the SQL DDL commands you've learned, using modified Backus-Naur form (BNF). BNF allows the many possible variations of a command to be compactly represented, so if you're not familiar with BNF, it's worth getting acquainted.

In the table, all SQL keywords appear in uppercase letters, and programmer-supplied names appear in lowercase letters. Brackets ([ ]) are used to enclose optional clauses of each command. You can include or omit the optional clauses according to need. Within the brackets, you may include individual choices, each separated from its neighbors by a bar (|). For example, the phrase

```
go [home | to work]
```

means you can write "go", "go home", or "go to work".

Braces ({}) are used to include alternative phrases. You must choose one, and only one, of the choices enclosed within the braces. For example, the phrase

```
go {home | to work}
```

means you can write "go home" or "go to work".

An ellipsis following a phrase enclosed in braces indicates that you can repeat the phrase any number of times. For example, the phrase

```
go {home | to work} …
```

means you can write "go home", "go home home", "go to work to work", "go home to work", "go work to home", and so on.

Finally, any phrase enclosed in angle brackets (<>) is defined elsewhere in the table. Look it up and substitute its definition. For example, the BNF statements

```
go <somewhere>
<somewhere>::= {home | to work}
```

mean you can write "go home" or "go to work", just as before. The special symbol (::=) is used to separate the name of a definition from the definition itself.

TABLE 9.3

SUMMARY OF **SQL DDL** COMMANDS.

ALTER TABLE table ADD COLUMN

  column type

  CONSTRAINT constraint

  {PRIMARY KEY

  |UNIQUE

  |NOT NULL

  |REFERENCES foreigntable [(foreignfield {, foreignfield} ...)]

  }

;

ALTER TABLE ADD CONSTRAINT constraint

  {PRIMARY KEY primary {, primary} ...)

  |UNIQUE (unique {, unique} ...)

  |NOT NULL (notnull {, notnull} ...)

  |FOREIGN KEY (ref {, ref} ...)

    REFERENCES foreigntable

    [(foreignfield {, foreignfield} ...)]

  }

;

ALTER TABLE DROP CONSTRAINT constraint ;

CREATE [unique] INDEX index ON table

(

  column [ASC|DESC]

  {, column [ASC|DESC]} ...

) [WITH PRIMARY | WITH DISALLOW NULL | WITH IGNORE NULL] ;

(continued)

TABLE 9.3

SUMMARY OF **SQL DDL** COMMANDS (*CONTINUED*).

CREATE TABLE table

(

  column type

   [CONSTRAINT constraint

    {PRIMARY KEY

    |UNIQUE

    |NOT NULL

    |REFERENCES foreigntable [(foreignfield {, foreignfield} ...)]

     }

   ]

  {, column type

   [CONSTRAINT constraint

    {PRIMARY KEY

    |UNIQUE

    |NOT NULL

    |REFERENCES foreigntable [(foreignfield {, foreignfield} ...)]

     }

   ]

  } ...

) ;

DROP INDEX index ON table ;

DROP TABLE table ;

The DBMaker Application

The DBMaker application is the vehicle you'll use for studying SQL DDL. Space doesn't permit me to show the entire program, but I'll show the highlights. The complete source code is on the CD-ROM, in the directory corresponding to this chapter.

Listing 9.1 shows the fields and **main( )** method of DBMaker. DBMaker uses menus, so the **DBMaker** class defines several menu-related fields, including a **MenuBar**, several **Menu**s, and a number of **MenuItem**s. Otherwise, it doesn't yet seem much different from other applications you've studied.

LISTING 9.1 FIELDS AND MAIN( ) METHOD OF DBMAKER.

```
import java.awt.*;
import java.awt.event.*;
import java.sql.*;

public class DBMaker extends Frame
implements ActionListener, Application
{
    MenuBar    theMenuBar      = new MenuBar( );

    Menu       theConnectMenu  = new Menu("Connect");
    MenuItem theOpenConnect    = new MenuItem(
                                     "Open Connection");
    MenuItem theCloseConnect   = new MenuItem(
                                     "Close Connection");
    MenuItem theExit           = new MenuItem("Exit");

    Menu       theTableMenu    = new Menu("Table");
    MenuItem theShowTable      = new MenuItem("Show Table");
    MenuItem theCreateTable    = new MenuItem("Create Table");
    MenuItem theAddColumn      = new MenuItem("Add Column");
    MenuItem theDropColumn     = new MenuItem("Drop Column");
    MenuItem theDropTable      = new MenuItem("Drop Table");

    Menu       theIndexMenu    = new Menu("Index");
    MenuItem theShowIndex      = new MenuItem("Show Indexes");
    MenuItem theCreateIndex    = new MenuItem("Create Index");
    MenuItem theDropIndex      = new MenuItem("Drop Index");

    Menu       theSQLMenu      = new Menu("SQL");
    MenuItem theDoQuery        = new MenuItem("Execute Query");
```

```
Label      theSource     = new Label( );
TextArea   theResult     = new TextArea(15, 64);
TextField theStatus      = new TextField(64);

Font       theFixedFont  = new Font("Courier",
                                Font.PLAIN, 12);

Connection         theConnection;
DatabaseMetaData   theDBMetaData;
Statement          theStatement;

public static void main(String args[ ])
{
    new DBMaker( ).init( );
}
```

The init( ) Method

Listing 9.2 shows the **init**( ) method, which builds the user interface. It's dominated by the code to establish the menus: setting the menu bar, adding the menus and menu items, and setting listeners for action events. Despite these differences, it follows the pattern that by now has become familiar.

LISTING 9.2   THE INIT( ) METHOD.

```
public void init( )
{
    setTitle("DBMaker");

    setMenuBar(theMenuBar);

    theMenuBar.add(theConnectMenu);
    theMenuBar.add(theTableMenu);
    theMenuBar.add(theIndexMenu);
    theMenuBar.add(theSQLMenu);

    theConnectMenu.add(theOpenConnect);
    theConnectMenu.add(theCloseConnect);
    theConnectMenu.addSeparator( );
    theConnectMenu.add(theExit);

    theTableMenu.add(theShowTable);
    theTableMenu.add(theCreateTable);
    theTableMenu.add(theAddColumn);
    theTableMenu.add(theDropColumn);
    theTableMenu.add(theDropTable);
```

```
        theIndexMenu.add(theShowIndex);
        theIndexMenu.add(theCreateIndex);
        theIndexMenu.add(theDropIndex);

        theSQLMenu.add(theDoQuery);

        add(theResult, "Center");
        add(theStatus, "South");

        theCloseConnect.setEnabled(false);
        theCloseConnect.setEnabled(false);
        theTableMenu    .setEnabled(false);
        theIndexMenu    .setEnabled(false);
        theSQLMenu      .setEnabled(false);

        theResult.setEditable(false);
        theResult.setFont(theFixedFont);
        theStatus.setEditable(false);

        theOpenConnect   .addActionListener(this);
        theCloseConnect  .addActionListener(this);
        theCreateTable   .addActionListener(this);
        theAddColumn     .addActionListener(this);
        theDropColumn    .addActionListener(this);
        theDropTable     .addActionListener(this);
        theExit          .addActionListener(this);
        theShowIndex     .addActionListener(this);
        theCreateIndex   .addActionListener(this);
        theDropIndex     .addActionListener(this);
        theShowTable     .addActionListener(this);
        theDoQuery       .addActionListener(this);

        addWindowListener(new WindowHandler(this));

        pack( );
        show( );
    }
```

The actionPerformed( ) Method

The **actionPerformed( )** method is shown in Listing 9.3. It responds to action events sent by menu items, invoking the method appropriate to each user request.

LISTING 9.3   THE ACTIONPERFORMED( ) METHOD.

```
public void actionPerformed(ActionEvent event)
{
    theStatus.setText("Status: OK");
    Object source = event.getSource( );
    if (source == theOpenConnect)      openConn( );
    else if (source == theCloseConnect) closeConn( );
    else if (source == theExit)        requestClose( );
    else if (source == theShowTable)    showTable( );
    else if (source == theCreateTable)  createTable( );
    else if (source == theAddColumn)    addColumn( );
    else if (source == theDropColumn)   dropColumn( );
    else if (source == theDropTable)    dropTable( );
    else if (source == theShowIndex)    showIndex( );
    else if (source == theCreateIndex)  createIndex( );
    else if (source == theDropIndex)    dropIndex( );
    else if (source == theDoQuery)      doQuery( );
}
```

The openConn( ) Method

The **openConn**( ) method, shown in Listing 9.4, opens a database connection. It uses the familiar **LoginDialog02** to accomplish this purpose. The method also enables and disables selected menu items to reflect the successful opening of a database connection.

LISTING 9.4   THE OPENCONN( ) METHOD.

```
public void openConn( )
{
    try
    {
        LoginDialog02 theLoginDialog02 = null;
        theLoginDialog02
          = new LoginDialog02("Open Connection",
            "jdbc:odbc:", this, true);
        theLoginDialog02.setVisible(true);
        if (theLoginDialog02.getStatus( ))
        {
            Class.forName (
              "sun.jdbc.odbc.JdbcOdbcDriver");
            if (theConnection != null)
                theConnection.close( );
            theConnection =
              DriverManager.getConnection(
                theLoginDialog02.getURL( ),
```

```
                    theLoginDialog02.getUser( ),
                    theLoginDialog02.getPassword( ));
                theDBMetaData
                  = theConnection.getMetaData( );
                theStatement
                  = theConnection.createStatement( );
            }
            theSource.setText("DSN: "
              + theLoginDialog02.getURL( ));
            theLoginDialog02.dispose( );
            theOpenConnect .setEnabled(false);
            theCloseConnect.setEnabled(true);
            theTableMenu    .setEnabled(true);
            theIndexMenu    .setEnabled(true);
            theSQLMenu      .setEnabled(true);
        }
        catch (SQLException sql)
          { handleError(sql); }
        catch (ClassNotFoundException ex)
          { handleError(ex); }
}
```

The closeConn( ) Method

The **closeConn( )** method, shown in Listing 9.5, closes a database connection. Like **openConn( )**, it enables and disables selected menu items to reflect the closing of the open connection.

LISTING 9.5   THE closeConn( ) METHOD.

```
public void closeConn( )
{
    try
    {
        if (theConnection != null)
            theConnection.close( );
        theOpenConnect .setEnabled(true);
        theCloseConnect.setEnabled(false);
        theCloseConnect.setEnabled(false);
        theTableMenu    .setEnabled(false);
        theIndexMenu    .setEnabled(false);
        theSQLMenu      .setEnabled(false);
    }
    catch (SQLException sql)  { handleError(sql); }
}
```

The showTable( ) Method

Listing 9.6 shows the **showTable( )** method, the first of several methods that, in response to a user request, do something using the open connection. The **showTable( )** method is responsible for displaying a report that shows the structure of a table selected by the user. A special dialog, **SelectTableDialog**, obtains the user's selection.

The method uses **DatabaseMetaData.getColumns( )** to generate a **ResultSet** that describes the table columns. From the **ResultSet**, it extracts columns that give the name, type, size, and scale of each column of the selected table. It also extracts a flag that tells whether each column can contain SQL nulls. It formats and displays the extracted information.

LISTING 9.6   THE SHOWTABLE( ) METHOD.

```
public void showTable( )
{
    try
    {
        SelectTableDialog st_dialog
          = new SelectTableDialog(this, theConnection);
        st_dialog.setVisible(true);
        String table_name = st_dialog.getTableName( );
        st_dialog.setVisible(false);
        st_dialog.dispose( );
        if (table_name == null) return;
        clear( );
        println(table_name);
        println( );

        ResultSet rs1 = theDBMetaData.getColumns(null,
          null, table_name, null);
        while (rs1.next( ))
        {
            String col_name
              = nonNull(rs1.getString(4));
            String type_name
              = nonNull(rs1.getString(6));
            String col_size
              = nonNull(rs1.getString(7));
            int    scale    = rs1.getInt(9);
            int    nullable = rs1.getInt(11);

            col_name = padTo(col_name, 24);
```

```
            print(col_name + " " + type_name
               + "(" + col_size + ", " + scale + ") ");
            if (DatabaseMetaData.columnNoNulls
               == nullable) print("Non-null");
            println( );
        }
        println("\nOK");
    }
    catch (SQLException sql) { handleError(sql); }
}
```

The createTable( ) Method

The **createTable**( ) method, shown in Listing 9.7, creates a new database table.
It prompts the user for the name of the table and information needed to create
a single table column using a special dialog, **CreateTableDialog**. After the table
has been created, the user can use the Table|Add Column menu item to add
columns to the table. The **doQuery**( ) method executes a generated SQL DDL
Create Table command.

LISTING 9.7   THE CREATETABLE( ) METHOD.

```
public void createTable( )
{
    CreateTableDialog ct_dialog =
      new CreateTableDialog(this, theConnection);

    ct_dialog.setVisible(true);
    ct_dialog.setVisible(false);

    boolean isStatusOK
      = ct_dialog.isStatusOK( );
    String  table_name
      = ct_dialog.getTableName( );
    String  col_name
      = ct_dialog.getColumnName( );
    String  col_type
      = nonNull(ct_dialog.getType( ));
    String  col_len
      = ct_dialog.getLength( );
    String  column_constraint
      = ct_dialog.getColumnConstraint( );
    String  table_constraint
      = ct_dialog.getTableConstraint( );

    ct_dialog.dispose( );
```

```
    if (isStatusOK)
    {
        if (table_name == null) return;
        String sql = "CREATE TABLE ";
        sql += table_name + " ( ";
        sql += col_name + " ";
        sql += col_type + " ";
        sql += col_len + " ";
        sql += column_constraint + " ) ";
        sql += table_constraint + " ;";
        doQuery(sql);
    }
}
```

The addColumn( ) Method

Listing 9.8 shows the **addColumn**( ) method, which adds a column to an existing table. Information on the column is obtained from the special dialog, **AddColumnDialog**. The **Alter Table Add Column** SQL DDL command is executed by means of the **doQuery**( ) method.

LISTING 9.8   THE ADDCOLUMN( ) METHOD.

```
public void addColumn( )
{
    AddColumnDialog ac_dialog =
      new AddColumnDialog(this, theConnection);

    ac_dialog.setVisible(true);
    ac_dialog.setVisible(false);

    boolean isStatusOK = ac_dialog.isStatusOK( );
    String table_name  = ac_dialog.getTableName( );
    String col_name     = ac_dialog.getColumnName( );
    String col_type     = nonNull(ac_dialog.getType( ));
    String col_len      = ac_dialog.getLength( );
    String constraint   = ac_dialog.getConstraint( );

    ac_dialog.dispose( );

    if (isStatusOK)
    {
        if (table_name == null) return;
        String sql = "ALTER TABLE ";
        sql += table_name + " ADD COLUMN ";
        sql +=  col_name + " ";
```

```
    sql += col_type + " ";
    sql += col_len + " ";
    sql += constraint + " ;";
    doQuery(sql);
    }
}
```

The dropColumn( ) Method

Listing 9.9 shows the **dropColumn**( ) method, used to drop a column from a database table. A special **DropColumnDialog** allows the user to identify the table and column. The SQL DDL **Alter Table Drop Column** command is used to accomplish the drop.

LISTING 9.9   THE DROPCOLUMN( ) METHOD.

```
public void dropColumn( )
{
    DropColumnDialog dc_dialog =
      new DropColumnDialog(this, theConnection);

    dc_dialog.setVisible(true);
    dc_dialog.setVisible(false);

    boolean isStatusOK = dc_dialog.isStatusOK( );
    String table_name  = dc_dialog.getTableName( );
    String col_name    = dc_dialog.getColumnName( );

    dc_dialog.dispose( );

    if (isStatusOK)
    {
        if (table_name == null || col_name == null)
            return;
        String sql = "ALTER TABLE ";
        sql += table_name + " DROP COLUMN ";
        sql += col_name + " ;";
        doQuery(sql);
    }
}
```

The dropTable( ) Method

The **dropTable**( ) method is shown in Listing 9.10. It is similar to the **dropColumn**( ) method, except that an entire table is dropped. The SQL DDL **Drop Table** command is used.

LISTING 9.10   THE DROPTABLE( ) METHOD.

```
public void dropTable( )
{
    SelectTableDialog st_dialog
      = new SelectTableDialog(this, theConnection);
    st_dialog.setVisible(true);
    String table_name = st_dialog.getTableName( );
    st_dialog.setVisible(false);
    st_dialog.dispose( );
    if (table_name == null) return;

    String sql = "Drop table " + table_name + " ;";
    doQuery(sql);
}
```

The showIndex( ) Method

The **showIndex**( ) method, shown in Listing 9.11, displays all the indexes defined in the open database. It uses the **DatabaseMetaData.getTables**( ) and **DatabaseMetaData.getIndexInfo**( ) methods to obtain its information. Although the JDBC API defines other methods that could provide additional useful information (e.g., **DatabaseMetaData.getExportedKeys**( )), the Microsoft Access ODBC driver does not support these. The index information is formatted and displayed in the **TextArea**.

LISTING 9.11   THE SHOWINDEX( ) METHOD.

```
public void showIndex( )
{
    try
    {
        clear( );
        println("Indexes");
        println( );

        DatabaseMetaData dbmeta
          = theConnection.getMetaData( );
        ResultSet rs1 = dbmeta.getTables(null, null,
          null, null);
        boolean first = true;

        while (rs1.next( ))
        {
            String table = nonNull(rs1.getString(3));
            String type  = nonNull(rs1.getString(4));
```

```
                if (!type.equals("TABLE")) continue;

            ResultSet rs2
              = theDBMetaData.getIndexInfo(null, null,
                table, false, true);
            while (rs2.next( ))
            {
                String  table_name
                  = nonNull(rs2.getString(3));
                boolean non_unique
                  = rs2.getBoolean(4);
                String  index_name
                  = nonNull(rs2.getString(6));
                short   index_type
                  = rs2.getShort(7);
                short   index_part
                  = rs2.getShort(8);
                String  col_name
                  = nonNull(rs2.getString(9));
                String  asc_desc
                  = nonNull(rs2.getString(10));

                if (DatabaseMetaData
                  .tableIndexStatistic == index_type)
                    continue;
                if (first)
                {
                    first = false;
                    println(
                        "Table                 "
                      + "Index                 "
                      + "Column                "
                      + "Flags");
                }

                if (index_part > 0)
                    index_name += "(" + index_part
                    + ")";

                print(padTo(table_name, 24));
                print(padTo(index_name, 24));
                print(padTo(col_name,   24));
                print(asc_desc);
                print(non_unique ? "" : " Unique");
                println( );
            }
```

```
        }
        println("\nOK");
    }
    catch (SQLException sql) { handleError(sql); }
}
```

The createIndex( ) Method

The **createIndex**( ) method, shown in Listing 9.12, creates an index on specified columns of a specified table. The **CreateIndexDialog**, which lets the user
select the table and columns, has an interesting user interface (not shown in this
chapter because of a lack of space) that is worth study. It displays two **Lists** side
by side, one showing columns of a selected table and one showing columns
selected as index keys. You can move entries from either **List** to the other by
clicking an appropriate button.

Based on the information received from the dialog, **createIndex**( ) uses the SQL
Create Index command to build the index.

LISTING 9.12   THE CREATEINDEX( ) METHOD.

```
public void createIndex( )
{
    String  index   = null;
    String  table   = null;
    String  keys[ ] = null;
    boolean unique  = false;
    String  type    = null;

    CreateIndexDialog ci_dialog
      = new CreateIndexDialog(this, theConnection);
    ci_dialog.setVisible(true);
    if (ci_dialog.isStatusOK( ))
    {
        index  = ci_dialog.getIndexName( );
        table  = ci_dialog.getTableName( );
        keys   = ci_dialog.getKeyNames( );
        unique = ci_dialog.isUniqueKey( );
        type   = ci_dialog.getType( );
    }
    ci_dialog.setVisible(false);
    ci_dialog.dispose( );
    if (index == null) return;
```

```
String sql = "CREATE ";
if (unique) sql += "UNIQUE ";
sql += "INDEX " + index + " ON " + table + "(";
boolean first = true;
for (int i = 0; i < keys.length; i++)
{
    if (!first) sql += ", ";
    sql += keys[i] + " ";
    first = false;
}
sql += ") WITH " + type + ";";
doQuery(sql);
}
```

The dropIndex( ) Method

Listing 9.13 shows the **dropIndex( )** method, which is used to drop an index from a specified table. It uses the SQL **Drop Index** command to accomplish its purpose.

LISTING 9.13   THE DROPINDEX( ) METHOD.

```
public void dropIndex( )
{
    try
    {
        SelectIndexDialog si_dialog
          = new SelectIndexDialog(this, theConnection);
        si_dialog.setVisible(true);
        String index_name = si_dialog.getIndexName( );
        si_dialog.setVisible(false);
        si_dialog.dispose( );
        if (index_name == null) return;

        int colon    = index_name.indexOf(": ");
        if (colon < 0)
            throw new SQLException("Internal error.");
        String table  = index_name.substring(0, colon);
        String index  = index_name.substring(colon + 2);

        String sql = "Drop index " + index + " on "
          + table + " ;";
        clear( );
        println("SQL: " + sql);
```

```
        int rows = theStatement.executeUpdate(sql);
        println("\nOK");
    }
    catch (SQLException sql)  { handleError(sql); }
}
```

The doQuery( ) Method

The **doQuery**( ) method, shown in Listing 9.14, is one of the most important methods in DBMaker, because it shows how to use the **Statement.execute**( ) method to execute an arbitrary SQL statement, which could be a query or DDL statement. DDL statements do not generate a SQL table, so the familiar **executeQuery**( ) method is not appropriate for executing them.

The **execute**( ) method returns a **boolean** that is **true** if the SQL command generated a **ResultSet**, and false otherwise. If the value is **true**, getResultSet( ) provides access to the **ResultSet**, which is processed in the usual way. If the value is **false**, the **getUpdateCount**( ) method is called. This method returns the number of rows updated by the SQL statement or the value -1. If the value is something other than -1, the number of rows updated is displayed.

The value -1 is needed because some SQL commands (for instance, those that invoke stored procedures) may return multiple result sets. Therefore, the process of calling **getResultSet**( ) or **getUpdateCount**( ) is repeated inside a **while** loop, to accommodate multiple result sets. At the bottom of the loop, the **getMoreResults**( ) method is used to advance to the next result set or update count. The value -1 indicates that all result sets have been processed, in which case a **break** is used to exit the **while** loop. Note that **getUpdateCount**( ) is enclosed in a **try-catch** block. Although the JDBC documentation does not suggest that this should be necessary, certain DDL commands return neither a result set nor an update count, which results in the throwing of a **SQLException**. The **try-catch** deals with this possibility, treating an exception as though the call to **getUpdateCount**( ) had succeeded.

LISTING 9.14 THE DOQUERY( ) METHOD.

```
public void doQuery( )
{
    GetSQLDialog sql_dialog = new GetSQLDialog(this);
    sql_dialog.setVisible(true);
    String sql = sql_dialog.getSQL( );
```

```
        sql_dialog.setVisible(false);
        sql_dialog.dispose( );
        if (sql.length( ) == 0) return;
        doQuery(sql);
}

public void doQuery(String sql)
{
    try
    {
        clear( );
        println("SQL: " + sql);
        println( );

        boolean is_result_set
            = theStatement.execute(sql);
        while (true)
        {
            if (is_result_set)
            {
                ResultSet rs
                    = theStatement.getResultSet( );
                if (rs != null)
                {
                    DisplayableResultSet03 dsr
                        = new DisplayableResultSet03(rs);
                    println(dsr.getString(true));
                }
            }
            else
            {
                try
                {
                    int update_count
                        = theStatement.getUpdateCount( );
                    if (update_count == -1) break;
                    println("" + update_count
                        + " rows updated.");
                }
                catch (SQLException done) { break; }
            }
            is_result_set
                = theStatement.getMoreResults( );
        }
    }
    catch (SQLException ex)  { handleError(ex); }
}
```

The TextArea-Related Methods

Listing 9.15 shows the methods used to display information in the **TextArea**. These allow familiar **println( )** and **print( )** calls, as well as a **cursorHome( )** method, which returns the cursor to the top left of the **TextArea**, and a **clear( )** method, which erases the current contents of the **TextArea**.

LISTING 9.15   THE TEXTAREA-RELATED METHODS.

```
public void cursorHome( )
{
    theResult.select(0, 0);
}

public void clear( )
{
    theResult.setText("");
}

public void println (String s)
{
    print(s + "\n");
}

public void println ( )
{
    print("\n");
}

public void print(String s)
{
    theResult.append(s);
}
```

The String-Related Methods

Listing 9.16 shows several **String**-related methods, including: **nonNull( )**, which replaces a null **String** with an empty one; **padTo( )**, which right pads a **String** to a specified length using spaces; and **space( )**, which returns a **String** containing the specified number of spaces.

LISTING 9.16   THE STRING-RELATED METHODS.

```
public String nonNull(String s)
{
    return (s != null) ? s : "";
}
```

```
public String padTo(String s, int n)
{
    int len = s.length( );
    if (len >= n) return s.substring(0, n);
    else return s + space(n - len);
}

public String space(int n)
{
    String result = "";
    for (int i = 1; i <= n; i++) result += ' ';
    return result;
}
```

The requestClose( ) and handleError( ) Methods

Listing 9.17 shows the **requestClose**( ) and **handleError**( ) methods. These are essentially identical to previous versions, shown here for completeness.

LISTING 9.17   THE REQUESTCLOSE( ) AND HANDLEERROR( ) METHODS.

```
public void requestClose( )
{
    closeConn( );
    setVisible(false);
    System.exit(0);
}

public void handleError(Throwable t)
{
    theStatus.setText("Error: " + t.getMessage( ));
    t.printStackTrace( );
}
}
```

The AddColumnDialog.loadTables( ) Method

Listing 9.18 shows the **loadTables**( ) method of the **AddColumnDialog** class. The method fills a **Choice** with items representing the names of database tables. It uses the **DatabaseMetaData.getTables**( ) method to obtain the table names, ignoring table types other than TABLE, so that system tables will not be included in the **Choice**.

LISTING 9.18   THE ADDCOLUMNDIALOG.LOADTABLES( ) METHOD.

```
public void loadTables( )
{
    theTables.removeAll( );
    try
    {
        DatabaseMetaData dbmeta
          = theConnection.getMetaData( );
        ResultSet rs1 = dbmeta.getTables(null, null,
          null, null);

        while (rs1.next( ))
        {
            String table = nonNull(rs1.getString(3));
            String type  = nonNull(rs1.getString(4));

            if (type.equals("TABLE"))
                theTables.add(table);
        }
    }
    catch (SQLException sql) { ; }
}
```

The AddColumnDialog.loadTypes( ) Method

Listing 9.19 shows the **loadTypes( )** method of the **AddColumnDialog** class. This method loads a **Choice** with the names of the data types implemented by the open database. It uses the local type names, rather than the standard SQL names. Column 2 of the result set (not used by **loadTypes( )**), however, contains a **short** value that indicates the standard SQL name. The possible values are defined in the class **java.sql.Types**.

LISTING 9.19   THE ADDCOLUMNDIALOG.LOADTYPES( ) METHOD.

```
public void loadTypes( )
{
    theType.removeAll( );
    theLengthTypes = new Vector( );
    try
    {
        DatabaseMetaData dbmeta =
          theConnection.getMetaData( );
        ResultSet rs1 = dbmeta.getTypeInfo( );
```

```
        while (rs1.next( ))
        {
            String name  = rs1.getString(1);
            String parms = rs1.getString(6);
            theType.add(name);
            if (parms != null &&
              parms.equals("MAX LENGTH"))
                theLengthTypes.addElement(name);
        }

        theDefaultType = null;
        if (theLengthTypes.indexOf("VARCHAR") >= 0)
            theDefaultType = "VARCHAR";
        else if (theLengthTypes.indexOf("TEXT") >= 0)
            theDefaultType = "TEXT";
        else if (theLengthTypes.indexOf("CHAR") >= 0)
            theDefaultType = "CHAR";
    }
    catch (SQLException sql) { ; }
}
```

The CreateIndexDialog.loadColumns( ) Method

Listing 9.20 shows the **loadColumns**( ) method of the **CreateIndexDialog** class. This method loads a **List** with the names of all the columns of a specified table, based on information obtained from **DatabaseMetaData.getColumns**( ). It appends ASC to each name to indicate that the column is to be sorted in ascending order; a user-interface function permits ASC to be changed to DESC.

LISTING 9.20   THE CREATEINDEXDIALOG.LOADCOLUMNS( )
                METHOD.

```
public void loadColumns( )
{
    theColumns.removeAll( );
    theKeys   .removeAll( );
    try
    {
        DatabaseMetaData dbmeta
          = theConnection.getMetaData( );
        String table = theTables.getSelectedItem( );
        if (table == null) return;
        ResultSet rs2 = dbmeta.getColumns(null, null,
          table, null);
```

```
        while (rs2.next( ))
        {
            String col = nonNull(rs2.getString(4));
            theColumns.add(col + " ASC");
        }
    }
    catch (SQLException sql) { ; }
}
```

The SelectIndexDialog.loadIndexes( ) Method

Listing 9.21 shows the **loadIndexes**( ) method of the **SelectIndexDialog** class. It loads a **List** with the names of every index defined in the database, using the **DatabaseMetaData.getTables**( ) method to identify all database tables and the **DatabaseMetaData.getIndexInfo**( ) method to obtain information on the indexes associated with each table.

LISTING 9.21   THE SELECTINDEXDIALOG.LOADINDEXES( ) METHOD.

```
public void loadIndexes( )
{
    theList.removeAll( );
    try
    {
        Hashtable hash = new Hashtable( );
        DatabaseMetaData dbmeta
          = theConnection.getMetaData( );
        ResultSet rs1 = dbmeta.getTables(null, null,
          null, null);
        boolean first = true;

        while (rs1.next( ))
        {
            String table = nonNull(rs1.getString(3));
            String type  = nonNull(rs1.getString(4));

            if (!type.equals("TABLE")) continue;

            ResultSet rs2 = dbmeta.getIndexInfo(null,
              null, table, false, true);
            while (rs2.next( ))
            {
```

```
                String  table_name
                  = nonNull(rs2.getString(3));
                String  index_name
                  = nonNull(rs2.getString(6));
                short   index_type
                  = rs2.getShort(7);

                if (index_type ==
                  DatabaseMetaData.tableIndexStatistic) continue;
                    hash.put(table_name + ": "
                    + index_name, "");
            }
        }
        Enumeration enum = hash.keys( );
        while (enum.hasMoreElements( ))
        {
            String index = (String) enum.nextElement( );
            theList.add(index);
        }
    }
    catch (SQLException sql) { ; }
}
```

Summary

The **Create, Drop,** and **Alter** verbs may be used to create, delete, and modify tables, indexes, and constraints. Constraints allow you to enforce rules that help ensure data is valid. Available constraints include **Primary Key, Unique, Not Null,** and **References.** The **References** constraint ensures the referential integrity of a primary-foreign key relationship.

10 SQL DATA MANIPULATION LANGUAGE

Т

he one unchanging characteristic of the world is change. Therefore, if the data stored in a database is to model the world accurately, the data must change. So far, none of the SQL statements you've learned in this book allows you to change database data. Your databases have modeled a static world, one where time is frozen. Some people may believe that the United States might be in better shape if only George Washington were president. All would concede, however, that a database that reports he *is* the president is out of date and grossly inaccurate.

In this chapter, you'll learn how to change database data. You'll use SQL's Data Manipulation Language (DML) to add, change, and delete table rows. You'll learn how to use prepared statements to speed execution of your SQL statements and how to use cursors to perform positioned updates and deletes.

Technically, the now-familiar **Select** is a DML statement. Although it does not change database contents, it does allow you to access and manipulate them, so categorizing it as a DML statement is reasonable from the standpoint of its function. It is also reasonable from the standpoint of its structure. The **Select** statement teams up with many of the same clauses that other DML statements team up with. Thus, the other DML statements (**Insert**, **Update**, and **Delete**) work pretty much the same as **Select**. Learning how to use them will be easy.

Because misuse of the SQL statements you'll learn in this chapter can destroy data, be sure to double-check your statements before executing them, and be sure you have a good backup copy of any important data stored on your system. Preventing data loss is usually much simpler than recovering lost data.

The Insert Statement

To add a new row to a table, use the **Insert** statement. As an example, I'll create a new table in the GuestBook database and insert some rows into it:

```
Create Table Visitors (VisitorName Varchar(50), VisitorEMail Varchar(50));

Insert Into Visitors Values ('Hamlet''s Father', 'deadking@elsinore.gov');

Select * From Visitors;
```

Results:

```
VisitorName          VisitorEMail

Hamlet's Father      deadking@elsinore.gov

(1 rows included)
```

The **Create** statement creates the Visitors table. It has two columns, both of which store up to 50 characters of data. The first column is named *VisitorName*, and the second, *VisitorEmail*. As the column names suggest, the new table will summarize information from the Visits table, which contains columns similar to those of the Visitors table, plus several additional columns.

Notice that the Visitors table was created without a primary key. You won't need to specify a primary key to use most of the SQL operations presented here. Later in the chapter, I'll show you how to delete the table and re-create it to include a primary key.

The **Insert** statement adds a row to the table. The statement specifies which columns are to receive values (VisitorName and VisitorEMail), and the **Values** clause gives a value for each of these columns. The VisitorName is *Hamlet's Father*, and his email is *deadking@elsinore.gov.*

Following the execution of **Insert**, perform a **Select** so you can see the results of the **Insert** statement. Just as promised, the new row appears as the only row of the Visitors table.

What if we wanted the new row to have a value for only one of its columns, giving the remaining column a SQL **null** as its value? The following query does just that:

```
Insert Into Visitors Values ('Polonius', Null);

Select * From Visitors;
```

Results:

```
VisitorName          VisitorEMail

Hamlet's Father      deadking@elsinore.gov
Polonius

(2 rows included)
```

Of course, you do not need to specify the null value. The following query has the same sort of result as the preceding one:

```
Insert Into Visitors (VisitorName) Values ('Horatio');
```

Results:

```
VisitorName          VisitorEMail
Hamlet's Father      deadking@elsinore.govPolonius
Horatio

(3 rows included)
```

What if you wanted to assign a value to the VisitorEMail column, giving the VisitorName column the null value? Just change the list of column names and values accordingly, as shown at the top of the next page.

```
Insert Into Visitors (VisitorEMail) Values ('rosencrantz@england.gov');
```

Results:

```
VisitorName          VisitorEMail

Hamlet's Father      deadking@elsinore.gov
Polonius
Horatio
                     rosencrantz@england.gov

(4 rows included)
```

Of course, this example assumes that nulls are allowed in the field that receives the null value. What happens when this is not the case? To find out, add a new column to the table, one that does not allow nulls, and then attempt to insert an incomplete row:

```
Alter Table Visitors Add Column Loyalty Varchar(16) Not Null;

Insert Into Visitors
  (VisitorName, VisitorEMail)
  Values ('Laertes', 'Laertes@france.gov');
```

Results:

```
Error: [Microsoft][ODBC Microsoft Access 97 Driver] The field
'Visitors.Loyalty' can't contain a Null value because the Required property
for this field is set to True.  Enter a value in this field.
```

Values are specified for two of the columns (VisitorName and VisitorEMail), but not for the third (Loyalty). Since the third column was given no value, it receives a SQL null as its value. However, the column is not allowed to contain null values, so the attempt to insert the row fails, and a **SQLException** is thrown.

Note that the four existing records have no value for Loyalty, even though the column is constrained to be non-null. To avoid this predicament, many databases forbid adding a column that includes the **Not Null** constraint. Even if your database does not have such a restriction, you should be careful about adding a column that is constrained to be non-null. If you do proceed, you should supply valid values for the null column as soon as possible.

Multirow Insert

Sometimes—as in the previous examples—it's convenient to insert new columns using values written within SQL commands. Often, however, you may want to load the rows of one table using values stored in another table.

```
Select VistorName, VisitorEMail, TimeOfVisit From Visits;
```

Results:

```
SeqNo  VisitorName      VisitorEMail            TimeOfVisit

1      Marcellus        marcellus@elsinore.gov  1649-08-02 06:00:00
2      Horatio          horatio@elsinore.gov    1649-08-02 06:00:00
3      Hamlet           hamlet@elsinore.gov     1649-08-02 06:05:00
4      Hamlet's Father  deadking@elsinore.gov   1649-08-02 06:10:00

(4 rows included)
```

Drop the Visitors table and re-create it. This time, include a primary key. The example will work fine without it, but every table should have a primary key, since this makes accessing records easier and, often, faster.

```
Drop Table Visitors;

Create Table Visitors
  (VisitorName Varchar(50) Constraint pk PRIMARY KEY,
   VisitorEMail Varchar(50)
);
```

Now, insert rows into the new table using values from the Visits table. Do this by placing a **Select** statement where the **Values** clause normally appears:

```
Insert Into Visitors
  (VisitorName, VisitorEMail)
  Select VisitorName, VisitorEMail From Visits;
```

Results:

```
VisitorName      VisitorEMail

Marcellus        marcellus@elsinore.gov
Horatio          horatio@elsinore.gov
```

```
Hamlet          hamlet@elsinore.gov
Hamlet's Father deadking@elsinore.gov
```

(4 rows included)

Each row of the Visits table is used to create a row of the Visitors table. Note that VisitorName was specified as a primary key when the Visitors table was created, which means its value must be unique for every row of the Visitors table. Suppose the same visitor had two rows in the Visits table, as is the case with Hamlet's Father:

```
Select VisitorName, VisitorEMail, TimeOfVisit From Visits;
```

Results:

```
SeqNo  VisitorName     VisitorEMail             TimeOfVisit

1      Marcellus       marcellus@elsinore.gov  1649-08-02 06:00:00
2      Horatio         horatio@elsinore.gov    1649-08-02 06:00:00
3      Hamlet          hamlet@elsinore.gov     1649-08-02 06:05:00
4      Hamlet's Father deadking@elsinore.gov   1649-08-02 06:10:00
5      Hamlet's Father deadking@elsinore.gov   1649-08-03 06:10:00
```

(5 rows included)

The SQL interpreter would attempt to create a row in the Visitors table for each of the rows. The primary key would not be unique, however, and an error would result. MS Access reports "General Error" when this occurs.

How could you resolve this problem? VisitorName is probably not the right choice for the primary key of the Visitors table. The better option might seem to be to use an artificial key and then index both the VisitorName and VisitorEMail columns. Then, however, you would have a distinct row in the Visitors table for each row in Visits, and you would likely have several rows with the same values for VisitorName and VisitorEMail.

The proper design is to use a composite primary key consisting of VisitorName and VisitorEMail. Of course, this takes you back to where you started. Many rows within Visits may share the same values for VisitorName and VisitorEMail. The solution is to use the **Group By** clause to insert only a single row in the Visitors table for a combination of values:

```
Create Table Visitors
  (VisitorName Varchar(50),
  VisitorEMail Varchar(50),
  Constraint pk PRIMARY KEY (VisitorName, VisitorEMail)
);

Insert Into Visitors
  (VisitorName, VisitorEmail)
  Select VisitorName, VisitorEMail
  From Visits
  GROUP BY VisitorName, VisitorEMail;
```

Results:

```
VisitorName         VisitorEMail

Hamlet              hamlet@elsinore.gov
Hamlet's Father     deadking@elsinore.gov
Horatio             horatio@elsinore.gov
Marcellus           marcellus@elsinore.gov

(4 rows included)
```

When using the **Select** statement to provide values for **Insert**, you can include expressions in the **Select** list. For example, let's change the email domain of the visitors from gov to gov.dk before loading their data into the Visitors table.

Now, drop and re-create the Visitors table. Don't bother to create a primary key, because the table will have a short life:

```
Drop   Table Visitors;

Create Table Visitors
  (VisitorName Varchar(50), VisitorEMail Varchar(50));

Insert Into Visitors
  (VisitorName, VisitorEmail)
  Select VisitorName, VisitorEMail+'.dk'
  From Visits;

Select * From Visitors;
```

Results:

```
VisitorName        VisitorEMail

Marcellus          marcellus@elsinore.gov.dk
Horatio            horatio@elsinore.gov.dk
Hamlet             hamlet@elsinore.gov.dk
Hamlet's Father    deadking@elsinore.gov.dk

(4 rows included)
```

You can even use literals to set values of columns that do not appear in the table used as a data source. For example, you can create a new column named Loyal and initialize it to the value Unknown:

```
Drop    Table Visitors;

Create Table Visitors
  (VisitorName Varchar(50),
   VisitorEMail Varchar(50),
   Loyal char(8)
);

Insert Into Visitors
  (VisitorName, VisitorEmail, Loyal)
  Select VisitorName, VisitorEMail, 'Unknown'
  From Visits;

Select * From Visitors;
```

Results:

```
VisitorName       VisitorEMail             Loyal

Marcellus         marcellus@elsinore.gov   Unknown
Horatio           horatio@elsinore.gov     Unknown
Hamlet            hamlet@elsinore.gov      Unknown
Hamlet's Father   deadking@elsinore.gov    Unknown

(4 rows included)
```

The Update Statement

Updating table rows is almost as easy as adding them. You can update rows by using the **Update** statement; the **Set** clause lets you specify the column values you want to update. Continuing the previous example, here is an **Update** that changes the value of the Loyal column from Unknown to Yes:

```
Update Visitors Set Loyal = 'Yes';

Select * From visitors;
```

Results:

VisitorName	VisitorEMail	Loyal
Marcellus	marcellus@elsinore.gov	Yes
Horatio	horatio@elsinore.gov	Yes
Hamlet	hamlet@elsinore.gov	Yes
Hamlet's Father	deadking@elsinore.gov	Yes

(4 rows included)

You can update several columns at once by including a list of assignments in the **Set** clause. The following query updates the values of the Loyal and the VisitorEMail columns, adding .dk to the end of the visitors' email addresses:

```
Update Visitors Set Loyal = 'Yes', VisitorEMail = VisitorEMail+'.dk';

Select * From Visitors;
```

Results:

VisitorName	VisitorEMail	Loyal
Marcellus	marcellus@elsinore.gov.dk	Yes
Horatio	horatio@elsinore.gov.dk	Yes
Hamlet	hamlet@elsinore.gov.dk	Yes
Hamlet's Father	deadking@elsinore.gov.dk	Yes

(4 rows included)

Conditional Update

When using a **Select** statement to report table rows, you use the **Where** clause to specify the rows you want to retrieve. The **Where** clause can be similarly used with the **Update** statement, specifying which rows you want to change. For example, assume you had discovered doubt of Marcellus' loyalty to Hamlet. You could update his table row by using this statement:

```
Update Visitors Set Loyal = 'Unknown' Where VisitorName = 'Marcellus';

Select * From Visitors;
```

Results:

```
VisitorName         VisitorEMail                        Loyal

Marcellus           marcellus@elsinore.gov.dk           Unknown
Horatio             horatio@elsinore.gov.dk             Yes
Hamlet              hamlet@elsinore.gov.dk              Yes
Hamlet's Father     deadking@elsinore.gov.dk            Yes

(4 rows included)
```

Note that, as desired, only Marcellus's row has been changed, and only its Loyal column has been changed. The values of the columns of the other rows are unchanged.

Of course, you can write more complex **Where** clauses. Since they work with **Update** exactly as they do with **Select**, and since you're thoroughly familiar with **Select**, you're an instant expert.

The Delete Statement

To delete table rows, you use…you guessed it: the **Delete** statement. Here is a simple query that deletes all the rows from the Visits table:

```
Delete From Visits;

Select * From Visits;
```

Results:

```
SeqNo  VisitorName  VisitorEMail  Comment  TimeOfVisit

(0 rows included)
```

Notice how effective the statement is. All the table rows have disappeared, just as ordered.

Recall the warning given at the beginning of the chapter: SQL does not prompt you to confirm an operation, such as this one, that removes or changes many table rows. It simply performs the operation. Before pressing the Enter key, be sure you've written what you intended. Once you've pressed Enter, it's too late to reconsider.

Conditional Delete

The **Where** clause can be used with a **Delete** statement to conditionally delete rows from a table. As an example, delete from the Visits table only those rows with a TimeOfVisit after Hamlet's. Here is the Visits table:

```
Select VisitorName, TimeOfVisit From Visits;
```

Results:

```
VisitorName        TimeOfVisit

Marcellus          1649-08-02 06:00:00
Horatio            1649-08-02 06:00:00
Hamlet             1649-08-02 06:05:00
Hamlet's Father    1649-08-02 06:10:00
Hamlet's Father    1649-08-03 06:10:00

(5 rows included)
```

Now do the conditional delete:

```
Delete From Visits Where TimeOfVisit < {ts '1649-08-01 06:05:00'};

Select VisitorName, TimeOfVisit From Visits;
```

Results:

```
VisitorName   TimeOfVisit

Marcellus     1649-08-02 06:00:00
Horatio       1649-08-02 06:00:00
Hamlet        1649-08-02 06:05:00
```

(3 rows included)

Though the query works generally as you might expect, note these peculiarities (fortunately, these will not affect you, unless you're working with dates prior to 1650 AD):

- *The sense of the inequality (<) is not as you would expect.* The statement seems to ask that rows *earlier* than August 1, 1649, be deleted. Apparently, because Access's internal representation of dates in this range is negative, later dates have *lower* values.

- *Although the date in the query is August 1, it is interpreted by Access as August 2.* This, too, seems to affect only dates prior to January 1, 1650.

As long as you're working with more recent dates, these problems should not arise. However, there is a lesson here that applies even if your interest is exclusively the twentieth century and beyond. The lesson is that things do not always work as you expect, even if your expectations are well grounded. When working with updates and deletes, you need to anticipate the possibility that things may go wrong. Even if you make no mistakes, your results may not be what "should" have happened. Plan for this by initially using **Select** in place of **Update** or **Delete**. That way, before you make any changes to the data, you can see what is going to happen. You may save yourself considerable anxiety in the process.

Prepared Statements

Although **Insert**, **Update**, and **Delete** statements resemble the **Select** statement in form, they are often used somewhat differently. It is common to insert, update, or delete a single record, specified by the **Where** clause of the statement, and then repeat the same operation with a slightly different **Where** clause. For example, you might use the following statement to give an employee a salary raise

```
Update Employees Set Salary = Salary * 1.1 Where EmployeeNo = 3 ;
```

and then do almost exactly the same for another employee:

```
Update Employees Set Salary = Salary * 1.1 Where EmployeeNo = 5 ;
```

You should avoid repeated operations when possible. Each such operation requires a table row to be delivered to your program, updated, and then retransmitted to the database. If many records are processed in this manner, the processing overhead can become substantial. Instead, use a **Where** clause that allows you to update an entire group at once:

```
Update Employees Set Salary = Salary * 1.1 Where State = 'CA' ;
```

This is not always possible, however. Sometimes, the nature of processing requires that you execute nearly the same statement over and over. To help reduce the overhead involved, JDBC provides a special class, **PreparedStatement**. It functions as a regular **Statement** class, except its contents are submitted to the SQL interpreter for compilation only once, saving the overhead involved in multiple compilations of the statement.

To change the parameters used in a **PreparedStatement**, as the EmployeeNo was changed in the example query, JDBC provides a simple parameter substitution mechanism. You write the query using question marks (?) as placeholders for values that will be supplied when the statement is executed. For example, the salary update query could be written

```
Update Employees Set Salary = Salary * ? Where EmployeeNo = ? ;
```

where the salary increase factor and the employee number are both represented using placeholders. Then, you use special methods of the **PreparedStatement** class to substitute values for the placeholders and execute the **PreparedStatement**.

Here's a short code example (I'll give a more elaborate one later):

```
String sql = "Update Employees "
  + "Set Salary = Salary * ? Where EmployeeNo = ? ;";
```

```
PreparedStatement ps = theConnnection.getPreparedStatement(sql);
ps.setString(1, "1.1");
ps.setString(2, "3");
ps.executeUpdate( );
```

Notice how the SQL command is specified at the time the **PreparedStatement** is created, so that it's not given as a parameter of the **executeUpdate( )** method (or the similar **execute( )** or **executeQuery( )** methods). A family of methods, shown in Table 10.1, is available to set parameter values, each member handling a different data type. In each method, the first parameter identifies a placeholder by position (relative to one), and the second parameter specifies the value that is to be bound to the placeholder. After all placeholders have had values bound to them, the SQL command is executed. Most types of values remain bound after the command is executed and don't need to be bounded again unless a new value is needed. This further increases the efficiency of the **PreparedStatement**. An example program later in this chapter demonstrates the performance improvement made possible by using a **PreparedStatement**.

TABLE 10.1

METHODS USED TO SET PREPAREDSTATEMENT PARAMETERS.

setAsciiStream(int, InputStream, int)

setBigDecimal(int, BigDecimal)

setBinaryStream(int, InputStream, int)

setBoolean(int, boolean)

setByte(int, byte)

setBytes(int, byte[ ])

setDate(int, Date)

setDouble(int, double)

setFloat(int, float)

setInt(int, int)

setLong(int, long)

setNull(int, int)

setObject(int, Object)

(continued)

	TABLE 10.1

METHODS USED TO SET PREPAREDSTATEMENT PARAMETERS (*CONTINUED*).

setShort(int, short)

setString(int, String)

setTime(int, Time)

setTimestamp(int, Timestamp)

setUnicodeStream(int, InputStream, int)

Positioned Updates And Deletes

SQL queries process an entire table in a single operation. Programs, by contrast, process a table one row at a time. Prepared statements accommodate the needs of programs by making it more efficient to process a row at a time. Another way SQL addresses the same problem is by providing *positioned updates* and *deletes*, which allow you to reference the current record of a result set and update or delete it. Not every database supports positioned updates and deletes. The **DatabaseMetaData** methods—**supportsPositionedUpdate( )** and **supportsPositionedDelete( )**—help you determine whether your database supports them. Each method returns **true** if the corresponding operation is supported, and **false** otherwise.

To use positioned updates or deletes, you must retrieve the name of the cursor used to identify the current record of the result set. You can use the **ResultSet.getCursorName( )** method to do this. The method returns a **String**, which you'll learn how to use in a moment.

Another way to accomplish the same result is to use the **Statement.set-CursorName( )** method to specify the name for the cursor used to reference the current row of any result set generated by the **Statement** clause. The method takes a **String** argument, which specifies the desired cursor name.

Once you have a cursor name, you can use a special form of the **Where** clause to uniquely identify a table row. For example, to update the Salary column of the current row of the result set (taken from the Employees table), you could write

```
Update Employees Set Salary = Salary * 1.1 Where Current Of cursor;
```

where *cursor* is the value returned by **getCursorName( )** (or the value passed to **setCursorName( )**).

Cursors may seem like an unqualified blessing. They do, however, have some disadvantages.

- *First, they have a deserved reputation for inefficiency.* If you can avoid row-at-a-time processing, do so. Of course, if this is not possible, using a **PreparedStatement** or a positioned update or delete is better than not doing so. In fact, you should use a **PreparedStatement** to accomplish your positioned update or delete whenever possible.

- *A second drawback is that, as mentioned, some databases do not support positioned operations.* Among these is Microsoft Access. If you're using Access to learn about SQL and JDBC, you'll be unable to explore positioned operations. Access does implement almost all other important JDBC functions.

- *A more serious drawback is that, at the time of writing, several common drivers do not handle positioned updates and deletes, although their **DatabaseMetaData** methods report that the positioned operations are supported by the underlying database.* When a positioned update or delete is issued, these drivers report that the connection is busy with another statement (that is, the one that generated the result set) and is unable to process the positioned operation. You can try to circumvent this by opening a second connection, but the cursor associated with the result set is tied to a given connection. You cannot access it across connections.

Presumably, this last drawback will soon be corrected. In the meantime, however, verify that your database and driver support positioned operations before basing the design of a program or system on the assumption that they do.

The GuestBook Applet

The latest incarnation of the ubiquitous GuestBook program is very different from its predecessors. It's implemented as an applet, rather than an application. Another difference is that it updates database information, whereas previous versions merely reported database information. Figure 10.1 shows the user interface of the applet.

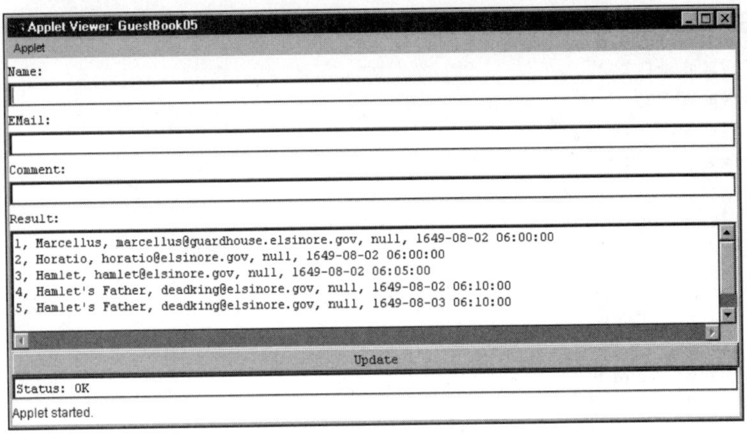

Figure 10.1
The GuestBook05 Applet.

The fact that GuestBook05 is implemented as an applet does not mean that you can immediately put it on your Web server and expect client browsers to use its functions. Applets are subject to a number of security restrictions, as will be explained in Chapter 14. Depending upon which browser you're using and how it's configured, you *may* be able to use GuestBook05 in that fashion. Between now and Chapter 14, however, you're advised to use the Java 1.1 appletviewer to experiment with example applets. The appletviewer fully supports Java 1.1 and, as long as you're loading the applet from your local hard disk, will not enforce security restrictions that prevent you from loading and running the applet. The same cannot be said today for browsers generally; hopefully, this will soon change.

Listing 10.1 shows the fields of the applet. These include a special **JDBC01** object that encapsulates data and methods used to access the database. I'll explain its structure in a moment. The GuestBook05 applet also has **TextField**s to obtain the name and email address of a visitor, as well as a comment left by the visitor. The remaining columns of the Visits table have values set programmatically, as you'll see later. The applet also has a button to trigger the insert operation, and a **TextArea** (**theText**) and **TextField** (**theStatus**) to monitor the operation of the applet.

GuestBook05 includes no **main( )** method, since it's an applet rather than an application. Similarly missing is code establishing a **WindowListener**, since this function is provided by the appletviewer, not the applet.

LISTING 10.1   FIELDS OF THE GUESTBOOK05 APPLET.

```
import java.applet.*;
import java.awt.*;
import java.awt.event.*;
import java.sql.*;

public class GuestBook05 extends Applet
implements ActionListener
{
    JDBC01      theJDBC;

    TextField theName;
    TextField theEMail;
    TextField theComment;

    Button      theUpdateButton;

    TextArea    theText;
    TextField theStatus;
```

The init( ) Method

As usual, the **init( )** method, which is shown in Listing 10.2, builds the user interface. To simplify placement and labeling of the components, **init( )** uses the **getLabeledComponent( )** method. It takes a **String** and a **Component** as arguments and returns a **Panel**, which includes the **Component**, and a **Label**, which takes its text from the **String**.

LISTING 10.2   THE INIT( ) METHOD.

```
public void init( )
{
    setFont(new Font("Courier", Font.PLAIN, 12));

    theName     = new TextField( );
    theEMail    = new TextField( );
    theComment = new TextField( );

    theUpdateButton = new Button("Update");

    theText     = new TextArea(15, 64);
    theStatus   = new TextField(64);

    setLayout(new BorderLayout( ));
    Panel input_panel = new Panel( );
```

```
input_panel.setLayout(new GridLayout(3, 1));
input_panel.add(getLabeledComponent("Name:",    theName));
input_panel.add(getLabeledComponent("EMail:",   theEMail));
input_panel.add(getLabeledComponent("Comment:", theComment));

Panel middle_panel = new Panel( );
middle_panel.setLayout(new BorderLayout( ));
middle_panel.add(getLabeledComponent("Result:", theText));

Panel bottom_panel = new Panel( );
bottom_panel.setLayout(new GridLayout(2, 1));
bottom_panel.add(theUpdateButton);
bottom_panel.add(theStatus);

add(input_panel,  "North");
add(middle_panel, "Center");
add(bottom_panel, "South");

theText  .setEditable(false);
theStatus.setEditable(false);

theUpdateButton.addActionListener(this);
}
```

The start( ) And stop( ) Methods

Since GuestBook05 is an applet, it has **start( )** and **stop( )** methods, shown in Listing 10.3, that the appletviewer invokes when the applet is opened and closed, respectively. The **start( )** method opens the database connection; the **stop( )** method closes it.

LISTING 10.3   THE START( ) AND STOP( ) METHODS.

```
public void start( )
{
    theJDBC = new JDBC01(theStatus);
    try
    {
        theJDBC.openConnection("jdbc:odbc:GuestBook", "", "");
        theJDBC.executeQuery("Select * From Visits;");
        theText.setText(theJDBC.dumpResult( ));
    }
    catch (SQLException sql) { ; }
}
```

```
public void stop( )
{
    try
    {
        theJDBC.closeConnection( );
    }
    catch (SQLException sql) { ; }
}
```

The actionPerformed( ) Method

Since the user interface has only one button, the **actionPerformed**( ) method, shown in Listing 10.4, is quite simple. In response to the user clicking the Update button, the method invokes the **doUpdate**( ) method.

LISTING 10.4   THE ACTIONPERFORMED( ) METHOD.

```
public void actionPerformed(ActionEvent event)
{
    theStatus.setText("Status: OK");
    Object source = event.getSource( );
    if (source == theUpdateButton) doUpdate( );
}
```

The doUpdate( ) Method

Listing 10.5 shows the **doUpdate**( ) method, which performs the most significant work of the applet. It begins by creating a **Timestamp** local variable, used to set the value of the TimeOfVisit column. It then creates a SQL **Insert** command that specifies the columns and values to be set, using the **getFieldList**( ) and **getValueList**( ) methods of **JDBC01** to simplify the task. I'll explain the operation of these two methods in the section on **JDBC01**.

The SeqNo column of the Visits table is not mentioned in the SQL command. It's a field of the COUNTER data type that serves as the primary key of the Visits table. Thus, the SQL interpreter automatically sets its value.

Once the SQL command is built, it is executed. Then, the updated contents of the table are retrieved and displayed so that correct operation of the applet can be verified.

LISTING 10.5 THE DoUPDATE( ) METHOD.

```
public void doUpdate( )
{
    java.util.Date today = new java.util.Date( );
    Timestamp      now   = new Timestamp(today.getTime( ));
    String         timestamp = "{ts '" + now.toString( ) + "'}";

    try
    {
        String sql = "Insert Into Visits " ;
        sql += theJDBC.getFieldList(
          new String [ ] { "VisitorName", "VisitorEMail", "Comment",
            "TimeOfVisit" }
        );
        sql += theJDBC.getValueList(
          new String  [ ] { theName.getText( ), theEMail.getText( ),
            theComment.getText( ), timestamp },
          new boolean [ ] { true,                true,
            true,                false      }
        );
        sql += " ;" ;

        theText.setText("Query: " + sql);
        int result = theJDBC.executeUpdate(sql);
        theText.append("Result =" + result + "\n\n");
        theJDBC.executeQuery("Select * From Visits;");
        theText.append (theJDBC.dumpResult( ));
    }
    catch (SQLException sql)
    {
        theStatus.setText(sql.getMessage( ));
    }
}
```

The getLabeledComponent( ) Method

The **getLabeledComponent( )** method, shown in Listing 10.6, is used by the **init( )** method to facilitate building the user interface. The method simplifies creating labeled fields.

LISTING 10.6 THE GETLABELEDCOMPONENT( ) METHOD.

```
public Panel getLabeledComponent(String text, Component comp)
{
    Panel p = new Panel( );
    p.setLayout(new BorderLayout( ));
```

```
        p.add(new Label(text), "North");
        p.add(comp, "Center");
        return p;
}
```

The JDBC01 Class

The **JDBC01** class encapsulates fields and methods commonly used in accessing a database. It helps isolate code specific to a program from general code that can be used in many programs. This makes the program easier and faster to write and understand.

Listing 10.7 shows **JDBC01**'s fields and its constructor. The constructor requires a reference to a **TextField** that will be updated with an error message when an error is discovered during execution of a SQL command.

LISTING 10.7   FIELDS AND CONSTRUCTOR OF THE JDBC01 CLASS.

```
import java.awt.*;
import java.sql.*;

public class JDBC01
{
String              theSource   = "";
String              theUser     = "";
String              thePassword = "";

Connection          theConnection = null;
DatabaseMetaData    theDBMetaData = null;
Statement           theStatement  = null;
ResultSet           theResultSet  = null;
ResultSetMetaData   theMetaData   = null;

TextField theStatus;

public JDBC01(TextField status)
{
    theStatus = status;
}
}
```

The openConnection( ) Method

Listing 10.8 shows the **openConnection( )** method. To provide generality and ease of use, the method obtains a **DatabaseMetaData** object that can be accessed through the field named *theDBMetaData,* and a **Statement** object that can be accessed through the field named *theStatement.*

LISTING 10.8   THE OPENCONNECTION( ) METHOD.

```
public void openConnection(String source, String user,
  String password)
throws SQLException
{
    theSource   = source;
    theUser     = user;
    thePassword = password;

    try
    {
        Class.forName (
          "sun.jdbc.odbc.JdbcOdbcDriver");
        if (theConnection != null)
            theConnection.close( );
        theConnection =
          DriverManager.getConnection(theSource, theUser,
            thePassword);
        theConnection.setTransactionIsolation(
          Connection.TRANSACTION_NONE);
        theDBMetaData
          = theConnection.getMetaData( );
        theStatement
          = theConnection.createStatement( );
        theResultSet = null;
        theMetaData = null;
        theStatus.setText("Status: OK");
    }
    catch (SQLException sql)
    {
        handleError(sql);
    }
    catch (ClassNotFoundException ex)
    {
        handleError(ex);
    }
}
```

The closeConnection( ) Method

The **closeConnection**( ) method, shown in Listing 10.9, contains no surprises.

LISTING 10.9   THE CLOSECONNECTION( ) METHOD.

```
public void closeConnection( )
throws SQLException
{
    try
    {
        if (theConnection != null)
            theConnection.close( );
    }
    catch (SQLException sql)  { handleError(sql); }
}
```

The executeQuery( ) And executeUpdate( ) Methods

The **executeQuery( )** and **executeUpdate( )** methods, shown in Listing 10.10, perform their usual functions. The **executeQuery( )** method immediately obtains a **ResultSetMetaData** object describing the result set and places its reference in the field named *theMetaData*.

LISTING 10.10   THE EXECUTEQUERY( ) AND EXECUTEUPDATE( ) METHODS.

```
public void executeQuery(String sql)
throws SQLException
{
    if (theResultSet != null)
      theResultSet.close( );
    theResultSet = theStatement.executeQuery(sql);
    if (theResultSet != null)
      theMetaData  = theResultSet.getMetaData( );
}

public int executeUpdate(String sql)
throws SQLException
{
    if (theResultSet != null)
      theResultSet.close( );
    theResultSet = null;
    theMetaData = null;
    int result = theStatement.executeUpdate(sql);
    return result;
}
```

The dumpResult( ) Method

The **dumpResult( )** method, shown in Listing 10.11, returns a **String** containing a formatted representation of the contents of the current result set. It loops over the columns of the **ResultSet**, concatenating a **String** representation of each column onto a result **String** that it ultimately returns.

LISTING 10.11   THE DUMPRESULT( ) METHOD.

```
public String dumpResult( )
throws SQLException
{
    String result = "";
    try
    {
        int column_count = theMetaData.getColumnCount( );
        while (theResultSet.next( ))
        {
            boolean first = true;
            for (int i = 1; i <= column_count; i++)
            {
                if (!first) result += ", ";
                result += theResultSet.getString(i);
                first = false;
            }
            result += "\n";
        }
    }
    catch (SQLException sql) { handleError(sql); }
    return result;
}
```

The getFieldList( ) Method

The **getFieldList( )** method, shown in Listing 10.12, is an unfamiliar method. It iterates through an array of field names, returning a comma-separated list suitable for use in a DML statement.

LISTING 10.12   THE GETFIELDLIST( ) METHOD.

```
String getFieldList(String [ ] fields)
{
    String result = "(";
    boolean first = true;
    for (int i = 0; i < fields.length; i++)
    {
```

```
        if (!first) result += ", ";
        first = false;
        result += fields[i];
    }
    result += ") ";
    return result;
}
```

The getValueList( ) Method

Listing 10.13 shows the **getValueList**( ) method, another unfamiliar method.
Its function is to return a **Values** clause that includes a comma-separated list of
values. Its input consists of parallel arrays. One, **values**, contains the text to be
placed in the list. The other, **isQuoted**, determines whether the corresponding
value should be surrounded by single quotes. This makes it easy to specify literals that may contain spaces.

The method also deals with the possibility that a quoted list item might contain
an embedded quote. In this event, it replaces the quote with a pair of quotes.
The SQL interpreter understands this convention, replacing the pair with a
single quote. Thus, the interpreter can handle literals, such as "Hamlet's", without producing a syntax error.

LISTING 10.13   THE GETVALUELIST( ) METHOD.

```
String getValueList(String [ ] values, boolean [ ] isQuoted)
{
    String result = "Values (";
    boolean first = true;
    for (int i = 0; i < values.length; i++)
    {
        if (!first) result += ", ";
        first = false;
        String value = values[i];
        if (isQuoted[i])
        {
            result += "'";

            // double any embedded single quotes
            int j;
            while ((j = value.indexOf('\'')) >= 0)
            {
                if (j > 0)
                {
                    result += value.substring(0, j);
                }
```

```
            result += "'";
            if (value.length( ) > j + 1)
            {
                value = value.substring(j + 1);
            }
            else
            {
                value = "";
            }
        }
        result += value + "'";
    }
    else
    {
        result += value;
    }
    }
    result += ") ";
    return result;
}
```

Utility Methods

Listing 10.14 shows three utility methods (**getNonNullString( )**, **nonNull( )**, and **handleError( )**). They do little of significance, but they are included anyway, for completeness.

LISTING 10.14   UTILITY METHODS.

```
String getNonNullString(int col)
throws SQLException
{
    return nonNull(theResultSet.getString(col));
}

String nonNull(String s)
{
    if (s != null) return s;
    return "";
}

public void handleError(Throwable t)
throws SQLException
{
    theStatus.setText("Error: " + t.getMessage( ));
    t.printStackTrace( );
    throw new SQLException(t.getMessage( ));
}
```

The PreppedMark Applet

The PreppedMark applet, which is shown in Figure 10.2, runs a benchmark that demonstrates the improved performance possible using a **PreparedStatement** object. The applet performs an equal number of row inserts, using a **Statement** or a **PreparedStatement**, as selected by the user. It displays the elapsed time (in milliseconds) taken by each query, permitting comparison of the results. As you can see from Figure 10.2, the **PreparedStatement** query is several times faster than the **Statement** query. Measured in time, the difference is only a couple of seconds. The applet, however, performs only 100 operations. If the applet performed 100,000 operations, the speed difference could become quite substantial. Databases that perform as many as 1 million inserts per day are not uncommon. In such a situation, you might need to use a **PreparedStatement** to meet processing schedules.

Listing 10.15 shows the fields of the PreppedMark applet. Like GuestBook05, it uses the **JDBC01** class to simplify database access.

LISTING 10.15   FIELDS OF THE PREPPEDMARK APPLET.

```
import java.applet.*;
import java.awt.*;
import java.awt.event.*;
import java.sql.*;

public class PreppedMark extends Applet
implements ActionListener
{
final static int OPERATIONS  = 100;

JDBC01    theJDBC;

TextField theNonPreppedTime;
TextField thePreppedTime;

Button    theNonPreppedButton;
Button    thePreppedButton;

TextField theStatus;
```

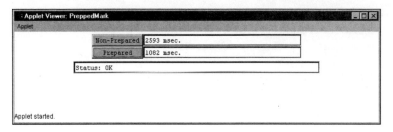

Figure 10.2
The PreppedMark applet.

The init( ) Method

Listing 10.16 shows the **init( )** method, which builds the user interface of PreppedMark. The user interface is a simple one, so the method presents no surprises.

LISTING 10.16   THE INIT( ) METHOD.

```
public void init( )
{
    setFont(new Font("Courier", Font.PLAIN, 12));

    theNonPreppedTime   = new TextField(40);
    thePreppedTime      = new TextField(40);
    theNonPreppedButton = new Button("Non-Prepared");
    thePreppedButton    = new Button("Prepared");
    theStatus           = new TextField(64);

    Panel p1 = new Panel( );
    p1.setLayout(new BorderLayout( ));
    p1.add(theNonPreppedTime,   "East");
    p1.add(theNonPreppedButton, "Center");

    Panel p2 = new Panel( );
    p2.setLayout(new BorderLayout( ));
    p2.add(thePreppedTime,   "East");
    p2.add(thePreppedButton, "Center");

    Panel p = new Panel( );
    p.setLayout(new GridLayout(2, 1));
    p.add(p1);
    p.add(p2);

    add(p,         "Center");
    add(theStatus, "South");
```

```
    theNonPreppedTime.setEditable(false);
    thePreppedTime   .setEditable(false);
    theStatus        .setEditable(false);

    theNonPreppedButton.addActionListener(this);
    thePreppedButton   .addActionListener(this);
}
```

The start( ) And stop( ) Methods

The **start( )** and **stop( )** methods, like those of GuestBook05, simply open or close the database connection, respectively. Listing 10.17 shows the methods.

LISTING 10.17   THE START( ) AND STOP( ) METHODS.

```
public void start( )
{
    theJDBC = new JDBC01(theStatus);
    try
    {
        theJDBC.openConnection("jdbc:odbc:GuestBookSS", "sa", "");
    }
    catch (SQLException sql) { ; }
}

public void stop( )
{
    try
    {
        theJDBC.closeConnection( );
    }
    catch (SQLException sql) { ; }
}
```

The actionPerformed( ) Method

The **actionPerformed( )** method, shown in Listing 10.18, invokes either the **doNonPrepped( )** method or the **doPrepped( )** method, based on which button the user clicks. The former performs insertions using a **Statement**, and the latter does so using a **PreparedStatement**.

LISTING 10.18   THE ACTIONPERFORMED( ) METHOD.

```
public void actionPerformed(ActionEvent event)
{
    theStatus.setText("Status: Working");
    Object source = event.getSource( );
```

```
    if (source == theNonPreppedButton)   doNonPrepped( );
    else if (source == thePreppedButton) doPrepped( );
    if (theStatus.getText( ).equals("Status: Working"))
        theStatus.setText("Status: OK");
}
```

The doNonPrepped( ) Method

The **doNonPrepped( )** method, shown in Listing 10.19, uses a **Statement** to perform insertions. To get a clean start, it first deletes all rows from the Visits table. It records the current time in a **Timestamp** object.

The method then enters a loop that will insert 100 rows. First, it places random values in column variables using the **Math.random( )** method. Although this results in strange, numeric column values, these are quite satisfactory for benchmarking. Then, the method builds and executes an **Insert** statement. The method repeats these steps until it has inserted all 100 rows.

Next, the method creates a second **Timestamp** object, capturing the current time. It then uses the **getTime( )** method to obtain a milliseconds value from each **Timestamp**, placing the elapsed time in milliseconds in a **TextField** so it can be viewed.

LISTING 10.19   THE DONONPREPPED( ) METHOD.

```
public void doNonPrepped( )
{
    try
    {
        String sql = "Delete From Visits ;";
        int result = theJDBC.executeUpdate(sql);

        java.util.Date begin_time = new java.util.Date( );
        for (int i = 0; i < OPERATIONS; i++)
        {
            String   name, email, comment, timestamp;
            Timestamp stamp;

            name    = "'" + Math.random( ) + "'";
            email   = "'" + Math.random( ) + "'";
            comment = "'" + Math.random( ) + "'";
            stamp = new Timestamp (
              new java.util.Date( ).getTime( )
            );
            timestamp = "{ts '" + stamp.toString( ) + "'}";
```

```
            sql = "Insert Into Visits " ;
            sql += theJDBC.getFieldList(
              new String [ ] { "VisitorName", "VisitorEMail", "Comment",
                              "TimeOfVisit" }
            );

            sql += theJDBC.getValueList(
              new String  [ ] { name, email, comment, timestamp },
              new boolean [ ] { true, true,   true,    false      }
            );
            sql += " ;" ;
            result = theJDBC.executeUpdate(sql);
        }

        java.util.Date end_time   = new java.util.Date( );
        long elapsed_time = end_time.getTime( ) - begin_time.getTime( );
        theNonPreppedTime .setText("" + elapsed_time + " msec.");
    }
    catch (SQLException sql)
    {
        theStatus.setText(sql.getMessage( ));
    }
}
```

The doPrepped( ) Method

The **doPrepped( )** method, shown in Listing 10.20, performs the same function as the **doNonPrepped( )** method, only it uses a **PreparedStatement** to
speed processing of the SQL **Insert**s. By comparing the results displayed in the
TextFields, the user can verify that the **PreparedStatement** is significantly faster
than the **Statement**.

LISTING 10.20   THE DOPREPPED( ) METHOD.

```
public void doPrepped( )
{
    try
    {
        String sql = "Delete From Visits ;";
        int result = theJDBC.executeUpdate(sql);
        //System.out.println("Deleted " + result + " records.");

        sql = "Insert Into Visits " ;
        sql += theJDBC.getFieldList(
          new String [ ] { "VisitorName", "VisitorEMail", "Comment",
                          "TimeOfVisit" }
        );
```

```
        sql += theJDBC.getValueList(
          new String  [ ] { "?",   "?",   "?",   "?"   },
          new boolean [ ] { false, false, false, false }
        );
        sql += " ;" ;

        PreparedStatement pstmt
          = theJDBC.theConnection.prepareStatement(sql);

        java.util.Date begin_time = new java.util.Date( );
        for (int i = 0; i < OPERATIONS; i++)
        {

            String    name, email, comment;
            Timestamp timestamp;

            name     = "'" + Math.random( ) + "'";
            email    = "'" + Math.random( ) + "'";
            comment  = "'" + Math.random( ) + "'";
            timestamp = new Timestamp (
              new java.util.Date( ).getTime( )
            );

            pstmt.setString(1, name);
            pstmt.setString(2, email);
            pstmt.setString(3, comment);
            pstmt.setTimestamp(4, timestamp);

            result = pstmt.executeUpdate( );
        }

        java.util.Date end_time   = new java.util.Date( );
        long elapsed_time = end_time.getTime( ) - begin_time.getTime( );
        thePreppedTime .setText("" + elapsed_time + " msec.");
    }
    catch (SQLException sql)
    {
        theStatus.setText(sql.getMessage( ));
    }
}
```

Summary

This chapter showed you how to use SQL **Insert**, **Update**, and **Delete** statements to maintain your data. You also learned how to use the **PreparedStatement** class to improve the efficiency of your SQL queries. The next chapter will show you how to write more powerful queries that you can use to retrieve and maintain data.

11

ADVANCED SQL QUERIES

Programming languages allow programmers to tackle problems a piece at a time, assembling complete solutions by bolting together a set of partial solutions. This helps programmers cope with complex problems by allowing them to focus first on one aspect of the problem, then on another, until they find a complete solution. In Java, the programmer can model complex object behaviors by writing high-level methods that call more basic methods, simplifying the programming task.

To help the programmer, SQL allows queries to contain other queries, called *subqueries* or *nested queries*. Subqueries allow SQL programmers to write sophisticated and powerful queries by combining queries that are more basic.

Because subqueries are so versatile, they are one of the most difficult aspects of SQL to master. A variety of forms is possible and each form has many variations. In this chapter, you'll learn the most important subquery forms and how you can combine them to form complete queries. Perhaps more important, you'll learn to understand subqueries written by others. Studying SQL queries written by others is the best way to continue your SQL education and is essential if you aspire to mastery of subqueries.

The example program for this chapter is an applet that lets you browse a database table. Unlike browser programs from earlier chapters, however, this applet lets you add, change, and delete rows from the table. You can use its structure as the starting point for many useful programs.

Subqueries

A subquery is nothing more than a query contained within another query. Subqueries come in two basic flavors: *uncorrelated* and *correlated*. An uncorrelated subquery is executed only once, returning either a single value or a set of values. In contrast, a correlated query is executed repeatedly, once for each row of the related table. Uncorrelated, single-value subqueries are the simplest variety.

Single-Value Subqueries

Suppose you wanted to know which employees are earning less than the average salary of all employees. To learn who they are, you would write two queries. The first would find the average salary, and the second would find the employees whose salaries are below the average. For example, you could write

```
Select Avg(Salary) As Average From Employees;
```

to find the average salary. As you know from Chapter 6, this query will generate a result set that includes a single row with a single column containing the average salary. Say the result was 100,000. You could take the result and use it in the second query like this:

```
Select Name, Salary From Employees Where Salary < 100000
  Order By Salary;
```

This query would list the names and salaries of the low-wage employees, from the lowest-paid to the highest-paid, exactly what was needed.

An uncorrelated, single-value subquery simply lets you perform both these steps in a single query. Here's how it's done:

```
Select Name, Salary From Employees
  Where Salary < (Select Avg(Salary) From Employees)
  Order By Salary ;
```

Notice how the query that computes the average salary

```
(Select Avg(Salary) From Employees)
```

is nested inside the other query. Like all subqueries, it is surrounded by paren-theses so you can easily spot its beginning and end. The nested query simply takes the place of the number (100,000) that appeared in the second of the two original queries.

That's all there is to writing uncorrelated, single-value queries. Instead of writ-ing a number, a text string, or other value in a query, you supply a subquery that retrieves the value. The more compact form afforded by the subquery stream-lines your programs, since only one call to **executeQuery( )** is required, rather than the two required without using a subquery. It also improves query perfor-mance because intermediate results don't have to be sent over the network. The cost is merely a little more effort in writing and understanding SQL.

Assume that the Employees table contains the following rows:

Name	Salary
Abigail Honest	60000
Bill Bonkers	60000
Fred Fearless	60000
Jumbo Jones	65000
Steve Giblet	70000
Ann Agram	75000
Sam TheMan	85000
Young Tom	90000
Adam Adams	120000
Eve Adams	130000
Sue Slewfoot	300000

Executing the query containing the subquery would return the following rows in the result set:

Name	Salary
Abigail Honest	60000
Bill Bonkers	60000
Fred Fearless	60000
Jumbo Jones	65000
Steve Giblet	70000

```
Ann Agram        75000
Sam TheMan       85000
Young Tom        90000
```

If you take the trouble to calculate it, you'll find that the average salary is a little more than $111,000. Only the eight employees with salaries under the average are listed by the query, exactly as desired.

In this example, the subquery was used inside the **Where** clause of another query. Subqueries can also be used inside the **Having** or **Select** clause of another query. I will show some examples in a moment. But first, I will elaborate on what's possible using subqueries in the **Where** clause. The first example was a subquery that returned a single value. What about a subquery that returns multiple values?

Multiple-Value Subqueries

Assume that the Employees and Assignments tables hold information about employees and their assignments to departments. The following query shows the data:

```
Select E.EmployeeNo, Name, DeptNo, HoursPerWeek, Salary
  From Employees E, Assignments A
  Where E.EmployeeNo = A.EmployeeNo
  Order BY E.EmployeeNo, DeptNo ;
```

Results:

EmployeeNo	Name	DeptNo	HoursPerWeek	Salary
1	Fred Fearless	2	40	60000
2	Adam Adams	3	40	120000
3	Eve Adams	3	40	130000
5	Jumbo Jones	2	40	65000
6	Sam TheMan	2	40	85000
8	Steve Giblet	4	40	70000
9	Bill Bonkers	1	20	60000
9	Bill Bonkers	2	40	60000
9	Bill Bonkers	3	20	60000
10	Sue Slewfoot	1	40	300000
11	Abigail Honest	2	20	60000
11	Abigail Honest	4	20	60000
12	Ann Agram	3	40	75000

Notice that two of the employees, Bill Bonkers and Abigail Honest, have multiple assignments. Bill is actually assigned to work a total of 80 hours per week, in three departments. Abigail works a regular 40-hour week, but divides her time between two departments.

Suppose you wanted to know which employees had one or more assignments of fewer than 40 hours per week. Using what you learned in Chapter 7, you could write a join query that gives the desired result:

```
Select Distinct E.EmployeeNo, Name From Employees E, Assignments
Where HoursPerWeek < 40 AND E.EmployeeNo = Assignments.EmployeeNo
Order By Name;
```

Results:

```
EmployeeNo Name

11         Abigail Honest
9          Bill Bonkers
```

Just as expected, Abigail and Bill are reported.

You could obtain the same result by using the following subquery:

```
Select Distinct EmployeeNo, Name
  From Employees
  Where EmployeeNo In
    (Select EmployeeNo From Assignments Where HoursPerWeek < 40)
  Order By Name ;
```

Here, the subquery produces a set of rows containing the employee numbers of all employees with at least one assignment that is less than full-time. This becomes the target list for the main query, which uses the **In** predicate. When the **In** predicate is true, this means the subquery also returned an employee number from the Employees table. This will occur only when the employee has a less-than-full-time assignment. The employee number and name of all such employees are included in the result set.

Notice the **Distinct** modifier placed after **Select**. This ensures that an employee, such as Abigail, who has two 20-hour assignments, will be included only once in the result set. Recall that **Distinct** suppresses duplicate result-set rows, eliminating any multiple hits returned by the subquery.

You can do some kinds of queries, such as this one, in a single step by using either a join or a subquery. Here the decision to use a subquery is not based on performance, but on style. In such a case, you should use whichever form seems clearer and less error-prone. Often, this will be the form that includes the subquery.

More Multiple-Value Subqueries: Not In, Any, And All

You can use several other predicates besides **In** with uncorrelated, multiple-value subqueries. For example, the **Not In** predicate has an effect opposite that of the **In** predicate. In the previous example, you could have used **Not In** to list those employees who *do not* have any less-than-full-time assignments:

```
Select Distinct EmployeeNo, Name
  From Employees
  Where EmployeeNo Not In
    (Select EmployeeNo From Assignments Where HoursPerWeek < 40)
  Order By Name ;
```

The **Any** predicate can be used with a comparison operator (=, >, <, <=, >=, or <>). When used with the equality operator (=), it has the same meaning as the **In** predicate. The following query finds the employees with less-than-full-time assignments:

```
Select Name from Employees
  Where EmployeeNo =
  Any (Select EmployeeNo From Assignments Where HoursPerWeek < 40) ;
```

When used with one of the other comparison operators, the **Any** predicate tests whether the comparison is true for at least one of the values returned by the subquery. Suppose you wanted to know which employees are working more hours per week than someone else. The following query would do just that:

```
Select Name, Sum(HoursPerWeek) As Hours
  From Employees E, Assignments A
  Where E.EmployeeNo = A.EmployeeNo
  Group By Name
  Having Sum(HoursPerWeek) >
    Any (Select Sum(HoursPerWeek) From Assignments Group By EmployeeNo);
```

Results:

```
Name              Hours

Bill Bonkers      80.0
```

The subquery generates one row for each employee represented in the Assignments table. The row includes the total hours per week worked by the employee. In the data shown earlier in the chapter, notice that everyone is working a total of 40 hours per week except poor Bill. His is the only row that contains a value other than 40. Therefore, he is the only one working more than anyone else, and he is the lone employee reported by the query.

Now look at some examples using the Skills and EmployeeSkills tables of the HRData database. Here are the contents of the Skills table:

```
Select * From Skills;
```

Results:

```
SkillNo    Skill

1          Requirements analysis
2          Java programming
3          C++ programming
4          Testing
5          Inspection
6          Writing
7          Sky diving
8          Computer programming
```

Here are the contents of the EmployeeSkills table:

```
Select * From EmployeeSkills Order By EmployeeNo, SkillNo;
```

Results:

```
EmployeeNo SkillNo

1          3
1          7
1          8
2          4
```

3	4
5	2
5	8
6	7
7	6
9	1
9	2
9	8
10	1
11	5
12	4
12	5

As a warm-up, join these tables with the Employees table to produce a list of employee names and skills:

```
Select E.EmployeeNo, Name, Skill
  From Employees E, EmployeeSkills ES, Skills S
  Where E.EmployeeNo = ES.EmployeeNo
    And ES.SkillNo = S.SkillNo
  Order By E.EmployeeNo, S.Skill;
```

Results:

EmployeeNo	Name	Skill
1	Fred Fearless	C++ programming
1	Fred Fearless	Computer programming
1	Fred Fearless	Sky diving
2	Adam Adams	Testing
3	Eve Adams	Testing
5	Jumbo Jones	Computer programming
5	Jumbo Jones	Java programming
6	Sam TheMan	Sky diving
7	Young Tom	Writing
9	Bill Bonkers	Computer programming
9	Bill Bonkers	Java programming
9	Bill Bonkers	Requirements analysis
10	Sue Slewfoot	Requirements analysis
11	Abigail Honest	Inspection
12	Anne Agram	Inspection
12	Anne Agram	Testing

Now, you can get down to business by writing a query that tells us which employees are computer programmers (skill #8) and which are sky divers (skill #7):

```
Select Distinct Name
   From Employees E, EmployeeSkills ES
   Where E.EmployeeNo = ES.EmployeeNo
     And SkillNo = 8
     And E.EmployeeNo In
       (Select EmployeeNo From EmployeeSkills Where SkillNo = 7)
   Order By Name;
```

Results:

```
Name

Fred Fearless
```

The subquery

```
(Select EmployeeNo From EmployeeSkills Where SkillNo = 7)
```

retrieves the employee number of each sky diver. The main query uses the **Where** clause to select only employees who are computer programmers (skill #8). It uses the **In** predicate to check whether a computer programmer is also a sky diver whose employee number is returned by the subquery.

Here is a similar query that finds computer programmers who are not also testers (skill #4):

```
Select Distinct Name
   From Employees E, EmployeeSkills ES
   Where E.EmployeeNo = ES.EmployeeNo
     And SkillNo = 8
     And E.EmployeeNo Not In
       (Select EmployeeNo From EmployeeSkills Where SkillNo = 4)
   Order By Name;
```

Results:

```
Name

Bill Bonkers
Fred Fearless
Jumbo Jones
```

Here is a query that finds employees skilled in requirements analysis (skill #1), who also have some other skill:

```
Select Distinct Name
  From Employees E, EmployeeSkills ES
  Where E.EmployeeNo = ES.EmployeeNo
    And SkillNo = 1
    And E.EmployeeNo In
     (Select EmployeeNo From EmployeeSkills Where SkillNo <> 1)
  Order By Name;
```

Results:

```
Name

Bill Bonkers
```

A similar query uses the **Not In** predicate to find testers who have no other skill:

```
Select Distinct Name
  From Employees E, EmployeeSkills ES
  Where E.EmployeeNo = ES.EmployeeNo
    And SkillNo = 4
    And E.EmployeeNo Not In
      (Select EmployeeNo From EmployeeSkills Where SkillNo <> 4)
  Order By Name;
```

Results:

```
Name

Adam Adams
Eve Adams
```

Now try some subqueries that use comparisons other than equality. First, use a join to see how salaries and skills are related:

```
Select Name, Salary, SkillNo
  From Employees E, EmployeeSkills ES
  Where E.EmployeeNo = ES.EmployeeNo
  Order By SkillNo, Name;
```

Results:

```
Name                 Salary      SkillNo

Bill Bonkers         60000       1
Sue Slewfoot         300000      1
Bill Bonkers         60000       2
Jumbo Jones          65000       2
Fred Fearless        60000       3
Adam Adams           120000      4
Anne Agram           75000       4
Eve Adams            130000      4
Abigail Honest       60000       5
Anne Agram           75000       5
Young Tom            90000       6
Fred Fearless        60000       7
Sam TheMan           85000       7
Bill Bonkers         60000       8
Fred Fearless        60000       8
Jumbo Jones          65000       8
```

Now find which computer programmer is earning the lowest salary:

```
Select Distinct Name
  From Employees E, EmployeeSkills ES
  Where E.EmployeeNo = ES.EmployeeNo
    And SkillNo = 8
    And Salary <= All
      (Select Salary
          From Employees E, EmployeeSkills ES
          Where E.EmployeeNo = ES.EmployeeNo
            And SkillNo = 8
      )
  Order By Name;
```

Results:

```
Name

Fred Fearless
```

The subquery retrieves the salary of each computer programmer (skill #8), and the <= **All** predicate limits the result set to the one programmer who makes no more than any other, Fred Fearless.

Next, find whether any testers (skill #4) are earning at least as much as every programmer:

```
Select Distinct Name
  From Employees E, EmployeeSkills ES
  Where E.EmployeeNo = ES.EmployeeNo
    And SkillNo = 4
    And Salary >= All
      (Select Salary
         From Employees E, EmployeeSkills ES
         Where E.EmployeeNo = ES.EmployeeNo
           And SkillNo = 8
    )
  Order By Name;
```

Results:

```
Name

Adam Adams
Eve Adams
```

The subquery again retrieves the salary of each programmer. The >= **All** predicate limits the result to only those testers whose salary is at least as much as every programmer.

As a final example of an uncorrelated subquery, find which Java programmers (skill #2) are earning at least as much as employees with writing skills (skill #6):

```
Select Distinct Name
  From Employees E, EmployeeSkills ES
  Where E.EmployeeNo = ES.EmployeeNo
    And SkillNo = 2
    And Salary >= ANY
      (Select Salary
         From Employees E, EmployeeSkills ES
         Where E.EmployeeNo = ES.EmployeeNo
           And SkillNo = 6
    )
  Order By Name;
```

Results:

```
Name

Bill Bonkers
```

Here the subquery retrieves the salary of every employee skilled in writing. The >= **Any** predicate tests whether a Java programmer earns at least as much as employees with writing skills. Bill is the only one who fits the profile.

You can use more than one subquery inside a main query. Say you wanted to know which nonmanagers earn more than a manager. Managers have their employee numbers stored in the Departments table, so you can list the managers and their salaries with this join:

```
Select Name, Salary
  From Employees E, Departments D
  Where E.EmployeeNo = D.ManagerID;
```

Results:

Name	Salary
Sue Slewfoot	300000
Sam TheMan	85000
Bill Bonkers	60000
Steve Giblet	70000

You can use a subquery to list the nonmanagers and their salaries:

```
Select Name, Salary
  From Employees
  Where EmployeeNo Not In
    (Select ManagerID From Departments);
```

Results:

Name	Salary
Fred Fearless	60000
Adam Adams	120000
Eve Adams	130000
Jumbo Jones	65000
Young Tom	90000
Abigail Honest	60000
Anne Agram	75000

Now, write a query that tells who the well-heeled nonmanagers are:

```
Select Name, Salary
  From Employees
```

```
Where EmployeeNo Not In
   (Select ManagerID From Departments)
   And Salary >= Any
   (Select Salary
      From Employees E, Departments D
      Where E.EmployeeNo = D.ManagerID
   );
```

Results:

```
Name            Salary

Adam Adams      120000
Eve Adams       130000
Young Tom        90000
```

The main query contains two uncorrelated subqueries. The first query

```
(Select ManagerID From Departments)
```

retrieves the ManagerID (that is, the employee number) of each manager. The main query uses this subquery with the **Not In** predicate to exclude managers.

The second subquery

```
(Select Salary
   From Employees E, Departments D
   Where E.EmployeeNo = D.ManagerID);
```

returns the salary of each manager. The main query uses the >= **Any** predicate to find only the employees who earn more than a manager.

Correlated Subqueries

The subqueries you have seen so far are uncorrelated, because they are evaluated only once. If a subquery references a column selected by the main query, the subquery must be reevaluated every time the column changes value. Such a subquery is *correlated*, because its evaluation is correlated with that of the main query.

Suppose you wanted to identify employees who have no work assignments. First, create such a situation by deleting Young Tom's work assignment:

```
Select From Assignments Where EmployeeNo = 7;
```

The following query containing a correlated subquery will discover that he has no assignments:

```
Select EmployeeNo, Name
  From Employees E
  Where Not Exists
    (Select * From Assignments A Where E.EmployeeNo = A.EmployeeNo) ;
```

Results:

```
EmployeeNo Name

7          Young Tom
```

This query has two novel aspects:

- The subquery contains a **Where** clause that compares the employee number in the Assignments table with the employee number in the Employees table. Notice that the subquery does not include the Employees table in its From list. The Employees table column values are taken from the main query. This means that the subquery must be reevaluated for every row of the Employees table, meaning that it's a correlated subquery.

- The **Not Exists** predicate is used to determine whether the subquery found returned no rows. If no rows were returned, the predicate is true; otherwise, it's false. (You can use the related **Exists** predicate to determine if a subquery returns at least one row. If so, the predicate is true; otherwise, it's false.)

As a whole, the query checks each row of the Employees table. The subquery is executed to see if a matching row is found in the Assignments table. If not, the employee number and name are included in the result set. In short, the query reports employees without assignments, just as desired.

Here is another query that uses a correlated subquery. This one reports employees who have an assignment that is longer than the average to their department. Since each department has at least one part-time worker, the average assignment is always less than 40 hours. The list, therefore, includes almost everyone.

```
Select Name, HoursPerWeek, DeptNo
  From Employees E, Assignments A
  Where E.EmployeeNo = A.EmployeeNo
  And HoursPerWeek >
```

```
(Select Avg(HoursPerWeek) From Assignments Where DeptNo = A.DeptNo)
Order By DeptNo ;
```

Results:

```
Name            HoursPerWeek DeptNo

Sue Slewfoot    40              1
Bill Bonkers    40              2
Jumbo Jones     40              2
Fred Fearless   40              2
Sam TheMan      40              2
Adam Adams      40              3
Ann Agram       40              3
Eve Adams       40              3
Steve Giblet    40              4
```

Here is the average assignment for each department, so you can verify the result of the previous query:

```
Select DeptNo, Avg(HoursPerWeek) As "Average" From Assignments
Group By DeptNo;
```

Results:

```
DeptNo      Average

1           30.0
2           36.0
3           35.0
4           30.0
```

Here is a query that uses a correlated subquery to report employees who have two or more work assignments:

```
Select Name
  From Employees E
  Where Exists
  (Select Count(*)
    From Assignments
    Where EmployeeNo = E.EmployeeNo
    Having Count(*) >= 2
  );
```

Results:

```
Name

Bill Bonkers
Abigail Honest
```

As usual, Bill and Abigail make the list. Each has at least two assignments, unlike the other employees, who have, at most, one.

As a final example of a correlated subquery, you'll list the number of skills possessed by each programmer. As a warm-up, first list the number of skills of each employee:

```
Select Name, Count(*) As "# Skills"
   From Employees E, EmployeeSkills ES
   Where E.EmployeeNo = ES.EmployeeNo
   Group By Name;
```

Results:

Name	# Skills
Abigail Honest	1
Adam Adams	1
Anne Agram	2
Bill Bonkers	3
Eve Adams	1
Fred Fearless	3
Jumbo Jones	2
Sam TheMan	1
Sue Slewfoot	1
Young Tom	1

Now all you have to do is limit the list to just those employees who possess skill #8 (computer programming). This is trickier than it might seem. If you simply include a **Where** clause that restricts the result to rows that specify skill #8, like this

```
Select Name, Count(*) As "# Skills"
   From Employees E, EmployeeSkills ES
   Where E.EmployeeNo = ES.EmployeeNo
     And SkillNo = 8
   Group By Name;
```

Results:

```
Name                 # Skills

Bill Bonkers         1
Fred Fearless        1
Jumbo Jones          1
```

the result includes *only* the row with SkillNo = 8, which distorts the count. A correlated query is the answer:

```
Select Name,
  (Select Count(*) As "# Skills"
     From EmployeeSkills ES2
     Where ES2.EmployeeNo = E.EmployeeNo
  ) As "# Skills"
  From Employees E, EmployeeSkills ES
  Where E.EmployeeNo = ES.EmployeeNo
    And SkillNo = 8
  Group By E.EmployeeNo, Name;
```

Results:

```
Name                 # Skills

Fred Fearless        3
Jumbo Jones          2
Bill Bonkers         3
```

The correlated query takes the value of **E.EmployeeNo** from the main query, much the way a method accepts an input argument. The correlated query is reevaluated for each employee (row) within the Employees table, returning the number of skills possessed by the employee. With that adjustment, the report works fine.

Subqueries In Other DML Statements

You can also use subqueries in the other DML statements—**Insert**, **Update**, and **Delete**. As an example, here is an **Update** that doubles the salary of any employee assigned to Department 3:

```
Update Employees
  Set Salary = 2 * Salary
  Where EmployeeNo In
    (Select EmployeeNo From Assignments Where DeptNo = 3) ;

Select E.EmployeeNo, Name, DeptNo, HoursPerWeek, Salary
  From Employees E, Assignments A
  Where E.EmployeeNo = A.EmployeeNo
  Order By E.EmployeeNo, DeptNo ;
```

Results:

EmployeeNo	Name	DeptNo	HoursPerWeek	Salary
1	Fred Fearless	2	40	60000
2	Adam Adams	3	40	240000
3	Eve Adams	3	40	260000
5	Jumbo Jones	2	40	65000
6	Sam TheMan	2	40	85000
8	Steve Giblet	4	40	70000
9	Bill Bonkers	1	20	120000
9	Bill Bonkers	2	40	120000
9	Bill Bonkers	3	20	120000
10	Sue Slewfoot	1	40	300000
11	Abigail Honest	2	20	60000
11	Abigail Honest	4	20	60000
12	Ann Agram	3	40	150000

By comparing the results above with the reports shown earlier in the chapter, you can verify that the employees assigned to Department 3, and only those assigned to Department 3, received the increase.

Sometimes, a problem seems too difficult to accomplish in a single SQL statement. In such a case, you can create a temporary table, using multiple DML statements to insert and update its contents. After retrieving the final result, the table can be dropped. Subqueries within DML statements are handy for such situations.

The EmpBrowser Applet

The EmpBrowser applet allows the user to navigate a simple table that contains employee information—viewing, adding, changing, and deleting records at will. Figure 11.1 shows the applet's user interface. Buttons control the operation of

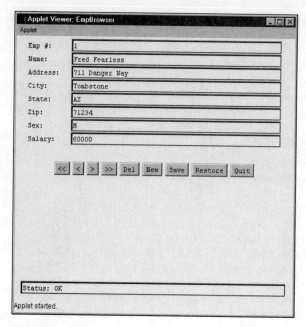

Figure 11.1
The user interface of the EmpBrowser applet.

the applet, which is based on similar read-only applets for viewing the Visits table, described in previous chapters.

Listing 11.1 shows the fields of the applet. These include **DBRecord**, which encapsulates information pertaining to a single employee record, and **theDB**, a **JDBC02** object that encapsulates database fields and methods.

The applet keeps track of its direction of movement through the table, so that **Select** operations can be minimized. The applet performs a **Select** only when the direction of movement changes or when a row is inserted, updated, or deleted. This makes operation of the applet quite efficient. Nevertheless, its code is simple.

In addition to the usual buttons for navigation, the applet includes a button to create a new (blank) record for insertion and a button for saving a modified record. The applet does not warn the user to save a changed record. Changes are lost if the user fails to click the Save button. If you prefer that the applet issue a warning, you can easily modify it to do so. The **TextEvent** will tell you whether a **TextField** has been changed. Before moving off a record that has been changed, the applet could show a dialog prompting the user to save the record or lose any changes made.

The applet also includes a Restore button that causes the Employees table to be re-created and loaded with sample data. This makes experimenting with the applet easy, since the table it updates can be easily returned to a known state.

LISTING 11.1   FIELDS OF THE EMPBROWSER APPLET.

```java
import java.applet.*;
import java.awt.*;
import java.awt.event.*;
import java.sql.*;

public class EmpBrowser extends Applet
implements ActionListener
{
    static final int BROWSING_FORWARD  = +1;
    static final int BROWSING_BACKWARD = -1;
    static final int FIELD_COUNT       =  8;

    Panel       theMainPanel = new Panel(new GridLayout(2, 1));
    Panel       theDataPanel = new Panel(new GridLayout(9, 1));

    TextField   txtEmpNo      = new TextField("",  6);
    TextField   txtEmpName    = new TextField("", 50);
    TextField   txtEmpAddress = new TextField("", 50);
    TextField   txtEmpCity    = new TextField("", 16);
    TextField   txtEmpState   = new TextField("",  2);
    TextField   txtEmpZip     = new TextField("",  5);
    TextField   txtEmpSex     = new TextField("",  1);
    TextField   txtEmpSalary  = new TextField("", 10);

    TextField [ ] theFields  =
      { txtEmpNo, txtEmpName, txtEmpAddress, txtEmpCity, txtEmpState,
        txtEmpZip, txtEmpSex, txtEmpSalary };

    Panel       theButtonPanel = new Panel(new FlowLayout( ));
    Button      theFirstButton = new Button("<<");
    Button      thePrevButton  = new Button("<");
    Button      theNextButton  = new Button(">");
    Button      theLastButton  = new Button(">>");
    Button      theDelButton   = new Button("Del");
    Button      theNewButton   = new Button("New");
    Button      theSaveButton  = new Button("Save");
    Button      theRestButton  = new Button("Restore");
    Button      theQuitButton  = new Button("Quit");
```

```
Panel        theStatusPanel  = new Panel(new BorderLayout( ));
TextField    theStatus       = new TextField(64);

JDBC02       theDB           = new JDBC02(theStatus);

DBRecord     theDBRecord     = new DBRecord(FIELD_COUNT);

int          theBrowseDirection = BROWSING_FORWARD;
boolean      haveResultSet   = false;
```

The init( ) Method

Listing 11.2 shows the **init( )** method, which builds the user interface. It uses the **getLabeledComponent( )** helper method to facilitate component placement. Rather than prompting for its data source, the URL is hard-coded in the program. This helps ensure that the program does not cause unintended damage to useful data.

LISTING 11.2   THE INIT( ) METHOD.

```
public void init( )
{
    setFont(new Font("Courier", Font.PLAIN, 12));

    add("Center", theMainPanel);
    add("South",  theStatusPanel);

    theMainPanel.add(theDataPanel);
    theMainPanel.add(theButtonPanel);

    theDataPanel.add(getLabeledComponent("Emp #:   ", txtEmpNo));
    theDataPanel.add(getLabeledComponent("Name:    ", txtEmpName));
    theDataPanel.add(getLabeledComponent("Address: ", txtEmpAddress));
    theDataPanel.add(getLabeledComponent("City:    ", txtEmpCity));
    theDataPanel.add(getLabeledComponent("State:   ", txtEmpState));
    theDataPanel.add(getLabeledComponent("Zip:     ", txtEmpZip));
    theDataPanel.add(getLabeledComponent("Sex:     ", txtEmpSex));
    theDataPanel.add(getLabeledComponent("Salary:  ", txtEmpSalary));

    theButtonPanel.add(theFirstButton);
    theButtonPanel.add(thePrevButton);
    theButtonPanel.add(theNextButton);
    theButtonPanel.add(theLastButton);
    theButtonPanel.add(theDelButton);
    theButtonPanel.add(theNewButton);
    theButtonPanel.add(theSaveButton);
```

```
    theButtonPanel.add(theRestButton);
    theButtonPanel.add(theQuitButton);

    theStatusPanel.add("Center", theStatus);

    theStatus .setEditable(false);

    theFirstButton.addActionListener(this);
    thePrevButton .addActionListener(this);
    theNextButton .addActionListener(this);
    theLastButton .addActionListener(this);
    theDelButton  .addActionListener(this);
    theNewButton  .addActionListener(this);
    theSaveButton .addActionListener(this);
    theRestButton .addActionListener(this);
    theQuitButton .addActionListener(this);

    try
    {
        theDB.openConnection("jdbc:odbc:Browser", "", "");
        theDBRecord = getFirstRecord( );
        if (theDBRecord != null)
        {
            theDBRecord.moveToScreen(theFields);
        }
    }
    catch (Exception e)
    {
        handleException(e);
    }
}
```

The stop( ) Method

The **stop**( ) method, shown in Listing 11.3, closes the database connection and hides the applet.

LISTING 11.3   THE STOP( ) METHOD.

```
public void stop( )
{
    try
    {
        theDB.closeConnection( );
    }
    catch (Exception e)
    {
```

```
        handleException(e);
    }
    setVisible(false);
}
```

The actionPerformed( ) Method

Listing 11.4 shows the **actionPerformed**( ) method, which detects button clicks
and invokes an appropriate method. The database navigation methods return a
reference to a **DBRecord**, which may be **null** if no record was found. The applet
updates its screen with new record contents only if a navigation method returns
a non-**null** value; otherwise, it displays an error message in the status **TextField**.

LISTING 11.4   THE ACTIONPERFORMED( ) METHOD.

```java
public void actionPerformed(ActionEvent event)
{
    statusOK( );
    Object source = event.getSource( );

    if (source == theFirstButton)
    {
        DBRecord first = getFirstRecord( );
        if (first != null)
        {
            theDBRecord = first;
            theDBRecord.moveToScreen(theFields);
        }
        else
            noRecordFound( );
    }
    else if (source == thePrevButton)
    {
        DBRecord prev = getPrevRecord( );
        if (prev != null)
        {
            theDBRecord = prev;
            theDBRecord.moveToScreen(theFields);
        }
        else
            noRecordFound( );
    }
    else if (source == theNextButton)
    {
        DBRecord next = getNextRecord( );
        if (next != null)
        {
```

```
            theDBRecord = next;
            theDBRecord.moveToScreen(theFields);
        }
        else
            noRecordFound( );
    }
    else if (source == theLastButton)
    {
        DBRecord last = getLastRecord( );
        if (last != null)
        {
            theDBRecord = last;
            theDBRecord.moveToScreen(theFields);
        }
        else
            theDBRecord.moveToScreen(theFields);
    }
    else if (source == theDelButton)
    {
        deleteRecord( );
    }
    else if (source == theNewButton)
    {
        newRecord( );
    }
    else if (source == theSaveButton)
    {
        saveRecord( );
    }
    else if (source == theRestButton)
    {
        restoreData( );
    }
    else if (source == theQuitButton)
    {
        stop( );
    }
}
```

The Navigation Methods

Listings 11.5 through 11.8 show the navigation methods. Where possible, the methods avoid executing a new **Select**, simply returning the next row of the current result set where appropriate. Backward movement through the table is implemented using a result set sorted in descending order by employee number.

LISTING 11.5   THE GETFIRSTRECORD( ) METHOD.

```
public DBRecord getFirstRecord( )
{
    DBRecord result = null;

    theBrowseDirection = BROWSING_FORWARD;

    try
    {
        theDB.executeQuery("SELECT * FROM Employees "
          + "ORDER BY employeeno;");

        if (theDB.nextRow( ))
        {
            result = new DBRecord(theDB.theResultSet);
            haveResultSet = true;
        }
        else
            noRecordFound( );
    }
    catch (Exception e)
    {
        handleException(e);
    }

    return result;
}
```

LISTING 11.6   THE GETLASTRECORD( ) METHOD.

```
public DBRecord getLastRecord( )
{
    DBRecord result = null;

    theBrowseDirection = BROWSING_FORWARD;
    haveResultSet = false;

    try
    {
        theDB.executeQuery("SELECT * FROM Employees "
          + " ORDER BY employeeno;");

        if (theDB.nextRow( ))
        {
            do
            {
```

```
            result = new DBRecord(theDB.theResultSet);
        }
        while (theDB.nextRow( ));
    }
    else noRecordFound( );
}
catch (Exception e)
{
    handleException(e);
}

return result;
}
```

LISTING 11.7   THE GETPREVRECORD( ) METHOD.

```
public DBRecord getPrevRecord( )
{
    DBRecord result = null;

    try
    {
        if (!haveResultSet || theBrowseDirection != BROWSING_BACKWARD)
        {
            theBrowseDirection = BROWSING_BACKWARD;

            theDB.executeQuery("SELECT * FROM Employees "
                + "WHERE employeeno < "
                + getEmployeeNo( )
                + " ORDER BY employeeno DESC;");
        }

        if (theDB.nextRow( ))
        {
            result = new DBRecord(theDB.theResultSet);
            haveResultSet = true;
        }
        else
            noRecordFound( );
    }
    catch (Exception e)
    {
        handleException(e);
    }

    return result;
}
```

LISTING 11.8   THE GETNEXTRECORD( ) METHOD.

```
public DBRecord getNextRecord( )
{
    DBRecord result = null;

    try
    {
        if (!haveResultSet || theBrowseDirection != BROWSING_FORWARD)
        {
            theBrowseDirection = BROWSING_FORWARD;

            theDB.executeQuery("SELECT * FROM Employees "
                + "WHERE employeeno > "
                + getEmployeeNo( )
                + " ORDER BY employeeno;");
        }
        if (theDB.nextRow( ))
        {
            result = new DBRecord(theDB.theResultSet);
            haveResultSet = true;
        }
        else
            noRecordFound( );
    }
    catch (Exception e)
    {
        handleException(e);
    }

    return result;
}
```

The deleteRecord( ) Method

The **deleteRecord**( ) method, shown in Listing 11.9, deletes the currently displayed record. To avoid problems that can occur when updating a row within the current result set, it first closes the result set. Technically, moving off the current row should be sufficient, but some drivers have bugs that require the result set to be closed. After the row is deleted, the method attempts to move to the next record and display it, taking into account the current direction of travel through the table.

LISTING 11.9 THE deleteRecord( ) METHOD.

```
public void deleteRecord( )
{
    try
    {
        theDB.closeResultSet( );
        haveResultSet = false;

        theDB.executeUpdate("DELETE FROM Employees "
          + "WHERE employeeno = "
          + getEmployeeNo( )
          + " ;") ;

        DBRecord next = new DBRecord(FIELD_COUNT);

        if (theBrowseDirection == BROWSING_FORWARD)
            next = getNextRecord( );
        else
            next = getPrevRecord( );

        theDBRecord = next;
        clearScreen( );

        if (next != null)
        {
            theDBRecord.moveToScreen(theFields);
        }
        else
            noRecordFound( );
    }
    catch (SQLException sql)
    {
        handleException(sql);
        return;
    }
}
```

The newRecord( ) Method

Listing 11.10 shows the **newRecord( )** method. This method, triggered by the New button, presents the user with a blank employee record, ready for input of new employee information. The Save button must be used to actually store the entered information on the database.

LISTING 11.10   THE NEWRECORD( ) METHOD.

```
public void newRecord( )
{
    clearScreen( );
    try
    {
        theDB.closeResultSet( );
    }
    catch (SQLException sql) { ; }
    haveResultSet = false;
}
```

The saveRecord( ) Method

The **saveRecord**( ) method, shown in Listing 11.11, writes a new or updated record to the database table. If an employee number was entered, the method deletes any previously existing record as the first step of processing. Generally, you should prompt the user to confirm such an operation before carrying it out, because an error could lead to deletion of the wrong record. This would complicate the example, however, so EmpBrowser does not include this function, which can be easily added if needed.

The record is then inserted into the database. If an employee number was not specified, the Insert field list is one that omits the employee number field, so Access can automatically assign the next available value to this Counter column. If an employee number was specified, however, it is used. Utility methods of the **JDBC02** class are used to build the Insert command. After updating the database, the method attempts to navigate to, and display, the next record.

LISTING 11.11   THE SAVERECORD( ) METHOD.

```
public void saveRecord( )
{
    haveResultSet = false;
    String sql;
    if (txtEmpNo.getText( ).length( ) > 0)
    {
        sql = "DELETE FROM Employees WHERE EmployeeNo = ";
        sql += txtEmpNo.getText( );
        sql += ";";
        try
        {
```

```
            theDB.executeUpdate(sql);
        }
        catch (SQLException e) { ; }

        sql = "INSERT INTO Employees ";
        String [ ] fields = new String[theFields.length];
        for (int i = 0; i < fields.length; i++)
            fields [i] = theFields [i].getText( );

        boolean [] quotes = new boolean [fields.length];
        for (int i = 0; i < fields.length; i++)
            quotes  [i] = true;

        sql += theDB.getValueList(fields, quotes);
    }
    else
    {
        sql = "INSERT INTO Employees ";
        sql += "(Name, Address, City, State, Zip, Sex, Salary) ";

        String [ ] fields = new String[theFields.length - 1];
        for (int i = 0; i < fields.length; i++)
            fields [i] = theFields [i + 1].getText( );

        boolean [] quotes = new boolean [fields.length];
        for (int i = 0; i < fields.length; i++)
            quotes  [i] = true;

        sql += theDB.getValueList(fields, quotes);
    }
    sql += ";";
    try
    {
        theDB.executeUpdate(sql);
        clearScreen( );

        DBRecord next = null;
        if (theBrowseDirection == BROWSING_FORWARD)
            next = getNextRecord( );
        else
            next = getPrevRecord( );
        if (next != null)
        {
            theDBRecord = next;
            theDBRecord.moveToScreen(theFields);
        }
```

```
        else
            noRecordFound( );
    }
    catch (SQLException sqlex)
    {
        handleException(sqlex);
    }
}
```

The getEmployeeNo( ) Method

The **getEmployeeNo**( ) method, shown in Listing 11.12, is used to obtain the value of the employee number contained in the **TextField**. It returns 0, indicating the first row of the table, if no employee number is present in the **TextField**.

LISTING 11.12   THE GETEMPLOYEENO( ) METHOD.

```
public String getEmployeeNo( )
{
    if (theDBRecord == null) return "0";
    if (theDBRecord.theFields[0] == null) return "0";
    return theDBRecord.theFields[0];
}
```

Miscellaneous Methods

Listing 11.13 shows miscellaneous methods used to clear the screen, display status messages, handle SQL exceptions, and build the user interface.

LISTING 11.13   MISCELLANEOUS METHODS.

```
public void clearScreen( )
{
    for (int i = 0; i < theFields.length; i++)
        theFields[i].setText("");
}

public void noRecordFound( )
{
    setStatus("Status: No record found.");
}

public void statusOK( )
{
    setStatus("Status: OK");
}
```

```
public void setStatus(String s)
{
    theStatus.setText(s);
}

public void handleException(Exception e)
{
    e.printStackTrace( );
}

public Panel getLabeledComponent(String s, Component c)
{
    Panel p = new Panel( );
    p.setLayout(new BorderLayout( ));
    p.add(new Label(s), "West");
    p.add(c, "Center");
    return p;
}
```

The restoreData( ) Method

The **restoreData**( ) method, shown in Listing 11.14, drops, re-creates, and loads the Employees table with a set of sample rows. After restoring the database table, the method attempts to display the first row of the table.

LISTING 11.14   THE RESTOREDATA( ) METHOD.

```
public void restoreData( )
{
    clearScreen( );
    haveResultSet = false;
    try
    {
        String sql;
        sql = "DROP TABLE Employees;";
        theDB.executeUpdate(sql);

        sql =  "create table employees (";
        sql += "employeeno counter constraint pk primary key, ";
        sql += "name varchar(50), ";
        sql += "address varchar(50), ";
        sql += "city varchar(16), ";
        sql += "state varchar(2), ";
        sql += "zip int, ";
        sql += "sex varchar(1), ";
        sql += "salary int ";
        sql += "); ";
        theDB.executeUpdate(sql);
```

```java
String [ ] [ ] data = new String [ ] [ ]
  {
      { "Fred Fearless",  "711 Danger Way",    "Tombstone",
      "AZ", "71234", "M", "60000"  },
      { "Adam Adams",      "1 Eden Circle",     "Paradise",
      "CA", "77701", "M", "120000" },
      { "Eve Adams",       "1 Eden Circle",     "Paradise",
      "CA", "77701", "F", "130000" },
      { "Bogus Blitzo",    "21 High Place",     "Easy Street",
      "CA", "16661", "M", "150000" },
      { "Jumbo Jones",     "17 Jungle Way",     "Redmond",
      "WA", "45624", "M", "65000"  },
      { "Sam TheMan",      "671 Careful Trail", "Santa Ona",
      "CA", "91732", "M", "85000"  },
      { "Young Tom",       "5542 Cushy Seat",   "Overstuff",
      "CA", "98235", "M", "90000"  },
      { "Steve Giblet",    "78 Turkey Plaza",   "Gravy",
      "CA", "93436", "M", "70000"  },
      { "Bill Bonkers",    "888 Frantic Lane",  "Anxiety",
      "CA", "95632", "M", "60000"  },
      { "Sue Slewfoot",    "86 Legal Tower",    "Highrise",
      "CA", "97655", "F", "300000" },
      { "Abigail Honest", "111 First Street",   "Integrity",
      "CA", "97633", "F", "60000"  },
      { "Ann Agram",       "22 Puzzle Box",     "Intellect",
      "CA", "95645", "F", "75000"  }
  };

boolean [ ] quotes = new boolean [ ]
  { true, true, true, true, true, true, true };

for (int i = 0; i < data.length; i++)
{

    sql = "INSERT INTO employees "
      + "(name, address, city, state, zip, sex, salary) "
      + theDB.getValueList(data[i], quotes)
      + ";" ;
    theDB.executeUpdate(sql);
}

theDBRecord = getFirstRecord( );
if (theDBRecord != null)
    theDBRecord.moveToScreen(theFields);
```

```
            theStatus.setText("Table restored.");
        }
        catch (SQLException e) { handleException(e); }

    }
```

The DBRecord Class

The **DBRecord** class, shown in Listing 11.15, encapsulates data and methods relating to database records. It's written to be flexible, so you can reuse it with few changes in building new applications.

You can build a new **DBRecord** using an **int** that specifies the number of fields (columns), a **ResultSet** that contains table rows, or an array containing references to **TextField**s column values.

Once a **DBRecord** has been established, it can be loaded with data from a **ResultSet** or an array of **TextField**s. Data can also be moved from the **DBRecord** into **TextField**s, permitting the display of a table row.

LISTING 11.15   THE DBRECORD CLASS.

```
class DBRecord
{
String [] theFields;

public DBRecord(int fields)
{
    theFields = new String [fields];
}

public DBRecord(ResultSet rs)
throws SQLException
{
    ResultSetMetaData meta = rs.getMetaData( );
    int fields = meta.getColumnCount( );
    theFields = new String[fields];

    for (int i = 1; i <= fields; i++)
    {
        theFields [i - 1] = nonNull(rs.getString(i));
    }
}

public DBRecord(TextField [ ] txt)
{
```

```
        theFields = new String[txt.length];

        for (int i = 1; i <= theFields.length; i++)
        {
            theFields [i - 1] = (txt [i - 1]).getText( );
        }
    }

    public void moveFromResultSet(ResultSet rs, TextField [ ] txt)
    throws SQLException
    {
        loadFromResultSet(rs);
        moveToScreen(txt);
    }

    public void loadFromResultSet(ResultSet rs)
    throws SQLException
    {
        for (int i = 1; i <= theFields.length; i++)
        {
            theFields [i - 1] = nonNull(rs.getString(i));
        }
    }

    public void moveFromScreen(TextField [ ] txt)
    {
        for (int i = 1; i <= theFields.length; i++)
        {
            theFields [i - 1] = (txt [i - 1]).getText( );
        }
    }

    public void moveToScreen(TextField [ ] txt)
    {
        for (int i = 1; i <= theFields.length; i++)
        {
            (txt [i - 1]).setText(theFields [i - 1]);
        }
    }

    public String nonNull(String s)
    {
        if (s != null) return s;
        return "";
    }
```

Summary

Subqueries are queries contained within other queries. Every subquery is one of two types: Uncorrelated subqueries are executed only once; correlated subqueries are executed repeatedly, once for each row of the related table. A subquery can return a single value or multiple values, which take the form of a table. The special predicates **In**, **Not In**, **Any**, **All**, **Exists**, and **Not Exists** are used to write subqueries. Subqueries can be used in **Insert**, **Update**, and **Drop** statements, as well as in the more common **Select** statement.

The result of a multiple-value subquery resembles a "virtual table" that is constructed when you run the subquery. The next chapter will teach you how to use another sort of virtual table, the view.

12
CREATING AND
USING VIEWS

This chapter deals with two SQL/JDBC facilities that are not fully supported by MS Access: views and stored procedures. The Access online documentation does not even mention views. Nevertheless, Access does let you create and use views, though sometimes in an idiosyncratic way. Access does not support stored procedures at all. If you want to try the examples dealing with stored procedures in this chapter, you will need a full-scale database, such as SQL Server.

Even if you don't have your own copy of a full-scale database, you will be able to study the example program for this chapter, an application that can execute SQL commands stored in text files. The application lets you create SQL scripts that you can execute repeatedly. This is a handy way to create small test databases that you can use to practice your SQL skills. By placing **Create** and **Insert** commands in a script, you can create database tables and load them with sample data. Then, after you have used **Insert**s, **Update**s, and **Delete**s to change the data, you can drop the tables and rerun the script to restore their original contents.

Using Views

SQL views are virtual tables—that is, database tables that appear to exist, but are actually subsets or combinations of real database tables. You can think of a view as a window into your database. For example, suppose that the Employees table contains information on employees working in several states, and that you often write queries that retrieve just the California employees. Each query must contain the **Where** clause

```
Where State = 'CA'
```

which is tiresome to write. You might even inadvertently omit it, leading to erroneous reports. To avoid this, you can create a view, based on the Employees table, that includes *only* the California employees. Once created, the view can be accessed just like a table, only you do not have to include the troublesome **Where** clause to restrict each query to California employees. Figure 12.1 shows how views work.

Views make queries easier to write and make the database easier to use. They're particularly handy when you find yourself joining tables repeatedly. As you learned in Chapter 8, database normalization, which requires you to split your data into separate tables, is essential for data integrity but a real nuisance when you want to retrieve data. By creating a view that joins tables split by normalization, you have the best of two worlds: Your data can be not only normalized, but it's also easy to access.

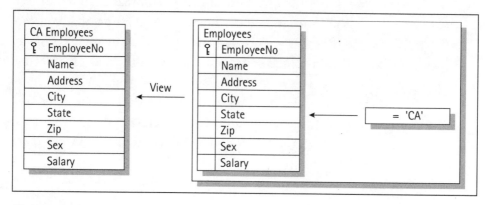

Figure 12.1
How views work.

Views let you protect yourself and others from changes to database structure. By creating a view that mimics the former database structure, you and your programs can continue to work as they did before, although the real structure of the database is now quite different.

Views are also useful because they can simplify complex tables and structures. By defining a view that contains only the columns a given user needs, you can avoid overwhelming the user with irrelevant information. As you'll learn in Chapter 13, you can also use views to implement security restrictions that prevent users from accessing or changing sensitive data. (Access, however, does not support this capability.)

Creating Views

Assume the Employees table has the following contents:

```
Select * From Employees;
```

Results:

```
EmployeeNo Name          Address         City       State Zip   Sex Salary

1          Fred Fearless 711 Danger Way  Tombstone  AZ    71234 M   60000
2          Adam Adams    1 Eden Circle   Paradise   CA    77701 M   240000
3          Eve Adams     1 Eden Circle   Paradise   CA    77701 F   260000
5          Jumbo Jones   17 Jungle Way   Redmond    WA    45624 M   65000
6          Sam TheMan    671 Careful Trail Santa Ona CA   91732 M   85000
7          Young Tom     5542 Cushy Seat Overstuff  CA    98235 M   90000
8          Steve Giblet  78 Turkey Plaza Gravy      CA    93436 M   70000
9          Bill Bonkers  888 Frantic Lane Anxiety   CA    95632 M   120000
10         Sue Slewfoot  86 Legal Tower  Highrise   CA    97655 F   300000
11         Abigail Honest 111 First Street Integrity CA   97633 F   60000
12         Ann Agram     22 Puzzle Box   Intellect  CA    95645 F   150000
```

To create a view, named Workers, that includes only selected columns of the Employees table, you write:

```
Create View Workers As Select EmployeeNo, Name, Salary From Employees;
```

Only the EmployeeNo, Name, and Salary columns are included in the view. Once you have created the view, you use it just like a table. For example, to list the rows of the view you write:

```
Select * From Workers;
```

Results:

```
EmployeeNo Name           Salary

1          Fred Fearless  60000
2          Adam Adams     240000
3          Eve Adams      260000
5          Jumbo Jones    65000
6          Sam TheMan     85000
7          Young Tom      90000
8          Steve Giblet   70000
9          Bill Bonkers   120000
10         Sue Slewfoot   300000
11         Abigail Honest 60000
12         Ann Agram      150000
```

If you like, you can think of the view as a subquery stored in the database. When you write a query that uses the view, SQL runs the stored subquery and returns the result set to the **From** clause of your query.

Views do not copy data and, therefore, do not occupy substantial amounts of space within a database. You may wish to delete a view simply to control clutter, however. The proper way to delete a view is using the **Drop View** statement:

```
Drop View Workers;
```

Unfortunately, Access rejects the standard syntax. If you try to drop a view under Access, you'll get an error message:

```
Error: [Microsoft][ODBC Microsoft Access 97 Driver]
Syntax error in DROP TABLE or DROP INDEX.
```

Because views behave so much like tables, the designers of Access decided to use **Drop Table**, instead of **Drop View**, to remove a view. The following works fine under Access, but most other databases require the standard **Drop View** statement to be used:

```
Drop Table Workers;
```

Views can be much more sophisticated than this simple example. Here's a view that chooses its columns *and* rows:

```
Create View Coasters As
   Select EmployeeNo, Name, Salary
      From Employees
      Where State = 'CA';

Select * From Coasters;
```

Results:

EmployeeNo	Name	Salary
2	Adam Adams	240000
3	Eve Adams	260000
6	Sam TheMan	85000
7	Young Tom	90000
8	Steve Giblet	70000
9	Bill Bonkers	120000
10	Sue Slewfoot	300000
11	Abigail Honest	60000
12	Ann Agram	150000

The real table used to define a view is called the *base table* of the view. Compare the query result just shown with the one from the base table shown earlier in the chapter, and verify that exactly the right rows were returned.

When you create a view, you can give the columns of the view new names, different from the column names of the base table. Unfortunately, the syntax required by Access is again nonstandard. Here's a view created using the standard syntax and the error returned by Access:

```
Create View Coasters (CNo, CName, CSalary) As
   Select EmployeeNo, Name, Salary From Employees
   Where State = 'CA';

Error: [Microsoft][ODBC Microsoft Access 97 Driver]
Syntax error in PARAMETER clause.
```

The view is intended to have three columns (CNo, CName, and CSalary) that are based on corresponding columns in the Employees table (EmployeeNo, Name, and Salary). The idiosyncratic syntax accepted by Access is this:

```
Create View Coasters As
   Select EmployeeNo As CNo, Name As CName, Salary As CSalary
```

```
   From Employees
   Where State = 'CA';

Select * From Coasters;
```

Results:

CNo	CName	CSalary
2	Adam Adams	240000
3	Eve Adams	260000
6	Sam TheMan	85000
7	Young Tom	90000
8	Steve Giblet	70000
9	Bill Bonkers	120000
10	Sue Slewfoot	300000
11	Abigail Honest	60000
12	Ann Agram	150000

You can also create columns of a view from expressions. For example, assume the Employees table stores the annual salaries of employees and that you want the view to return monthly salaries instead. You can write:

```
Create View Coasters As
   Select EmployeeNo As CNo, Name As CName,
     Salary/12 As CMSalary
   From Employees
   Where State = 'CA';
```

Results:

CNo	CName	CMSalary
2	Adam Adams	20000.0
3	Eve Adams	21666.6666666667
6	Sam TheMan	7083.33333333333
7	Young Tom	7500.0
8	Steve Giblet	5833.33333333333
9	Bill Bonkers	10000.0
10	Sue Slewfoot	25000.0
11	Abigail Honest	5000.0
12	Ann Agram	12500.0

As you will see in the next section, including expressions in views has some important consequences.

I began the chapter by remarking on the value of views that join tables. Here is an example that joins the Skills table with the EmployeeSkills table, making it easier to write a query that reports employee skills:

```
Create View EmployeeSkillsView As
   Select EmployeeNo, Skill
   From EmployeeSkills ES, Skills S
   Where ES.SkillNo = S.SkillNo;

Select Name, Skill
   From Employees E, EmployeeSkillsView ESV
   Where E.EmployeeNo = ESV.EmployeeNo
   Order By E.EmployeeNo, ESV.Skill;
```

Results:

Name	Skill
Fred Fearless	C++ programming
Fred Fearless	Computer programming
Fred Fearless	Sky diving
Adam Adams	Testing
Eve Adams	Testing
Jumbo Jones	Computer programming
Jumbo Jones	Java programming
Sam TheMan	Sky diving
Young Tom	Writing
Bill Bonkers	Computer programming
Bill Bonkers	Java programming
Bill Bonkers	Requirements analysis
Sue Slewfoot	Requirements analysis
Abigail Honest	Inspection
Ann Agram	Inspection
Ann Agram	Testing

If you like, you can go a step further by defining a view based on another view, rather than a real table. Here is how to use this trick and make the previous query easier still:

```
Create View NameSkillView As
   Select Name, Skill
   From Employees E, EmployeeSkillsView ESV
   Where E.EmployeeNo = ESV.EmployeeNo
   Order By E.EmployeeNo, ESV.Skill;
```

Now you can list the names of employees and their skills with nothing more than

```
Select * From NameSkillView;
```

which will give the same result as the previous query. Judicious definition of views can really cut down on the work needed to access tables and on the potential for error. This last query is much simpler and safer than the form needed without the use of views:

```
Select Name, Skill
  From Employees E, EmployeeSkills ES, Skills S
  Where E.EmployeeNo = ES.EmployeeNo
    And ES.SkillNo = S.SKillNo
  Order By E.EmployeeNo, ES.SkillNo;
```

One note of caution is in order. Some databases restrict the clauses that can be used in defining a view, prohibiting **Order By**, **Having**, and other clauses. Access allows **Order By**, but you'll need to check your documentation if you're using some other database.

Inserting, Updating, And Deleting Viewed Tables And Views

Creating and using views to access database tables is straightforward—until you consider the possibility of changing the data in the base table or the view. At that point, things get interesting. Some simple cases work well. I'll show these first, and then I'll address the problems.

Return to the example view, Coasters, defined to include selected rows and columns of the Employees table. Update the name of an employee via the Employees table. Here's what happens:

```
Update Employees
  Set Name = 'Anne Agram'
  Where EmployeeNo = 12;

Select * From Coasters
  Where CNo = 12;
```

Results:

```
CNo    CName          CMSalary
12     Anne Agram     12500.0
```

The view reflects the change.

Now try a riskier operation. Recall that the view defined monthly salary (CMSalary) as 1/12 the annual salary stored in the Employees table. Update the annual salary and see what happens:

```
Update Employees
   Set Salary = 120000
   Where EmployeeNo = 12;

Select * From Coasters
   Where CNo = 12;
```

Results:

```
CNo    CName          CMSalary
12     Anne Agram     10000.0
```

Notice that the view returns the monthly amount that corresponds to the updated annual amount. However, what happens if you update the view, rather than the base table?

```
Update Coasters Set CMSalary = 5000 Where CNo = 12;

Error: [Microsoft][ODBC Microsoft Access 97 Driver] Can't update
'CMSalary'; field not updatable.
```

Because the CMSalary column is a computed amount, Access will not allow you to update it. In many ways, views act the same as tables, but this example shows that they do not always do so. The illusion they offer is a good one, but not a perfect one. In principle, a database system could perform such an update by running the computation in reverse, calculating the annual salary as 12 times the monthly salary. Most databases will not go this "extra mile," however. They will simply forbid the operation.

This same principle governs **Inserts**. Access forbids the insertion of new row in the view:

```
Insert Into Coasters (CNo, CName, CMSalary)
Values (200, 'No Man', 5000) ;
```

Results:

```
Error: [Microsoft][ODBC Microsoft Access 97 Driver] Can't update
'CMSalary'; field not updatable.
```

The insertion would require a corresponding change to the base table (Employees), and Access refuses to compute the annual salary from the monthly salary.

These problems stem from the decision to include monthly salary in the view. If you revise the view to include annual salary—so its structure more closely matches that of the base table—and then retry the operation, here's what will happen:

```
Drop Table Coasters;

Create View Coasters As
   Select EmployeeNo As CNo, Name As CName, Salary As CSalary
   From Employees
   Where State = 'CA';

Update Coasters
   Set CSalary = 5000
   Where CNo = 12;
```

This time, Access allows the operation, since CSalary is a column, rather than an expression. However, the **Insert** operation still fails, though for a new reason:

```
Insert Into Coasters (CNo, CName, CSalary)
Values (200, 'No Man', 60000) ;

Error: [Microsoft][ODBC Microsoft Access 97 Driver]
The field 'Employees.Address' can't contain a Null value
because the Required property for this field is set to True.
Enter a value in this field.
```

Adding the row to the view would require a corresponding row to be added to the base table, Employees. However, the base table includes several columns (for example, Address) that do not appear in the view. Some of these columns are required and must not contain the SQL null value. You have no way to specify values for these columns when inserting a row into the view; therefore, insertions into the view are not allowed.

Rules For Modification Of Views

The ANSI standard defines five rules that govern modifications to views. Some databases, including Access, relax these rules somewhat, allowing some operations forbidden by the rules. An operation that violates these rules, however, is apt to be nonportable.

The ANSI SQL standard states that a view is read-only (that is, it cannot be modified) if the **Create View** statement includes any of the following:

- The Distinct modifier in the **Select** list

- A **Group By** or **Having** clause

- An expression in the **Select** list

- A reference to more than one table

- A reference to a view that is read-only

According to these rules, you should be able to modify the last example view

```
Create View Coasters As
   Select EmployeeNo As CNo, Name As CName, Salary As CSalary
   From Employees
   Where State = 'CA';
```

because it includes none of the prohibited constructs. Nevertheless, you cannot add new rows to the view, because of required columns of the base table that do not appear in the view. The fact that a view can be modified does not mean that *any* operation is permitted, only that *some* are permitted. The simple rule of thumb is that you should not depend upon being able to update a view.

Using Stored Procedures

So far, you have seen two kinds of objects used to execute SQL commands: **Statements** and **PreparedStatements**. The time has come to meet the third and final such object, **CallableStatement**. You can use the **CallableStatement** object to execute *stored procedures*, special queries stored inside the database. The database administrator usually creates stored procedures, making them available to users and programmers. Although Access does not support stored procedures, every full-scale database does.

JDBC provides a special escape syntax for calling stored procedures, helping overcome differences in syntax requirements of databases. Two forms are defined. You use the first for stored procedures that return no value. Even stored procedures that return no value are capable of generating result sets, which are processed in the usual way. The JDBC syntax is:

```
{call proc [(x1, x2, …)]}
```

Note that the square brackets ([ ]) indicate that the parameters are optional; the brackets are not to be included in the query string. For stored procedures that return a value, use the following syntax:

```
{? = call proc [(x1, x2, …)]}
```

Again, the brackets should not appear in the actual query string.

If the question mark (?) included in the second form reminds you of the placeholders used with **PreparedStatements**, you are correct. The **CallableStatement** interface implements the **PreparedStatement** interface, so **CallableStatements** are a great deal like **PreparedStatments**. The arguments used with a **CallableStatement** can be hard-coded or can take the form of placeholders, the values of which can be specified using the **setXXXX( )** methods of the **PreparedStatement** interface.

The only difference of significance between the use of **PreparedStatements** and **CallableStatements** is that the parameters of a **PreparedStatement** are all input values passed to the query. In contrast, the parameters of a **PreparedStatement** may be input values passed to the query, output values returned by the query, or input-output values passed to the query and then updated by it. The return value specified in the second form of the JDBC escape syntax is an example of an output parameter.

To set up the linkage necessary to obtain an output value (or updated input-output value), the **CallableStatement.registerOutParameter( )** method is called before execution of the **CallableStatement**. After execution, values are obtained using **getXXXX( )** methods.

The **registerOutParameter( )** method takes two or three parameters:

- The first is the sequential number of the placeholder for the output value.

- The second is an **int** that specifies the SQL data type of the output value.

- When the output parameter has the **NUMERIC** or **BIGDECIMAL** type, a third parameter specifies the scale (number of fractional digits) in the value.

The **java.sql.Types** class defines values used to specify data types, as summarized in Table 12.1. When getting the actual value using **Callable-Statement.getXXXX( )**, the method used must correspond to the registered data type of the value. Table 12.2 summarizes the methods of the **CallableStatement** interface.

TABLE 12.1

DATA–TYPE CODES DEFINED IN JAVA.SQL.TYPES.

BIGINT

BINARY

BIT

CHAR

DATE

DECIMAL

DOUBLE

FLOAT

INTEGER

LONGVARBINARY

LONGVARCHAR

NULL

(continued)

TABLE 12.1

DATA-TYPE CODES DEFINED IN JAVA.SQL.TYPES (CONTINUED).

NUMERIC

OTHER

REAL

SMALLINT

TIME

TIMESTAMP

TINYINT

VARBINARY

VARCHAR

TABLE 12.2

SUMMARY OF CALLABLESTATEMENT METHODS.

Method	Function
getBoolean (int)	Get the value of a BIT parameter as a boolean.
getByte(int)	Get the value of a TINYINT parameter as a byte.
getBytes(int)	Get the value of a SQL BINARY or VARBINARY parameter as a byte[ ].
getDate(int)	Get the value of a SQL DATE parameter as a java.sql.Date object.
getDouble(int)	Get the value of a DOUBLE parameter as a double.
getFloat(int)	Get the value of a FLOAT parameter as a float.
getInt(int)	Get the value of an INTEGER parameter as an int.
getLong(int)	Get the value of a BIGINT parameter as a long.
getObject(int)	Get the value of a parameter as an object.
getShort(int)	Get the value of a SMALLINT parameter as a short.
getString(int)	Get the value of a CHAR, VARCHAR, or LONGVARCHAR parameter as a String.
getTime(int)	Get the value of a SQL TIME parameter as a java.sql.Time object.

(continued)

TABLE 12.2

SUMMARY OF CALLABLESTATEMENT METHODS (*CONTINUED*).

getTimestamp(int)	Get the value of a SQL TIMESTAMP parameter as a java.sql.Timestamp object.
registerOutParameter (int, int)	Register an out parameter, other than a NUMERIC or BIGDECIMAL.
registerOutParameter (int, int, int)	Register a NUMERIC or BIGDECIMAL out parameter.
wasNull()	Return true if the last value fetched was SQL NULL.

Listing 12.1 shows how output values are registered and obtained. The next section presents a complete program that executes stored procedures.

LISTING 12.1   REGISTERING AND OBTAINING OUTPUT VALUES.

```
CallableStatement cs
  = theConnection.prepareCall("{call getSomeStuff(?, ?)}";
cs.registerOutParameter(1, Types.INTEGER);
cs.registerOutParameter(2, Types.DECIMAL, 2);
cs.executeQuery( );
int x = cs.getInt(1);
BigDecimal y = cs.getBigDecimal(2, 2);
```

The CallableDemo Applet

The CallableDemo applet allows you to execute several of the standard stored procedures supplied with Microsoft SQL Server. You cannot use the applet with Access, since Access does not support stored procedures. Figure 12.2 shows the user interface of the applet. Buttons allow the user to execute stored procedures that require no parameters. Text fields allow the user to type a parameter that is passed to a stored procedure. Pressing Enter causes execution of the corresponding stored procedure. To understand the details of each stored procedure, consult the SQL Server online documentation.

The CallableDemo applet, shown in Listing 12.2, builds its user interface using two arrays: one containing names of SQL Server stored procedures that take no parameters, and the other containing names of stored procedures that take one input parameter. The applet creates a **Button** for each no-parameter procedure and a **TextField** for each one-parameter procedure.

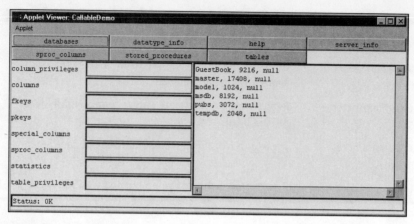

Figure 12.2
The user interface of the CallableDemo applet.

Preparation and execution of the **CallableStatement** and retrieval of results are accomplished in the **actionPerformed**( ) method. The technique is the same as that shown in Listing 12.1.

LISTING 12.2   THE CALLABLEDEMO APPLET.

```java
import java.applet.*;
import java.awt.*;
import java.awt.event.*;
import java.sql.*;

public class CallableDemo extends Applet
implements ActionListener
{
    Connection        theConnection;
    String            theSQL;
    CallableStatement theCallable;
    ResultSet         theResult;
    ResultSetMetaData theMeta;

    String [] theButtonProcs =
    {
        "databases",
        "datatype_info",
        "help",
        "server_info",
        "sproc_columns",
        "stored_procedures",
        "tables"
    };
```

```
String [] theTextProcs =
{
    "column_privileges",
    "columns",
    "fkeys",
    "pkeys",
    "special_columns",
    "sproc_columns",
    "statistics",
    "table_privileges"
};

TextField theStatus   = new TextField(64);
TextArea  theTextArea = new TextArea(5, 64);

public void init( )
{
    setFont(new Font("Courier", Font.PLAIN, 12));
    setLayout(new BorderLayout( ));

    Panel pb = new Panel(new GridLayout(0, 4));
    for (int i = 0; i < theButtonProcs.length; i++)
    {
        Button b = new Button(theButtonProcs[i]);
        pb.add(b);
        b.addActionListener(this);
    }

    add(pb, "North");

    Panel p1 = new Panel(new GridLayout(0, 1));
    Panel p2 = new Panel(new GridLayout(0, 1));

    for (int i = 0; i < theTextProcs.length; i++)
    {
        TextField t = new TextField(24);
        t.setName(theTextProcs[i]);
        p1.add(t);
        p2.add(new Label(theTextProcs[i]));
        t.addActionListener(this);
    }

    Panel p = new Panel(new BorderLayout( ));
    p.add(p2, "West");
    p.add(p1, "East");
    add(p, "West");
```

```
        add(theTextArea, "Center");
        add(theStatus,   "South");

        theTextArea.setEditable(false);
        theStatus  .setEditable(false);

        try
        {
            theStatus.setText("Status: OK");
            Class.forName ("sun.jdbc.odbc.JdbcOdbcDriver");
            theConnection =
              DriverManager.getConnection("jdbc:odbc:GuestBookSS",
                "sa", "");
        }
        catch (SQLException ex)          { handleException(ex); }
        catch (ClassNotFoundException ex) { handleException(ex); }
    }

    public void actionPerformed(ActionEvent e)
    {
        theStatus.setText("Status: OK");
        Object source = e.getSource( );
        if (source instanceof Button)
        {
            String label = ((Button) source).getLabel( );
            theSQL = "{call sp_" + label + "}";
            try
            {
                theCallable = theConnection.prepareCall(theSQL);
                theResult   = theCallable.executeQuery( );
                theMeta     = theResult.getMetaData( );
                theTextArea.setText(dumpResult( ));
            }
            catch (SQLException ex) { handleException(ex); }
        }
        if (source instanceof TextField)
        {
            TextField t = (TextField) source;
            String name = t.getName( );
            String parm = t.getText( );
            theSQL = "{call sp_" + name + " (?)}";
            System.out.println("SQL: " + theSQL);
            try
            {
                theCallable = theConnection.prepareCall(theSQL);
                theCallable.setString(1, parm);
```

```
                        System.out.println("parm #1: " + parm);
                        theResult = theCallable.executeQuery( );
                        theMeta   = theResult.getMetaData( );
                        theTextArea.setText(dumpResult( ));
                }
                catch (SQLException ex) { handleException(ex); }
        }
    }

    public String dumpResult( )
    throws SQLException
    {
        if (theResult == null) return "";
        String result = "";
        try
        {
            int column_count = theMeta.getColumnCount( );
            while (theResult.next( ))
            {
                boolean first = true;
                for (int i = 1; i <= column_count; i++)
                {
                    if (!first) result += ", ";
                    result += theResult.getString(i);
                    first = false;
                }
                result += "\n";
            }
        }
        catch (SQLException sql) { handleException(sql); }
        return result;
    }

    public void handleException(Throwable t)
    {
        theStatus.setText("Error:   " + t.getMessage( ));
        t.printStackTrace( );
    }
}
```

The BatchQuery Application

The BatchQuery application, shown in Figure 12.3, lets you store SQL statements in a file for later execution. These scripts are handy for creating the small test databases needed to check out database applications when they are being

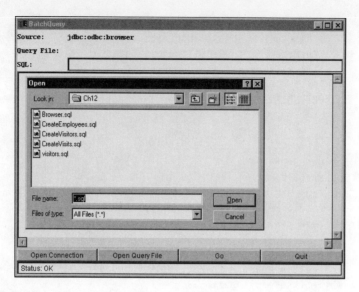

Figure 12.3
The user interface of the BatchQuery application.

written or revised. The application includes an Open Query button that brings up a file dialog, letting the user select the script to be executed. It also includes a Go button that initiates execution of the query. The SQL statement last executed appears in a **TextField**, facilitating correction of the script when necessary because of errors.

Listing 12.3 shows the fields of the BatchQuery application. BatchQuery uses a slightly modified version of the **JDBC01** class described in the previous chapter. It also defines a **FileReader** used to read SQL scripts.

LISTING 12.3   FIELDS OF THE BATCHQUERY APPLICATION.

```
import java.awt.*;
import java.awt.event.*;
import java.sql.*;
import java.io.*;

class BatchQuery extends Frame
implements ActionListener
{
    Panel      topPanel    = new Panel( );
    Panel      sourcePanel = new Panel( );
    Panel      queryPanel  = new Panel( );
    Panel      sqlPanel    = new Panel( );
```

```
Panel      mainPanel   = new Panel( );
Panel      bottomPanel = new Panel( );
Panel      buttonPanel = new Panel( );

Font       topFont     = new Font("Courier", Font.BOLD,  12);
Font       resultFont = new Font("Courier", Font.PLAIN, 12);

Label      theSource     = new Label( );
Label      theQueryFile = new Label( );
TextField  theSQL        = new TextField( );
TextArea   theResult     = new TextArea(15, 80);
Button     btnOpenDB   = new Button("Open Connection");
Button     btnOpenFile = new Button("Open Query File");
Button     btnGo       = new Button("Go");
Button     btnQuit     = new Button("Quit");
TextField  theStatus     = new TextField( );

JDBC02         theJDBC     = new JDBC02(theStatus);
String         theFileName = "";
BufferedReader theReader   =null;
```

The main( ) And init( ) Methods

The **main( )** and **init( )** methods, shown in Listing 12.4, contain no surprises. As usual, the program builds the user interface using nested **Panel**s, so that resizing the window does not distort the component layouts.

LISTING **12.4**   THE MAIN( ) AND INIT( ) METHODS.

```
public static void main(String args[])
{
    new BatchQuery( ).init( );
}

public void init( )
{
    setTitle("BatchQuery");

    topPanel.setFont(topFont);
    theResult.setFont(resultFont);

    add("North",  topPanel);
    add("Center", mainPanel);
    add("South",  bottomPanel);

    topPanel.setLayout(new GridLayout(3, 1));
    topPanel.add(sourcePanel);
```

```
        topPanel.add(queryPanel);
        topPanel.add(sqlPanel);

        sourcePanel.setLayout(new BorderLayout( ));
        sourcePanel.add("West", new Label("Source: "));
        sourcePanel.add("Center", theSource);

        queryPanel.setLayout(new BorderLayout( ));
        queryPanel.add("West", new Label("Query File:"));
        queryPanel.add("Center", theQueryFile);

        sqlPanel.setLayout(new BorderLayout( ));
        sqlPanel.add("West", new Label("SQL: "));
        sqlPanel.add("Center", theSQL);

        mainPanel.setLayout(new BorderLayout( ));
        mainPanel.add("Center", theResult);

        bottomPanel.setLayout(new BorderLayout( ));
        bottomPanel.add("North", buttonPanel);
        bottomPanel.add("South", theStatus);

        buttonPanel.setLayout(new GridLayout(1, 4));
        buttonPanel.add(btnOpenDB);
        buttonPanel.add(btnOpenFile);
        buttonPanel.add(btnGo);
        buttonPanel.add(btnQuit);

        theSQL   .setEditable(false);
        theResult.setEditable(false);
        theStatus.setEditable(false);

        btnGo.setEnabled(false);

        addWindowListener(new WindowAdapter( )
            {
                public void windowClosing(WindowEvent event)
                {
                    requestClose( );
                }
            }
        );

        btnOpenDB  .addActionListener(this);
        btnOpenFile.addActionListener(this);
        btnGo      .addActionListener(this);
        btnQuit    .addActionListener(this);
```

```
while (!openConnection( )) ; // null statement

pack( );
show( );
}
```

The actionPerformed( ) Method

The **actionPerformed**( ) method, shown in Listing 12.5, invokes methods to open a new database connection, open a new SQL script file, initiate execution of an open SQL script file, or quit the program.

LISTING 12.5   THE ACTIONPERFORMED( ) METHOD.

```
public void actionPerformed(ActionEvent event)
{
    theStatus.setText("Status: OK");
    Object source = event.getSource( );
    if (source == btnOpenDB)        openConnection( );
    else if (source == btnOpenFile) openFile( );
    else if (source == btnGo)       doQuery( );
    else if (source == btnQuit)     requestClose( );
}
```

The openConnection( ) Method

Listing 12.6 shows the **openConnection**( ) method, which opens a new database connection. The **JDBC02** object will automatically close any previous connection. The method obtains connection information from the user by means of a **LoginDialog02**, seen in previous programs (e.g., DBMaker, in Chapter 9).

LISTING 12.6   THE OPENCONNECTION( ) METHOD.

```
public boolean openConnection( )
{
    LoginDialog02 theLoginDialog02 = null;
    try
    {
        theSource.setText("");
        theResult.setText("");
        theLoginDialog02
          = new LoginDialog02("BatchQuery: "
            + "Please select the data source:",
            "jdbc:odbc:browser", this, true);
        theLoginDialog02.setVisible(true);
        if (theLoginDialog02.getStatus( ))
        {
```

```
        theSource.setText(theLoginDialog02.getURL( ));
        theJDBC.openConnection(theLoginDialog02.getURL( ),
            theLoginDialog02.getUser( ),
            theLoginDialog02.getPassword( ));
    }
    theLoginDialog02.dispose( );
    return true;
}
catch (SQLException sql)
{
    theStatus.setText(sql.getMessage( ));
}
if (theLoginDialog02 != null) theLoginDialog02.dispose( );
return false;
}
```

The openFile( ) Method

The **openFile**( ) method, shown in Listing 12.7, uses a **FileDialog** to assist the user in choosing the desired SQL script file. The dialog initially displays only files with the .sql extension, but the user can override this behavior if desired. The method saves the name of the selected file in **theFileName** and displays it in the **TextField** named **theQueryFile**.

LISTING 12.7   THE OPENFILE( ) METHOD.

```
public void openFile( )
{
    FileDialog filedlg = new FileDialog(this, "Open Query File",
      FileDialog.LOAD);
    filedlg.setFile("*.sql");
    filedlg.show( );
    theFileName = filedlg.getDirectory( ) + filedlg.getFile( );
    theQueryFile.setText(filedlg.getFile( ));
    filedlg.hide( );
    filedlg.dispose( );
    btnGo.setEnabled(true);
    theSQL.setText("");
}
```

The doQuery( ) Method

Listing 12.8 shows the **doQuery**( ) method. This method opens the file specified by the user and reads it line by line, accumulating the lines in a buffer (**sql**). When a line ends with a semicolon (;), the contents of the buffer are passed to the **executeSQL**( ) method.

Some SQL interpreters define a special **go** command used to signal that execution should start. The BatchQuery application does not provide this feature, but it would be simple to implement, if desired.

LISTING 12.8   THE DOQUERY( ) METHOD.

```
public void doQuery( )
{
    try
    {
        if (theReader != null) theReader.close( );
        theReader = null;
        theReader = new BufferedReader(new FileReader(theFileName));
        String sql = "";
        String line;
        while (true)
        {
            line = theReader.readLine( );
            if (line == null) break;
            sql += line;
            if (line.endsWith(";"))
            {
                executeSQL(sql);
                sql = "";
            }
        }
        if (sql.length( )> 0) executeSQL(sql);
        theSQL.setText("");
    }
    catch (FileNotFoundException fnf)
    {
        theStatus.setText("Error:  File not found ("
          + theFileName + ")");
    }
    catch (IOException io)
    {
        theStatus.setText("Error: " + io.getMessage( ));
    }
    catch (SQLException sqlex) { ; }
    try
    {
        theReader.close( );
    }
    catch (IOException io) { ; }
    btnGo.setEnabled(false);
}
```

The executeSQL( ) Method

The **executeSQL( )** method, shown in Listing 12.9, uses the **JDBC02.execute( )** method to execute the SQL command passed as its only parameter. The method sends output of the command to **System.out**, which can be redirected to a file if desired, by means of an operating-system command option.

LISTING 12.9   THE EXECUTESQL( ) METHOD.

```
public void executeSQL(String sql)
throws SQLException
{
    theSQL.setText(sql);
    try
    {
        System.err.println("SQL: " + sql);
        boolean result;
        result = theJDBC.execute(sql);
        System.out.println(theJDBC.dumpResult( ));
    }
    catch (SQLException sqlex)
    {
        theStatus.setText("Error: " + sqlex.getMessage( ));
        sqlex.printStackTrace( );
        throw new SQLException(sqlex.getMessage( ));
    }
}
```

The requestClose( ) Method

The **requestClose( )** method, shown in Listing 12.10, is used to shut down the application. It hides the application **Frame**, calls the **JDBC.closeConnection( )** method to close the database connection, and terminates.

LISTING 12.10   THE REQUESTCLOSE( ) METHOD.

```
public void requestClose( )
{
    setVisible(false);
    try
    {
        theJDBC.closeConnection( );
    }
    catch (SQLException sql) { ; }
    System.exit(0);
}
```

Summary

In this chapter, you learned how to create and use views and how to call database stored procedures. You also learned how to write an application that lets you save SQL queries in a disk file. The next chapter will describe some subtle problems that can arise when multiple users access the same data, and will show you how to use *transactions*, a SQL facility designed to overcome these problems.

13

MULTIUSER CONSIDERATIONS

G rocery shopping right after work, when the market is crowded, barely resembles shopping at midnight, when no one is around except the store clerks. During the late afternoon rush, people jostle one another, compete for the last good tomatoes, and cut ahead of one another in the checkout lines. The shopping trip takes much longer to complete, and you may not get everything you wanted. When multiple users share access to a database, they can experience some of the same frustrations. Their transactions may take longer to complete and may interfere with those of other users, leaving the database in an inconsistent state.

To minimize such problems, relational databases implement special mechanisms that facilitate the sharing of data. This chapter describes two such mechanisms:

- *Transactions*—These let you group a series of operations into a single unit. When a transaction cannot be completed, any operations performed up to the point of failure can be rolled back, returning the database to its original state. The transaction becomes an all-or-nothing operation that cannot leave the database in a partially updated, inconsistent state even if it fails.

- *Transaction isolation levels*—These are "rules of engagement" for database transactions. They establish policies that regulate the likelihood that one transaction will interfere with another. By choosing a high level of transaction isolation, you can ensure that your database will remain consistent, even though many users are competing to update the same data.

This chapter includes two example programs. Because MS Access has only limited support for transaction isolation, the programs are best run using SQL Server or some other full-function database. You can, however, run them using MS Access; you simply won't be able to explore the full range of transaction isolation levels. The first of the two programs, DBAnomalies, demonstrates how nonisolated transactions can break a database, leaving it in an inconsistent state. The second program, TransDemo, lets you experiment with transactions running at different isolation levels. You can see the danger of using low isolation levels and also the reduced throughput that results from using high isolation levels.

Transactions

Assume you're responsible for an employee database that holds data, including the job title and salary of employees. Suppose an employee receives a promotion that entails a salary increase. You need to update the JobTitle and Salary columns. These columns could be stored in separate tables, in which case you would use a pair of queries like this:

```
Update Employees    Set JobTitle = 'Programmer II'
  Where EmployeeNo = 1234
Update Compensation Set Salary   = '85000'
  Where EmployeeNo = 1234
```

It's possible that, right after the first **Update** statement completes, something might go wrong with the database or the database connection. Perhaps a network glitch causes a few lost packets. In such a case, the database server might know that it missed something, but it might not know what. The second query would never complete, and the salary would not be updated. Of course, the user of the application program might see an error message of some sort, but that's no guarantee that the user would understand the error message and properly act on it.

The network error has left the database in an inconsistent state. The database is said to have suffered a *data integrity* error. Someone running a report to determine the average salary of programmers will receive incomplete information. The error may not be discovered for many days and the salary not properly updated. In the meantime, many faulty reports could be generated.

A partially completed **Update** is like coming home from the market having bought your spouse's favorite cookies, but no milk. You would have been better off to have come directly home. Your spouse wants all or nothing: either cookies *and* milk, or neither cookies nor milk.

To avoid problems of this sort, relational databases let you group queries and other database operations as a unit called a *transaction*. As the database operations of the transaction are performed, the database keeps track of them. Should anything go wrong, the database will cause a **SQLException** to be thrown. The programmer can **catch** the exception and use a special *rollback* operation that undoes the completed operations of the transaction. In effect, the rollback erases the transaction. It restores any changed records to the values they had before the transaction was begun. It also undeletes any records deleted by the transaction and deletes any records added by it.

To tell the database that a transaction is complete, the programmer uses a special *commit* operation. Once a transaction has been committed, it can no longer be rolled back, so the database does not need to continue tracking it. Together, the **commit( )** and **rollback( )** methods give programmers the support needed to avoid data integrity problems resulting from partially complete updates.

The JDBC **Connection** interface provides several methods used in working with transactions. These are shown in Table 13.1.

TABLE 13.1

JDBC CONNECTION METHODS FOR WORKING WITH TRANSACTIONS.

Method	Function
void commit( ) throws SQLException	Commits the current transaction, releasing all locks.
boolean getAutoCommit( ) throws SQLException	Returns the auto-commit status.

(continued)

TABLE 13.1
JDBC CONNECTION METHODS FOR WORKING WITH TRANSACTIONS (*CONTINUED*).

Method	Function
int getTransactionIsolation( ) throws SQLException	Gets the current transaction isolation level (see Table 13.2).
void rollback( ) throws SQLException	Rolls back the current transaction, releasing all locks.
int setAutoCommit (boolean commit) throws SQLException	Sets the auto-commit status to the specified value.
void setTransactionIsolation (int level) throws SQLException	Sets the current transaction isolation level (see Table 13.2).

A transaction is automatically begun by the execution of a SQL statement and ended by calling the **commit( )** method or the **rollback( )** method. The **commit( )** method makes any changes made by a transaction permanent. The **rollback( )** method discards the changes made by a transaction.

When a database connection is first established, the auto-commit status is set to **true**. This mode of operation causes **commit( )** to be automatically called following execution of each SQL statement. To make full use of the JDBC transaction facility, you should use the **setAutoCommit( )** method to set the auto-commit status to **false**. If desired, you can use the **getAutoCommit( )** method to determine the current auto-commit status.

The **setTransactionIsolation( )** and **getTransactionIsolation( )** methods are presented in the next section, which also explains the concept of database locks. The example program that appears near the end of this chapter shows how the various transaction handling methods are used.

Concurrency

You've seen what results when a series of **Update** operations is partially completed and how transactions can be used to avoid that result. Unfortunately, this isn't the end of the matter: Another cause can produce a similar result. Just as a highly aggressive cantaloupe-loving shopper might take the last ripe cantaloupe from your shopping cart when you're not looking, concurrent database transactions can interfere with one another, leading to data integrity problems. The SQL countermeasure aimed at such problems provides policies that keep transactions at arm's length, reducing mutual interference. The countermeasure is known as *transaction isolation levels*.

To understand transaction isolation levels, you need to know about the three kinds of data integrity problems that can arise when transactions concurrently access data. These are:

- Dirty reads

- Nonrepeatable reads

- Phantom reads

Dirty Reads

Say two transactions, A and B, are accessing the same database table. Transaction A begins by changing a row of the table. Shortly thereafter, Transaction B reads the same table row. Assume that as Transaction A continues, a problem occurs and Transaction A is rolled back. Transaction B now has an incorrect value for the table row, one that does not correspond to the value stored in the database. Transaction B may simply report the incorrect data, or it may go on to perform **Update**s based on the incorrect value for the table row—in which case the database may be left in an inconsistent state. A data integrity problem exists.

The cause of the problem is the willingness of the database to supply Transaction B with the value of an updated row resulting from an uncommitted transaction, called a *dirty read*. Figure 13.1 illustrates the dirty read. SQL provides a mechanism, implemented by the JDBC API, that prevents dirty reads. If enabled, this mechanism would have prevented Transaction B from viewing the updated row until Transaction A was committed. The next sections look at the remaining data integrity problems that arise from concurrent database access and consider the JDBC API facilities that prevent them.

Nonrepeatable Reads

Nonrepeatable reads arise as follows. Suppose that Transaction B reads a table row. While Transaction B is busy performing other operations, Transaction A

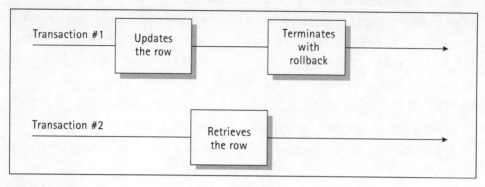

Figure 13.1
A dirty read.

updates the row read by B and commits. If B rereads the row, it will obtain a different value than before. B's reading of the table is said to be *nonrepeatable*. Figure 13.2 illustrates how nonrepeatable reads occur.

You might think you could easily avoid this problem by avoiding multiple reads, but it's not that simple. Reads are hidden within many SQL operations, and many queries implicitly involve multiple reads. For example, an **Update** must read the value of a row before the row can be updated; **Update**s include an implicit read. An **Update** that includes subqueries may perform multiple reads: one for the **Update** operation and one (or more) for each subquery.

Because avoiding multiple reads is not always possible, SQL includes a facility that prevents nonrepeatable reads. I'll present this facility in a moment, after

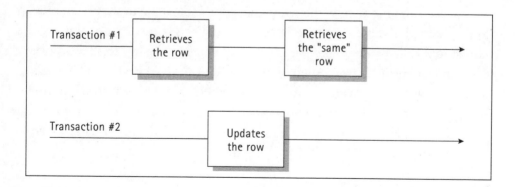

Figure 13.2
A nonrepeatable read.

looking at the final type of data integrity problem arising from concurrent database access.

Phantom Reads

Phantom reads can occur when a database is concurrently accessed. Say Transaction B is a query that selects all the records of employees working in California. While Transaction B is working with this result, suppose Transaction A adds a record for a new employee that works in California. If Transaction B again queries the database for California employees, the new record will appear in the result set. Hence, the transaction will obtain a result inconsistent with the original result. The phenomenon is known as a *phantom read*, since the new record appears unexpectedly. Figure 13.3 illustrates how phantom reads can occur. The next section shows how you can avoid dirty reads, nonrepeatable reads, and phantom reads.

Transaction Isolation Levels

SQL defines five transaction isolation levels that can be used to prevent data integrity problems resulting from concurrent database access. Not all databases, however, support every level. The **DatabaseMetaData.supportsTransactionIsolationLevel( )** method can determine which levels are supported. The DBAnalyzer program of Chapter 5 shows how this can be done.

The isolation level that applies to a transaction depends on the levels of other concurrently executing transactions. A transaction running at a low isolation

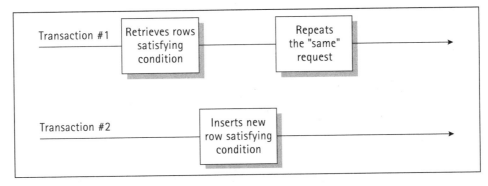

Figure 13.3
A phantom read.

level can spoil everything. Therefore, to obtain the protection afforded by the transaction isolation facility, you must ensure that your database supports the desired isolation level and that no concurrent transactions operate at a lower level of isolation.

Table 13.2 shows the isolation levels supported by SQL-JDBC. The **Connection** interface defines **static final int**s that have these same names, used with the **setTransactionIsolation( )** and **getTransactionIsolation( )** methods.

The lowest level, **TRANSACTION_NONE**, is not commonly used. It disables transaction processing, including the rollback and commit facility. The remaining levels prevent the data integrity problems presented in the preceding section. For example, the **TRANSACTION_READ_COMMITTED** isolation level prevents dirty reads, while the **TRANSACTION_NON_REPEATABLE_READ** isolation level prevents both dirty reads and nonrepeatable reads. The highest level, **TRANSACTION_SERIALIZABLE**, prevents each of the possible data integrity problems arising from concurrent database access.

When a database connection is established, the transaction isolation level is set to a default value determined by the database driver. For Microsoft Access, this is **TRANSACTION_READ_COMMITTED**. This is also the highest level of isolation supported by Access, which has a limited repertoire of transaction isolation levels. You can select a desired level by calling the **setTransaction Isolation( )** method, which is best done right after establishing the connection. The example program at the end of this chapter shows how this is done.

TABLE 13.2

TRANSACTION ISOLATION LEVELS.

Level	Dirty Reads	Nonrepeatable Reads	Phantom Reads
TRANSACTION_NONE	Yes	Yes	Yes
TRANSACTION_READ_UNCOMMITTED	Yes	Yes	Yes
TRANSACTION_READ_COMMITTED	No	Yes	Yes
TRANSACTION_NON_REPEATABLE_READ	No	No	Yes
TRANSACTION_SERIALIZABLE	No	No	No

Problems With Transactions

Because the **TRANSACTION_SERIALIZABLE** level prevents each of the possible data integrity problems of concurrent access, why might you choose a lower level of isolation? Running at a lower level of isolation does incur some risk that one or another of the data integrity problems of concurrent access may arise. Running at a high level of transaction isolation, however, incurs a performance penalty. Designing efficient database applications requires making an informed trade-off that balances concerns for data integrity against concerns for application performance. To see why this is so, you need to know a bit about how transaction isolation levels are implemented.

LOCKING

Most databases implement transaction isolation by means of a mechanism called *locking*. Locking allows, for example, one transaction to access a table while temporarily preventing other transactions from accessing the table. The other transactions are said to be locked out. Locking allows transactions to operate more independently, by reducing the number of database operations that can take place concurrently.

A wide variety of locking strategies is employed by various databases. These differ principally in the type of database object that is locked. Some databases lock entire tables, while others lock individual rows. A compromise approach locks all rows stored near a particular row, while allowing other transactions free access to other rows. The locking strategy used by a database has important implications for performance.

PERFORMANCE

Locks are held for the duration of a transaction. A lock is not released until the transaction completes by committing or rolling back its **Update**s. While a lock is held, other transactions cannot access the locked object. They must wait for the transaction that owns the lock to complete, at which point its locks will be released.

Transaction efficiency is affected by the choice of objects locked by a database. A database that applies locks to entire tables may perform poorly when many transactions execute concurrently, particularly if many of the transactions manipulate the same table. The transactions may spend much time waiting their turns for access to the table of mutual interest. A database that locks rows rather than tables is likely to handle concurrent transactions more efficiently, since transactions are less likely to have to wait on one another.

The level of transaction isolation also affects transaction efficiency. Generally, a transaction that operates at a high level of isolation will hold more locks (or locks on bigger objects, such as entire tables) than a transaction that operates at a low level of isolation. Thus, the higher the level of transaction isolation, the more time transactions are apt to spend waiting on one another.

A programmer using JDBC has no means of directly specifying the objects locked by a database. Instead, the database will choose a locking strategy based on the isolation level specified for each transaction. Simple databases may implement only a limited number of isolation levels, depending upon relatively high-level locks to ensure data integrity. Such an approach is common among lower-priced databases, which do not efficiently handle concurrent transactions.

DEADLOCK

A potentially more serious result of database locking is the possibility of a *deadlock*, a situation in which two (or more) transactions hold locks that prevent the other from proceeding. Suppose two transactions—call them A and B—are each interested in records having primary keys 1 and 2. Assume that A accesses and locks Record 1 and that B accesses and locks Record 2. Now, neither can complete. Transaction A will wait for Record 2 to become available. This will not occur, however, until Transaction B completes. But Transaction B will not complete, since it is waiting for Record 1 to become available, and this will not occur until Transaction A completes. In other words, Transaction A cannot complete until after Transaction B completes, and Transaction B cannot complete until after Transaction A completes. The transactions are deadlocked.

Most databases are capable of detecting such a situation. They differ, however, in their approaches to resolving deadlocks. A popular approach is simply to cancel one of the transactions. Its changes are then rolled back, either by the database or the application program, and the other transaction is allowed to proceed. The canceled transaction can then be reexecuted, and all will be well.

Good application design strives to avoid deadlocks, because databases do not detect them instantly. Consequently, frequent deadlocks may lead to poor application response time. Of course, designing an application system in such a way that deadlocks are unlikely requires detailed knowledge of the database that hosts the application. This is not a job for a mere mortal, but one for a bona fide database guru.

Software defects in drivers and other systems software sometimes cause deadlocks even in application systems that have been correctly designed and implemented. This is particularly true of relatively new drivers, such as those supporting JDBC. Knowing something about how deadlocks arise can be helpful to you in diagnosing such unfortunate situations. If two transactions seem blocked, but canceling one of them allows the other to proceed, you should suspect that a deadlock is involved.

The DBAnomalies Applet

Now that you have a framework for understanding database transactions, you are ready to see how they are implemented using JDBC. The DBAnomalies applet, the first of two example programs in this chapter, lets you see firsthand how important transaction isolation can be. It implements transactions that are apt to produce dirty reads, nonrepeatable reads, and phantom reads, letting you execute the transactions at selected levels of isolation. The applet is best run using SQL Server or another full-capability database, because MS Access supports only a limited range of transaction isolation levels. Even with Access, however, you can observe the effects of dirty reads and see how transaction isolation can prevent them.

The User Interface

The user interface of the DBAnomalies applet is shown in Figure 13.4. The applet provides a **Choice** that lets you select the transaction isolation level. To use the applet, select an isolation level and then click the button corresponding to the type of anomaly you want to study: dirty reads, nonrepeatable reads, or phantom reads. The applet will open a database connection and attempt to set the transaction isolation level you selected. The database may not support the selected level, so the actual level is displayed in a **Label** at the top of the applet's window. The applet then executes a transaction that attempts to produce the selected anomaly. A blow-by-blow commentary is sent to the **TextArea** that

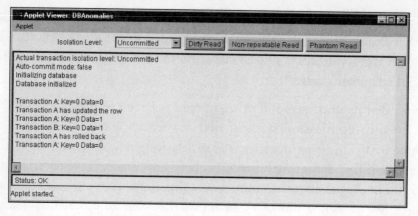

Figure 13.4
The user interface of the DBAnomalies applet.

occupies the middle of the applet's window. By studying the commentary, you can determine whether the transaction isolation level was effective in avoiding the anomaly. Of course, Table 13.2 correctly predicts every result. The applet simply allows you to observe the results. It also shows you how to accomplish many useful transaction-related JDBC operations.

Listing 13.1 shows the fields and the **init( )** method of the DBAnomalies applet. There are few surprises. The applet uses **final static Strings**, such as **NONE**, to display the actual transaction isolation level. The relevant code appears in the **openConnection( )** method. The **init( )** method uses the **Strings** to initialize the **Choice** component (**theIsoLevel**) used to select the transaction isolation level.

To support concurrent transactions, the applet opens two database connections. It creates arrays to hold a **Connection**, **Statement**, and **ResultSet** for each.

LISTING 13.1 FIELDS AND INIT( ) METHOD OF THE DBANOMALIES APPLET.

```
import java.applet.*;
import java.awt.*;
import java.awt.event.*;
import java.sql.*;

public class DBAnomalies extends Applet
implements ActionListener
{
```

```java
static final String NONE        = "None";
static final String UNCOMMITTED = "Uncommitted";
static final String COMMITTED   = "Committed";
static final String REPEATABLE  = "Nonrepeatable";
static final String SERIALIZABLE = "Serializable";

Choice    theIsoLevel                = new Choice( );
Button    theDirtyReadButton         = new Button("Dirty Read");
Button    theNonRepeatableReadButton =
  new Button("Nonrepeatable Read");
Button    thePhantomReadButton       = new Button("Phantom Read");

TextArea  theText   = new TextArea(15, 80);
TextField theStatus = new TextField(64);

Connection [ ] theConnection = new Connection [2];
Statement  [ ] theStatement  = new Statement  [2];
ResultSet  [ ] theResult     = new ResultSet  [2];

public void init( )
{
    Panel p = new Panel(new FlowLayout( ));
    p.add(new Label("Isolation Level: "));
    p.add(theIsoLevel);
    p.add(theDirtyReadButton);
    p.add(theNonRepeatableReadButton);
    p.add(thePhantomReadButton);

    setLayout(new BorderLayout( ));
    add(p, "North");
    add(theText, "Center");
    add(theStatus, "South");

    theIsoLevel.add(UNCOMMITTED);
    theIsoLevel.add(COMMITTED);
    theIsoLevel.add(REPEATABLE);
    theIsoLevel.add(SERIALIZABLE);

    theText  .setEditable(false);
    theStatus.setEditable(false);

    theDirtyReadButton         .addActionListener(this);
    theNonRepeatableReadButton.addActionListener(this);
    thePhantomReadButton       .addActionListener(this);

    statusOK( );
}
```

The **actionPerformed( )** method, shown in Listing 13.2, captures **ActionEvent**s, originating with the **Buttons**, and dispatches an appropriate method that performs a transaction designed to produce the anomaly designated by the **Button**. Before dispatching the transaction method, **actionPerformed( )** clears the **TextArea** by setting its contents to a null **String**. It also resets the **TextField** that displays status information, setting its contents to "Status: OK" by means of the **statusOK( )** method. After a transaction method has completed, **actionPerformed( )** sets the **TextArea** cursor to the top of the **TextArea** by using the methods **setSelectionStart( )** and **setSelectionEnd( )**. This makes it easier to read the commentary posted to the **TextArea** by the transaction method.

LISTING 13.2   THE ACTIONPERFORMED( ) METHOD.

```
public void actionPerformed(ActionEvent event)
{
    Object source = event.getSource( );
    theText.setText("");
    statusOK( );
    if (source == theDirtyReadButton)              dirty ( );
    else if (source == theNonRepeatableReadButton) repeat ( );
    else if (source == thePhantomReadButton)       phantom( );
    theText.setSelectionStart(0);
    theText.setSelectionEnd  (0);
}
```

The Transaction Methods

Listing 13.3 shows the transaction methods. Each button-selectable anomaly has one method: The **dirty( )** method attempts to produce a dirty read; the **repeat( )** method attempts to produce a nonrepeatable read; and the **phantom( )** method attempts to produce a phantom read. Of course, if the user has selected a sufficiently high level of transaction isolation, no anomaly will result.

To support concurrent transactions, the **openConnection( )** method opens two database connections. The fields holding **Connection**, **Statement**, and **ResultSet** objects are parallel arrays and must be indexed when referenced. Each transaction method uses the [0] element of the parallel arrays for the transaction that writes data and the [1] element for the transaction that only reads data. The data access methods each accept a parameter that has a corresponding value. For example, the method invocation

```
openConnection(0);
```

uses the [0] elements of the parallel arrays to hold the resulting **Connection**, **Statement**, and **ResultSet** objects.

Most of the drivers used to test the applet caused it to hang if high levels of transaction isolation were selected. This is apparently due to a deadlock condition that remains undetected because both participating transactions are running on a single host. Hopefully, this flaw will be corrected in future releases of the drivers. To prevent inconvenient deadlocks in the meantime, each method includes code that attempts to avoid such a situation, returning with an error message when a high level of isolation is selected. This technique may fail when a database does not implement the selected level of isolation. In such an event, you may need to use the Windows task manager to terminate the applet.

LISTING 13.3 THE TRANSACTION METHODS.

```
public void dirty( )
{
    openConnection(0);
    try
    {
        int level = theConnection[0].getTransactionIsolation( );
        if (level == Connection.TRANSACTION_READ_COMMITTED
         || level == Connection.TRANSACTION_REPEATABLE_READ
         || level == Connection.TRANSACTION_SERIALIZABLE)
        {
            theStatus.setText("Invalid choice: "
              + "Cannot generate this anomaly "
              + "at the specified isolation level.");
            return;
        }
    }
    catch (SQLException sqlex)
    {
        handleException(sqlex);
    }

    createTable( );
    openConnection(1);
    releaseLocks( );

    readDB(0);
    updateDB(0, 1);
    readDB(0);
    readDB(1);
    closeConnection(1);
```

```
                    rollbackDB(0);
        readDB(0);
        closeConnection(0);
}

public void repeat( )
{
    openConnection(0);
    try
    {
        int level = theConnection[0].getTransactionIsolation( );
        if (level == Connection.TRANSACTION_REPEATABLE_READ
         || level == Connection.TRANSACTION_SERIALIZABLE)

    {
            theStatus.setText("Invalid choice: "
              + "Cannot generate this anomaly "
              + "at the specified isolation level.");
            return;
        }
    }
    catch (SQLException sqlex)
    {
        handleException(sqlex);
    }

    createTable( );
    openConnection(1);
    releaseLocks( );

    readDB(0);
    readDB(1);
    updateDB(0, 1);
    readDB(0);
    commitDB(0);
    closeConnection(0);

    readDB(1);
    closeConnection(1);
}

public void phantom( )
{
    openConnection(0);
    try
    {
```

```
        int level = theConnection[0].getTransactionIsolation( );
        if (level == Connection.TRANSACTION_SERIALIZABLE)
        {
            theStatus.setText("Invalid choice: "
              + "Cannot generate this anomaly "
              + "at the specified isolation level.");
            return;
        }
    }
    catch (SQLException sqlex)
    {
        handleException(sqlex);
    }

    createTable( );
    openConnection(1);
    releaseLocks( );

    readAllDB(1);
    insertDB(0, 1, 0);
    commitDB(0);
    closeConnection(0);

    readAllDB(1);
    closeConnection(1);
}
```

Opening And Closing The Database

Listing 13.4 shows the **openConnection**( ) method. This method is a bit different from versions used in earlier example programs, because it uses a set of
three parallel arrays to store its results, as explained earlier. It also uses
setTransactionIsolationLevel( ) to set a desired isolation level. Because the
database may not support the desired level, the method obtains the actual isolation level by using **getTransactionIsolationLevel**( ) and displays the result in
the applet window.

After setting the isolation level, the method turns off auto-commit by using the
setAutoCommit( ) method. It does this after setting the isolation level, because
tests found that some database drivers reset auto-commit when the isolation
level is changed. A program that sets auto-commit and then sets the isolation
level may lose its auto-commit setting.

LISTING 13.4   THE openConnection( ) METHOD.

```
public void openConnection(int i)
{
    String source   = "jdbc:odbc:GuestBookSS";
    String user     = "sa";
    String password = "sa";
    try
    {
        closeConnection(i);
        Class.forName("sun.jdbc.odbc.JdbcOdbcDriver");
        theConnection [i]
          = DriverManager.getConnection(source, user, password);
        theStatement  [i] = theConnection[i].createStatement( );
        theResult     [i] = null;

        int level = Connection.TRANSACTION_NONE;
        if      (theIsoLevel.getSelectedItem( ).equals(UNCOMMITTED))
            level = Connection.TRANSACTION_READ_UNCOMMITTED;
        else if (theIsoLevel.getSelectedItem( ).equals(COMMITTED))
            level = Connection.TRANSACTION_READ_COMMITTED;
        else if (theIsoLevel.getSelectedItem( ).equals(REPEATABLE))
            level = Connection.TRANSACTION_REPEATABLE_READ;
        else if (theIsoLevel.getSelectedItem( ).equals(SERIALIZABLE))
            level = Connection.TRANSACTION_SERIALIZABLE;

        try
        {
            theConnection [i].setTransactionIsolation(level);
        }
        catch (SQLException sqlex) { ; }

        level = theConnection[i].getTransactionIsolation( );

        if (i == 0)
        {
            String slevel = "(invalid)";
            if (level == Connection.TRANSACTION_NONE)
                slevel = "None";
            else if (level == Connection.TRANSACTION_READ_UNCOMMITTED)
                slevel = "Uncommitted";
            else if (level == Connection.TRANSACTION_READ_COMMITTED)
                slevel = "Committed";
            else if (level == Connection.TRANSACTION_REPEATABLE_READ)
                slevel = "Non-repeatable";
            else if (level == Connection.TRANSACTION_SERIALIZABLE)
                slevel = "Serializable";
```

```
            theText.append("Actual transaction isolation level: "
                + slevel + "\n");
        }

        theConnection[i].setAutoCommit(false);

        if (i == 0)
            theText.append("Auto-commit mode: "
                + theConnection[i].getAutoCommit( ));
    }
    catch (SQLException sqlex)
    {
        handleException(sqlex);
    }
    catch (Exception ex)
    {
        theStatus.setText("Error: " + ex.getMessage( ));
        ex.printStackTrace( );
        stop( );
    }
}
```

Listing 13.5 shows the **closeConnection( )** method. The method avoids attempting to close a **null Connection** or a **Connection** that is already closed. It also rolls back any pending changes before closing the database.

LISTING 13.5   THE CLOSECONNECTION( ) METHOD.

```
public void closeConnection(int i)
{
    try
    {
        if(theConnection [i] != null && ! theConnection[i].isClosed( ))
        {
            theConnection[i].rollback( );
            theConnection[i].close( );
        }
        theConnection[i] = null;
    }
    catch (SQLException sqlex)
    {
        handleException(sqlex);
    }
}
```

Listing 13.6 shows the **createTable( )** method. The applet uses this method to fully initialize the Anomalies table every time a new transaction is executed. This way, no transaction is affected by the possibly inconsistent state resulting from a previous transaction. The method drops and re-creates the table, inserting a single record with a key value of 0 and a data value of 0. Note that **create-Table( )** uses the **commit( )** method to commit its changes before returning.

LISTING 13.6   THE CREATETABLE( ) METHOD.

```
public void createTable( )
{
    theText.append("\nInitializing database");
    try
    {
        theStatement[0].executeUpdate("DROP TABLE Anomalies");
    }
    catch (SQLException sqlex) { ; }
    try
    {
        theStatement[0].executeUpdate("CREATE TABLE Anomalies "
          + "(theKey INTEGER PRIMARY KEY, theData INTEGER);");
        theStatement[0].executeUpdate("INSERT INTO Anomalies "
          + "(theKey, theData) VALUES (0, 0)");
        theConnection[0].commit( );
        theText.append("\nDatabase initialized\n");
    }
    catch (SQLException sqlex)
    {
        handleException(sqlex);
        rollbackDB(0);
    }
}
```

Accessing The Data

Listing 13.7 shows the data access methods the applet uses:

- **readDB( )**—Reads a record from the Anomalies table

- **readAllDB( )**—Reads records of the Anomalies table, returning only those records that have a data value of 0

- **updateDB( )**—Updates the data value of a record of the Anomalies table to a specified value

- **insertDB( )**—Adds a record to the Anomalies table

None of these methods actually commits any database changes. Thus, they can be flexibly used to construct transactions that perform commits or rollbacks at designated points by including the commit or rollback call within the transaction code.

LISTING 13.7   THE DATA ACCESS METHODS.

```
public void readDB(int i)
{
    try
    {
        theResult[i] = theStatement[i]
          .executeQuery("SELECT theKey,theData FROM Anomalies "
          +  "WHERE theKey=0");
        if (theResult[i] == null) return;
        if (! theResult[i].next( )) return;
        int the_key  = theResult[i].getInt(1);
        int the_data = theResult[i].getInt(2);
        theText.append("\nTransaction " + getTransID(i) + ": Key="
          + the_key + " Data=" + the_data);
        theResult[i].close( );
    }
    catch (SQLException sqlex)
    {
        String message = sqlex.getMessage( );
        theText.append("\nTransaction " + getTransID(i) + " read error:"
          + message);
    }
}

public void readAllDB(int i)
{
    try
    {
        theResult[i] = theStatement[i]
          .executeQuery("SELECT theKey,theData FROM Anomalies "
          +  "WHERE theData=0");
        if (theResult[i] == null) return;
        while (theResult[i].next( ))
        {
            int the_key  = theResult[i].getInt(1);
            int the_data = theResult[i].getInt(2);
            theText.append("\nTransaction " + getTransID(i) + ": Key="
              + the_key + " Data=" + the_data);
        }
        theResult[i].close( );
```

```
    }
    catch (SQLException sqlex)
    {
        String message = sqlex.getMessage( );
        theText.append("\nTransaction " + getTransID(i) + " read error:"
          + message);
    }
}

public void updateDB(int i, int data)
{
    try
    {
        theStatement[0].executeUpdate("UPDATE Anomalies "
          + "SET theData = " + data + " WHERE theKey = 0");
        theText.append("\nTransaction " + getTransID(i)
          + " has updated the row");
    }
    catch (SQLException sqlex)
    {
        String message = sqlex.getMessage( );
        theText.append("\nTransaction " + getTransID(i)
          + " update error:" + message);
    }
}

public void insertDB(int i, int key, int data)
{
    try
    {
        theStatement[0].executeUpdate("INSERT Anomalies "
          + "(theKey, theData) VALUES(" +
          key + ", " + data + ")");
        theText.append("\nTransaction " + getTransID(i)
          + " has inserted a row");
    }
    catch (SQLException sqlex)
    {
        String message = sqlex.getMessage( );
        theText.append("\nTransaction " + getTransID(i)
          + " update error:" + message);
    }
}
```

The commitDB( ), rollbackDB( ), And releaseLocks( ) Methods

Listing 13.8 shows the methods used to commit and roll back database changes—**commitDB( )** and **rollbackDB( )**. A third method, **releaseLocks( )**, uses the **Connection.commit( )** method to release all locks held by a connection, committing any pending changes in the process.

LISTING 13.8   THE COMMITDB( ), ROLLBACKDB( ), AND RELEASELOCKS( ) METHODS.

```
public void commitDB(int i)
{
    try
    {
        theConnection[i].commit( );
        if (i == 0)
            theText.append("\nTransaction A has committed");
    }
    catch (SQLException sqlex)
    {
        if (i == 0)
            handleException(sqlex);
    }
}

public void rollbackDB(int i)
{
    try
    {
        theConnection[i].rollback( );
        if (i == 0)
            theText.append("\nTransaction A has rolled back");
    }
    catch (SQLException sqlex)
    {
        if (i == 0)
            handleException(sqlex);
    }
}

public void releaseLocks( )
{
    try
    {
        theConnection[0].commit( );
    }
```

```
    catch (SQLException sqlex) { ; }
    try
    {
        theConnection[1].commit( );
    }
    catch (SQLException sqlex) { ; }
}
```

Miscellaneous Methods

Listing 13.9 shows miscellaneous methods of the DBAnomalies applet. The
getTransID( ) method translates an index value of 0 or 1 to the **String** "A" or
"B", facilitating the labeling of output commentary sent to the **TextArea**. The
statusOK( ) method places a message indicating nominal status in the **TextField**
used to display status information (**theStatus**). The **handleException( )** method
is a familiar friend, used to display a status message describing a **SQLException**.

LISTING **13.9**   MISCELLANEOUS METHODS.

```
public String getTransID(int i)
{
    String [ ] trans_id = { "A", "B" };
    return trans_id [i];
}


public void statusOK( )
{
    theStatus.setText("Status: OK");
}


public void handleException(Exception ex)
{
    theStatus.setText("Error: " + ex.getMessage( ));
}
```

The TransDemo Applet

The second example program for this chapter is the TransDemo applet. It lets
you execute transactions that consist of **Read**s and **Update**s, and commit or roll
back the result. By running two (or more) copies of the applet, you can explore
many aspects of concurrent transaction processing.

The User Interface

The user interface of the TransDemo applet is shown in Figure 13.5. The buttons let you perform common transaction steps:

- The Read button lets you read a database record.

- The Update button lets you update a database record.

- The Commit button lets you commit a transaction.

- The Rollback button lets you roll back a transaction.

- The Batch Update button lets you initiate a series of read and update operations, performed as a series of transactions.

- The Reset Data button lets you restore the database table used by the program to its original state.

- The Reopen DB button lets you close the current database connection and open a new one. It's useful for recovering from errors.

In addition, the applet displays important status information, including:

- Whether an uncommitted transaction is pending

- Whether an update anomaly has been detected during a batch update

- The average time per transaction during a batch update

- The count of transactions remaining in a currently executing batch update

- The SQL status

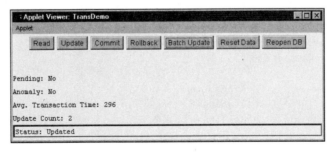

Figure 13.5
The user interface of the TransDemo applet.

The fields and **init( )** method of the applet are shown in Listing 13.10. A **final static int** sets the number of transactions performed in a batch update. You can choose a different value by changing the field's initializer. Otherwise, there's nothing new here.

LISTING 13.10   FIELDS AND INIT( ) METHOD OF THE TRANSDEMO APPLET.

```
import java.applet.*;
import java.awt.*;
import java.awt.event.*;
import java.sql.*;

public class TransDemo extends Applet
implements ActionListener
{
    final static int BATCHSIZE = 25;

    Button        theReadButton      = new Button("Read");
    Button        theUpdateButton    = new Button("Update");
    Button        theCommitButton    = new Button("Commit");
    Button        theRollbackButton  = new Button("Rollback");
    Button        theBatchButton     = new Button("Batch Update");
    Button        theResetButton     = new Button("Reset Data");
    Button        theReopenButton    = new Button("Reopen DB");

    Label         thePending         = new Label("Pending: No");
    Label         theAnomaly         = new Label("Anomaly: No");
    Label         theAverage         =
      new Label("Avg. Transaction Time: ?");
    Label         theCount           = new Label( );
    TextField     theStatus          = new TextField(64);

    String theSource   = "jdbc:odbc:TransDemo";
    String theUser     = "";
    String thePassword = "";

    Connection    theConnection  = null;
    Statement     theStatement   = null;
    ResultSet     theResultSet   = null;

    public void init( )
    {
        Panel p1 = new Panel(new FlowLayout( ));
```

```
            p1.add(theReadButton);
            p1.add(theUpdateButton);
            p1.add(theCommitButton);
            p1.add(theRollbackButton);
            p1.add(theBatchButton);
            p1.add(theResetButton);
            p1.add(theReopenButton);

            Panel p2 = new Panel(new GridLayout(0, 1));
            p2.setFont(new Font("Courier", Font.PLAIN, 12));

            p2.add(thePending);
            p2.add(theAnomaly);
            p2.add(theAverage);
            p2.add(theCount);
            p2.add(theStatus);

            setLayout(new BorderLayout( ));
            add(p1,          "Center");
            add(p2,          "South");

            theReadButton    .addActionListener(this);
            theUpdateButton  .addActionListener(this);
            theCommitButton  .addActionListener(this);
            theRollbackButton.addActionListener(this);
            theBatchButton   .addActionListener(this);
            theResetButton   .addActionListener(this);
            theReopenButton  .addActionListener(this);

            openConnection( );
        }
```

Listing 13.11 shows the **actionPerformed( )** method. As usual, the method dispatches a working method based on which button the user clicked.

LISTING 13.11 THE ACTIONPERFORMED( ) METHOD.

```
public void actionPerformed(ActionEvent event)
{
    Object source = event.getSource( );
    theStatus.setText("Status: OK");
    try
    {
        if      (source == theReadButton)     readDB ( );
        else if (source == theUpdateButton)   updateDB( );
        else if (source == theCommitButton)   commitDB( );
        else if (source == theRollbackButton) rollbackDB( );
```

```
            else if (source == theBatchButton)     batchDB( );
            else if (source == theResetButton)     resetDB( );
            else if (source == theReopenButton)    openConnection( );
        }
    catch (SQLException sqlex)
    {
        handleException(sqlex);
    }
}
```

Opening The Database

Listing 13.12 shows the **openConnection( )** method. The method first checks whether a connection is already open, in which case it uses the **rollback( )** and **close( )** methods to terminate the connection.

For variety, the method uses a variant form of the **getConnection( )** method. This form permits specification of property name-value pairs, as described in Chapter 5. Only the **userid** and **password** properties are used.

The transaction isolation is set to **TRANSACTION_READ_COMMITTED**, which is the default value (and highest value) supported by MS Access. If you have access to another database, you may wish to experiment by using other values. Even if you're using Access, you may want to experiment with the **TRANSACTION_READ_UNCOMMITTED** isolation level.

Note that there is no companion **closeConnection( )** method. To close the database connection, the applet relies on the **finalize( )** methods implemented by the JDBC objects. This is a generally unsafe practice. Because the database table updated by the applet contains no useful data, however, no problem will arise. Omitting the method makes the program somewhat shorter and simpler.

LISTING 13.12   THE OPENCONNECTION( ) METHOD.

```
public void openConnection( )
{
    theStatus.setText("Status: OK");

    try
    {
        if (theConnection != null && ! theConnection.isClosed( ))
        {
            theConnection.rollback( );
            theConnection.close( );
        }
    }
```

```
    catch (SQLException sqlex) { ; }

    try
    {
        Class.forName("sun.jdbc.odbc.JdbcOdbcDriver");

        java.util.Properties pprops = new java.util.Properties( );
        pprops.put("user", theUser);
        pprops.put("password", thePassword);

        if (theConnection != null)
            theConnection.close( );

        theConnection =
            DriverManager.getConnection(theSource, pprops);

        TheStatement =
            theConnection.createStatement( );

        theResultSet = null;

        theConnection.setTransactionIsolation(
          Connection.TRANSACTION_READ_COMMITTED);
        theConnection.setAutoCommit(false);
        readDB( );
    }
    catch (ClassNotFoundException cnfex)
    {
        System.err.println("Can't locate database driver.");
        stop( );
        destroy( );
    }
    catch (SQLException sqlex)
    {
        handleException(sqlex);
    }
}
```

Accessing The Data

The methods used to access database records are shown in Listing 13.13. These include **updateDB( )**, which increments a counter in the database record, and **readDB( )**, which reads a database record. The **updateDB( )** method contains two SQL **Update** statements, each incrementing the counter by one. This is subtly different from using a single **Update** statement that increments the counter by two. During the hiatus between the two **Update** statements, another transaction may read the incomplete updated record, simulating what could happen during a complex, multistep transaction. The same situation could not occur, of course, if a single **Update** were used. The two statements are divisible, though the single statement would not be. To make the divisible operation even more so, the method pauses for five seconds (five iterations of a 1,000-millisecond delay) between the two updates.

When a database record is read, the counter is checked for parity. The counter should always be even, since it starts at zero and is incremented twice by each invocation of the **updateDB( )** method. A read occurring in the midst of an **Update** transaction may, however, fetch a partially updated record with an odd value. A **Label** is updated to reflect the presence or absence of such an **Update** anomaly.

LISTING 13.13 THE DATA ACCESS METHODS.

```
public void updateDB( )
throws SQLException
{
    theStatus.setText("Status: Updating .");
    thePending.setText("Pending: Yes");
    theStatement.executeUpdate(
      "UPDATE trans SET update_count = update_count + 1 "
        + "WHERE key_value = 1");
    for (int i = 1; i <= 5; i++)
    {
        try
        {
            Thread.sleep(1000);
        }
        catch (Exception ex) { ; }
        theStatus.setText(theStatus.getText( ) + " .");
    }
    theStatement.executeUpdate(
      "UPDATE trans SET update_count = update_count + 1 "
        + "WHERE key_value = 1");
    theStatus.setText("Status: Updated");
    readDB( );
}

public void readDB( )
throws SQLException
{
```

```
    if (theStatement != null)
        theStatement.close( );
    theStatement = theConnection.createStatement( );
    theResultSet = theStatement.executeQuery(
      "SELECT update_count FROM trans WHERE key_value = 1");
    if (theResultSet != null)
    {
        theResultSet.next( );
        int update_count = theResultSet.getInt(1);
        theCount.setText("Update Count: " + update_count);
        if (update_count % 2 == 1)
            theAnomaly.setText("Anomaly: Yes");
        else
            theAnomaly.setText("Anomaly: No");
        theResultSet.close( );
    }
}
```

Transaction Commit And Rollback

Listing 13.14 shows the **commitDB( )** and **rollbackDB( )** methods, used, respectively, to commit or roll back transactions. A **Label** component (**thePending**) is updated to reflect the absence of a pending update following a commit or rollback. The **updateDB( )** method updates this **Label** to reflect the presence of a pending update.

LISTING 13.14   THE COMMITDB( ) AND ROLLBACKDB( ) METHODS.

```
public void commitDB( )
throws SQLException
{
    theConnection.commit( );
    thePending.setText("Pending: No");
}

public void rollbackDB( )
throws SQLException
{
    theConnection.rollback( );
    thePending.setText("Pending: No");
}
```

Executing A Transaction Batch

Listing 13.15 shows the **batchDB( )** method, which performs a series of divisible updates of the sort performed by **updateDB( )**. A smaller time delay than that used in **updateDB( )** avoids unnecessarily lengthy execution of the method. Tests show the smaller value is generally capable of generating an update anomaly when concurrent transactions are executing at a low level of isolation (for example, **TRANSACTION_READ_UNCOMMITTED**).

LISTING 13.15   THE BATCHDB( ) METHOD.

```
public void batchDB( )
throws SQLException
{
    java.util.Date begin = new java.util.Date( );
    for (int i = 1; i <= BATCHSIZE; i++)
    {
        theStatus.setText("Updating (" + (BATCHSIZE - i) + ") .");
        thePending.setText("Pending: Yes");
        theStatement.executeUpdate(
          "UPDATE trans SET update_count = update_count + 1 "
          + "WHERE key_value = 1");
        for (int j = 1; j <= 5; j++)
        {
            try
            {
                Thread.sleep(50);
            }
            catch (Exception ex) { ; }
            theStatus.setText(theStatus.getText( ) + " .");
        }
        theStatement.executeUpdate(
          "UPDATE trans SET update_count = update_count + 1 "
          + "WHERE key_value = 1");
        commitDB( );
        java.util.Date now = new java.util.Date( );
        long elapsed = now.getTime( ) - begin.getTime( );
        theAverage.setText("Avg. Transaction Time: " + elapsed / i);
    }
    theStatus.setText("Status: Updated");
}
```

Resetting The Database

Listing 13.16 shows the **resetDB( )** method, which uses an **Update** to reset the database counter value to zero. You'll need it to replace an odd counter value once an anomaly has occurred. Listing 13.17 shows the **handleException( )** method, which prints a stack trace and displays an error message describing any **SQLException**s detected.

LISTING 13.16   THE RESETDB( ) METHOD.

```
public void resetDB( )
{
    try
    {
        rollbackDB( );
        theStatement.executeUpdate("UPDATE trans SET update_count = 0 "
          + "WHERE key_value = 1");
        commitDB( );
        readDB( );
    }
    catch (SQLException sqlex) { ; }
    theStatus.setText("Status: OK");
}
```

LISTING 13.17   THE HANDLEEXCEPTION( ) METHOD.

```
public void handleException(Exception e)
{
    e.printStackTrace( );
    theStatus.setText("Error: " + e.getMessage( ));
}
```

Summary

This chapter introduced some important subtleties involving concurrent access to a database. You learned how to use the **commit( )** and **rollback( )** methods to group SQL statements into transactions. You also learned how various transaction isolation levels help you avoid database anomalies resulting from dirty reads, nonrepeatable reads, and phantom reads. The next chapter takes up some more important real-world database issues, including security and recovery.

DATABASE SECURITY AND RECOVERY

Using a database centralizes data, presenting many advantages, but also posing a few complications. One such complication is security—once the data is stored in one place, everyone knows where to find it, including both legitimate and potential illegitimate users. To be useful, a database must ensure that only legitimate users gain access to sensitive data. If every worker could set his or her own salary by simply updating the database at will, chaos would ensue. The situation could get even more exciting if workers could change the salaries of other workers.

Of course, most organizations don't allow such access to their databases. Most organizations, in fact, strive to prevent workers from even learning the salaries of other employees. Several states have privacy laws that impose upon the employer an obligation to keep employees' personal information private. Failure to establish adequate data security can cost a company money in several ways—from fraud to fines.

One advantage to centralizing data is that repairing a damaged database is easier. When data is scattered in several files stored on several systems, recovery is sometimes possible only in principle—bringing every record of every file back to a completely consistent state might take more time than it's worth. Storing

435

data centrally simplifies recovery considerably. When you buy a database, you'll get one or more recovery tools that can help you restore it to service after a mishap.

This chapter describes the security and recovery features and functions provided by modern databases. This is a difficult task, because database vendors display a notable lack of consistency in their approaches to security and recovery. The ANSI SQL standard specifies only a minimal set of security functions, and a number of vendors have ignored even that. Microsoft is one such vendor; Microsoft Access uses an almost entirely idiosyncratic approach to database security.

Rather than describing the security and recovery functions of Access, which neither conform to the SQL standard nor generalize well to other databases, I'll focus primarily on the SQL standard. To avoid a vague and general presentation, I'll offer examples based mainly on Microsoft SQL Server. Like other databases, SQL Server has its share of idiosyncrasies in its handling of security and recovery. It does, however, implement the security functions specified by the SQL standard. In that sense, its security and recovery features are as close to standard as those of any other database.

The disadvantage of this approach is that you must have SQL Server to run the examples in this chapter. If you don't have access to SQL Server, you may be able to get a copy inexpensively. At the time of this writing, Microsoft is offering a 120-day evaluation copy of SQL Server, which can be downloaded from the Microsoft World Wide Web site. The download is large—about 35MB— but it will afford you the temporary access to SQL Server you need to run the examples.

Alternatively, you might consider purchasing Microsoft Visual Studio, which includes a copy of a developer's edition of SQL Server. Finally, you might acquire a copy of another database, such as Sybase SQL Anywhere, which is often available inexpensively. Although the example programs will not run without modification on a database other than SQL Server, you will find porting them to a new database to be instructive.

Data Control Language (DCL)

SQL's Data Control Language (DCL) lets you control access to these database management functions:

- Select
- Insert
- Update
- Delete
- References

The first four of these are familiar DML verbs. The last, **References**, was mentioned in Chapter 9. It can be used in a DDL statement to define a constraint that enforces referential integrity.

Using DCL, you can control who is allowed to use these verbs on a given table. The **Insert** and **Update** verbs can even be restricted at the column level. For example, you could prohibit users outside the payroll department from using the **Select** verb on the Employees table. This would prevent them from accessing the sensitive information contained in the table. You might choose to allow any worker in the payroll department to use **Select** on the Employees table, but you might restrict use of the **Insert**, **Update**, and **Delete** verbs to only those workers who are authorized to make changes to employee data. Or, you might allow workers very wide access, prohibiting them only from using **Insert** and **Update** on the Salary column of the Employee table. You'll learn exactly how to enforce such restrictions later in the chapter.

A number of databases allow the database administrator to control access to additional functions beyond those identified in the SQL standard. For example, every database somehow restricts access to the DDL **Create** verb, which was described in Chapter 9. Many databases simply allow only the database administrator to use **Create**. Microsoft SQL Server, in contrast, allows the database administrator to specify others who are allowed to use **Create**. To learn exactly which functions your database allows you to control, consult the documentation for your database.

User Identification

To enforce the restrictions put in place using DCL, a database must have some way of positively identifying each database user. A common way to accomplish this is to have each user identify himself or herself by means of a user ID and a password when the database connection is established. The **DriverManager.get Connection**( ) method supports this approach, by providing parameters that contain the user ID and password. Such a facility is all the SQL standard requires.

SQL Server uses a somewhat more elaborate scheme, based on logins, users, and groups. The user ID and password supplied to **getConnection**( ) grant a user access to SQL Server itself, but do not in themselves grant access to any database. When using SQL Server, the user ID is more properly known as a *login*. Each database maintains a list of authorized users and the SQL Server login that corresponds to each. Each database also keeps track of which privileges each user is allowed.

Separating logins from user names makes maintaining the database easier. To see why this is so, first consider the situation where the login and user name are identical. If the payroll department has three workers—John, Sue, and Fran— each must have a login to SQL Server. Each must also have a corresponding user ID within the payroll database. Suppose John leaves and is replaced by Frank. The database administrator must delete John's login and user name, and create new ones for Frank. The database administrator must also ensure that all the permissions previously held by John are established for Frank. This can be a time-consuming and error-prone task.

The better way is to take advantage of the fact that logins and user names can be different. Since John, Sue, and Fran have the same duties and responsibilities, you can create a single database user named *Clerk* that has the permissions needed by all three people. This single user name can be associated with the logins for John, Sue, and Fran, giving them the permissions they need. Now, when John leaves and Frank replaces him, the database administrator's job is much simpler: Delete John's login, add a new login for Frank, and associate Frank's login with the Clerk user name. The permissions associated with Clerk do not need to be changed at all.

GROUPS

Groups are another way of simplifying the work of the database administrator. When added to the database, a user can be made part of a group; otherwise, the user automatically joins a built-in group named *public*. SQL Server allows the database administrator to grant permissions to groups as well as users. Any permission granted to the public group is available to every user of the database.

Groups can also be used to simplify granting of permissions to classes of users. For example, the payroll database might have a group named *Clerk,* and the users John, Sue, and Fran might belong to the group. Replacing John with Frank is again easy, since Frank obtains all necessary permissions as soon as he is joined to the Clerk group. You'll see how to do so later in this chapter.

SPECIAL USERS

SQL Server supports a number of special users, including:

- SA

- DBO

- Guest

The special capabilities of these users are described in the following sections.

THE SA USER

The database administrator of a SQL Server system is the user known as SA, for *system administrator.* You don't need to create the SA user, since one automatically exists. You should, however, change the password associated with the SA user to a value known only to the database administrator.

Logging into SQL Server as SA and providing the proper password gives the user unrestricted access to every SQL Sever function. SA can perform certain functions, such as reconfiguring or shutting down SQL Server, that no other user can do.

THE DBO USER

The user who creates a database becomes the database owner (DBO). You don't have to create a user named DBO; the user who creates the database is automatically known as DBO. The DBO of a database has full privileges for that database, including the ability to:

- Allow users to access the database
- Grant users permission to access tables and columns of the database
- Create groups
- Assign users to groups

Often, the database administrator logs in as SA and creates a database. In such a case, SA becomes the DBO of the database.

THE GUEST USER

By creating a user named *guest*, the owner of a database (that is, the DBO user) allows general access to the database by users not otherwise authorized. If a user without a valid user name attempts to access a database that includes a guest user, the user will be allowed to use the database and will be accorded the permissions assigned to guest. When the guest user name is created, guest inherits the permissions assigned to the public group.

Granting Privileges

The SQL **Grant** statement allows you to grant privileges to users. Its general form is

```
Grant privileges On table To user
```

where *privileges* can include any of the following:

```
All
Select
Delete
Insert [ (column [, column] … ) ]
Update [ (column [, column] … ) ]
References [ (column [, column] … ) ]
```

More than one *privilege* can be listed; the individual privileges must be separated by commas. The *table* can name either a table or a view. The *user* can reference a group name or user name or can have the value **public**. For example, the following grants the user Clerk use of the **Select** statement on the Employees table:

```
Grant Select On Employees To Clerk
```

To grant the user John the ability to update the Name column of the Employees table, you could use the following statement:

```
Grant Update (EmployeeName) On Employees To John
```

To grant all privileges to all users of the Employees table, you could use:

```
Grant All On Employees To Public
```

Of course, granting so many rights to so many users is usually unwise. The old saying, "Not everything that can be done should be done," should be kept in mind when defining security policies. The best course is to give each user only the privileges actually needed.

The References Privilege

The **References** privilege is a bit unusual and requires special explanation. Suppose that a company is about to award end-of-year bonuses and has directed a database programmer to develop and run a query that determines which employees will receive bonuses. The programmer has put the employee numbers and names of those who will receive bonuses in a table named Bonuses. Because the identities of the bonus earners are to be kept secret, the database administrator has granted **Select** privileges on the Bonuses table only to the programmer. To prevent tampering, **Update** and **Insert** privileges have been similarly restricted.

You really want to know whether you're one of the lucky few, because the special sale on drag boats at Tony's Marine will be over before the winners are announced. If you knew for certain you were going to receive a bonus, you would put a down payment on that 25-foot racer you've been admiring. The price is too good to pass up if you could be sure you could swing the monthly payments. After pondering the problem, you discover a hole in the security arrangements and proceed to exploit it (apparently, you're better known for your technical ingenuity than your good character).

First, you create a table containing a foreign key that references the Bonuses table:

```
Create Table Winners
  (Employeeno Int Constraint fk1 References Bonuses(EmployeeNo);
```

Then, you attempt to insert a record for each employee into the Winners table. For most employees, the attempt will fail because the foreign-key constraint requires a corresponding record in the Bonuses table. Records for bonus winners, however, will be successfully inserted into the Winners table. When the query is finished, the Winners table will contain the employee number of each employee who is to receive a bonus. You simply check the table for your own employee number and then either race down to Tony's or start reminding the boss what a productive worker you are.

If you were the database administrator in such a case, you would want to prevent someone from cleverly exploiting this security hole. The SQL standard gives you exactly the mechanism you need: the **References** privilege. This privilege is necessary to reference a table using a foreign key. If only the responsible programmer has the **References** privilege to the Bonuses table, others cannot create a table that has a foreign key pointing into the Bonuses table. As the administrator, you want no unauthorized users to have **Select**, **Update**, **Insert**, or **References** privileges on the Bonuses table. The best way to make sure no unauthorized users have these privileges is to use the **Revoke** statement, which you will see shortly.

The Grant Option

Sometimes, you may want to give a user—to whom you've granted a privilege—the ability to grant that privilege to others. By including the clause **With Grant Option** in the original **Grant**, you allow the grantee to grant the privilege to others. For example, the following statement not only allows John to update the Salary column, it allows him to grant this privilege to others:

```
Grant Update(Salary) On Employees To John With Grant Option
```

Now John can pass the privilege on to Mary:

```
Grant Update(Salary) On Employees To Mary
```

Revoking Privileges

To rescind a granted privilege, you can use the **Revoke** statement, which has the following form:

```
Revoke privileges On table From user
```

Privileges, *table*, and *user* take the same form used in the **Grant** command. If the user has granted privileges to others, these privileges are not automatically revoked. If you wish them to be revoked, you specify the **Cascade** option:

```
Revoke privileges On table From user Cascade
```

To revoke the ability to grant a privilege, you can use this form:

```
Revoke Grant Option For privileges On table From user
```

Using Grant And Revoke Together

Often, using **Grant** followed by **Revoke** (or the reverse) is simpler than writing a single more complex statement. Using **Grant** and **Revoke** together can make you a more productive database administrator. Suppose you are responsible for the EmployeeInfo table, and you want the following distribution of privileges:

- Everyone should be able to select data from the table.

- Only the clerks in the Human Resources Department (John and Sally) should be able to insert new data or update data in the table.

- No one, not even the clerks in the Human Resources Department, should be able to update an employee number.

The following SQL statements establish the desired privileges:

```
Grant Select, Insert
  On EmployeeInfo
  To John, Sally;
Grant Update
  On EmployeeInfo (Name, Address, City, State, Zip, Phone)
  To John, Sally;
Grant Select
  On EmployeeInfo
  To Alice, Bob, Cindy, David, Elizabeth, Fred, Georgia, Harry, Ima,
  Jerry, Keri, Lee, Michele, Norbert, Olivia, Paul;
```

Using **Grant** and **Revoke** together makes the job simpler:

```
Grant Select On EmployeeInfo To Public;
Grant Insert, Update
  On EmployeeInfo To John, Sally;
Revoke Update
  On EmployeeInfo(EmployeeNo)
  From John, Sally;
```

The first approach requires you to list the columns of the EmployeeInfo table and the users. This is not necessary in the second form, which is therefore more compact and less subject to change.

Encryption

Restricting data access privileges using **Grant** and **Revoke** doesn't make your data entirely safe. Some databases store data in special files that can be read only by system or database administrators. Microsoft Access, however, stores its data in ordinary files; hackers can get in and discover information that the database administrator has tried to keep secret. SQL access privileges cannot prevent such an invasion, since the hacker never logs into the database.

You can protect your Access database against this threat by *encrypting* it. When data is encrypted, its characters are replaced using an encryption algorithm and a string of text known as the *key*. Someone trying to read the encrypted data will see an apparently random series of characters that is entirely unreadable. To read the data, it must be *decrypted* using the same key used to encrypt it. One of the risks in encrypting data is that you may forget the key. If you do, you won't be able to recover the original data.

Access provides an encryption facility that chooses a key for you, eliminating the possibility that you will forget it. Moreover, Access decrypts data only when it is accessed and only when the user has the necessary data access privileges. Once you have encrypted an Access database, you will not likely need to decrypt it. (Because decryption is automatic, there's little point in manually decrypting.)

To encrypt an Access database, you use the Security|Encrypt/Decrypt Database menu item. You can put the encrypted database in a new file, or you can replace the original database with the encrypted one.

SQL Server also stores its data in ordinary files, but SQL Server databases cannot be hacked so easily. When the database server is active, it keeps an exclusive lock on the file holding the database. The operating system will prevent any process other than the database server process from accessing the database.

Of course, a determined hacker would not be put off so easily and would probably seek some way to terminate the database process so that the lock would be removed. Only an administrator can start or stop the SQL Server database process, however, so the hacker would need to find a way to become an administrator of the system that hosts the SQL Server database. Although most users of Access databases are users of the system that hosts the database, most users of SQL Server databases do not even have a login account on the system that hosts the SQL Server database. A would-be hacker must penetrate several layers of software protection to compromise a SQL Server database. Data held in a SQL Server database, therefore, is reasonably secure from unauthorized access.

Backup

From time to time, a database is likely to suffer damage from power failures, media failures, or other causes. Often, the database system will report the damage; sometimes, erratic operation may lead the database administrator to conclude that the database has been damaged. In either case, the administrator has two options:

- Restore the database from a backup.

- Run a database recovery program.

Choosing between these options is simple if you have no backup copy of the database, but this is a situation to be avoided. The administrator should ensure that the database is regularly backed up, that the backup media are kept safe, that they are stored at some distance from the database itself, and that the process produces usable backups. Just in case, you should keep several generations of backups, because backups can be faulty. Also, damage to a database sometimes does not become evident right away. If your only backup is not usable or if it contains the image of a damaged database, you are in a most unpleasant situation.

Backing up an Access database is simple. If you have a copy of the MDB file, you have a backup of the database. You can simply copy small databases onto a floppy diskette. For larger databases, you may want to use a commercial backup program.

Before making the backup, you should ensure that no one is using the database; otherwise, the backup may contain inconsistent data. An example may help you see the need for this precaution. Assume you have a database that contains two tables—A and B—and that a user is posting transactions that update both tables. If you begin copying the database just before a transaction is posted, you may copy Table A before the transaction commits and Table B after the transaction commits. If you later restore your copy of the database, you will find that the database is inconsistent: The transaction that was posted as you made the backup is missing its update to Table A.

More sophisticated database systems, such as SQL Server, provide special backup utilities that help avoid such problems. To back up a SQL Server database, start the SQL Enterprise Manager, select a server, and choose the Tools|Backup|Restore menu item. SQL Enterprise Manager also lets you schedule backups for automatic execution at predetermined times. For details, consult the SQL Server documentation.

Database Recovery

You can recover a database by restoring a backup copy or by running the special repair program included with most database systems. Either operation involves some risk—for example, restoring an old copy of a database over a perfectly up-to-date and intact database is not a good idea. Restoring a backup usually entails losing any transactions posted to the database after the backup copy was made. If this is not acceptable, you need to have some method, such as a printed activity log, for identifying and recovering such transactions. Sophisticated database systems, such as SQL Server, provide an automated transaction log. If this log is intact, it can be used to recover the database fully. Often, however, a power failure or other incident that compromises database integrity will compromise the integrity of the log as well.

Since the recovery process is itself risky, you should make a backup copy of your database before beginning any recovery procedure. When all is said and done, you may find that the point at which you started is preferable to any destination reachable using the best backup copies and repair programs available.

To restore an Access database, you simply copy the MDB file from the backup media to the host system. To repair an Access database, the administrator uses the Database Utilities|Repair Database menu item.

SQL Server automatically repairs its databases, if necessary, every time SQL Server is restarted. To restore a SQL Server database, start the SQL Enterprise Manager, select a server, and choose the Tools|Backup/Restore menu item. You should consult the SQL Server *Administrator's Companion* before attempting to recover a SQL Server database.

Event Logs And Audits

Most database systems provide event logs and audit trails that record important events. The database log will tell you when the server was started and stopped, when connections were refused owing to an insufficient number of licenses, when media failures occurred, when database recoveries were performed, and other important information.

Though Access does not provide such facilities, SQL Server provides two distinct logs for errors:

- *The SQL Server error log*—Viewed using the SQL Enterprise Manager or a text editor
- *The Windows NT application log*—Viewed using the Windows NT Event Viewer

Applet Security

You can write Java programs as applets or as applications. Each has its benefits and drawbacks. The chief benefit of applets is that they are downloaded from a server every time they are run. The user, therefore, always runs the most current version of an applet. This makes software version control much simpler than when using applications.

On the other hand, applets loaded across the network are subject to a number of security restrictions not imposed on applications. These restrictions are intended to prevent a hacker from using an applet to compromise the security or integrity of a client system. Some of these restrictions, however, have unintended side effects that hamper applets, at least when they are run inside current-generation browsers. Browser authors have promised that future generations of browsers will have more flexible security mechanisms that can be configured to meet specific needs.

Restrictions

Applets loaded from your local hard drive can do just about anything an application can do. Applets downloaded from a Web server are not allowed to:

- Create a top-level window that is not plainly marked as an *untrusted window*

- Obtain the user name or home directory name

- Read, write, delete, or rename files on the client system

- Create a directory; list a directory; check to see whether a specific file exists; or obtain size, type, or modification time-stamp information about a file on the client system

- Create a network connection to any computer other than the one that served the applet

- Listen for, or accept, network connections to the client system

- Run a program, load a dynamic library, or cause the Java interpreter to exit

- Create a thread outside the **ThreadGroup** of the applet

- Create a **ClassLoader** or **SecurityManager**

- Specify network control functions, such as **ContentHandlerFactory**, **SocketImplFactory**, or **URLStreamHandlerFactory**

- Define any system properties

- Define classes that are part of system packages

The restrictions that most affect designers and programmers of Java-based software are those that deal with access to classes and hosts. These are discussed in more detail in the following sections.

ACCESS TO CLASSES

Applets are restricted from defining classes that are part of system packages. Most current browsers seem to understand system packages as those named beginning with *java* or *sun*. As a consequence, most browsers consider the JDBC classes of **java.sql** to be system packages. This may pose no obvious problem; but at the time of writing, browsers generally do not implement the **java.sql** package. Because of the security restriction, you cannot simply send the **java.sql** class files along with the class files of an application. The browser will refuse to accept your offer, since it consists of system classes.

How, then, do you persuade the browser to allow your applet to perform JDBC operations? One approach is to hack the source code of the **java.sql** classes, renaming the classes so the browser will understand them as benign. Symantec has taken this approach in its Visual Café and Visual Café Pro products, naming the JDBC classes as part of the package **symjava.sql** rather than **java.sql**. Of course, purchasing a product like Visual Café or Visual Café Pro is probably easier than determining, by reading your license agreement, whether you have the legal right to recompile the **java.sql** classes as part of a different package.

When browsers include built-in support for the **java.sql** package, this problem will disappear. Fortunately, better solutions are available, which I will present shortly. First, I'll explain the other major restriction placed on applets.

ACCESS TO HOSTS

Applets are also restricted from making network connections to hosts other than the host that served the applet. This restriction closes the door on all sorts of potential mischief, but it also constrains the possible configurations for Java-based client-server systems. For example, assume that Host A stores the CLASS files for the applets that make up a client-server application system and that it also runs an HTTP server that distributes the applets to users who request them. Now, assume that Host B stores the SQL Server database for the application. Problem: The applets served by Host A are not allowed to open a connection to Host B; therefore, the applets cannot access the SQL Server database.

Of course, you can resolve this problem simply by hosting the SQL Server database on Host A, along with the applets and the HTTP server. If you have multiple databases, however, they must *all* reside on the same host.

You'll end up with a monolithic architecture that resembles those of the main-frame era rather than the modern, distributed computing era that Java promises to support.

Solutions

Fortunately, there are solutions to applet security, other than twisting your software into an architectural pretzel. Two, to be exact. The first, and presently more realistic, is based on the use of special middleware drivers. The second is based on capabilities promised for the coming generation of browsers.

DRIVERS AND MIDDLEWARE

The most workable and popular solution to the Java security dilemma is the three-tier architecture presented in Chapter 1. Rather than communicating directly with a database server, your applets can communicate with a middleware server. The middleware server can reside on the same host system as the CLASS files and HTTP server; however, it can communicate on behalf of an applet with database servers on many other hosts. The middleware server frees your databases from the requirement that they reside on a single host. With middleware, your architecture can be a truly distributed one.

Quite a few middleware products are available, and their numbers are growing. Javasoft maintains a Web page that lists such products. Consult the page for up-to-date information about what's available. So that you can experiment with middleware and see for yourself how it works, several representative products are included on the CD-ROM that accompanies this book.

BROWSER CONFIGURATIONS

Browser authors have promised that the coming generation of browsers will be more configurable than the current generation. New-generation browsers will have flexible security managers that allow the user to relax the imposed security restrictions, establishing a customized security policy. For example, the user will be able to create a list of hosts that applets are allowed to contact, apart from the host that served the applet. Applets may also be able to read and write files into a specified directory, giving them a little more access to the computing capabilities of the client.

The DBGuard Applets

The DBGuard applets will help you explore the SQL security facilities provided by SQL Server. The applets also demonstrate use of several stored procedures included with SQL Server. They will not work with Access, since it does not implement the **Grant** and **Revoke** statements. The applets' source code is too long to be completely included in this chapter, so only excerpts are shown. Complete source code is included on the CD-ROM.

Fifteen source files make up the DBGuard family of applets:

- DBGuard—Acts as a menu, facilitating access to the other applets
- AddGroup—Allows you to add user groups
- AddLogin—Allows you to add user logins
- AddUser—Allows you to add users
- AddUserToGroup—Allows you to assign users to groups
- DB—Manages access to the database
- DropGroup—Allows you to delete user groups
- DropLogin—Allows you to delete logins
- DropUser—Allows you to delete users
- GrantRights—Allows you to grant rights
- ListGroups—Allows you to list user groups
- ListLogins—Allows you to list user logins
- ListRights—Allows you to list user rights
- ListUsers—Allows you to list users
- RevokeRights—Allows you to revoke rights

The DB.getResult( ) Method

The **DB.getResult( )** method, shown in Listing 14.1, returns a **Vector** that contains the entire contents of a **ResultSet**, representing each row as an array of **Strings**. This method makes repeatedly traversing retrieved data easy, and it is used by other methods of the DBGuard applets.

LISTING 14.1   THE DB.GETRESULT( ) METHOD.

```
DB.getResult( );
public Vector getResult( )
throws SQLException
{
    Vector result = new Vector( );
    ResultSetMetaData rsm = theResultSet.getMetaData( );
    int cols = rsm.getColumnCount( );
    while (theResultSet.next( ))
    {
        String [ ] row = new String [cols];
        for (int i = 1; i <= cols; i++)
        {
            row [i - 1] = theResultSet.getString(i);
        }
        result.addElement(row);
    }
    return result;
}
```

The DB.getParameterValue( ) Method

The **DB.getParameterValue( )** method, shown in Listing 14.2, retrieves parameters from the HTML file used to start an applet. The driver name, database URL, user name, and password are passed to each applet using parameters of the <APPLET> HTML tag.

LISTING 14.2   THE DB.GETPARAMETERVALUE( ) METHOD.

```
public static String getParameterValue(Applet applet, String name)
{
    String value = applet.getParameter(name);
    if (value != null) return value;
    return "";
}
```

Using The Stored Procedures

SQL Server provides a set of stored procedures that you can use to update security information. Among these are the following stored procedures invoked by DBGuard applets:

- SP_ADD_LOGIN—Adds a new login, demonstrated by the AddLogin applet

- SP_ADD_USER—Adds a new user, demonstrated by the AddUser applet

- SP_ADD_GROUP—Adds a new user group, demonstrated by the AddGroup applet

- SP_CHANGEGROUP—Changes the group to which a user is assigned, demonstrated by the AddUserToGroup applet

- SP_DROPGROUP—Deletes a user group, demonstrated by the DropGroup applet

- SP_DROPUSER—Deletes a user, demonstrated by the DropUser and DropLogin applets

Consult the SQL Server documentation to learn which parameters each stored procedure uses. Once you know which parameters to supply, using these stored procedures via JDBC is straightforward.

Listing Groups

Listing groups, logins, rights, and users is more challenging than using the stored procedures to update them. The relevant information is contained in three SQL Server tables that you can query using ordinary SQL statements:

- *SysUsers*—Records information about users, including user ID, group ID, and name

- *SysLogins*—Records each valid login name

- *SysObjects*—Records the ID, name, and type of various system objects. System objects include rights assigned to users

The SQL Server documentation provides additional helpful information about these tables.

The **ListGroups.list( )** method in Listing 14.3 shows how to obtain a list of users and groups. The method uses a **Select** to obtain the user ID, group ID, and name of each user from the SysUsers table. It then uses the **getResult( )** method to retrieve a **Vector** containing the result of the **Select**, which it traverses, extracting the elements for which the user ID is the same as the group ID. These elements give the ID and name of each group, so the method stores them in a **Vector**, named *group*, for later use.

A second traversal using **getResult( )** examines the elements for which the user ID and group ID are distinct. These elements give the names and IDs of the users in each group. The **Vector** group retrieves the group name that corresponds to the group ID. The group name and user name are then appended to the output **TextArea, theGroups.**

LISTING 14.3 THE LISTGROUPS.LIST( ) METHOD.

```
public void list( )
{
    try
    {
        theGroups.setText("");
        theStatus.setText(OK);
        theDB.openConnection (theDriver, theURL, theUser, thePassword);
        theDB.executeQuery("SELECT uid, gid, name FROM sysusers");
        Vector result = theDB.getResult( );
        Vector group  = new Vector( );
        for (int i = 0; i < result.size( ); i++)
        {
            String [ ] row = (String [ ]) result.elementAt(i);
            if (row[0].equals(row[1]))
            {
                group.addElement(new String [ ] { row[1], row[2] } );
            }
        }
        theDB.closeConnection( );
        theGroups.append("\n");
        for (int i = 0; i < group.size( ); i++)
        {
            String [ ] element = (String [ ]) group.elementAt(i);
            String gid  = element [0];
            String name = element [1];
            theGroups.append(name + ":\n");
            for (int j = 0; j < result.size( ); j++)
            {
                String [ ] row = (String [ ]) result.elementAt(j);
                if (row[1].equals(gid) && ! row[0].equals(row[1]))
                {
                    theGroups.append("    " + row[2] + "\n");
                }
            }
        }
    }
    catch (SQLException sqlex)
    {
```

```
        sqlex.printStackTrace(System.err);
        theStatus.setText("Error: " + sqlex.getMessage( ));
    }
}
```

Listing Logins

The **ListLogins.list( )** method uses a similar approach to list the logins associated with a database. Its task is simpler, because no lookups of IDs are required;
the SysLogins table contains the login names themselves. The method is shown
in Listing 14.4.

LISTING 14.4   THE LISTLOGINS.LIST( ) METHOD.

```
public void list( )
{
    try
    {
        theLogins.setText("");
        theStatus.setText(OK);
        theDB.openConnection (theDriver, theURL, theUser, thePassword);
        theDB.executeQuery("SELECT name FROM syslogins");
        Vector result = theDB.getResult( );
        for (int i = 0; i < result.size( ); i++)
        {
            String [ ] row = (String [ ]) result.elementAt(i);
            theLogins.append(row[0] + "\n");
        }
        theDB.closeConnection( );
    }
    catch (SQLException sqlex)
    {
        sqlex.printStackTrace(System.err);
        theStatus.setText("Error: " + sqlex.getMessage( ));
    }
}
```

Listing Rights

The **ListRights.listRights( )** method lists the rights assigned to database
users. Rather than accessing the relevant tables directly, it uses several subsidiary
methods:

- **getUsers( )**—Returns a **Hashtable** containing the ID number and name of
  each database user.

- **getObjects( )**—Returns a **Hashtable** containing the ID number, name, and type of each database object.

- **getRights( )**—Returns a **Vector** containing the ID number of each database object, along with the ID number of the related user, a code for the right (action), a code for the object type, and a list of related columns.

The method is shown in Listing 14.5.

LISTING 14.5   THE LISTRIGHTS.listRights( ) METHOD.

```
public void listRights( )
{
    try
    {
        theRightList.setText("");
        theStatus.setText(OK);
        theDB.openConnection (theDriver, theURL, theUser, thePassword);
        Hashtable users  = getUsers  ( );
        Hashtable objs   = getObjects( );
        Vector    rights = getRights ( );
        theDB.closeConnection( );
        for (int i = 0; i < rights.size( ); i++)
        {
            String [ ] row = (String [ ]) rights.elementAt(i);
            String id     = row[0];
            String uid    = row[1];
            String action = row[2];
            String type   = row[3];
            String cols   = row[4];
             theRightList.append(
               "User " + getUserName(users, uid)
              + " " + getRightType(type)
              + " privilege " + theActionType.getActionTypeName(action)
              + " on object " + getObjectName(objs, id)
              + " ("
              + theObjectType.getObjectTypeName(getObjectType(objs, id))
              + ") applying to "
              + getColumnInfo(cols)
              + "\n");
        }
    }
    catch (SQLException sqlex)
    {
        sqlex.printStackTrace(System.err);
        theStatus.setText("Error: " + sqlex.getMessage( ));
    }
}
```

The **ListRights.getObjects( )** method is shown in Listing 14.6. The **ListRights.getUsers( )** and **ListRights.getRights( )** methods are similar and, therefore, not shown.

From the SysObjects table, the method retrieves information on all database objects. The ID, name, and type of each object is placed in a **Hashtable** that uses the ID as a key. If you know the ID of an object, you can use the **Hashtable** to obtain its name and type. Simple wrapper methods **getObjectName( )** and **getObjectType( )**, not shown here, make interrogating the **Hashtable** easy. These wrapper methods are used by the **listRights( )** method and others.

LISTING 14.6   THE LISTRIGHTS.GETOBJECTS( ) METHOD.

```
public Hashtable getObjects( )
throws SQLException
{
    theDB.executeQuery("SELECT id, name, type FROM sysobjects");
    Vector objs = theDB.getResult( );
    Hashtable result = new Hashtable( );
    for (int i = 0; i < objs.size( ); i++)
    {
        String [ ] row = (String [ ]) objs.elementAt(i);
        String id    = row[0];
        String name  = row[1];
        String type  = row[2];
        result.put(id, new String [ ] { name, type });
    }
    return result;
}
```

Listing Users

The **ListUsers.list( )** method, shown in Listing 14.7, places a list of database users in the **TextArea** known as **theUsers**. The method obtains its information from the SysUsers table, which contains the user ID, group ID, and name of each database user.

LISTING 14.7   THE LISTUSERS.LIST( ) METHOD.

```
public void list( )
{
    try
    {
        theUsers.setText("");
        theStatus.setText(OK);
```

```
theDB.openConnection (theDriver, theURL, theUser, thePassword);
theDB.executeQuery("SELECT uid, gid, name FROM sysusers");
Vector result = theDB.getResult( );
for (int i = 0; i < result.size( ); i++)
{
    String [ ] row = (String [ ]) result.elementAt(i);
    if (!row[0].equals(row[1]))
        theUsers.append(row[2] + "\n");
}
theDB.closeConnection( );
}
catch (SQLException sqlex)
{
    sqlex.printStackTrace(System.err);
    theStatus.setText("Error: " + sqlex.getMessage( ));
}
}
```

Summary

This chapter presented a number of issues that you must deal with when deploying database applications in the real world. You learned how to use the SQL DCL commands, **Grant** and **Revoke**, to control access to SQL databases. You also learned about such important considerations as database encryption, backup, recovery, and logging. Finally, you saw how Java applets could use stored procedures and special tables of a SQL Server database to report and maintain information on users and privileges.

You're now equipped to write your own applications using SQL and JDBC. The best ways to continue learning are to write code and study how it works, and to study code written by others. I hope this book has been helpful in getting you quickly, but thoroughly, acquainted with SQL. Happy developing!

QUICK REFERENCE TO SQL STATEMENTS

This appendix gives an alphabetical quick reference to the SQL language, as implemented for Microsoft Access and Microsoft SQL Server. You should consult the documentation provided by Microsoft for additional available options and details of the operation of each statement. If you are using a database other than Access or SQL Server, you can use this appendix as a rough guide to the syntax of SQL statements. You should also consult the documentation provided by your database vendor for more accurate and detailed information specific to your database.

Alter Table

The **Alter Table** statement allows you to add a column or constraint to a table, or drop a column or constraint from a table.

Microsoft Access

```
Alter Table table
Add Column field type[(size)] [Not Null]


|
Add Constraint single-field_constraint


|
Add Constraint multiple-field_constraint
```

```
|
Drop Column field

|
Drop Constraint constraint

Single-field constraint:

Constraint name
{
    Primary Key
    | Unique
    | Not Null
    | References foreigntable
      [(foreignfield1, foreignfield2)]
}

Multiple-field constraint:

Constraint name{
    Primary Key (primary1
      [, primary2 [, …]])
    | Unique (unique1
      [, unique2 [, …]])
    | Not Null (nonnull1
      [, nonnull2 [, …]])
    | Foreign Key (ref1
       [, ref2 [, …]])
        References foreigntable
          [(foreignfield1
          [, foreignfield2 [, …]])])
}
```

Microsoft SQL Server

```
Alter Table [database.[owner].]table_name
[With Nocheck]
[Add
{
    column_definition [column_constraint] …
    [, column_definition [column_constraint] … ] …
}


|
Add table_constraint [, table_constraint] …
```

```
|
Drop [Constraint] constraint_name
  [, constraint_name2] …
```

Create Database

The **Create Database** statement allows you to create a new database.

Microsoft Access

Create Database is not available as a Microsoft Access SQL statement. Launch the Access application and use File|New Database.

Microsoft SQL Server

```
Create Database name
[On {default | device} [= size] [, device [= size]] …]

[Log On device [= size] [, device [= size]] …]

[For Load]
```

Create Index

The **Create Index** statement allows you to add an index to a database table.

Microsoft Access

```
Create [ Unique ] Index index On table
    (field [Asc|Desc]
    [, field [Asc|Desc], …])[With
    { Primary | Disallow Null | Ignore Null }
]
```

Microsoft SQL Server

```
Create [Unique]
[Clustered | Nonclustered]
Index indexname
On [[database.]owner.]tablename      columnname [, columnname]…)
[With
    [Fillfactor = x]
    [[,] Ignore_Dup_Key]
    [[,] {Sorted_Data | Sorted_Data_Reorg}]
```

```
       [[,] {Ignore_Dup_Row | Allow_Dup_Row}]]
[On segmentname]
```

Create Table

The **Create Table** statement allows you to add a table to a database.

Microsoft Access

```
Create Table table (
field1 type [(size)] [Not Null] [index1]

[, field2 type [(size)] [Not Null] [index2]

[, …]]

[, Constraint multifieldindex [, …]])
```

Microsoft SQL Server

```
Create Table [database.[owner].]tablename
(
{colname datatype [Null | Not Null | Identity[(seed, increment)]]
[
[Constraint constraint]

[Default {expression
     | niladic-function
     | Null}
     [For col_name]]


|
[Primary Key [Clustered
     | Nonclustered]
     (col_name
     [, col_name2
     […, col_name16]])
     [On Segment]]


|
[Unique [Clustered
     | Nonclustered]
     (col_name
     [, col_name2
     […, col_name16]])]
```

```
|
[[Foreign Key
    (col_name
    [, col_name2
    [..., col_name16]])]
    References [owner.]ref_table
        [(ref_col
        [, ref_col2
        [..., ref_col16]])]
    [On segment]]


|
[Check [Not For Replication] (expression)]


] ...


[, next_column
[next_constraint] ... ] ...]


[Primary Key [Clustered
    | Nonclustered]
    (col_name
    [, col_name2
    [..., col_name16]])
    [On segment]]


|
[Unique [Clustered
    | Nonclustered]
    (col_name
    [, col_name2
    [..., col_name16]])]


|
[[Foreign Key
    (col_name
    [, col_name2
    [..., col_name16]])]
    References [owner.]ref_table
        [(ref_col
        [, ref_col2
        [..., ref_col16]])]
    [On segment]]


|
[Check [Not For Replication] (expression)]
```

```
] …
)
[On segment]
```

The niladic functions provided by Microsoft SQL Server are: **Current_Timestamp**, **System_User, Current_User, User,** and **Session_User**.

Create View

The **Create View** statement allows you to define a view that is based on the result of a **Select** statement.

Microsoft Access

The view facility is not officially supported by Microsoft Access.

Microsoft SQL Server

```
Create View [owner.]view
[(column [, column]…)]
[With Encryption]
As select
[With Check Option]
```

Delete

The **Delete** statement allows you to delete rows from a table.

Microsoft Access

```
Delete [table.*] From table Where criteria
```

Microsoft SQL Server

```
Delete [From] { [[database.]owner.] {table | view}}
[Where {condition | Current Of cursor}]
```

Drop Database

The **Drop** statement allows you to delete a database.

Microsoft Access

Drop is not available as a Microsoft Access SQL statement. Use a system command prompt window or the file explorer to delete the MDB file containing the database.

Microsoft SQL Server

```
Drop Database name [, name …]
```

Drop Index

The **Drop Index** statement allows you to delete an index.

Microsoft Access

```
Drop Index index On table
```

Microsoft SQL Server

```
Drop Index [owner.]table.index
[, [owner.]table.index] …
```

Drop Table

The **Drop Table** statement allows you to delete a table, along with all its rows.

Microsoft Access

```
Drop Table table
```

Microsoft SQL Server

```
Drop Table [[database.]owner.]tablename
[, [[database.]owner.]tablename] …
```

Drop View

The **Drop View** statement allows you to delete a view.

Microsoft Access

The view facility is not officially supported by Microsoft Access.

Microsoft SQL Server

```
Drop View [owner.]view [, [owner.]view] …
```

Grant

The **Grant** statement allows you to give users permission to use SQL statements or access database objects.

Microsoft Access

The **Grant** statement is not supported by Microsoft Access, which uses a security mechanism unlike that specified by the SQL standard.

Microsoft SQL Server

Two distinct forms of the **Grant** statement are available. The first is used to give permission to use specified SQL statements:

```
Grant {All | statementlist}
To {Public | {userorgroup [, userorgroup] … }}
```

The *statementlist* can include any of the following entries:

```
Create Database, Create Default, Create Procedure, Create Rule,
Create Table, Create View, Dump Database, Dump Transaction
```

Multiple entries within the *statementlist* are separated by commas.

The second form of the **Grant** statement is used to give users permission to access database objects:

```
Grant {All | permissionlist}
On {table [(columnlist)]
  | view [(columnlist)]
  | storedprocedure
  | extendedstoredprocedure}
To {Public | {userorgroup [, userorgroup] … }}
```

The *permissionlist* can include any of the following entries:

```
Select, Insert, Delete, Update, References
```

Multiple entries within the *permissionlist* are separated by commas.

Insert

The **Insert** statement allows you to add new rows to a table.

Microsoft Access

```
Insert Into table [(field1[, field2[, ...]])]
Values (value1[, value2[, ...])
```

Microsoft SQL Server

```
Insert [Into] {[[database.]owner.]{table | view}}
[(columnlist)]
{
  Default Values
  | Values (
            Default
            | expression [, Default | expression] …
           )
  | select
}
```

Revoke

The **Revoke** statement allows you to withdraw permission to use SQL statements or access database objects.

Microsoft Access

The **Revoke** statement is not supported by Microsoft Access, which uses a security mechanism unlike that specified by the SQL standard.

Microsoft SQL Server

Two distinct forms of the **Revoke** statement are available. The first is used to withdraw permission to use specified SQL statements:

```
Revoke {All | statementlist}
From {Public | {userorgroup [, userorgroup] … }}
```

The *statementlist* can include any of the following entries:

```
Create Database, Create Default, Create Procedure, Create Rule,
Create Table, Create View, Dump Database, Dump Transaction
```

Multiple entries within the *statementlist* are separated by commas.

The second form of **Revoke** is used to withdraw permission to access database objects:

```
Revoke {All | permissionlist}
On {table [(columnlist)]
  | view [(columnlist)]
  | storedprocedure
  | extendedstoredprocedure}
From {Public | {userorgroup [, userorgroup] … }}
```

The *permissionlist* can include any of the following entries:

```
Select, Insert, Delete, Update, References
```

Multiple entries within the *permissionlist* are separated by commas.

Select

The **Select** statement allows you to access the rows of one or more tables that satisfy specified conditions.

Microsoft Access

```
Select
[All | Distinct | DistinctRow | Top n Percent]
{ *
  | table.*
  | [table.]field1 [As alias1] [, [table.]field2 [As alias2] [, …]]
} [INTO [newtable]]
[From {table | alias} [, [table | alias] …] [In database]]
[Where condition]
[Group By [All] {column | expression} [, [column | expression]] … ]
[Having condition]
[Order By {column | position | label} [Asc | Desc]]
[With Owneraccess Option]
```

Microsoft SQL Server

```
SELECT
[ALL | DISTINCT]
{ *
  | [alias1 =] [table.]field1 [, [alias2 =] [table.]field2] …
}[INTO [newtable]]
[FROM {table | view}
    [[, {table2 | view2}
    […, {table16 | view16}]]]
[Where condition]
[Group By [All] {column | expression} [, [column | expression]] … ]
[Having condition]
[Order By {column | position | label} [Asc | Desc]]
[Compute row (column) [, row (column)] …
  [By column [, column] …]
[For Browse]
```

Update

The **Update** statement allows you to change the value of columns within selected rows of a table.

Microsoft Access

```
Update tableSet
{
  column = {expression | Default | Null}
  [, column = {expression | Default | Null}] …
}
[Where condition ]
```

Microsoft SQL Server

```
Update { [[database.]owner.]{table | view}}
Set [{table | view}]
{
  column = {expression | Default | Null}
  [, column = {expression | Default | Null}] …
}
[Where {condition | Current Of cursor}]
```

Use Database

The **Use Database** statement allows you to dynamically select a database.

Microsoft Access

Access does not support dynamic selection of databases. Open a separate connection to each database needed by your application.

Microsoft SQL Server

```
Use database
```

QUICK REFERENCE TO SQL FUNCTIONS

B

This appendix gives an alphabetical quick reference to the functions included in SQL, as implemented for Microsoft Access. You should consult the documentation provided by Microsoft for additional available functions, and for options and details of operation of each function. If you are using a database other than Access, you can use this appendix as a rough guide to the SQL functions. You should also consult the documentation provided by your database vendor for more accurate and detailed information specific to your database.

TABLE B.1

MICROSOFT ACCESS SQL FUNCTIONS.

Name	Meaning
ABS(x)	Returns the absolute value of the number x.
ASCII(x)	Returns the numeric value of the ASCII character x.
ATAN(x)	Returns the angle (in radians) whose tangent is the number x.
CEILING(x)	Returns the smallest integer not less than the number x.
CHAR(x)	Returns the character whose ASCII code is given by the number x.

(continued)

MICROSOFT ACCESS SQL FUNCTIONS (*CONTINUED*).

Name	Meaning
CONCAT(x, y)	Returns the result of concatenating string y onto the end of string x.
COS(x)	Returns the cosine of the angle given by x (in radians).
CURDATE(x)	Returns the current date.
CURTIME(x)	Returns the current time.
DAYOFMONTH(x)	Returns the day of month (1–31) specified by the date x.
DAYOFWEEK(x)	Returns the number that represents the day of the week (Sunday = 1) specified by the date x.
DAYOFYEAR(x)	Returns the day of year (1–366) specified by the date x.
EXP(x)	Returns the base of natural logarithms (e) raised to the power x.
FLOOR(x)	Returns the largest integer not greater than the number x.
HOUR(x)	Returns the hour specified by the time x.
LCASE(x)	Returns the result of converting string x to lowercase.
LEFT(x, y)	Returns the leftmost y characters of string x.
LENGTH(x)	Returns the length of string x.
LOCATE(x, y)	Returns the index of string y in string x, or 0 if y is not found in x.
LOG(x)	Returns the natural logarithm of x.
LTRIM(x)	Returns the string x with any leading (left) spaces removed.
MINUTE(x)	Returns the minute specified by the time x.
MOD(x, y)	Returns the remainder of the division of x by y.
MONTH(x)	Returns the month (1–12) specified by the date x.
NOW(x)	Returns a timestamp containing the current date and time.
POWER(x, y)	Returns the number x raised to the power y.
RAND( )	Returns a random number from 0.0 (inclusive) to 1.0 (exclusive).
RIGHT(x, y)	Returns the rightmost y character(s) of string x.
RTRIM(x)	Returns the string x with any trailing (right) spaces removed.
SECOND(x)	Returns the number of seconds specified by the time x.

(continued)

MICROSOFT ACCESS SQL FUNCTIONS (*CONTINUED*).

Name	Meaning
SIGN(x)	Returns -1, 0, or 1 according to the sign of x.
SIN(x)	Returns the sine of the angle given by x (in radians).
SPACE(x)	Returns a string containing the number of spaces specified by x.
SQRT(x)	Returns the square root of the number x.
SUBSTRING(x, y, z)	Returns the substring of string x, beginning at position y and having length z.
TAN(x)	Returns the tangent of the angle given by x (in radians).
UCASE(x)	Returns the result of converting string x to uppercase.
WEEK(x)	Returns the week of year (1-53) specified by the date x.
YEAR(x)	Returns the year specified by the date x.

QUICK REFERENCE TO MICROSOFT ACCESS DATA TYPES

This appendix gives a quick reference to the data types supported by SQL, as implemented for Microsoft Access. You should consult the documentation provided by Microsoft for additional information. If you are using a database other than Access, you should consult the documentation provided by your database vendor for more accurate and detailed information specific to your database.

TABLE C.1

DATA TYPES SUPPORTED BY MICROSOFT ACCESS.

Java Type	Access Type	SQL Type	Method
String	Text	VARCHAR	getString( )
String	Memo	LONGVARCHAR	getASCIIStream( )
java.sql.Numeric	Number	NUMERIC	getNumeric( )
boolean	Yes/No	BIT	getBoolean( )
byte	Byte	TINYINT	getByte( )
short	Integer	SMALLINT	getShort( )

(continued)

475

TABLE C.1

DATA TYPES SUPPORTED BY MICROSOFT ACCESS (*CONTINUED*).

Java Type	Access Type	SQL Type	Method
int	Long	INTEGER	getInt( )
long	Long	BIGINT	getLong( )
float	Single	REAL	getFloat( )
double	Double	DOUBLE	getDouble( )
byte[ ]	OLE Object	VARBINARY, LONGVARBINARY	getBytes( ), getBinaryStream( )
java.sql.Date	Date/Time	DATE	getDate( )
java.sql.Time	Date/Time	TIME	getTime( )
java.sql.Timestamp	Date/Time	TIMESTAMP	getTimeStamp( )

INDEX

Symbols

::=, 277
<>, 277
{}, 277
[], 277, 284
*, 68
?, 313, 384

A

Abstract Windowing Toolkit (AWT)
   components, 46
Access. *See* Microsoft Access.
Access methods, data, 420–422
Access ODBC driver
   support of API calls, 271
Acceptable values. *See* Domains and Constraints.
Accessor methods, 216
ActionListener interface, 56, 106
actionPerformed( ) method, 60–61, 83, 89, 108–
   109, 134, 173, 209–210, 212, 217, 282–283,
   320, 330–331, 358–359, 395, 414, 427–428
Adapter class, 105
Add command, 34
addColumn( ) method, 287–288
AddColumnDialog, 287
AddColumnDialog class, 296, 297
AddColumnDialog.loadTables( )
   method, 296–298
addFocusListener( ) method, 208
Aggregates, 154–157
Aliases, 194–195
All predicates, 345-346
Alter Table Add Column command, 287-288

Alter Table statement, 459–461
And operator, 74
Anomalies, 241–243, 430.
   See also DBAnomalies.
ANSI standards, 12, 164, 199, 383-384, 436
Any predicates, 340, 347
Applets, 45. *See also* Program names.
   CallableDemo, 387–391
   DBAnomalies, 411–424
   DBGuard, 451–458
   EmpBrowser, 353–371
   GuestBook05, 316–328
   PreppedMark, 328–334
   security issues, 447–451
   TransDemo, 424–433
Application interface, 105–106
Application object, 105, 214
Applications. *See also* Program names.
   programming interface (API), 13
   programs, defined, 14
   programs, initializing in Java, 49
Architectures. *See also* Client-Server Architectures.
   defined, 15
   three-tier, 94, 450
Arithmetic operations, 163
Artificial keys. *See* Keys.
As clauses, 155, 194
Assignments table, 159, 187, 191, 244–246,
   273–276, 349-353
Asterisks (*) in queries, 68
Attributes, defined, 27
Audits, 447
Auxiliary table, 240
AWT thread, 108, 134

Solutions for Your World

It's easy to get lost in the online universe, but *INTERNET JAVA & ACTIVEX ADVISOR* will guide you in the right direction. Written by expert developers, every issue brings you vital information on the latest products and technologies necessary for staying ahead of the Internet Revolution. Take a look at what you'll get each month when you subscribe today:

New Product Reviews
What works and what doesn't

Developer News
What's happening and what's important

Feature Articles
Developer insights on the products you use

It's A Big Online World.